Fodor's

PUERTO VALLARTA

WELCOME TO
PUERTO VALLARTA

Sunbathing and sipping margaritas is just one of many ways to spend a vacation in Puerto Vallarta. Mexico's prettiest resort town is also one of its most diverse. Old Vallarta—El Centro and the Zona Romántica—is a goldmine of quirky boutiques and winding cobblestone streets. In Marina Vallarta, shopping centers and deluxe hotels spread around the city's yacht marina. And from Costalegre to the Riviera Nayarit, miles of sandy beaches and scores of stellar restaurants and lively nightclubs, surrounded by historic mountain towns, keep visitors returning again and again.

TOP REASONS TO GO

★ **Resorts:** Everything from luxurious beachfront high-rises to quaint boutique hideaways.

★ **Nightlife:** Vallarta after dark is one of Mexico's best party scenes.

★ **Beaches:** From lively town beaches to secluded natural havens, each beach is unique.

★ **Golf:** A top golf destination with exclusive links and accessible courses for all players.

★ **Water Sports:** Windsurfing, snorkeling, and scuba diving are just a few top options.

★ **El Malecón:** PV's seaside boardwalk is always a lovely stroll, especially at sunset.

Fodor's PUERTO VALLARTA

Publisher: Amanda D'Acierno, *Senior Vice President*

Editorial: Arabella Bowen, *Editor in Chief*; Linda Cabasin, *Editorial Director*

Design: Tina Malaney, *Associate Art Director*; Chie Ushio, *Senior Designer*; Ann McBride, *Production Designer*

Photography: Jennifer Arnow, *Senior Photo Editor*; Mary Robnett, *Photo Researcher*

Production: Linda Schmidt, *Managing Editor*; Evangelos Vasilakis, *Associate Managing Editor*; Angela L. McLean, *Senior Production Manager*

Maps: Rebecca Baer, *Senior Map Editor*; David Lindroth and Mark Stroud, Moon Street Cartography, *Cartographers*

Sales: Jacqueline Lebow, *Sales Director*

Marketing & Publicity: Heather Dalton, *Marketing Director*; Katherine Punia, *Publicity Director*

Business & Operations: Susan Livingston, *Vice President, Strategic Business Planning*; Sue Daulton, *Vice President, Operations*

Fodors.com: Megan Bell, *Executive Director, Revenue & Business Development*; Yasmin Marinaro, *Senior Director, Marketing & Partnerships*

Copyright © 2015 by Fodor's Travel, a division of Random House LLC

Editors: Perrie Hartz, Douglas Stallings

Writers: Federico Arrizabalaga, Luis Domínguez

Production Editor: Evangelos Vasilakis

6th Edition 5 6 5 7 1 4 0

ISBN 978-1-101-87814-9

ISSN 1558-8718   5/15

SPECIAL SALES

This book is available at special discounts for bulk purchases for sales promotions or premiums. For more information, e-mail specialmarkets@penguinrandomhouse.com

PRINTED IN THE UNITED STATES OF AMERICA

10 9 8 7 6 5 4 3 2 1

CONTENTS

CONTENTS

ABOUT THIS GUIDE

Fodor's Recommendations

Everything in this guide is worth doing—we don't cover what isn't—but exceptional sights, hotels, and restaurants are recognized with additional accolades. **Fodor's Choice** ★ indicates our top recommendations; and **Best Bets** call attention to notable hotels and restaurants in various categories. Care to nominate a new place? Visit Fodors.com/contact-us.

Trip Costs

We list prices wherever possible to help you budget well. Hotel and restaurant price categories from **$** to **$$$$** are noted alongside each recommendation. For hotels, we include the lowest cost of a standard double room in high season. For restaurants, we cite the average price of a main course at dinner or, if dinner isn't served, at lunch. For attractions, we always list adult admission fees; discounts are usually available for children, students, and senior citizens.

Hotels

Our local writers vet every hotel to recommend the best overnights in each price category, from budget to expensive. Unless otherwise specified, you can expect private bath, phone, and TV in your room. For expanded hotel reviews, facilities, and deals visit Fodors.com.

Top Picks	Hotels &
★ **Fodor's**Choice	**Restaurants**
	🏨 Hotel
Listings	↳ Number of
✉ Address	rooms
✉ Branch address	⊠ Meal plans
☎ Telephone	✕ Restaurant
🖶 Fax	⚑ Reservations
⊕ Website	👔 Dress code
✉ E-mail	⊟ No credit cards
🎟 Admission fee	$ Price
⊙ Open/closed	
times	**Other**
Ⓜ Subway	⇨ See also
✛ Directions or	☞ Take note
Map coordinates	🏌 Golf facilities

Restaurants

Unless we state otherwise, restaurants are open for lunch and dinner daily. We mention dress code only when there's a specific requirement and reservations only when they're essential or not accepted. To make restaurant reservations, visit Fodors.com.

Credit Cards

The hotels and restaurants in this guide typically accept credit cards. If not, we'll say so.

EUGENE FODOR

Hungarian-born Eugene Fodor (1905–91) began his travel career as an interpreter on a French cruise ship. The experience inspired him to write *On the Continent* (1936), the first guidebook to receive annual updates and discuss a country's way of life as well as its sights. Fodor later joined the U.S. Army and worked for the OSS in World War II. After the war, he kept up his intelligence work while expanding his guidebook series. During the Cold War, many guides were written by fellow agents who understood the value of insider information. Today's guides continue Fodor's legacy by providing travelers with timely coverage, insider tips, and cultural context.

EXPERIENCE
PUERTO VALLARTA

1

WELCOME TO PUERTO VALLARTA

TOP REASONS TO GO

★ **Legendary restaurants:** Eat barbecued snapper with your feet in the sand or chateaubriand with a killer ocean view.

★ **Adventure and indulgence:** Ride a horse, mountain-bike, or go four-wheeling in the mountains, dive into the sea, and relax at an elegant spa—all in one day.

★ **Natural beauty:** Enjoy the physical beauty of Pacific Mexico's prettiest resort town, where cobblestone streets disappear into emerald green hills with the big, sparkling bay below.

★ **Authentic art:** PV's artists and artisans—from Huichol Indians to expats—produce a huge array of exceptional folk treasures and fine art.

★ **Diverse nightlife:** Whether you're old, young, gay, straight, mild, or wild, PV's casual and unpretentious party scene has something to entice you after dark.

1 Zona Romántica. South of the Cuale River, the Zona Romántica (Romantic Zone, including Col. E. Zapata) has PV's highest density of restaurants and tourist-oriented shops.

2 El Centro. Rising abruptly from the sea are the hilly, cobblestone streets of El Centro (Downtown), lined with white-washed homes and shops.

3 Zona Hotelera. Facing a busy avenue, the Zona Hotelera (Hotel Zone) has malls, businesses, and high-rise hotels.

4 Marina Vallarta. The shopping centers and deluxe hotels of Marina Vallarta are sandwiched between a golf course and the city's main yacht marina.

5 Olas Altas. On the southern edge of PV are the upscale residential neighborhoods of Amapas and Conchas Chinas, located on both sides of Highway 200.

6 Nuevo Vallarta. This area just north of PV is composed mainly of golf courses, exclusive condos, and luxurious restaurants, and has the second-highest number of hotels in the country.

7 Riviera Nayarit. Just north of Nuevo Vallarta, Riviera Nayarit has pristine beaches, luxurious resorts, and dozens of laid-back towns loved by artists, hippies, surfers, and celebrities.

8 South of Puerto Vallarta. This area stretches all the way to Mismaloya. South of El Tuito, Cabo Corrientes has tiny towns and gorgeous beaches.

9 Costalegre. A series of secluded bays and white-sand beaches located south of PV in Jalisco, with a few luxury resorts and hotels in Barra de Navidad.

10 San Blas. A region North of Riviera Nayarit, this rustic area has a few basic attractions but lots of "Old Mexico" culture and striking natural beauty.

11 Inland Mountain Towns. There are a few historic and tiny former mining towns within the Sierra Madre.

12 Guadalajara. Often called "The Mexican's Mexico," Guadalajara is a vibrant, culturally rich city teeming with activity.

13 Tlaquepaque. A touristy yet quaint town filled with local arts and crafts as well as some great shopping.

Bucerías

Playa Bucerías

Mezcales

Nuevo Vallarta

*Bahía de
Banderas*

NAYARIT
JALISCO

Mountain Time Zone
Central Time Zone

**MARINA
VALLARTA**

Marina Vallarta
Playa el Salado

Playa del Oro

**ZONA
HOTELERA**

Playa las Glorias

Playa Camarones

Playa Olas Altas

Playa Los Muertos

EL CENTRO

Puerto Vallarta

Playa Los Amapas

Playa Conchas Chinas

**ZONA
ROMÁNTICA**

Playa los
Estacas

Playa
Gemelas

OLAS ALTAS

Los Arcos

Mismaloya

0 _____ 6 mi

0 _____ 6 km

GETTING ORIENTED

The original town, Old Vallarta, sits at the center of 42-km (26-mile) Bahía de Banderas, Mexico's largest bay, in Jalisco State. From here, the Sierra Madre foothills dive into the sea. Mountain-fed rivers nourish tropical deciduous forests as far north as San Blas, in Nayarit State. South of PV the hills recede from the coast, and the drier tropical thorn forest predominates south to Barra de Navidad.

PUERTO VALLARTA PLANNER

The Scene

Mexico's second-most-visited destination after the Cancún/Playa del Carmen area, Puerto Vallarta is touristy. That said, this isn't a spring-break destination. Yes, twentysomethings party all night. But a sense of decorum and civic pride keeps things reasonably restrained. Most tour companies, restaurants, and hotels are run by locals who are happy to have you—tourism is PV's only real industry.

Fast Facts

Nickname: Foreigners call it PV or Vallarta. A *vallartense* (person from Puerto Vallarta), however, is known as a *pata salada* (literally, salty foot).

State: PV is in the state of Jalisco, whose capital is Guadalajara.

Population: 255,861

Latitude: 20°N (same as Cancún, Mexico; Port-au-Prince, Haiti; Hanoi, Vietnam)

Longitude: 105°W (same as Regina, Saskatchewan; Denver, Colorado; El Paso, Texas)

Logistics

Getting Here: Aeropuerto Internacional de la Ciudad de México (Benito Juárez; airport code: MEX) is the main airport to fly into. Puerto Vallarta's small international Aeropuerto Internacional Gustavo Díaz Ordáz (PVR) is 7.5 km (4½ miles) north of downtown.

Flights: Flights with stopovers in Mexico City can take the entire day. There are nonstop flights from a few U.S. cities, including Atlanta (Delta), Los Angeles (Alaska Air, American Airlines via Mexicana de Aviación), San Francisco (Alaska Air, United, Mexicana), Seattle (Alaska Air), Phoenix (US Airways), Houston (Continental), Dallas (American), Denver (Frontier Air, United), Chicago ORD (American Airlines), and Kansas City, Missouri (Frontier Air).

Flying times are about 2¾ hours from Houston, 3 hours from Los Angeles, 3½ hours from Denver, 4 hours from Chicago, and 8 hours from New York.

On the Ground: Vans provide transportation from the airport to PV hotels. There is a zone system with different prices for downtown PV, the Zona Hotelera, Marina Vallarta, etc. You can buy a taxi voucher at the stands inside the terminal. Head for an official taxi kiosk, which will have zone information clearly posted.

Renting a Car: Rates range from $19 a day and $120 a week to $50 a day and $300–$400 a week, excluding insurance. It's essential to get Mexican auto insurance for liability. Navigating the steep hills of Old Vallarta can be difficult, and traffic tends to be bad in peak season (December through April). If you're heading out of Puerto Vallarta, there are several well-kept toll roads called *carreteras* (major highways) that lead in and out of major cities like Guadalajara—most of them are four lanes wide. Roads leading to, or in, Nayarit and Jalisco include highways connecting Nogales and Mazatlán; Guadalajara and Tepic; and Mexico City, Morelia, and Guadalajara. Tolls between Guadalajara and Puerto Vallarta (334 km [207 miles]) total about $25. You can also hire a taxi with a driver (who generally doubles as a tour guide) through your hotel.

Hotels

Puerto Vallarta is the center for area beach hotels. Look for smaller budget hotels downtown, and oceanfront high-rise hotels to the north in the Hotel Zone, Marina Vallarta, and Nuevo Vallarta. Even farther north, Riviera Nayarit is where to go for unique B&Bs, boutique hotels, and some truly luxurious villas.

Boutique Hotels: Small boutique hotels are another option in PV, especially in the Zona Romántica and El Centro.

Chain Hotels: In PV these have excellent rates and can be good last-minute options. Chains include the Holiday Inn/InterContinental Group, Marriott, Sheraton, and various Starwood chains, like Westin and St. Regis.

Apartments/Villas: When shared by a few couples, a spacious villa can save you a lot on upscale lodging and on meals. Villas often come with great amenities like stereo systems, pools, maid service, and air-conditioning.

Restaurants

There are many good hotel-based restaurants in PV, but most of the city's top spots are independent and can be found in El Centro or Zona Romántica. There are also several good spots in Marina Vallarta and north along the Riviera Nayarit.

Prices: Most restaurants offer lunch deals with special menus at great prices, though at more traditional spots, the lunch menu may not be available before 1 or 1:30 pm. If you're dining at a small restaurant or beachside bar, make sure to have some bills in your wallet; these casual places tend to be cash-only.

Cuisine: Everything from haute cuisine to casual fare is available. Some of the best food is found outside of fancy restaurants and familiar chain eateries at the street-side tacos stalls and neighborhood *fondas,* unassuming spots serving Mexican comfort food.

Restaurant-lounges: Many PV restaurants combine dining and dancing, with a ground-floor eatery and a dance club above.

Beach Dining: For those who prefer dining alfresco (and wearing flip-flops), almost every popular beach has a *palapa* shanty or two selling fish fillets and snacks, sodas, and beer.

When to Go

High season (aka dry season) is December through April; the resorts are most crowded and expensive during this time. If you don't mind afternoon showers, temperatures in the 80s and 90s F (high 20s and 30s C), and high humidity, rainy season (late June through October) is a great time to visit. Hotel rates drop by as much as 40%, and there aren't any crowds.

Summer sees the best diving, snorkeling, and surfing conditions. By August the coast and inland forests are green and bursting with blooms. Afternoon rains clean the streets; waterfalls and rivers outside of town spring into action. On the downside, heat and humidity are high, some businesses close shop in the hottest months (August and September), and nightlife slacks off.

Climate

The proximity of mountains to the coast increases humidity. From Puerto Vallarta north to San Blas there's jungly terrain (officially, tropical deciduous forest). South of PV the mountains recede from the coast, making that area's thorn-forest ecosystem drier but still hot and humid.

PUERTO VALLARTA TOP ATTRACTIONS

Dining Out

(A) Dozens of top chefs have restaurants in PV, and each November sees the International Gourmet Festival, with guest chefs, recipes, and ideas from around the globe. Seaside family-owned eateries grill fish right off the boat, and tiny city cafés have great eats at bargain prices. And a number of street-side stalls are as hygienic as five star-hotel restaurants.

Beaches

(B) The diversity of beaches that the Puerto Vallarta–Riviera Nayarit region offers is outstanding. From intimate beaches with crystal clear water and no waves, to long stretches of white sand beach and fantastic breaks, there is a beach for every taste.

Water Sports

(C) Dive the varied landscape of Las Marietas Islands, angle for billfish, or take a boat ride. Look for humpbacks in winter and dolphins year-round. Swim, snorkel, or learn to surf or sail. Nuevo Vallarta

and Bucerias are the soul and heart of the national kite-surf scene, while Punta Mita is the best spot to practice the increasingly popular Paddle Surf.

Sensational Sunsets

(D) Sip a cocktail to live music at busy Los Muertos Beach or enjoy a cold beer at El Solar in Playa Camarones while watching the sunset. For dramatic views from high above the sea, head to Barcelona Tapas or Vista Guayabitos (⇨ *Chapter 4*). Both serve dinner and drinks.

Late Nights, Latino Style

(E) Much of Vallarta is geared to the gringo palate; however, there's plenty of authentic spice too. Enjoy a mojito at La Bodeguita del Medio, on the malecón. Dine on roast pork, black beans, and fried plantains before heading for the dance floor. Thursday and Friday, take a taxi to J&B Dance Club for $4 dance lessons from 8 to 9 pm. Otherwise hang at La Bodeguita until around 11, when the Latino crowds

start to arrive at J&B for a late night of cumbia, salsa, and merengue.

Artsy Vallarta

(F) The cultural scene in Puerto Vallarta is quite impressive. Thursday night is artWalk night; spend a relaxing evening walking through the cobblestone streets of Downtown Vallarta while visiting a series of sophisticated art galleries and enjoying a glass of wine or tequila. If you're lucky, you may get the chance to chat with the artists. Teatro Vallarta offers top-quality plays, concerts, and conferences, while Act II presents an interesting mix of cabaret and theater shows.

Hilltop Retreats

(G) 4,000 feet above sea level are the mountain towns east of PV. Admire the elegant simplicity of tiny San Sebastián; in Talpa, visit the diminutive Virgin of Talpa statue, revered throughout Mexico for petitions granted. Road access is relatively easy, but you can still charter a plane to these towns or to Mascota, where you can sample homemade *raicilla*—second cousin of tequila. For an unforgettable experience (at least until your thigh muscles recover), take a horseback expedition *(⇨ Chapter 7)* into forests. Rancho Charro and Rancho Ojo de Agua have full-day excursions.

Canopy Tours

Canopy tours are action-packed rides, where, fastened to a zip line high off the ground, you fly from tree to tree—blue sky above, ribbons of river below, and, in between, a forest of treetops and a healthy shot of adrenaline.

GAY PUERTO VALLARTA

Puerto Vallarta is a gay old town. Mexico's most popular gay destination draws crowds of "Dorothy's friends" from both sides of the Río Grande and from the Old World as well.

The Romantic Zone is the hub for rainbow bars and sophisticated, gay-friendly restaurants. Here, many foreigners have relocated to PV to fulfill their ultimate fantasy in the form of bistro, bar, or B&B. International savvy (and financial backing) teamed up with Mexican sensibilities has produced a number of successful gay businesses.

Gay hotels offer entertainment that allows you to party on-site without having to worry about getting "home." In addition to gay properties such as Blue Chairs and Casa Cupula, hotels like Los Cuatro Vientos, in Centro, and Quinta María Cortez above Playa Conchas Chinas (⇨ Chapter 5) are gay-friendly.

Clubbing may be the favorite pastime in the Romantic Zone, but there's more than one way to cruise Vallarta. Gay boat tours keep the libations flowing throughout the day, and horses head for the hills for bird's-eye views of the beach.

THE BEACH SCENE

The undisputed king of daytime beach action is **Blue Chairs** (⊠ South end of Los Muertos Beach, Col. E. Zapata, Zona Romántica).

Next door, the green umbrellas blend with the blue; at this end of the beach, though, it's pretty much gay no matter what color the umbrellas. This is PV's most popular rainbow beach scene, a magnet for first-timers as well as those sneaking away from social obligations in Guadalajara.

GET THE SCOOP

Gay Guide Vallarta (⊕ www.gayguidevallarta.com) is an excellent and occasionally opinionated source of information about gay-friendly and gay-owned hotels, restaurants, and nightlife.

Gay PV (⊕ www.gaypv.mx) is a free gay guide to the vibrant LGBT lifestyle in Puerto Vallarta, which you can find all around Zona Romántica.

Cruises

Boana Hot Springs (⊠ Boana Torre Malibu Condo-Hotel, Calle Amapas 325, Col. E. Zapata ☎ 322/222–0999 ⊕ www.boana. net) offers a twice-weekly romantic hot spring tour ($75). Included are transportation, a candlelight dinner, and open bar. In high season tours operate Tuesday and Friday, leaving at 4:45 pm and returning to PV at midnight. To hold a spot, make a deposit in person at Boana's office in Boana Torre Malibu, behind Blue Chairs on Highway 200 just south of the Romantic Zone.

Diana's Gay Cruise (☎ 322/222–1510; 866/514–7969 in U.S. for reservations ⊕ www.dianastours.com) is a booze-and-beach cruise (Thursdays and most Fridays in high season) popular with lesbians and gays. Straights are also welcome, but minors are not. Go for the swimming, snorkeling, and lunch on the beach at Las Animas or another area beach, or for the unlimited national-brand beers and mixed drinks. Most of the time is spent on the boat. It's easiest to reserve tickets ($80) online using PayPal. Private tours are also available.

SNAPSHOT OF PUERTO VALLARTA

Geography

Puerto Vallarta sits at the center point of C-shaped Banderas Bay. Spurs from the Sierra Cacoma run down to the sea, forming a landscape of numerous valleys. This highly fractured mountain range is just one of many within the Sierra Madre—which runs from the Rockies to South America. Sierra Cacoma sits at the juncture of several major systems that head south toward Oaxaca State. Forming a distinct but related system is the volcanic or transversal volcanic axis that runs east to west across the country—and the globe. Comprising part of the so-called Ring of Fire, this transverse chain includes some of the world's most active volcanoes. Volcán de Fuego, southeast of Puerto Vallarta in Colima State, and the giant Popocateptl, near the Gulf of Mexico, are active. Visible from PV are the more intimate Sierra Vallejo and the Sierra Cuale ranges, to the north and south, respectively.

Heading down to the sea from these highlands are a number of important rivers, including the Ameca and the Mascota, which join forces not far from the coast at a place called Las Juntas (The Joining). Now mostly dry, the Ameca forms the boundary between Jalisco and Nayarit states. The Cuale River empties into the ocean at Puerto Vallarta, dividing the city center in two. In addition to boasting many rivers, the area is blessed with seasonal and permanent streams and springs.

Banderas Bay, or Bahía de Banderas, is Mexico's largest bay, at 42 km (26 miles) tip to tip. The northern point, Punta Mita, is in Nayarit State. Towns at the southern extreme of the bay, at Cabo Corrientes (Cape Currents)—named for the frequently strong currents off its shore—are accessible only by boat or dirt roads. The mountains backing the Costalegre are part of the Sierra Madre Occidental range. The hilly region of eroded plains has two main river systems: the San Nicolás and Cuitzmala.

Several hundred miles east of Banderas Bay, Guadalajara—capital of Jalisco State—occupies the west end of 5,400-foot Atemajac Valley, which is surrounded by mountains. Just south of Guadalajara, Lake Chapala is Mexico's largest natural lake.

Flora

The western flanks of the Sierra Madre and foothills leading down to the sea have tropical deciduous forest. At the higher levels are expanses of pine-oak forest. Many species of pines thrive in these woods, mixed in with *encinos* and *robles,* two different categories of oak. Walnut trees and *oyamel,* a type of fir, are the mainstays of the lower *arroyos,* or river basins.

Along the coast magnificent *huanacaxtle,* also called *parota* (in English, monkey pod or elephant ear tree), mingle with equally huge and impressive mango as well as kapok, cedar, tropical almond, tamarind, flamboyant, and willow. The brazilwood tree is resistant to insects and, therefore, ideal for making furniture. *Matapalo,* or strangler fig, are common in this landscape. As its name hints, these fast-growing trees embrace others in a death grip; once the matapalo is established, the host tree eventually dies.

Colima palms, known locally as *guaycoyul,* produce small round nuts smashed for oil or sometimes fed to domestic animals. Mango, avocado, citrus, and guava are found in the wild. Imported trees and bushes often seen surrounding homes and

small farms include Indian laurel, bamboo, and bougainvillea.

The coastal fringe north of San Blas is surprisingly characterized by savannas. Guinea grass makes fine animal fodder for horses and cows. Lanky coconut trees line roads and beaches. Watery coconut "milk" is a refreshing drink, and the meat of the coconut, although high in saturated fat, can be eaten or used in many types of candy. Another drink, *agua de tuba,* is made from the heart of the palm; the trunk is used in certain types of construction. Mangroves in saltwater estuaries provide an ecosystem for crabs, crustaceans, and birds.

South of Banderas Bay, thorn forest predominates along the coastal strip, backed by tropical deciduous forest. Leguminous trees like the *tabachin,* with its bright orange flowers, have long, dangling seedpods used by indigenous people as rattles. Other prominent area residents are the acacias, hardy trees with fluffy puffballs of light yellow blooms. The dry forest is home to more than 1,100 species of cacti. The *nopal,* or prickly pear cactus, abounds; local people remove the spines and grill the cactus pads or use them in healthful salads. The fruit of the prickly pear, called *tuna,* is used to make a refreshing drink, *agua de tuna.*

Fauna

Hunting, deforestation, and the encroachment of humans have diminished many once-abundant species. In the mountains far from humankind, endangered margay, jaguar, and ocelot hunt their prey, which includes spider monkeys, deer, and peccaries. More commonly seen are skunks, raccoons, rabbits, and coyote. The coatimundi is an endearing little animal that lives in family groups, often near streambeds. Inquisitive and alert, they resemble tall, slender prairie dogs. Along with the tanklike, slow-moving armadillo, the sandy-brown coatimundi is among the animals you're most likely to spot without venturing too deep within the forest. Local people call the coatimundi both *tejón* and *pisote* and often keep them as pets.

Poisonous snakes include the Mexican rattlesnake and the fer-de-lance. Locals call the latter *cuatro narices* (four noses) because it appears to have four nostrils. It's also called *nauyaca;* the bite of this viper can be deadly. There are more than a dozen species of coral snakes with bands of black, yellow, and red in different patterns. False corals imitate this color scheme to fool their predators, but unless you're an expert, it's best to err on the side of caution.

The most famous of the migratory marine species is the humpback whale, here called *ballena jorobada,* or "hunchback" whale. These leviathans grow to 51 feet and weigh 40 to 50 tons; they travel in pods, feeding on krill and tiny fish. In a given year the females in area waters may be either mating or giving birth. During their annual migration of thousands of miles from the Bering Sea, the hardy creatures may lose some 10,000 pounds, or approximately 10% of their body weight. Hunted nearly to extinction in the 1900s, humpbacks remain an endangered species.

A few Bryde whales make their way to Banderas Bay and other protected waters near the end of the humpback season, as do some killer whales (orca) and false killer whales. Bottlenose, spinner, and pantropic spotted dolphins are present pretty much year-round. These acrobats

love to bow surf just under the water's surface and to leap into the air. Another spectacular leaper is the velvety-black manta ray, which can grow to 30 feet wide. Shy but lovely spotted eagle rays hover close to the ocean floor, where they feed on crustaceans and mollusks. Nutrient-rich Pacific waters provide sustenance for a wide range of other sea creatures. Among the most eye-catching are the graceful king angelfish, iridescent bumphead parrotfish, striped Indo-Pacific sergeants and Moorish idols, and the funny-looking guinea fowl puffer and its close relative, the equally unusual black-blotched porcupine fish.

The varied landscape of Nayarit and Jalisco states provides a tapestry of habitats for some 350 species of birds. In the mangroves, standouts are the great blue heron, mangrove cuckoo, and vireo. Ocean and shorebirds include red-billed tropic birds as well as various species of heron, egret, gulls, brown and blue-footed boobies, and frigate birds. Military macaws patrol the thorn forests, and songbirds of all stripes live in the pine-oak forests. About 40% of the birds in the Costalegre region are migratory. Among the residents are the yellow-headed parrot and the Mexican wood nymph, both threatened species.

Environmental Issues
The biggest threat to the region is deforestation of the tropical dry forest. Slash-and-burn techniques are used to prepare virgin forest for agriculture and pasturing of animals. This practice is counterproductive, as the thin soil fails to produce after the mulch-producing trees and shrubs have been stripped.

The tropical dry forests (also called tropical thorn forest) are now being deforested due to the increasing tourism and human population. Controlled ecotourism offers a potential solution, although failed projects in the area have significantly altered or drained salt marshes and mangrove swamps.

The dry forest is an extremely important ecosystem. It represents one of the richest in Mexico and also one with the highest level of endemism (plant and animal species found nowhere else). Several species of hardwood trees, including the Pacific coast mahogany and Mexican kingwood, are being over-harvested for use in the building trade. The former is endangered and the latter, threatened.

South of Puerto Vallarta in the Costalegre are two adjacent forest reserves that together form the 32,617-acre Chamela–Cuixmala Biosphere Reserve. Co-owned and managed by nonprofit agencies, private companies, and Mexico's National University, UNAM, the reserve protects nine major vegetation types, including the tropical dry forest, tropical deciduous forest, and semi-deciduous forest. A riparian environment is associated with the north bank of the Cuixmala River. Within the reserve there are approximately 72 species considered at risk for extinction, including the American crocodile and several species of sea turtle.

Hojonay Biosphere Reserve was established by the Hojonay nonprofit organization to preserve the jaguar of the Sierra de Vallejo range and its habitat. The 157,060-acre reserve is in the foothills and mountains behind La Cruz de Huanacaxtle and San Francisco, in Nayarit State.

There are no tours or casual access to either of the reserves, which serve as buffers against development and a refuge for wildlife.

The People

The population of Puerto Vallarta is overwhelmingly of mestizo (mixed Native American and white/European) descent. According to the 2010 census, fewer than 1% of Jalisco residents speak an indigenous language. Compare that to nearby states: Michoacán with 3.6%; Guerrero with about 14%; and Oaxaca, where more than 33% of the inhabitants converse in a native language. Those indigenous people who do live in Jalisco State are small groups of Purépecha (also called Tarascans), in the south. The Purépecha were among the very few groups not conquered by the Aztec nation that controlled much of Mesoamerica at the time of the Spanish conquest.

Although not large in number, the indigenous groups most associated with Nayarit and Jalisco states are the Cora and their relatives, the Huichol. Isolated in mountain and valley hamlets and individual *rancherías* (tiny farms) deep in the Sierra Madre, both have, to a large extent, maintained their own customs and culture. According to the CDI (Comisión Nacional Para el Desarrollo de los Pueblos Indígenas, or National Commission for the Development of Native Peoples), there are about 24,390 Cora in Durango, Zacatecas, and Nayarit states, and some 43,929 Huichol, mainly in Nayarit, Jalisco, and Durango. Nearly 70% of the culturally related groups speak their native language.

No matter their background, you'll notice nearly all locals have a contagiously cheery outlook on life. There's an explanation for that: In 1947 a group of prominent vallartenses was returning along twisty mountain roads from an excursion to Mexico City. When the driver lost control and the open-sided bus plunged toward the abyss, death seemed certain. But a large rock halted the bus's progress, and Los Favorecidos (The Lucky Ones), as they came to be known, returned to Puerto Vallarta virtually unharmed. Their untrammeled gestures of thanks to the town's patron saint, the Virgin of Guadalupe, set the precedent for this animated religious procession. Today, all Puerto Vallartans consider themselves to be Los Favorecidos, and thus universally blessed—hence, the story goes, their optimism. For those of us fortunate enough to visit, taking home a bit of that spiritual magnetism can be the best souvenir.

The Magic of Mexico

To say that Mexico is a magical place means more than saying it's a place of great natural beauty and fabulous experiences. Cities like Catemaco, in Veracruz, have a reputation for their *brujos* and *brujas* (male and female witches, respectively) and herbal healers (*curanderos/curanderas*). But Mexicans use these services even in modern Mexico City and Guadalajara and in tourist towns like Puerto Vallarta. Some might resort to using a curandera to reverse *mal de ojo,* the evil eye, thought to be responsible for a range of unpleasant symptoms, circumstances, disease, or even death.

A *limpia,* or cleansing, is the traditional cure for the evil eye. The healer usually passes a raw chicken or turkey egg over the sufferer to draw out the bad spirit. Green plants, like basil, or branches from certain trees can also be used, drawing the greenery over the head, front, and back to decontaminate the victim. Prayer is an essential ingredient.

Some cures are of a more practical nature. Mexican herbalists, like their colleagues

around the world, use tree bark, nuts, berries, roots, and leaves to treat everything from dandruff to cancer. *Epazote*, or wormseed, is a distinctly flavored plant whose leaves are used in cooking. As its English name implies, its medicinal task is to treat parasites.

Most folk wisdom seems to draw from both fact and, if not fiction, at least superstition. Breezes and winds are thought to produce a host of negative reactions: from colds and cramps to far more drastic ailments like paralysis. Some people prefer sweating in a car or bus to rolling down the window and being hit by the wind, especially since mixing hot and cold is something else to be avoided. Even worldly athletes may refuse a cold drink after a hot run. Sudden shock is thought by some to cause lasting problems.

Although it doesn't take a leap of faith to believe that herbal remedies cure disease and Grandma's advice was right on, some of the stuff sold in shops is a bit "harder to swallow." It's difficult to imagine, for example, that the sky-blue potion in a pint-size bottle will bring you good luck, or the lilac-color one can stop people from gossiping about you. Those that double as floor polish seem especially suspect.

Whether magic and prophecy are real or imagined, they sometimes have concrete results. Conquistador Hernán Cortés arrived on the east coast of Mexico in 1519, which correlated to the year "One Reed" on the Aztec calendar. A few centuries prior to Cortés's arrival, the benevolent god-king Quetzalcoatl had, according to legend, departed the same coast on a raft of snakes, vowing to return in the year One Reed to reclaim his throne.

News of Cortés—a metal-wearing godman accompanied by strange creatures (horses and dogs) and carrying lightning (cannons and firearms)—traveled quickly to the Aztec capital. Emperor Moctezuma was nervous about Quetzalcoatl's return and his reaction to the culture of war and sacrifice the Aztecs had created. In his desire to placate the returning god, Moctezuma ignored the advice of trusted counselors and opened the door for the destruction of the Aztec empire.

La Vida Loca

Living the good life in Mexico—specifically in and around Banderas Bay—seems to get easier year by year. Americans and Canadians are by far the biggest groups of expats. In addition to those who have relocated to make Mexico their home, many more foreigners have part-time retirement or vacation homes here. A two-bedroom property in a gated community by the sea begins at around $230,000. You could get more modest digs for less; at the upper end of the spectrum, the sky's the limit.

The sheer number of foreigners living in Puerto Vallarta facilitates adventures that were much more taxing a decade or two ago, like building a home or finding an English-speaking real estate agent or lawyer. Contractors and shopkeepers are used to dealing with gringos; most speak good to excellent English. The town is rich with English-language publications and opportunities for foreigners to meet up for events or volunteer work.

WEDDINGS AND HONEYMOONS

Mexico is a growing wedding and honeymoon destination for Canadians and Americans. Many area hotels—from boutiques to internationally known brands—offer honeymoon packages and professional wedding planners. Although there's an obligatory civil ceremony that must accompany the Big Event, you can get married in a house of worship, on a beach, at a hotel chapel, or on a yacht or sailboat.

The Big Day

Choosing the Perfect Place. Puerto Vallarta—including resorts to the north along the Riviera Nayarit and south along the Costalegre—is one of Mexico's most popular wedding and honeymoon destinations. Many couples choose to marry on the beach, often at sunset because it's cooler and more comfortable for everyone; others chuck the whole weather conundrum and marry in an air-conditioned resort ballroom.

The luxury of enjoying your wedding and honeymoon in one place has a cost: You may find it hard to have some alone time with your sweetie with all your family and friends on hand. Consider booking an all-inclusive, which has plenty of meal options and activities to keep your guests busy. This will make it easier for them to respect your privacy and stick to mingling with you and your spouse at planned times. Among PV's best options for on-site, catered weddings are the Marriott CasaMagna, the Westin, the Villa Premiere, and Casa Velas. Le Kliff and El Dorado restaurants offer stunning views from their wedding-reception areas; Las Caletas offers unique beachfront weddings accessed by boat through Vallarta Adventures.

Wedding Attire. Some women choose a traditional full wedding gown with veil, but more popular and comfortable—especially for an outdoor wedding—is a simple sheath or a white cotton or linen dress that will breathe in the tropical heat. Some brides, of course, opt for even less formal attire: anything from a sundress to shorts or a bathing suit.

Weddings on the beach are best done barefoot, even when the bride wears a gown. Choose strappy sandals for a wedding or reception that's not on the sand, and forget the notion of stockings—it's usually too hot and humid. Whatever type of gown you choose, it's best to both purchase and get any alterations done before leaving home. Buy a special garment bag and hand-carry your dress on the plane. Don't let this be the one time in your life that your luggage goes missing at great personal cost.

Time of Year. Planning according to the weather can be critical for a successful PV wedding. If you're getting married in your bathing suit, you might not mind some heat and humidity, but will your venue—and your future mother-in-law—hold up under a summer deluge? We recommend substituting the traditional June wedding that's so suitable for New England and Nova Scotia with one held between late November and February or March. April through mid-June is usually dry but extremely hot and humid. Summer rains begin to fall in mid-June. Sometimes this means a light sprinkle that reduces heat and humidity and freshens the trees; other times it means a torrential downpour that immediately floods the streets. Although hurricanes are rarer along the Pacific than the Caribbean, they can threaten September through early November. For

an outdoor wedding, establish a detailed backup plan in case the weather lets you down.

Finding a Wedding Planner. Hiring a wedding planner will minimize stress for all but the simplest of ceremonies. A year or more in advance, the planner will, among other things, help choose the venue, recommend a florist, and arrange for a photographer and musicians. The most obvious place to find a wedding planner is at a resort hotel that becomes wedding central: providing accommodations for you and your guests, the wedding ceremony venue, and the restaurant or ballroom for the reception. But you can also hire an independent wedding coordinator; just do a Web search for "Puerto Vallarta wedding" and you'll get tons of hits. Unless you're fluent in Spanish, make sure the person who will be arranging one of your life's milestones speaks and understands English well. Ask for references, and check them.

When interviewing a planner, talk about your budget, and ask about costs. Are there hourly fees or one fee for the whole event? How available will the consultant and his or her assistants be? Which vendors do they use and why? How long have they been in business? Request a list of the exact services they'll provide, and get a proposal in writing. If you don't feel this is the right person or agency for you, try someone else. Cost permitting, it's helpful to meet the planner in person.

Requirements. Getting a bona fide wedding planner will obviously facilitate completing the required paperwork and negotiating the legal requirements for marrying in Mexico. Blood work must be done upon your arrival, but not more than 14 days before the ceremony. All documents must be translated by an authorized translator from the destination, and it's important to send these documents certified mail to your wedding coordinator at least a month ahead of the wedding. You'll also need to submit an application for a marriage license as well as certified birth certificates (bring the original with you to PV, and send certified copies ahead of time). If either party is divorced or widowed, an official divorce decree or death certificate must be supplied. The bride, groom, and four witnesses will also need to present passports and tourist cards.

Jalisco State has additional requirements; for this reason some couples choose to have the civil ceremony in Nayarit State (Nuevo Vallarta or anywhere north of there) and then the "spiritual" ceremony in the location of their choice. Since church weddings aren't officially recognized in Mexico, even for citizens, a civil ceremony is required in any case, thus making your marriage valid in your home country as well. Another option is to be married (secretly?) in a civil ceremony in your own country and then hold the wedding event without worrying about all the red tape.

The Honeymoon

If you've chosen a resort wedding, you and many of the guests may be content to relax on-site after the bustle and stress of the wedding itself. Puerto Vallarta has a huge variety of accommodations, from name-brand hotels with spas and multiple swimming pools to three-bedroom B&Bs in the moderate price range. Many properties have special honeymoon packages that include champagne and strawberries on the wedding night, flowers in the room, spa treatments, or other sorts of pampering and earthly pleasures.

KIDS AND FAMILIES

What better way to bond with your kids than splashing in the pool or the sea, riding a horse into the hills, or zipping through the trees on a canopy tour? Puerto Vallarta may be short on sights, but it's long on outdoor activities like these. It also has a huge range of accommodation options: everything from B&Bs that leave lunch and dinner wide open for a family on the go to all-inclusive resorts where picky eaters can be easily indulged and kids of all ages can be kept engaged by activities or kids' clubs.

Places to Stay

Resorts: Except those that exclude children entirely, most of Vallarta's beach resorts cater to families and have children's programs. The Sol Meliá is great for little kids, as it offers lots of games and activities geared toward them; there's not so much of interest to teens here. The Marriott is kid-friendly, offering children's menus at most of its restaurants and kids' clubs for the 4-to-13 set. In addition to things like Ping-Pong, tennis, and volleyball, kids absolutely love liberating tiny turtle hatchlings into the sea during the summer/early fall turtle season.

At the high end of the price spectrum, Four Seasons has plenty for the kids to do, as well as golf and spa appointments for Mom and Dad. The protected, almost private beach here is great for the children, who also love floating on inner tubes in the ring-shaped swift-water swimming pool. The children's center, with loads of cool games and computer programs, keeps kids of all ages entertained.

South of Vallarta, Dreams is a great place for an all-inclusive family vacation, with movies on the beach and loads of activities for adults and children. Kids enjoy the secluded beach (parents needn't worry about them wandering off), the giant-screen TV on the beach for movies or ball games, and the treasure hunts and weekly overnight campouts.

Old Vallarta (El Centro and Colonia E. Zapata, aka Zona Romántica) consists mainly of moderate to budget hotels. Independent families are often drawn to such properties on or near Los Muertos Beach. Playa Los Arcos, for instance, is right on the sand; Eloisa, with its inexpensive studios (with kitchenettes) and suites, is a block from the bay.

Vacation Rentals: Apartments, condos, and villas are an excellent option for families. You can cook your own food (a big money saver), spread out, and set up a home away from home, which can make everyone feel more comfortable. If you decide to go the apartment- or condo-rental route, be sure to ask about the number and size of the swimming pools and whether outdoor spaces and barbecue areas are available.

Funky Yelapa, south of PV, has only a few hotels; most people rent homes—ranging from spartan to less spartan—via the Internet; the site ⊕ *www.yelapa. info* has a wide range of rentals. **Boutique Villas** (☎ *322/209–1992 or 866/560–2281* ⊕ *www.boutiquevillas.com*) is an excellent resource for quality condos and villas in a variety of price ranges. Even in the winter (high) season, you can get a nice two-bedroom, two-bath condo for $150 a night. Add great locations, satellite TV in every bedroom, daily maid service, and the use of washer and dryer, and the value is obvious. You can even get your own cook who will do the shopping as well.

Beaches

Los Muertos Beach is a good bet for families who want access to snacks and water-sports rentals, and there are (usually) lifeguards here, too. Families favor the north end near Playas Olas Altas (the south end is the gay beach), but there's plenty of sand and sun for all. The all-inclusive resorts of Nuevo Vallarta rent water-sports equipment for use at a long, wide beach that continues all the way to Bucerías. The scene here is very laid-back, involving more lounging than anything else.

Water Activities

If you surf, or want to learn, Sayulita is a good option. There are also many good surfing beaches off the point at Punta Mita as well as around San Blas and Barra de Navidad.

Year-round you can catch glimpses of manta rays leaping from the water and dolphins riding the wakes of bay cruises. Winter sees whale-watching expeditions on which you can spot humpbacks and, occasionally, orcas.

Turtle season is summer through late fall; children love to take part in liberating the tiny hatchlings. Larger resort hotels on turtle-nesting beaches often encourage guests to participate in this, and wildlife operators offer turtle tours.

There's snorkeling (though sometimes lots of little jellyfish join you in the hot summer months) around Los Arcos just south of PV, at the Marietas Islands off Punta Mita, and at other beaches north and south. Divers haunt these spots, too, in addition to farther-away destinations.

PV's yachts and *pangas* (skiffs) are available for shore- or deep-water fishing excursions. Nuevo Vallarta has a much smaller fleet based at Paradise Village marina. In small towns like Mismaloya, Boca de Tomatlán, Rincón de Guayabitos, Sayulita, Tenacatita, and Barra de Navidad, you contract with local fishermen on or near the beach for angling expeditions.

Land Activities

Puerto Vallarta proper has a lovely botanical garden with a river in which kids can splash. In the hills behind town, you can go on horseback, mountain-bike, ATV, dune-buggy, or canopy-tour adventures. Golf courses range from private links at Punta Mita to fun and accessible courses in Nuevo Vallarta and Marina Vallarta. There are excellent courses to the south at El Tamarindo and Barra de Navidad.

After Dark

Nightly in high season musicians, clowns, and mimes perform at PV's Los Arcos amphitheater. Walk along the malecón en route, stopping to enjoy an ice cream, admire the sunset, or pose for pictures beside a sculpture.

Dinner shows often offer Mexican-theme buffets, mariachi music, and, sometimes, cowboys doing rope tricks. The pirate-theme vessel *Marigalante* has both day and evening cruises that kids love. PV has three modern movie theaters with English-language movies; note, though, that animated films or those rated "G" are usually dubbed in Spanish, as kids aren't fond of subtitles.

GREAT
ITINERARIES

Each of these itineraries fills one day. Together they touch on some of PV's quintessential experiences, from shopping to getting outdoors to just relaxing at the best beaches and spas.

Romancing the Zone

Head south of downtown to the Zona Romántica for a day of excellent shopping and dining. Stop at Isla del Río Cuale for trinkets and T-shirts, and have an island breakfast overlooking the stream at the River Cafe.

■TIP➔ **Most of the stores in the neighborhood will either ship your oversize prizes for you or expertly pack them and recommend reputable shipping companies.**

Crossing the pedestrian bridge nearest the bay, drop nonshoppers at Los Muertos Beach. They can watch the fishermen on the small pier, lie in the sun, sit in the shade with a good book, or walk south to the rocky coves of **Conchas Chinas Beach,** which is good for snorkeling when the water is calm. Meanwhile, shoppers head to **Calle Basilio Badillo** and surrounding streets for folk art, housewares, antiques, clothing, and accessories. End the day back at Los Muertos with dinner, drinks, and live music.

■TIP➔ **Some of the musicians at beachfront restaurants work for the restaurant; others are freelancers. If a roving musician (or six) asks what you'd like to hear, find out the price of a song. Fifty pesos (around $4) is typical.**

Downtown Exploration

Puerto Vallarta hasn't much at all in the way of museums, but with a little legwork, you can get a bit of history. Learn about the area's first inhabitants at the tiny but tidy **Museo Arqueológico** (closed Sunday), with information in English. From the museum, head downtown along

the newest section of the **malecón,** which crosses the river. About four blocks north, check out the action in the main plaza and Los Arcos amphitheater. At the **Iglesia de Nuestra Señora de Guadalupe,** you can pay your respects to the patron saint of the city (and the country).

Strolling farther north along the malecón is like walking through a sculpture garden: Look for the statue of a boy riding a sea horse (it's become PV's trademark), and *La Nostalgia,* a statue of a seated couple, by noted PV artist Ramiz Barquet. Three figures climb a ladder extending into the air in Sergio Bustamante's *In Search of Reason.* One of the most elaborate sculptures is by Alejandro Colunga: *Rotunda del Mar* has more than a dozen fantastic figures—some with strange, alien appendages—seated on chairs and pedestals of varying heights.

A Day of Golf and Steam

Puerto Vallarta is one of Mexico's best golfing destinations. And what better way to top off a day of play than with a steam, soak, and massage? At the southern end of the Costalegre, Tamarindo has a great course (18 holes) and a very good spa. The closest spas to the greens of Marina Vallarta and the Vista Vallarta are those at the Westin Regina and the CasaMagna Marriott, which has gorgeous new facilities. The El Tigre course is associated with the Paradise Village resort, whose reasonably priced spa is open also to those who golf at Mayan Palace, just up the road, and at Flamingos, at the far northern edge of Nuevo Vallarta.

■TIP➔ **Ask your concierge (or look online) to find out how far ahead you can reserve, and then try for the earliest possible tee time to beat the heat. If the course you choose doesn't have a club**

pool, you can have lunch and hang at the pool at the resorts suggested above or get a massage, facial, or other treatment (always reserve ahead).

A Different Resort Scene

If you've got wheels, explore a different sort of beach resort. After breakfast, grab beach togs, sunscreen, and other essentials for a day at a beach north of town. Before heading out, those with a sweet tooth should make a pit stop at PV's Pie in the Sky, which has excellent pie, chocolate, and other sugar fixes. (There's another Pie in the Sky in Bucerías, as well as a Los Chatos cake and ice cream shop.)

About an hour north of PV, join Mexican families on the beach at **Rincón de Guayabitos,** on attractive Jaltemba Bay. Play in the mild surf; walk the pretty, long beach; or take a ride in a glass-bottom boat to **El Islote,** an islet with a small restaurant and snorkeling opportunities. Vendors on Guayabitos beach sell grilled fish, sweet breads, and chilled coconuts and watermelon from their brightly colored stands.

On the way back south, stop in the small town of **San Francisco** (aka San Pancho) for dinner. You can't go wrong at La Ola Rica or the more sophisticated Cafe del Mar (brush the sand off your feet for that one). In high season and especially on weekend evenings, one of the two will probably have live music.

■ TIP→ Take a water taxi out for a look at El Islote, where with luck you might spot a whale between December and March.

LIZ + RICHARD

The affair between Richard Burton and Elizabeth Taylor ignited tourism to PV, which was an idyllic beach town when they first visited in 1963. Taylor tagged along when Burton starred in *The Night of the Iguana,* shot in and around Mismaloya beach. The fiery Welsh actor purchased Casa Kimberley (Calle Zaragoza, a few blocks behind the cathedral) for Liz's 32nd birthday and connected it to his home across the street with a pink-and-white "love bridge." Taylor owned the house for 26 years and left most of her possessions behind when she sold it. Casa Kimberley later became a B&B and is now part of Hacienda San Angel (⇨ *Chapter 5).*

FESTIVALS AND EVENTS

January

El Día de los Santos Reyes. El Día de los Santos Reyes (January 6) was the day of gift-giving in Latin America until Santa Claus invaded from the North. Although many families now give gifts on Christmas or Christmas Eve, Three Kings Day is still an important celebration. The children receive token "gifts of the Magi." *Atole* (a drink of finely ground rice or corn) or hot chocolate is served along with the *rosca de reyes*, a ring-shaped cake. The person whose portion contains a tiny baby Jesus figurine must host a follow-up party on Candlemass, February 2.

February

Festival de Música San Pancho. The four-day Festival de Música San Pancho is an amalgam of the area's best regional musicians; snowbirds also participate. The free jamboree is usually held in mid- to late February. The event has featured bluegrass, blues, jazz, funk, and standards in addition to cumbia and Mexican classics. Look for flyers around town. San Pancho is 50 minutes north of downtown Puerto Vallarta. ⊕ *sanpanchomusicfest. wordpress.com.*

Campeonato Nacional Charro Vallarta (*National Charro Championship*). *Charros* (cowboys) from all over Mexico compete in the four-day Campeonato Nacional Charro Vallarta. In addition to men's rope and riding tricks and the female competitors, there are mariachis, a parade, and exhibitions of charro-related art. Admission is $7–$12. ⊕ *centrode eventosvallarta.com.*

May

Restaurant Week. Restaurants lower their prices for two weeks at the beginning of low season during Restaurant Week, also known as the May Food Festival.

June

Día de la Marina. June 1 is Día de la Marina. Like other Mexican ports, PV celebrates Navy Day with free boat rides (inquire at the Terminal Marítima or the XII Zona Naval Militar, just to the south). Watch colorfully decorated boats depart to make offerings to sailors lost at sea.

July and August

San Antonio de Padua. Barra de Navidad celebrates its patron saint, San Antonio de Padua, the week preceding July 13 with religious parades, mass, street parties, and fireworks. ⊠ *Barra de Navidad.*

Cristo de los Brazos Caídos. Cristo de los Brazos Caídos is honored August 30–September 1 in much the same way as St. Anthony.

September

Celebration of Independence. The Celebration of Independence is held on September 15 and 16, beginning on the evening of September 15 with the traditional *Grito de Dolores*. It translates as "Cry of Pain," but it also references the town of Dolores Hidalgo, where the famous cry for freedom was uttered by priest Miguel Hidalgo. Late in the evening on September 15 there are mariachis, speeches, and other demonstrations of national pride. On September 16, witness parades and charros on horseback through the main streets of town.

October

Historic Center artWalk. One of the most traditional events in dowtown Vallarta is the Historic Center artWalk, which showcases artwork at several dozen galleries. The galleries stay open late, sometimes offering an appetizer or snack, wine, beer, or soft drinks. Browse among the paintings, jewelry, ceramics, glass, and folk art while hobnobbing with some of

PV's most respected artists. If you don't have a map, pick one up from one of the perennially participating galleries, which include Galería Whitlow, Corsica, Colectika, Galería Pacífico, Galería Caballito de Mar, PV Santana, The Loft, and Galería de Ollas. This walk is held every Wednesday from 6 pm to 10 pm, from the last week of October until late May. ⊕ *www. vallartaartwalk.com.*

Bucerias Art Walk. North of Nuevo Vallarta, Bucerías Art Walk is on Thursday nights from the last week of October until late April, 7–9 pm. Participating galleries are on Boulevard Lázaro Cárdenas 62 around Calle Galeana. ⊕ *www. thebuceriasartwalk.com.*

November and December

Fodor's Choice ★ **International Gourmet Festival.** The International Gourmet Festival is one of PV's biggest events. ☎ *322/222–2247* ⊕ *www.festivalgourmet.com.*

Home Tours. Mid-November through the end of April, three-hour villa tours by the International Friendship Club get you inside the garden walls of some inspiring PV homes. English-speaking guides lead groups on air-conditioned buses Tuesday and Wednesday, from December to March. Tours depart at 10:30 am. Lunch is included. The fee benefits local charities. ⊠ *Calle Olas Altas 513* ☎ *322/222–5466* ⊕ *ifctoursforvallarta.com* ⌲ *$35.*

Fiestas de la Virgen de Guadalupe. Puerto Vallarta's most important celebration of faith—and also one of the most elaborate spectacles of the year—is Fiestas de la Virgen de Guadalupe, designed to honor the Virgin of Guadalupe, the city's patron saint and the patroness of all Mexico. Exuberance fills the air as the end of November approaches and each participating business organizes its own procession.

The most elaborate ones include allegorical floats and papier-mâché *matachines,* or giant dolls (for lack of a better phrase), and culminate in their own private mass. Groups snake down Calle Juárez from the north or the south, ending at the Cathedral in Old Vallarta. ⊠ *Centro.*

DID YOU KNOW?

Sunset is considered a prime hour to stroll the malecón—or any other stretch of sand or boardwalk—to watch the water, town, and mountains change color as dusk settles in.

2

EXPLORING
PUERTO VALLARTA

Updated
by Luis
Domínguez

The reason Puerto Vallarta is one of the most popular tourist destinations is the fact that it is so much more than just another simple beach destination with an exceptional climate, vast beaches, and cold beer. You can have a great vacation here, stay half a year, come every high season, or just settle down, and there will always be something new to see, visit, experience, and explore.

There are incredible petroglyphs in Altavista, about an hour and a half north of Puerto Vallarta; charming and picturesque towns like Sayulita, San Pancho, and Bucerias, loved by surfers, artists, and laid-back people; ecological conservation zones with endangered species near Boca de Tomates and in the Marina area; various croc sanctuaries; a botanical garden and a zoo for those who look for off-the-beaten-track experiences. Puerto Vallarta itself is packed with little places to discover and enjoy after you get bored with sunbathing and sipping margaritas. The malecón has been refurbished recently and you can simply linger lazily for about 15 city blocks, or tour the sculptures, art walk, shop around, watch clown shows and folkloric dancers, visit the oldest restaurants in town, and walk as far as Los Muertos beach and step on the new pier. The Romantic Zone is one of the trendiest areas of the city. Around Basilio Badillo Street is the place to eat out and hang around with friends.

Puerto Vallarta is constantly reinventing itself while preserving its natural charms as a slightly chaotic, fun town that never stops surprising visitors.

ORIENTATION AND PLANNING

GETTING ORIENTED

Puerto Vallarta town is located in the center of Mexico's largest bay. Bahía de Banderas is 42 kilometers (26 miles) long and combines beach attractions with spectacular mountain views, as the Sierra Madre foothills descend into the blue waters of the Pacific Ocean. The northern part is called Riviera Nayarit and in the south, on the way to Manzanillo, there is a series of different beaches and bays, baptized as "the Virgin Coast" of Mexico, Costalergre. ⇨ *For detailed information on getting to and around Puerto Vallarta, see Travel Smart.*

PLANNING

WHEN TO GO

Puerto Vallarta is an all-year-round destination as far as exploring is concerned, and you may even enjoy the fact that there are not so many other tourists visiting the same places at the same time. Also prices tend to mysteriously go down in the rainy season. However, it cannot be denied that there is much more going on in Puerto Vallarta between November and May, the so-called high season, than during the rest of the year. So, if you consider yourself an independent explorer, who doesn't care about hot weather, rainy afternoons, and storms at night, feel free to explore Vallarta any time you want. But if you need more guidance and organized tours and entertainment, you should stick to high season dates.

GETTING HERE AND AROUND

The best way to move along the bay and to explore it is by car, and if you don't have your own, you should definitely consider renting one. Things to see in the northern part of Banderas Bay, as well as southern attractions, are not always easily accessible by bus, and also finding a bus stop may be quite a challenge. However, the beautiful downtown and the Zona Romántica can be perfectly done using public transport or simply on foot.

TOURS

Although Puerto Vallarta is an ideal place to visit on your own and without limitations of a guided visit, there are some occasions in which it would be highly beneficial for you to take advantage of some already organized tours and activities such as Puerto Vallarta's artWalk, Southside Shuttle on Basilio Badillo, the Malecón Public Sculpture Tour, or the popular Tequila Express train ride and distillery tour.

Tequila Express. On the nine-hour Tequila Express train ride, blue agave fields zip by as you sip tequila and listen to roving mariachis. After a distillery tour, there's lunch, folk dancing, and *charro* (cowboy) demonstrations. Make reservations up to a month ahead; from outside Mexico you'll need to use Ticketmaster, which adds an 8% surcharge. ⊠ *Camara de Comercio, Av. Vallarta 4095, Guadalajara* ☏ *33/3880–9090, 33/3818–3800 Ticketmaster* ⊕ *www.tequilaexpress.com.mx.*

Puerto Vallarta Tourism Board & Convention and Visitors Bureau. Before you visit and when you arrive, contact the Puerto Vallarta Tourism Board & Convention and Visitors Bureau. ⊠ *Local 18 Planta Baja, Zona Comercial Hotel Canto del Sol, Zona Hotelera, Las Glorias* ☎ *322/224–1175, 888/384–6822 in U.S.* ⊕ *www.visitpuertovallarta.com.*

Riviera Nayarit Convention & Visitors Bureau. Riviera Nayarit Convention & Visitors Bureau is a friendly source of info for the area between San Blas and Nuevo Vallarta. ⊠ *Paseo de los Cocoteros 85 Sur, Local I-8, Paradise Plaza, Nuevo Vallarta* ☎ *322/297–2516* ⊕ *www.riviera nayarit.com.*

Bay of Banderas/Nuevo Vallarta Tourism Office. For information about the area between Nuevo Vallarta and Punta de Mita, contact the Bay of Banderas/Nuevo Vallarta Tourism Office, wedged between the Gran Velas and Marival hotels. To avoid the small parking fee, tell the attendant you're visiting the tourism office. ⊠ *Paseo de los Cocoteros & Blvd. Nuevo Vallarta* ☎ *322/297–1006.*

PUERTO VALLARTA

ZONA ROMÁNTICA

The Romantic Zone is one of the hippest areas of Puerto Vallarta, popular not only with tourists but also with local residents, ensuring a buzz all year round. The area has many of Puerto Vallarta's must-sees.

The recent renovation of Basilio Badillo Street marked the beginning of its climb to fame. It was widened and lit up. All the establishments got on board with the transformation and worked on reinventing their images. Every other Friday in high season, the whole town seems to be on Basilio Badillo; from 6 to 10 pm the Southside Shuffle occurs. The idea is to shuffle between art galleries, boutiques, and other venues, enjoy what you see, and shop. And all that with free wine and delicious appetizers.

The oldest Farmers' Market in town is also in the Romantic Zone and takes place from 9:30 am to 2 pm at Lazaro Cárdenas Park (only in high season). You can buy all kinds of freshly baked products, artisanal foods, handmade clothing, jewelry, and crafts.

Another attraction in the area is a series of events called Viva Vallarta, celebrated at the Lazaro Cárdenas Park every Wednesday in high season. From 7 pm to 11 pm, you get a great opportunity to get to know Mexican culture and folklore through shows and games, and also to meet local artists. Gourmet food and drinks are sold through the evening and are catered by the best restaurants in town.

Don't miss the relatively new pier, Los Muertos Pier, inaugurated in January 2013. The spot was where the first wooden pier of Vallarta was built in the 1960s for the cast and crew of the film *The Night of the Iguana.* That ramshackle construction was replaced 30 years later by a concrete structure, which became the departure point for boats going to southern coastal destinations. In 2010, the city decided to renovate again. The result was the current sleek pier, resembling a soaring sail that projects 320 feet into the ocean. Apart from serving as a landing dock, it includes pedestrian pathways, plenty of seating, colorful lighting, and a waterfront promenade.

TOP ATTRACTIONS

Fodor'sChoice **El Malecón.** If you have visited Puerto Vallarta before, maybe you remem-
★ ber that its malecón used to have cars between the boardwalk and the shops and nightclubs. But in 2012 Puerto Vallarta's beloved walkway underwent a huge renovation that closed it to traffic and transformed it into a highly enjoyable (and quiet) pedestrian walkway. The scene now takes in runners, skaters, and bicyclists, as well as traditional bronze sculptures. There is talk of reopening it to cars to cater to local businesses negatively affected by the loss of traffic, but for now you can enjoy it as a lovely pedestrian promenade. ⊠ *Paseo Diaz Ordaz, Zona Romántica.*

Los Muertos Pier. There was a time when Los Muertos Pier was a sad piece of concrete extending a few meters into the sea, but that changed in 2013 when it was replaced by a beautifully designed pier that underwent years of renovations. The new pier was an instant hit and has become one of the most recognizable landmarks in Puerto Vallarta. It's perfect for a romantic walk, for reading a book while listening to the sound of the waves, and for viewing at night when it lights up the buzzing Los Muertos Beach. Oh, and it also serves as a pier! You can get a boat from here to visit the amazing beaches south of Puerto Vallarta, such as Yelapa, Quimixto, Las Animas, and many more. ⊠ *End of Francisca Rodriguez St., Zona Romántica.*

EL CENTRO

Downtown Puerto Vallarta is the main attraction of the whole Banderas Bay, with lots of things to do and explore. If your last visit to Puerto Vallarta was a couple of years ago, you won't recognize the city. It still has that old charm, but it has been enhanced with some first-world improvements.

The new malecón is the most noticeable change. It has been totally renovated, closed to traffic, and embellished with big planters full of colorful flowers, bushes, and palm trees. Now you can rent a bike for two or three, and even a stroller or a wheelchair. The malecón extends from Hotel Rosita to the new pier and maintains all the old, well-known establishments as well as the entertainment: street performers, Papantla birdmen, sand sculptures, and many others. Almost all the clubs and bars took advantage of the renovating period to update their businesses.

The Church of Our Lady of Guadalupe is an obligatory stop in the historic center. Recently it got a new crown and looks splendid over the city skyline. After your visit, relax at the Main Square just one block from the parish where you can eat an ice cream. On Sunday there is live music and dancers performing the traditional danzón.

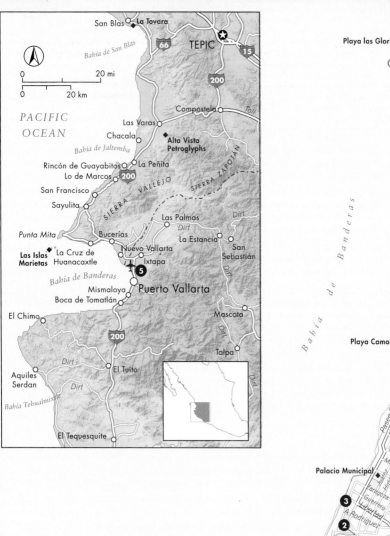

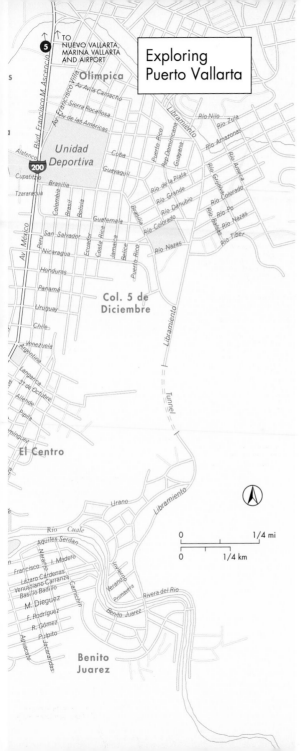

Exploring
Puerto Vallarta

A section of El Malecón, the iconic waterfront boardwalk that extends down the coastline to Los Muertos beach.

You'll spot art galleries all over the city and, in the high season, you can attend an artWalk. From November to April, stroll from one gallery to the next and enjoy local art together with a free cup of wine, a shot of tequila, and some appetizers. The participating galleries are labeled on the outside walls and you can get a free map along the way. Be sure to check ahead on which days you can chat with the artists.

The natural island on the Cuale River with restaurants, a museum, an art gallery, and countless shops and souvenir stands is another must-see. If you want to buy some more crafts at affordable prices go to the Municipal Market on the north side of the island. It has lots to choose from: pottery, jewelry, embroidered clothing, and many food stands.

TOP ATTRACTIONS

Archaeological Museum. Pre-Columbian figures and Indian artifacts are on display at the Archaeological Museum. There's a general explanation of Western Pacific cultures and shaft tombs and abbreviated but attractive exhibits of Aztatlán and Purépecha cultures and the Spanish conquest. ⊠ *Western tip of Isla Río Cuale, Centro* ✉ *By donation* ☉ *Mon.–Sat. 10–6.*

Church of Our Lady of Guadalupe. The Church of Our Lady of Guadalupe is dedicated to the patron saint of Mexico and of Puerto Vallarta. The holy mother's image, by Ignacio Ramírez, is the centerpiece of the cathedral's slender marble altarpiece. The brick bell tower is topped by a lacy-looking crown that replicates the one worn by Carlota, short-lived empress of Mexico. The wrought-iron crown toppled during an earthquake that shook this area of the Pacific Coast in October 1995 but was soon replaced with a fiberglass version, supported, as was the original, by a squadron of stone angels. This was replaced with a newer and larger rendition in October 2009. ⊠ *Calle Hidalgo 370, between Iturbide and Zaragoza, Centro* ☎ *322/222–1326* ⊕ *parroquiadeguada-lupepv.com* ⊗ *7:30 am–9 pm daily.*

ZONA HOTELERA

Puerto Vallarta is a tourist destination with all kinds of accommodations to enjoy, but you will find the greatest concentration of hotels in the Hotel Zone. Zona Hotelera, as the locals call it, stretches along Francisco Medina Ascencio Avenue, from the Puerto Vallarta Maritime Terminal to the Sheraton Buganvilias Resort. The creation of the Hotel Zone moved the tourist accommodations outside the downtown boundaries, allowing the historic center to remain relatively untouched.

Although most of the hotels are not brand new, they are all on the beach and offer spectacular ocean views over Banderas Bay, making them highly popular among Vallarta visitors. The latest additions to the area are numerous skyscrapers with oceanfront exclusive condominiums that are often available for short-term vacation rentals.

Zona Hotelera is loved by joggers. They often start their route at the beginning of the river walk, located between Plaza Peninsula and the Holiday Inn, and continue to a calm residential area called Fluvial Vallarta across the street. Another option is to follow Medina Ascencio to the city's public stadium, Agustin Flores Contreras, at the very end of the Hotel Zone (in front of the Sheraton Buganvilia Resort). Medina Ascencio is partially closed at certain hours on Sunday, when cars are replaced by bicyclists, walkers, and joggers.

Beach lovers will enjoy the many interconnected beaches of the Hotel Zone. There are several points of access along Medina Ascencio Avenue, but the easiest way is to park your car between Plaza Peninsula and the Holiday Inn. Plaza Peninsula is also the biggest shopping plaza in the area, perfect for buying souvenirs.

MARINA VALLARTA

Marina Vallarta is a beachfront model tourist community located next to the Puerto Vallarta International Airport, between a golf course and a marina. It was created at the end of the 1980s and was quickly "copied" by other tourist destinations such a Cancún, Los Cabos, Mazatlán, and Ixtapa. It functions almost as a self-sustainable entity, where tourists can find absolutely everything they may need during vacation including restaurants, bars, shops, and the Plaza Marina shopping center with a Comercial Mexicana supermarket.

Marina Vallarta is a pleasant area to visit on a lazy afternoon. If you arrive by car, you will first notice a big whale sculpture at the main entrance, designed by Octavio González in the 1990s and sponsored by local Marina businessmen. You may park your car at the Nima Bay building, which has numerous shops, cafés, and restaurants that cater to both tourists and locals. Nima Bay opens to a marina promenade, where the main attraction is a lighthouse with a bar at the top, at the end of

Puerto Vallarta's Art Walk

A series of bronze sculptures stretches along the sea walk and are the most photographed elements of the city. In contrast to traditional sculptures in museums, these can be touched and even climbed and this close contact has already given many of them a bright bronze luster.

The "Millenium" spiral sculpture created by Mathis Lidice is located at the beginning of the malecón and represents history and the passage of time. DNA at its base depicts the origin of life and the dove of peace at the top symbolizes hope for the future. There are various historical characters included in the design, such as Charlemagne and Nezahualcoyotl.

"Origin and Destination" is a project by Pedro Tello composed of five sculptures that represent the beginnings of humanity. The boat represents humanity's search for new horizons; the chimera depicts the rise of machines; the whale shows the rise of humanity in the new millennium; and the obelisk represents the work of humanity through time and history.

The "Nostalgia" sculpture was the first one installed on the malecón and it depicts a couple on a bench, looking towards the sea. Many locals look at this piece of art nostalgically, remembering the love story between the artist Ramiz Barquet and his wife Nelly.

"La Naturaleza Como Madre" (Nature as Mother) is an abstract sculpture by Adrian Reynoso that shows a wave with some human characteristics on a spiral shell and symbolizes the evolution of our planet with nature as the controlling force.

"El Sutil Come Piedras" (The Subtle Rock-Eater) by Jonas Gutierrez is a friendly, chubby man sculpted in metal and rock, reminding observers of happy childhoods and the enjoyment of every single discovery.

"El Unicornio de la Buena Fortuna" (The Good Fortune Unicorn) by Anibal Riebeling dates back to 2011. Its sleek and curvy shape makes it look like a natural part of the malecón.

"Tritón y Sirena," by Carlos Espino, depicts the Greek God of the sea, earthquakes, and the sea-nymph Amphitrite, his wife.

"La Rotonda del Mar" by a famous artist, Alejandro Colunga, is one of the most loved sculpture collections in PV. Both locals and tourists like to take pictures with his work while sitting in one of the anthropomorphic chairs.

"En Búsqueda de la Razón" (In Search of Reason), by Sergio Bustamante, was inaugurated in 1999 for the new millennium. It shows two children climbing a bronze ladder and their mother begging them to get down. The sculpture attracts lots of kids, and tourists flock to it in search of good photo ops.

"El Caballito del Mar" (The Seahorse), by Rafael Zamarripa, has been in Puerto Vallarta since 1976 and has become the city's symbol. After the renewal of the malecón, the Seahorse was moved to a better spot on the promenade with more visibility.

"La Fuente de la Amistad" (The Friendship Fountain), by James "Bud" Bottoms, is right next to Los Arcos del Malecón. It was created to celebrate the sisterhood between Puerto Vallarta and the city of Santa Barbara, California. The dolphins are inspired by a local native myth in which the earth goddess Hutash created a rainbow to help some travelers cross to the mainland. As some of them looked down, they fell off the bridge and were transformed into dolphins. Since then dolphins and humans have been considered brothers in local folklore.

"Los Bailarines de Puerto Vallarta" (Puerto Vallarta Dancers), by Jim Demetro, has been part of the malecón since 2006 and was inspired by the colorful costumes of the Xiutla Municipal Folkloric Ballet, made up of children and teenagers from Puerto Vallarta.

"Erizados" (Sea Urchins), by Blu (Maritza Vázquez), can be found in the new extension of the malecón and shows a connection between Puerto Vallarta and the sea. The sculpture was set up on the malecón as part of a temporary exhibition, but the locals liked it so much that the artist decided to leave it there.

"San Pascual Bailón" (Saint Paschal Baylon) is another curious sculpture by Ramiz Barquet, and depicts the patron saint of cooks. Saint Paschal Baylon was a Franciscan monk who sanctified cooking and baking and distributed the leftovers among the poor.

"Lorena Ochoa," by Octavio González Gutiérrez, was placed on the malecón in 2012 to commemorate the sporting career of Lorena Ochoa, a talented golfer from Jalisco, who ranked first in the world for several years.

"The Washer Woman," by Jim Demetro, can be found on the wall surrounding the Molino de Agua Condominium, next to the Cuale River. The sculpture shows a woman washing her clothes on a rock in a river next to a water mill, the way it's still done by some people.

There is a guided sculpture tour every Tuesday organized by Galeria Pacifico that will provide you with interesting historical and artistic insight. It starts at 9:30 am at the Rosita Hotel, where the first sculpture "Millennium" is located. You may also do the tour by yourself.

Sculptures stand against a stunning view of the ocean at La Rotonda del Mar on El Malecón.

Timón Street. The promenade stretches along modern vessels and offers numerous restaurants for breakfast, lunch, and dinner. This is also an ideal place to go on a fishing tour. Renting a boat is extremely easy, and you will surely be approached by many people offering you one.

If you come with your own boat, Marina Vallarta rents many slips on a daily, weekly, or monthly basis with all basic services such as electricity, satellite TV, honey barge, water, laundry services, an 88-ton travel lift, and security. For more information contact the Harbormaster: ☎ 322/221–0722.

Sports lovers will appreciate the 18-hole golf course designed by Joe Finger that offers a typical Vallarta experience with stellar ocean and mountain views.

WORTH NOTING

Estero El Salado. You know how in New York they reserved a huge piece of much-coveted land for Central Park? Well, something like that happened in Puerto Vallarta with the Estero El Salado. This estuary right in the middle of the city has been declared a protected area featuring spectacular examples of biodiversity. Boat tours go deep into El Salado from Tuesday to Saturday at 11 am and 3 pm. Get ready to see plenty of crocodiles up close and personal in their natural habitat, as well as a variety of birds and impressive vegetation. There is a museum and a tower offering stunning views of the estuary and the city. Call or write ahead (via the website) to book a tour. ⊠ *Marina Vallarta* ☎ *322/226–2878* ⊕ *www.esterodelsalado.org* ✉ *$25; check website for different discounts.*

OLAS ALTAS

On the southern board of Puerto Vallarta, just behind the famous Los Muertos Beach and the new pier, you will find the upscale residential neighborhoods of Amapas and Conchas Chinas. They are located on both sides of Highway 200 and enjoy either the whitest beaches of the bay or the best panoramic ocean views. The beaches are fun to visit and explore, with impressive boulders, little coves, and rocky grottos, and you can access them from the highway or on foot from Los Muertos Beach via a small trail. However, the lack of restaurants, showers, toilets, and other facilities don't make these beaches ideal for long stays.

The higher zones are incredible observation points and can be easily accessed through one of two entrances on the left side of the road. Simply take either of them and drive as high as you can, stopping whenever you feel like. At the top, turn round and get some spectacular shots of the bay or of the high-end villas.

NUEVO VALLARTA

15 km (9 miles) north of Puerto Vallarta.

Nuevo Vallarta is one of the fastest growing beach destinations of Mexico and has the second-highest number of hotels in the country. The countryside is composed mainly of vast golf courses, exclusive condominiums, luxurious restaurants, marinas, and miles of golden beaches. This is a great place to try all kinds of water sports such as surfing, scuba diving, kayaking, and paddle- and kite surfing. The hotels and resorts in the area also hide world-class spas and renowned restaurants.

The golf courses of Nuevo Vallarta are among the best in the world. El Tigre (par 72), designed by Robert von Hagge, has 18 holes, 144 sand traps distributed over 7,329 yards of Bermuda 419-covered terrain, and nine artificial lakes. Even the most experienced golfers find it challenging.

The Grand Mayan development has the Nayar Golf Club, another spectacular course designed by Jim Lipe and redesigned by Jack Nicklaus. Here you get 6,936 yards with nine holes and fine Bermuda 417 grass.

Two marinas, Nuevo Vallarta Marina and Paradise Village Marina, are also worth a visit. They can accommodate around 500 vessels and the latter is certified as the cleanest marina in the country. Beautiful ships, natural surroundings, and luxurious properties alongside should be enough to attract your attention. But if not, the marinas are home to numerous species such as herons, ducks, pelicans, and seagulls, as well as enormous crocodiles that swim freely between boats. If you don't disturb them, you shouldn't be disturbed either.

Nature lovers can also enjoy turtle releases. Olive Ridley and leatherback turtles come to the beaches of Nuevo Vallarta to lay their eggs, spurring the development of a turtle sanctuary near Bahia del Sol Resort that guarantees their protection. From August to January nightly releases are organized if any eggs have hatched. To participate, ask the reception staff at Bahia del Sol (☎ *322/297–9527*) for details.

RIVIERA NAYARIT

Riviera Nayarit has been gaining recognition in the last few years and is now seriously competing with Puerto Vallarta for visitors. It boasts 322 km (200 miles) of pristine beaches, luxurious resorts, and dozens of little laid-back towns loved by artists, hippies, surfers, and celebrities. There are some areas that deserve special recognition for everything they have to offer.

FLAMINGOS

21 km (13 miles) north of Puerto Vallarta.

Flamingos is a mega development just behind Nuevo Vallarta and it boasts the longest beach in Banderas Bay that starts at the Ameca River (the border between Jalisco and Nayarit) and stretches up to Bucerías. This beach is lined with numerous hotels and condominiums and also has an 18-hole golf course. The Comercial Mexicana shopping center offers everything that you may need during your stay. Visit the Cocodrilario El Cora in the La Coartada Lagoon to observe local efforts to research and preserve the area's crocodile population.

BUCERÍAS

2 km (1 mile) north of Flamingos.

Bucerías resembles Puerto Vallarta when it was smaller and less famous. You have beautiful beaches, great restaurants, a lively art scene, residential and commercial areas, an art walk, and a farmers' market every Saturday. The Lázaro Cárdenas six-block street is the heart of this community and it's also where you can find the best restaurants, art galleries, and handicraft stores. The beach is preferred by families as there are no big waves and the waters are shallow near the coastline. There are many points where you can rent paddle surf or surf boards on your own, or take some classes.

LA CRUZ DE HUANACAXTLE

7 km (4 miles) north of Bucerías.

La Cruz de Huanacaxtle, or simply La Cruz if it is too hard to pronounce, is a typical fishing village that is slowly becoming the next popular destination in Banderas Bay. It has a modern world-class marina with slips for 400 vessels, a seaside promenade, many gourmet restaurants, and the best farmers' market in the bay. To get there, take the Punta Mita exit on Highway 200, almost immediately after passing Bucerías. In addition to the must-see farmers' market, you may also want to visit the fresh seafood market located right at the entrance. Osos's Restaurant, located in the middle of the farmers' market, offers incredible views over the marina and delicious gourmet seafood. Beaches are not the area's strongest points. La Manzanilla Beach is usually very crowded and the sand is hard and grey. Alamar Beach is less crowded and has a renowned bar called Sandzibar.

PUNTA MITA

17 km (10 miles) north of La Cruz de Huanacaxtle.

Punta Mita is the farthest point of Banderas Bay, located at the very tip. It's well loved by jet-setters and the famous for luxurious hotels—the Punta Mita Four Seasons hotel, the St. Regis Resort, and many exclusive developments are here. It is probably the best place in the bay to try all kinds of aquatic activities, including paddle boarding, surfing, fishing, and scuba diving. Almost every restaurant at the coast offers rental services and classes. Punta Mita is also the departure point for whale-watching excursions in winter months or boats heading for the Marietas Islands. The upscale Punta Mita development hosts luxury restaurants, but you will need a prior reservation to be able to access the resort. Hotel guests and members can enjoy two Jack Nicklaus Signature golf courses with spectacular views and challenging holes.

WORTH NOTING

Marietas Islands. This group of small islands just in front of Punta Mita at the northern end of Banderas Bay has been called "the most idyllic bomb site," because it was once used for military testing by the Mexican government. But the incredible caves created by the bombings are now the delight of tourists. Today the islands are protected, declared an area of great biodiversity by world-famous oceanographer Jacques Cousteau. Only a 20-minute boat trip away from Punta Mita, here you can practice snorkeling, scuba diving, and paddle surfing, and visit "Love Beach," a hidden artificial beach only accessible for those willing to get off the boat and swim to reach it. During winter season, a visit to the islands almost certainly guarantees a glimpse of humpback whales rejoicing in the warm waters of Banderas Bay. ✉ *off the coast of Punta Mita.*

SAYULITA

17 km (10 miles) north of Punta Mita.

You can get to Sayulita, the next famous spot along Riviera Nayarit, by taking a loop that passes through Litibú with its white-sand beaches. The town is also next to the breathtaking Tranquila resort, which has a spectacular golf course. You can travel to Sayulita by public transport, taking a Compostela bus from Walmart in front of the Maritime Terminal in Puerto Vallarta. Sayulita is a funky small town, extremely popular with surfers and healthy-living enthusiasts. Local businesses offer yoga classes, surfing, organic food shops, and numerous charming bars and restaurants with live music. It is becoming more and more popular with tourists and is gaining a trendier look every year.

WORTH NOTING

Alta Vista Petroglyphs. Even though it's not a typical excursion for tourists, the Alta Vista petroglyphs offer an interesting and different day in the outdoors. Discovered by the National Institute of Anthropology and History, the petroglyphs are a series of drawings set in stone in what seems to have been a ceremonial center for the ancient people of the Texcoquines. The petroglyphs possibly represent a 1,500-year historical span. Nowadays, the indigenous Huichol people still visit the site to celebrate different rituals. The self-guided tour ends up at the majestic "King's Pool," a naturally formed pool surrounded by cube-like stones. You can finish your history-rich excursion with a refreshing swim in the crystal-clear waters. This is a hard-to-find place, so make sure you have a reliable guide. ⊠ *North of Sayulita.*

SAN PANCHO/SAN FRANCISCO

7 km (4 miles) north of Sayulita.

Five minutes north of Sayulita is San Pancho, or San Francisco as locals call it. This is a smaller town, but equally creative and laid-back. It is popular with communities of artists and writers, and boasts numerous environmental organizations as well as art and music festivals—most of them at the end of December. Tercer Mundo Avenue hosts most of the local businesses and galleries, but exploring other streets also can be very rewarding. One of two polo fields in the area is located in San Pancho (the other one in Costalegre). La Patrona organizes seasonal polo matches every Saturday in winter and spring. The beach in San Francisco is wide and long, but the waves tend to be higher than in other regions, making it very attractive for advanced surfers.

JALTEMBA BAY

26 km (16 miles) north of San Pancho/San Francisco.

Jaltemba Bay hosts two important tourist spots: Rincón de Guayabitos and La Peñita de Jaltemba. Rincón de Guayabitos enjoyed the peak of its fame in the 1990s, but nowadays it still remains popular, especially among Canadian tourists and expats. The bay resembles a giant swimming pool, with almost no waves, and tranquil, clean waters. The beach is family-friendly and you will see many young people playing soccer or volleyball, while the little ones build sand castles with their parents. You should also visit the Coral and Cangrejo islands with their beautiful natural landscapes and numerous bird species, including pelicans, seagulls, and blue-footed boobies. The waters surrounding the islands are ideal for snorkeling and scuba diving. La Peñita is located right behind Guayabitos and maintains the charm of a small Mexican town. You can buy almost anything on the main avenue (Emiliano Zapata) and the Thursday street market in winter and spring months is an obligatory stop on your trip.

SOUTH OF PUERTO VALLARTA

All the way to Mismaloya, the hotels of the Zona Hotelera Sur hug the beach or overlook it from cliff-side aeries. South of El Tuito, Cabo Corrientes hides tiny towns and gorgeous, untrammeled beaches.

LOS ARCOS

9 km (5 miles) south of Puerto Vallarta.

Los Arcos National Marine Park is located in the southern part of Banderas Bay, just between the Mismaloya and Las Gemelas beaches. These beautiful granite islands attract thousands of visitors each year. The protected area is ideal for snorkeling and diving, and you won't believe that it is the deepest part of the bay. Some places can reach up to 480 meters (1,600 feet) under water. The islands are breeding grounds for many birds, such as pelicans, bobos, parrots, and many others, but the greatest diversity lies beneath the water surface: admire a spectacle of colors created by different species of fish and corals. John Huston filmed some parts of the movie *The Night of the Iguana* with Los Arcos in the background. There are several companies in Puerto Vallarta that organize tours to Los Arcos and include all the necessary aquatic equipment.

MISMALOYA

12 km (7 miles) south of Los Arcos.

Mismaloya is the first important stop after Conchas Chinas and this is the place that made Puerto Vallarta famous. Director John Huston chose this little hamlet as a setting for his movie *The Night of the Iguana* in 1963, and that is when and where it all started. The whole crew, including Elizabeth Taylor and Richard Burton, fell in love with the village, whose name in Náhautl means, "the place where they grab fish with their hands." It wasn't long after the movie came out that tourists started to come. A few year later, *Predator* with Arnold Schwarzenegger was filmed nearby in a jungle known as El Edén. Nowadays, the remains of the original sets are not accessible to the public, but there is a large Barceló hotel on the beach, rustic palapa bars and restaurants, and a small village to explore with more spots to grab something to eat, if you are not looking for sophisticated restaurants.

BOCA DE TOMATLÁN

4 km (2 miles) south of Mismaloya.

Almost immediately after Mismaloya, you will find the small fishing village of Boca de Tomatlán, the most important departure point for reaching southern destinations accessible only by boat, such as Las Ánimas, Yelapa, or Quimixto. Boca de Tomatlán is the last beach town accessible from Vallarta by public transportation. It is very small, but offers beautiful views over the cove with dolphins coming for a visit in the winter season and a few palapa restaurants located on the beach, with delicious seafood and sun umbrellas for rent. It is a good place to spend a quiet day on the beach.

VALLARTA BOTANICAL GARDENS

8 km (5 miles) east of Boca de Tomatlán.

If you decide to get a bit away from the coast, following the same Highway 200 you will find yourself in one of the most beautiful places in Puerto Vallarta. This not-so-little paradise is about 30 minutes from Puerto Vallarta's historic district, and you can also get to the gardens by public transportation, catching the bus headed for "El Tuito" at the corner of Carranza and Aguacate streets in the Romantic Zone. The fare costs 20 pesos (around $1.50) and the bus departs every half an hour.

Puerto Vallarta Botanical Gardens. On 20 acres of land 19 km (12 miles) south of town, the Puerto Vallarta Botanical Gardens features more than 3,000 species of plants. Set within the tropical dry forest at 1,300 feet above sea level, its trails lead to a stream where you can swim. You can also see palm, agave, and rose gardens; a tree fern grotto; an orchid house; and displays of Mexican wildflowers and carnivorous plants. There is free parking and a free guided tour daily at 1 pm, from December through Easter. The lovely, open-sided Hacienda de Oro restaurant serves an array of starters as well as pizza and Mexican dishes. Beverages include wine and a full bar. Visit the website to arrange a four-hour birding (via ATV) or hiking tour with lunch, for $85 per person. A taxi here will cost about $20, but for less than a dollar, you can take the "El Tuito" bus from the corner of Aguacate and Venustiano Carranza streets. ■ TIP→ **Slather on insect repellent before you go, and take some with you.** This is the jungle, and *jejenes* (no-see-ums), mosquitoes, and other biting bugs will definitely attack. ⊠ *Carretera a Barra de Navidad Km 24, Las Juntas y Los Veranos, Olas Altas* ☏ *322/223–6182* ⊕ *www.vbgardens.org* ✉ *$5* ⊗ *Tues.–Sun. 9–5* ⊗ *Closed Mon.*

EL TUITO

20 km (12 miles) east of Vallarta Botanical Gardens.

Continuing your trip south, you will soon get to El Tuito, the capital of Cabo Corrientes—still close enough to consider it a day trip from Puerto Vallarta (40 minutes from downtown). El Tuito is a very small but charming town with everything you might want to explore within two blocks of the plaza. All the buildings are painted with a mixture of local clays, which gives them a uniform orange look. Enjoy the day walking on the cobblestone streets and shopping for organic coffee, artisanal cheese, and delicious raicilla.

LAS ÁNIMAS

30 km (18 miles) west of El Tuito.

Coming back to the coasts, there is a series of beach destinations accessible only by boat from either Mismaloya or Boca de Tomatlán.

The first stop is Las Ánimas, a small sand beach perfect for swimming and diving. It offers beautiful coral formations, varied marine fauna, and several little restaurants on shore. Some visitors decide to take a hike from Boca, but water taxis are a more comfortable option, especially if you are not travelling very lightly.

QUIMIXTO

2 km (1 mile) south of Las Ánimas.

Quimixto is the second destination and one of the most "virgin" ones. PV locals love to unwind here and spend a lazy day away from "civilization." It has a 10-meter-high waterfall, perfect for swimming, as well as options to hike or go horseback riding. There's also a restaurant zone with simple Mexican treats and beverages.

LAS CALETAS

2 km (1 mile) south of Quimixto.

Following south, you'll come upon this beach, most famous for its exclusive show by Vallarta Adventures, Rhythms of the Night, a Las Vegas-level spectacle. The show, which is actually a tour based on ancient traditions, starts in Nuevo Vallarta at Vallarta Adventures Center or at the Maritime Terminal. During the day, Vallarta Adventures also organizes sea lion encounters at the same beach.

MAJAHUITAS

2 km (1 mile) south of Las Caletas.

Majahuitas is a tiny cove with a beautiful beach. Unless you decide to stay at the Majahuitas resort located there, there are no services or facilities available, but you may simply enjoy the white-sand beach and crystalline water.

YELAPA

5 km (3 miles) south of Majahuitas.

Yelapa is the most famous spot of the southern destinations and has its own office at the end of the Los Muertos Pier. The area enjoys the same latitude as Hawaii, but everybody compares it to Tahiti. There is a small town, a beach, and a large creek with waterfalls where the Tuito River ends. Some people come and stay for six months, but for most it is a perfect one-day or weekend destination with places to sleep and eat—telephones and electricity are very recent additions. Loved by artists and free spirits alike, the town has Spanish language, yoga, writing, drumming, meditation, art, and many other classes. And another, quite unexpected, activity that you may enjoy is croquet. There is even a Croquet Club with annual tournaments that have been going on for over two decades.

COSTALEGRE

Costalegre is a series of bays, white-sand beaches, and capes located south of Puerto Vallarta in Jalisco. Different beaches that form part of Costalegre are also known as the virgin beaches, and are definitely worth visiting.

MAYTO

96 km (59 miles) south of Puerto Vallarta.

Mayto is probably the most spectacular of all the Costalegre beaches. Just imagine 15 km (9 miles) of white sand and extreme beauty, with nothing around but two small hotels at the entrance and sea turtles breeding grounds. You can camp and for an extra charge you will be allowed to use the restrooms at the little hotels. Don't forget to buy your own provisions beforehand, as there are no stores or restaurants in Mayto. If you book ahead, you may also participate in the release of newborn turtles.

COSTA MAJAHUAS

108 km (67 miles) south of Mayto.

Here you will find Chalacatepec Beach and La Peñita Pintada (Painted Lil'Rock) that owes its name to a natural cavity with various ancient paintings. Both places are also famous for their turtle conservation programs.

BAHÍA DE CHAMELA

25 km (15 miles) south of Costa Majahuas.

Bahía de Chamela is an undeveloped bay with several islands accessible only by boat. They are exotic bird reserves, too, and great spots for snorkeling and diving.

COSTA CAREYES

14 km (8 miles) south of Bahía de Chamela.

Costa Careyes is the luxurious part of Costalegre with its diversity of spas, aquatic sports facilities, and upscale accommodations. This large coast also hosts two Bermuda grass fields and stables for 150 polo horses. Cuixmala is a stunning private estate and one of the most important ecological reserves. Located on 25,000 acres, the area has 1,200 plant species, 72 species of mammals, and 270 types of birds. There are also many small beaches with hidden grottos to explore and the estate offers plenty of activities to choose from, such as kayaking, snorkeling, and fishing.

TENACATITA BAY

36 km (22 miles) south of Costa Careyes.

Tenacatita Bay is one of the largest bays in Mexico and offers seven beautiful and not-so-developed beaches; La Manzanilla, Tenacatita, and Boca de Iguanas are the most famous ones. It is one of very few places in Mexico where, in winter months, you can observe both sunrise and sunset over the sea. The whole bay is famous for sports fishing, snorkeling, and diving.

BARRA DE NAVIDAD

42 km (26 miles) south of Tenacatita Bay.

Barra de Navidad is the biggest urban development in Costalegre. It offers all types of accommodations, including the exclusive Grand Bay Hotel, as well as plenty of palapa restaurants. In many of them you will be able to choose the fish you want for lunch from the restaurant's pools. A traditional pineapple filled with shrimp is a delicious must-have after a stroll down the local malecón.

3

BEACHES

Updated by Luis Domínguez

Throughout the region, from the Riviera Nayarit to the Costalegre, long, flat beaches invite walking, and reefs and offshore breaks draw divers, snorkelers, and surfers. In places, untouristy hideaways with little to distract you beyond waves lapping the shore may be accessible by land or by sea. Omnipresent seafood shanties are perfect vantage points for sunsets on the sand.

Although Pacific Mexico's beaches aren't the sugar-sand, crystal-water variety of the Caribbean, they're still lovely. The water here is relatively unpolluted, and the oft-mountainous backdrop is majestic.

PV sits at the center of horseshoe-shaped Bahía de Banderas (Banderas Bay), the second-largest bay in North America (after the Hudson). Exquisitely visible from cliff-side hotels and restaurants, the bay's scalloped coast holds myriad coves and small bays perfect for shelling, sunning, swimming, and engaging in more strenuous activities.

At Zona Hotelera beaches and a few popular stretches of sand north and south of PV proper, you can parasail, take boat rides, or Jet Ski; some beaches lend themselves to kayaking, boogie boarding, paddle surfing, or snorkeling. Foothills that race down to the sea are crowded with palms and cedars, and the jungle's blue-green canopy forms a highly textured background to the deep-blue ocean. Dozens of creeks and rivers follow the contours of these hills, creating estuaries, mangrove swamps, and other habitats.

South of Cabo Corrientes the mountains recede from the coast. Lovely yet lonely beaches and bays are fringed, as elsewhere in and around PV, by dry, tropical thorn forest with a variety of plants. Several species of whales cruise down in winter, and turtles spawn on the beaches from late summer into fall.

GO FOR:	IN PV:	NORTH OR SOUTH OF PV:
Wildlife	Los Arcos; Marina Vallarta (for turtles in season)	Islas Marietas (Punta de Mita); Playa Careyes and nearby beaches (for turtles in season)
Snorkeling	Los Arcos; Playa Conchas Chinas	Islas Marietas; Quimixto; Playa Mora
Walking or Jogging	Playa los Muertos; Playa Camarones	Nuevo Vallarta; Bucerías; Flamingos; Boca de Iguanas; Playa Tenacatita; Barra de Navidad; San Patricio–Melaque (Bahía de Navidad)
Calm, Swimmable Waters	Hotel pools; Conchas Chinas	Boca de Tomatlán; Playa los Ayala; Rincón de Guayabitos (Bahía de Jaltemba); Playa Chalacatepec; Punta Perula; Boca de Iguanas; Tenacatita; San Patricio–Melaque
Surfing	Olas Altas (best April–September)	El Anclote (Punta de Mita); Playa La Lancha; Sayulita; San Pancho; Quimixto; Barra de Navidad
Eating/Drinking with Locals	Playa Los Muertos; Playa Camarones (but not right on the beach)	El Anclote; La Manzanilla; Boca de Tomatlán; Chacala; Rincón de Guayabitos (Bahía de Jaltemba); Punta Perula; Playa Tenacatita; Colimilla (Barra de Navidad)

PUERTO VALLARTA

PV beaches are varied. Downtown's main beach, Los Muertos, is a fun scene, with shoulder-to-shoulder establishments for drinking and eating under the shade. There's year-round action, although water-sports equipment rentals may be available on weekends only during the rainy season. The itinerant vendors are present year-round, however, and can be annoying. Olas Altas Beach, which runs north from Los Muertos, has the same grainy brown sand but fewer vendors and services and sometimes waves big enough to surf or boogie. During vacation periods it's just as lively as Los Muertos Beach. North of the malecón and Hotel Rosita, Playa Camarones has become one of the best beaches in town, as it was the first one to get a Playa Limpia (Clean Beach) Certification from the federal government.

Hotel Zone beaches offer adults opportunities to play with aquatic toys, especially in high season. The sand here is often pocked with rocks, depending on the season and tides, and the beach is narrow in places. The beach at Marina Vallarta, between PV and Nuevo Vallarta, is swimmable but mainly uninspired except for the beach toys and hotels that offer refreshments. Again, sand here is lacking in front of some hotels, especially at high tide.

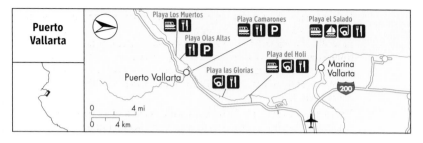

South of Vallarta proper are Conchas Chinas, a few smaller beaches, and Mismaloya. The wild beaches farther south (on the north side of Cabo Corrientes, from Las Animas to Yelapa) didn't have electricity until the 1970s or later. They tend to fill up with day-trippers between December and April but are well worth a visit.

At Los Muertos as well as beaches in the Hotel Zone and Marina Vallarta, you can find Jet Skis, parasailing, and banana-boat rides daily in high season (December–April) and on weekends year-round.

GETTING HERE AND AROUND

You can readily access Downtown and Hotel Zone beaches from the street. Take a bus or a cab, or drive your car. There's coveted curbside parking, or you can pay by the hour at the Benito Juárez parking structure: it's just north of the Cuale River at the malecón and Calle Rodríguez, under Parque Lázaro Cárdenas, and across from Olas Altas Beach. The Hidalgo Street parking structure, near Playa Camarones a few blocks from the north end of the malecón, is another option.

BEACHES KEY	
🚤	Boat tours
🅰	Camping
🎣	Fishing
🐎	Horseback riding
🅿	Parking
🚻	Restroom
⛵	Sailing
🚿	Showers
🤿	Snorkel/Scuba
🏄	Surfing
🏊	Swimming

In Marina Vallarta, main public beach access (with on-street parking) is between the airport and the Marina Golf Course. There's also a paid parking lot between the Marival and Grand Velas hotels, by the Nuevo Vallarta tourism office. In Bucerías, there is direct access to the beaches from almost every street.

ZONA ROMÁNTICA

Paralleling the Zona Romántica, Playa los Muertos is PV's most popular beach, where restaurants and bars have music, vendors sell barbecued fish on a stick, and people cruise the boardwalk.

Playa los Muertos. PV's original happenin' beach has nice bay views, and as action central, it's definitely PV's most engaging beach. Facing Vallarta's South Side (south of the Río Cuale), this flat beach hugs the Zona Romántica and runs about 1½ km (1 mile) south to a rocky point called El Púlpito. ■TIP➔ **The steps (more than 100) at Calle Púlpito lead to a lookout with a great view of the beach and the bay.**

Joggers cruise the cement boardwalk early morning and after sunset; vendors stalk the beach nonstop, hawking kites, jewelry, and serapes as well as hair-braiding and alfresco massage. Their parade can range from entertaining (good bargainers can get excellent deals) to downright maddening. Bar-restaurants run the length of the beach; the bright blue umbrellas at the south end belong to Blue Chairs resort, the hub of PV's effervescent gay scene.

The surf ranges from mild to choppy with an undertow; the small waves crunching the shore usually discourage mindless paddling. Strapping young men occupy the lifeguard tower, but the service isn't consistent. The Los Muertos Pier underwent a recent facelift and it's now one of PV's main landmarks and a prime spot for romantic night walks. Jet Skis zip around but stay out beyond the small breakers so they aren't too distracting to swimmers and sunbathers. Guys on the beach offer banana-boat and parasailing rides. **Facilities:** lifeguards, banana-boat rides, Jet Skis, parasailing; food concessions. **Best for:** partiers; surfing; sunset. ⊠ *Zona Romántica.*

Playa Olas Altas. The name means "high waves beach," but the only waves suitable for bodysurfing, boogie boarding, or, occasionally, surfing small waves are near the Cuale River, at the north end of this small beach. Although "Olas Altas" more often refers to the neighborhood of bars and businesses near the ocean south of the Río Cuale, it is also the name of a few blocks of sand between Daiquiri Dick's restaurant and the Río Cuale. The beach attracts fewer sunbathers than Los Muertos but is otherwise an extension of that beach, and it gets lively during holidays with sunbathers and impromptu snack stands and shaded tables on the sand. There are good views of the recently renovated Los Muertos Pier and spectacular lighting at night. Facing Olas Altas Beach near Lázaro Cárdenas plaza are open-air stands selling beach accessories, small grocery stores, and beach-facing bar-restaurants. **Facilities:** food concessions, parking (at Parque Lázaro Cárdenas). **Best for:** sunset; swimming. ⊠ *Zona Romántica.*

EL CENTRO

Playa Camarones. A long, flat brown sand beach that literally means Shrimp Beach, Playa Camarones was the first urban beach in the country to receive the Playa Limpia (Clean Beach) certification by the federal government. The certification means that the beach will always have a lifeguard present, trash bins, clean bathrooms, and handicap accessibility. Its location attracts many locals: parallel to the malecón between the Hotel Rosita and the Buenaventura Hotel. The shore is always changing—it could be rock-strewn in the morning and clear later when the tide goes out. Watch for whales in winter, too, from trendy beachfront El Solar Bar or from the Barracuda Restaurant, next door. Although the waves are gentle, there are strange currents here, which should discourage all but strong swimmers. What you see here most often are small groups of men and boys surf casting. **Facilities:** lifeguard, banana-boat rides, SUP paddle boards, Jet Skis, parasailing;

For shaded surf-side relaxation, grab a table under an umbrella at Playa Olas Altas.

food concessions, toilets, trash bins, street parking and private parking at Parque Hidalgo. **Best for:** sunset; surfing; walking. ⊠ *Centro*.

ZONA HOTELERA

The beaches in the Hotel Zone can be lively during holidays and high season but have less to recommend them the rest of the year. Beach erosion is a problem here, and some of the hotels' beaches have little or no sand at high tide.

Playa del Holi. The high-rise-backed Zona Hotelera beach goes by several monikers—mainly **Playa del Holi** but also **Playa Peninsula** around the Holiday Inn and Fiesta Americana hotels. Most people, however, just refer to each piece of beach by the hotel that it faces. Interrupted here and there by breakwaters, this fringe of gray-beige sand is generally flat but slopes down to the water. Winds and tides sometimes strew it with stones that make it less pleasant. Hit hard by Hurricane Kenna in 2002, the Sheraton, at the south end of the strip, had tons of sand deposited on its beach in 2005; it is, therefore, sandier than its neighbors, although still pocked with smooth, egg-size rocks. Some of the hotels, in particular Hotel Pelícanos and Canto del Sol, have no beach in front of their property; the water laps right at the hotel breakwater, even at low tide. **Facilities:** banana-boat rides, Jet Skis, parasailing, snorkeling; food concessions. **Best for:** snorkeling; walking; sunset. ⊠ *Zona Hotelera*.

MARINA VALLARTA

Playa el Salado. At Marina Vallarta, Playa El Salado—facing the Grand Velas, Sol Meliá, Marriott, Mayan Palace, and Westin hotels—is sandy but in spots very narrow. Colorful in high season with parasailers and with windsurfers rented or lent at area hotels, these beaches are actually more fun when crowded than when solitary. During fine weather and on weekends, and daily during high season, you can rent Jet Skis and pack onto colorful banana boats for bouncy tours of 10 minutes or longer. Some hotels rent small sailboats, sailboards, and sea kayaks to guests and to nonguests.

BEACH OF THE DEAD

There are several versions of how Playa los Muertos got its name. One says that around the time it was founded, members of a local tribe attacked a mule train laden with silver and gold from the mountain towns, leaving the dead bodies of the muleteers on the beach. A version crediting pirates with the same deed seems more plausible. In 1935, anthropologist Dr. Isabel Kelly postulated that the site used to be a cemetery.

In late summer and early fall, there are opportunities to view turtle-protection activities. **Facilities:** banana-boat rides, Jet Skis, kayaking, sailing, snorkeling; food concessions. **Best for:** sunset; windsurfing; walking. ⊠ *Marina Vallarta.*

OLAS ALTAS

Playa Conchas Chinas. Frequented mainly by visitors staying in the area, this beach has a series of rocky coves with crystalline water. Millions of tiny white shells, broken and polished by the waves, form the sand; rocks that resemble petrified cow pies jut into the sea, separating one patch of beach from the next. These individual coves are perfect for reclusive sunbathing and, when the surf is mild, for snorkeling around the rocks; bring your own equipment. It's accessible from Calle Santa Barbara, the continuation of the cobblestone coast road originating at the south end of Los Muertos Beach, and also from Carretera 200 near El Set restaurant. Swimming is best at the cove just north of La Playita de Lindo Mar, below the Hotel Conchas Chinas (where the beach ends), as there are fewer rocks in the water. You can walk—be it on the sand, over the rocks, or on paths or steps built for this purpose—from Playa Los Muertos all the way to Conchas Chinas. **Facilities:** none. **Best for:** swimming; snorkeling; sunset. ⊠ *Olas Altas.*

NUEVO VALLARTA

One wide, flat, sandy beach stretches from the mouth of the Ameca River north for miles, past the Nuevo Vallarta hotels (including the new developments at the north end, called Flamingos) and into the town of Bucerías. The generally calm water is good for swimming and, when conditions are right, bodysurfing or boogie boarding. Activities are geared to all-inclusive-hotel guests north of Paradise Village marina.

Guys on the beach rent water-sports equipment, as do most of the hotels.

GETTING HERE AND AROUND

In Nuevo Vallarta, park on the street or in the lot of the tourism office (50 pesos), between Grand Velas and Marival hotels. Buses arrive here as well, but the all-inclusive hotels that predominate cater to guests only, so bring your own supplies. It's a cinch to install yourself anywhere on Bucerías's long beach, especially on the south side, where there's plenty of street-side parking. As most of the beaches north of here are off the main road, they are easiest to access by car (or taxi), although buses are frequent and drop passengers along the highway at the entrance to town.

FAMILY **Playa Nuevo Vallarta.** Several kilometers of pristine beach face the hotels of Playa Nuevo Vallarta. In the fall, a fenced-off turtle nesting area provides relief for the endangered ocean dwellers. Jet Skis whiz by, kids frolic in the roped-off water nearest the beach, and waiters tend to vacationers lounging in recliners in front of their respective hotels. The wide, flat sandy stretch is perfect for long walks. In fact, you could walk all the way to Bucerías, some 8 km (5 miles) to the north. Most of the hotels here are all-inclusives, so guests generally move between their hotel pool, bar, and restaurant, and the beach in front. All-inclusive programs mean that nonguests are barred from the bars and restaurants. This beach recently received certification by the Mexican government as a "Clean Beach." **Facilities:** banana-boat rides, Jet Skis, parasailing; lifeguards, parking, toilets, showers, trash bins. **Best for:** walking; swimming; sunset. ⊠ *Nuevo Vallarta.*

RIVIERA NAYARIT

At the northern end of Bahía de Banderas and farther into Nayarit State, to the north, are long, beautiful beaches fringed with tall trees or scrubby tropical forest. Only the most popular beaches like Rincón de Guayabitos have much in the way of water-sports equipment rentals, but even the more secluded ones have stands or small restaurants serving cold coconut water, soft drinks, beer, and grilled fish with tortillas. Surfing is big at Sayulita and Punta de Mita, where some of the best spots are accessible only by boat.

GETTING HERE AND AROUND

A new road (rather, the improvement of an old, narrow dirt-and-gravel road) connects Punta Mita to Sayulita and, from there, rejoins Highway 200 to San Francisco and points to the north. However, if your destination is north of Punta Mita, there's no need to follow the coast road to the point. Simply bear right instead of left after Bucerías, continuing on Carretera 200.

NUEVO VALLARTA TO PUNTA MITA

Flamingos. Officially known as Nuevo Vallarta Norte, Flamingos, as called by locals, is the only beach in the Riviera Nayarit holding the coveted international Blue Flag certification. Located between Nuevo Vallarta and Bucerías, Flamingos is a string of relatively new hotels facing the broad, brown-sand beach that is virtually identical to those of its neighbors to the north and south. Shacks on the sand rent water-sports equipment, while showers serve to clean up guests returning to their high-rise, mainly all-inclusive hotels. At the south end of the beach, driftwood and the occasional scurrying crab are more obvious than in the manicured areas by the hotels. As one approaches Nuevo Vallarta, elaborate homes begin to spring up like solitary mushrooms, inhabited by those who can afford and desire privacy. **Facilities:** boogie boards, banana-boat rides, Jet Skis, parasailing; lifeguard, restrooms, showers, food concessions, beach club, handicap accessible. **Best for:** swimming; walking; windsurfing. ⊠ *Nuevo Vallarta.*

FAMILY **Playa Bucerías.** Eight kilometers (5 miles) north of Nuevo Vallarta, the substantial town of Bucerías attracts flocks of snowbirds, and this has encouraged the establishment of rental apartments and good restaurants. The surf is usually gentle enough for swimming, and a small shore break is sometimes suitable for body surfing. Beginning surfers occasionally arrive with their longboards. It's Banderas Bay's chosen beach for kite surfing, and hosts the largest national tournament of this sport in May. Backed by a fringe of beautiful coconut palms, the long beach is wide enough that it remains viable even at high tide. There are beautiful views of the arms of blue Banderas Bay to the north and south. The town is divided by an *arroyo* (dry river bed). On the north side, small shops face the main street, Avenida del Pacífico, while restaurants face the beach; many have tables on the sand. As the bay curves north toward La Cruz de Huanacaxtle, these businesses soon give way to small hotels, condo complexes, and single-family homes. If you have a car, parking is easiest south of the arroyo, where streets off the main beach access road, Avenida Lázaro Cárdenas, dead-end at the beach. From the south end of Bucerías you can walk all the way south to the Nayarit–Jalisco state line, created by the Ameca River. This walk of several hours takes you past the high-rise hotel developments at Flamingos and Nuevo Vallarta. Bucerías Beach has been recently certificated by the federal government as a "Clean Beach." **Facilities:**

food concessions, restrooms, lifeguard, trash bins. **Best for:** walking; swimming; windsurfing. ⊠ *Bucerías.*

FAMILY   **Playa La Manzanilla.** On this crescent of soft, gold sand half a mile long, kids play in the shallow water while their parents float in the calm green water without a care. Cold drinks and so-so food are served at several seafood shacks on the sand. Protected by the Piedra Blanca headland to the north, the beach is at the northernmost edge of the town of La Cruz de Huanacaxtle. Named for a cross made of superresilient wood (*huanacax-tle*, which translates to "ear pod," "elephant ear," or "monkey ear tree"), most people simply call the town "La Cruz." What was a rough little fishing village now has a 400-slip private marina aptly named Marina Riviera Nayarit at La Cruz (⊕ *www.marinarivieranayarit.com*). It was launched in 2008 as part of the Riviera Nayarit development plan. Like it or not, homey La Cruz is growing and becoming more sophisticated. **Facilities:** beach umbrellas, boating, fishing, inner tubes; food concessions, parking. **Best for:** walking; sunset. ⊠ *La Cruz de Huanacaxtle.*

Destiladeras. A classic in the region's beach scene and favorite of locals, this beach stretches a few miles north of Piedra Blanca headland. It's a wide, 1½-km-long (1-mile-long) beach with powder-soft beige sand and sometimes good waves for bodysurfers and boogie boarders. It's a pretty scene with the blue mountains to the north and south and the area's ubiquitous coconut palms framing views of the sky. On weekends and holidays, vendors prepare and sell yummy barbecue-blackened shrimp and fish kebabs, fresh fruit, and ceviche. A new development called Nahui was built above the beach and it brought with it better facilities for the beach. At the north end of the beach, **Punta el Burro** is a popular surf spot often accessed by boat from Punta Mita. **Facilities:** food concessions, bathrooms, trash bins, parking. **Best for:** surfing; swimming; sunset. ⊠ *La Cruz de Huanacaxtle.*

FAMILY   **El Anclote.** The most accessible beach at Punta de Mita and considered to be surf central is El Anclote, whose name means "the big anchorage." Just a few minutes past the gated entrance to the tony Four Seasons and St. Regis hotels, the popular beach has a string of restaurants—once simple shacks but today of increasing sophistication and price. This is a primo spot for viewing a sunset. The surf is calmed by several rock jetties and is shallow for quite a way out, so it's a good spot for children and average to not-strong swimmers; however, the jetties have also robbed sand from the beach. There's a long, slow wave for beginning surfers; you can rent boards and take lessons from outfitters in town. Most of the jewelry and serape sellers and fishermen looking for customers have moved—or been moved—off the beach to more official digs in buildings along the same strip or facing the Four Seasons. Accessible from El Anclote (or the adjacent town of **Corral del Risco**), more than half a dozen great surf spots pump year-round; most are accessible only by boat. Punta de Mita is the northernmost point of Banderas Bay, about 40 km (25 miles) north of Puerto Vallarta. **Facilities:** fishing, snorkeling, surfing, paddle surfing; food concessions, showers, parking. **Best for:** snorkeling; surfing; sunset. ⊠ *Punta Mita.*

Islas Marietas. Since Jacques Cousteau pointed out the amazing biodiversity of this pair of small islands, they've been designated a protected area by the Mexican government and have become a must for snorkelers and divers who favor the relatively clear waters and abundance of fish and coral. In winter, especially January through March, these islands, about a half hour offshore from El Anclote, are also a good place to spot orcas and humpback whales, which come to mate and give birth. Las Marietas is the destination for fishing, diving, and snorkeling; in addition, sea-life-viewing expeditions set out from El Anclote and Corral de Risco as well as from points up and down Banderas Bay. Don't miss the Love Beach, a secluded stretch of sand only accessible by swimming or snorkeling; the legend says that it was created during a weapon test by the Mexican army, which made a hole in the island and created a unique beach. Truth or not, it's a piece of beauty. **Facilities:** none. **Best for:** snorkeling; solitude; swimming. ⊠ *Off the coast of Punta Mita.*

WATER-TOY PRICES
Prices for water toys in and around Vallarta are fairly consistent:
Jet Skis: $45–$50 per half hour (one or two riders)
Parasailing: $35–$40 for a 10-minute ride
Banana-boat rides: $12–$20 for a 10-minute ride (usually four-person minimum)
Hobie Cat or small sailboat: $35–$45 per hour
Kayak: $9–$15 per hour single; $15–$22 per hour double
Boogie Board: $5 per hour

NORTH OF BANDERAS BAY

Real estate north of the bay began booming in the late '80s, although due to the worldwide recession, sales have tapered off and there are many "for sale" signs on single-family homes and condos. Still, Mexicans continue to sell family holdings, jaded gringos build private homes, and speculators from around the globe grab land on and off the beach. Changes notwithstanding, the Nayarit coast continues to enchant, with miles of lovely beaches bordered by arching headlands and hamlets drowsing in the tropical sun.

Playa de Sayulita. The increasingly popular town and beach of Sayulita is about 45 minutes north of PV on Carretera 200, just about 19 km (12 miles) north of Bucerías and 35 km (22 miles) north of the airport. Despite the growth, this small town is still laid-back and retains its surfer-friendly vibe. Fringed in lanky palms, Sayulita's curvaceous beach hugs the small bay. A decent shore break here is good for beginning or novice surfers; the left point break is more challenging. Skiffs on the beach have good rates for surfing or fishing safaris in area waters, and you can rent surfboards and snorkeling gear. **Facilities:** fishing, snorkeling, surfing; food concessions, restrooms, showers. **Best for:** surfing; partiers; walking. ⊠ *Sayulita.*

Playa de San Pancho. Ten minutes north of Sayulita is the town of San Francisco, known to most people by its nickname, San Pancho. Its beach

stretches between headlands to the north and south and is accessed at the end of the town's main road, Avenida Tercer Mundo. At the end of this road, on the beach, a couple of casual restaurants have shaded café tables on the sand where locals and visitors congregate. You'll sometimes see men fishing from shore with nets as you walk the 1½-km-long (1-mile-long) stretch of coarse beige sand. There's an undertow that should discourage less-experienced swimmers. A small reef break sometimes generates miniature waves for surfing (especially in September), but this isn't a surf spot. In fact the undertow and the waves, which are too big for family splashing and too small for surfing, have probably helped maintain the town's innocence—until now. Popular with a hip crowd, San Pancho has just a few hotels but a growing number of good restaurants. **Facilities:** food concessions, showers, toilets. **Best for:** surfing; walking; sunset. ⊠ *Ten minutes north of Sayulita, San Francisco.*

Lo de Marcos. About 8 km (5 miles) north of San Pancho, Lo de Marcos is a humble town of quiet, wide streets. It fills up on weekends and holidays with Mexican families renting the bungalow-style motel rooms that predominate; a few RV parks on the beach attract long-term snowbirds. The town's main beach is flat and dark, but the sand is generally clean. There are small waves, not big enough for surfing but just right for splashing around. A small restaurant on the beach serves sodas, snacks, and the usual seafood suspects. Note that the once-popular playas **Las Minitas** and **Los Venados** are closed for private development. **Facilities:** food concessions. **Best for:** walking; swimming. ⊠ *San Pancho.*

Playa los Ayala. Playa los Ayala has a level beach, mild surf, and an excellent view of Isla del Coral, to which glass-bottom boats ferry passengers for about $9 (100 pesos) per person. There are small hotels and plenty of seaside palapas for shade and basic sustenance. On weekends, holidays, and in high season take a ride on a banana boat; most any time you can find a skiff owner to take you to Playa Frideritas or Playa del Toro, two pretty beaches for bathing that lie around the headland to the south and are accessible only by boat. You can walk, however, over the hill at the south end of the beach to a seafood restaurant on a small scallop of beach called Playa Frideras. **Facilities:** banana-boat rides, boating; food concessions. **Best for:** swimming; walking. ⊠ *A few miles north of Sayulita.*

FAMILY **Rincón de Guayabitos.** A little over a mile north of Los Ayala along the highway, Guayabitos bustles with legions of Mexican families on weekends and holidays; foreigners take up residence during the winter months. The main street, Avenida Nuevo Sol, has modest hotels, inexpensive restaurants, and scores of shops that all seem to sell the same cheap bathing suits and plastic beach toys. One block closer to the sea are more hotels along with some vacation homes right on the sand. Colorfully painted stands on the beach sell fresh chilled fruit and coconuts; others serve up fresh grilled fish on the cheap. This lovely beach bounded by headlands and the ocean is tranquil and perfectly suited for swimming. You can also arrange turtle and whale-watching excursions as well as boat rides to explore the coast or to Isla del Coral, just offshore. ■TIP→ **The boatmen who ferry passengers for a few hours' sunbathing on Isla del Coral may fail to mention that the restaurant there opens only in high season. Although there's usually a lady or two on the sand selling ceviche, bring a picnic lunch just in case.** **Facilities:** boating, fishing, snorkeling; food concessions. **Best for:** swimming; snorkeling; walking. ⊠ *Sayulita.*

La Peñita. Contiguous with Guayabitos, at the north end of the Jaltemba Bay, La Peñita has fewer hotels and a beach that's often abandoned save for a few fishermen. Its name means "little rock." The center for area business, La Peñita has banks, shoe stores, and ice cream shops; a typical market held each Thursday offers knock-off CDs, polyester clothing, and fresh fruits and vegetables. **Facilities:** none. **Best for:** walking; swimming. ⊠ *Sayulita.*

Boca de Naranjo. A couple of miles north of La Peñita, a dusty road leads to this long, secluded sandy beach with excellent swimming. The rutted dirt road from the highway, although only about 4 km (2½ miles) long, takes almost a half hour to negotiate in most passenger cars. Enjoy great views of the coastline from one of nearly a dozen seafood shanties. Turtles nest here in August and September. There are rumors of a major development here in the near-ish future. **Facilities:** restaurants. **Best for:** swimming; walking. ⊠ *5 km (3 miles) north of La Peñita, Sayulita.*

Chacala. Some 30 km (19 miles) north of Rincón de Guayabitos, Chacala is another 9 km (5 miles) from the highway through exuberant vegetation. You can dine or drink at the handful of eateries right on the beach, take in the soft-scented sea air and the green-blue sea, or bodysurf and boogie board. Swimming is safest under the protective headland to the north of the cove; surfing is often very good, but you have to hire a boat to access the point break. The beach is long but rather narrow when the tide is in. **Facilities:** food concessions. **Best for:** surfing; swimming. ⊠ *30 km (19 miles) north of Rincón de Guayabitos, Sayulita.*

SOUTH OF PUERTO VALLARTA

While coastal Nayarit is jumping on the development bandwagon, the isolated beaches of Cabo Corrientes and those of southern Jalisco—some surrounded by ecological reserves—continue to languish in peaceful abandon. Things here are still less formal, and aside from the super-posh resorts like El Careyes, El Tamarindo, and Las Alamandas, whose beaches are off-limits to nonguests, words like "laid-back" still apply.

At popular Rincón de Guayabitos beach, you'll share umbrella space with locals and visitors alike.

Long sandy beaches are frequented by fishermen and local people relaxing at seafood shanties. They usually allow shelling, snorkeling, fishing, and trips to nearby islands and beaches only accessible by sea. Having a car is helpful for exploring multiple beaches, although local bus service is available if you have no problem with riding through the tropics without air-conditioning.

GETTING HERE AND AROUND

Catch a green bus to Conchas Chinas, Mismaloya, or Boca de Tomatlán from the southwest corner of Calle Basilio Badillo and Constitución in PV. Give the driver sufficient notice when you want to get off; pulling over along the narrow highway is challenging.

There are several ways to reach the beaches of southern Banderas Bay. Party boats (aka booze cruises) and privately chartered boats leave from Marina Vallarta's maritime terminal and generally hit Las Animas, Quimixto, Majahuitas, and/or Yelapa. You can also hire a water taxi from Boca de Tomatlán ($6 one way, usually on the hour 9 am through noon and again starting in early afternoon), from the Los Muertos Pier ($20 round-trip, 11 am and in high season at 10:15 am and 11 am), or from the tiny pier next to Hotel Rosita ($20 round-trip, 11:30 am). ■TIP→ Note that weather and other variables can affect the water-taxi schedules.

For maximum time at the beach of your choice and minimum frustration, head out early and relax over a soda or coffee at Boca de Tomatlán as you wait for the next available skiff to depart. Catch the 4 pm taxi from Los Muertos to Yelapa only if you're planning to spend the night; it won't return until the next day. You can hire *pangas* (skiffs) at

Boca, Mismaloya, or Los Muertos. The price depends on starting and ending points but runs about $35 per hour for up to eight passengers.

It's best to have your own car for exploring the Costalegre, as many beaches are a few kilometers—down rutted dirt roads—from the highway. However, if you want to hang out in the small but tourist-oriented towns of San Patricio–Melaque, Barra de Navidad, and La Manzanilla, you don't necessarily need wheels.

SOUTHERN BANDERAS BAY

Fodor'sChoice
★ **Playa Palmares.** This is the first beach to be awarded the prestigious Blue Flag certification, a program run by the Foundation for Environmental Education. To get a Blue Flag a beach needs to meet 32 criteria regarding water quality, environmental education, environmental management, and safety and services. Located 6 km (3 miles) south of Puerto Vallarta's downtown, Playa Palmares is a pristine stretch of beach, good for swimming and equipped with all the necessary services. **Facilities:** food concessions; restrooms, showers, parking. **Best for:** swimming; walking; sunset. ⊠ *South of Puerto Vallarta, Olas Altas.*

Playa Mismaloya. It was in this cove that *The Night of the Iguana* was made. Visitors from the '70s remember parking their vans on the sand

> ### TURTLE RESCUE
>
> **Grupo Ecológico de la Costa Verde** (*Green Coast Ecological Group*). In San Pancho, Grupo Ecológico de la Costa Verde works to save the olive ridley, leatherback, and eastern Pacific green turtles. Volunteers patrol beaches, collect eggs, maintain the nursery, tabulate data, and educate the public. (Apply any time during the year, via the website, for an assignment June through November.) Call or check their website to see if slide shows to raise awareness and funds are happening during your stay. ⊠ *Av. Latino América 102, San Francisco, San Pancho* ☎ *311/258-4100* ⊕ *www. project-tortuga.org.*

and eating fish plucked from the sea for week after blissful week. Unfortunately, construction of the big, tan Hotel La Jolla de Mismaloya at the north end of the once-pristine bay has stolen its Shangri-La appeal, and to add insult to injury, in 2002, Hurricane Kenna stole much of the soft beige sand. Nonetheless, the place retains a certain cachet. It also has views of the famous cove from a couple of seafood restaurants on the south side of a wooden bridge over the mouth of the Río Mismaloya.

Sun-seekers kick back in wooden beach chairs, waiters serve up food and drink on the sand, massage techs offer their (so-so) services alfresco. Chico's Dive Shop sells dive packages and boat trips and rents snorkel gear, boogie boards ($10 for the day for either), and double sea kayaks ($20 per hour). Barceló La Jolla de Mismaloya has day passes for nonguests that are valid from 9 am to 6 pm: $60 gets you use of facilities (pool, gym, game room, an hour of kayaking), plus food and drink. In the afternoons locals hang out at this beach, the kids playing in the sand while the moms wait for their men to return from fishing expeditions and touring gigs. The beach is about 13 km (8 miles) south of

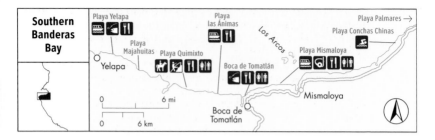

PV. The bus drops you on the highway, and it's a 200-yard walk from there down a dirt road to the beach. The tiny village of Mismaloya is on the east side of Carretera 200. **Facilities:** boating, diving, kayaking, snorkeling; food concessions, toilets (portable toilets on road to beach). **Best for:** swimming; snorkeling. ⊠ *South of Puerto Vallarta, Mismaloya.*

Playa Boca de Tomatlán. This is the name of both a small village and a deep, V-shaped, rocky bay that lie at the mouth ("boca" means mouth) of the Río Horcones, about 5 km (3 miles) south of Mismaloya and 17 km (10½ miles) south of PV. Water taxis leave from Boca to the southern beaches; you can arrange snorkeling trips to Los Arcos. As far as most visitors are concerned, this is mainly the staging area for water taxis with nowhere else to hang out. However, this dramatic-looking bay fringed in palm trees does have a rustic appeal. Grocery stores sell chips, Cokes, and plastic water toys for tots; a handful of informal seaside cafés cluster at the water's edge. At very low tide only, it's possible for adventurers and cheapskates to walk south from Boca to Playa Las Animas (about 40 minutes) along a small path at waters' edge. You certainly don't want to be on this path, however, when the tide begins to come in, as the rocks behind it are steep and sharp. **Facilities:** fishing; food concessions, toilets. **Best for:** swimming. ⊠ *South of Puerto Vallarta, Mismaloya.*

FAMILY **Playa las Animas.** There's lots to do besides sunbathe at this beach and town 15 minutes south of Boca de Tomatlán. Framed in oak, coconut, and pink-flowering *amapa* trees, the brown-sand beach is named "The Souls" because pirate graves were reportedly located here many years ago. Along the 1-km-long (½-mile-long) beach are piles of smooth, strange rocks looking an awful lot like petrified elephant poo. Because of its very shallow waters, Las Animas is often referred to as *la playa de los niños* (children's beach), and it tends to fill up with families on weekends and holidays. They come by water taxi or as part of half- or full-day bay cruises. Five or six seafood eateries line the sand; a few will lend their clients volleyballs to use on sand courts out front. You can also rent Jet Skis, ride a banana boat, or soar up into the sky behind a speedboat while dangling from a colorful parachute. **Facilities:** banana-boat rides, boating, Jet Skis, parasailing; food concessions. **Best for:** swimming; walking; sunset. ⊠ *South of Puerto Vallarta, Mismaloya.*

Quimixto. Between the sandy stretches of Las Animas and Majahuitas, and about 20 minutes by boat from Boca de Tomatlán, Quimixto has a narrow, rocky shoreline that attracts few bathers. Tour boats stop here, and their clients usually have a meal at one of the seafood eateries facing the beach. Horses by the dozens are standing by to take passengers to Quimixto Falls (about $13 round-trip). It's only slightly longer than the 25-minute ride to walk there. You can bathe at the base of the energetic falls; the pool is enclosed by sheer rock walls. Be careful of the current during the rainy season, when the water crashing into the pool tends to push swimmers toward the rock walls. Before proceeding to the falls, have a cool drink at the casual restaurant; consuming something is obligatory to gain access. During stormy weather or a full moon there's a fun, fast wave at Quimixto's reef, popular with surfers but, because of its inaccessibility, rarely crowded. **Facilities:** horseback riding, surfing; food concessions, toilets. **Best for:** surfing; walking. ⊠ *South of Puerto Vallarta, Mismaloya.*

Majahuitas. Between the beaches of Quimixto and Yelapa and about 35 minutes by boat from Boca de Tomatlán, this small beach is the playground of people on day tours and guests of the exclusive Majahuitas Resort. There are no services for the average José; the lounge chairs and toilets are for hotel guests only. Palm trees shade the white beach of broken, sea-buffed shells. The blue-green water is clear, and there's sometimes good snorkeling around the rocky shore. **Facilities:** none. **Best for:** snorkeling; swimming. ⊠ *South of Puerto Vallarta, Mismaloya.*

Yelapa. This secluded village and ½-km-long (¼-mile-long) beach is about an hour southeast of downtown PV and a half hour from Boca de Tomatlán—by boat, of course. A half-dozen seafood *enramadas* (thatch-roof huts) edge its fine, clean grainy sand. Phones and electricity arrived in Yelapa around the turn of the 21st century. Believe it or not, it's the largest and most developed of the north Cabo Corrientes towns, with quite a few rustic rooms and houses for rent by the day, week, or month. ■TIP➔ **That said, bring all the money you'll need, as there's nothing as formal as a bank.**

The beach slopes down to the water, and small waves break right on the shore. In high season and during holidays, there are water-sports outfitters. From here you can hike 20 minutes into the jungle to see the small Cascada Cola del Caballo (Horse Tail Waterfall), with a pool at its base for swimming. (The falls are often dry near the end of the dry season, especially April–early June.) A more ambitious expedition of several hours brings you to less-visited, very beautiful Cascada del Catedral (Cathedral Falls). Beyond that, Yelapa is, for the most part, *tranquilisimo*: a place to just kick back in a beach chair and sip something cold. Seemingly right when you really need it, Cheggy or Agustina, the pie ladies, will show up with their homemade lime, coconut, or nut creations. **Facilities:** boating, fishing, parasailing; food concessions. **Best for:** swimming; walking. ⊠ *Yelapa.*

CABO CORRIENTES

Just south of the end of Banderas Bay are the lovely beaches of pristine, wonderful Cabo Corrientes. These take an effort to visit, as well as a sturdy, high-clearance vehicle. Public transportation comes here and back once a day from the small town of El Tuito (40 km [25 miles] south of PV) along a partially paved but mainly rutted dirt-and-gravel road.

Grab a boat ride right off the beach at Boca de Tomatlán.

Playa Mayto. Thirty-eight kilometers (23 miles) down a passable road from El Tuito, this gorgeous beach is several miles long, embraced on either end by a rocky point. The sand is grainy but clean and slopes down to meet the rough to semirough surf. Despite the slope of the beach, this is a great place for a long walk or shore fishing. In late summer and fall there's a turtle camp where volunteers protect the eggs of the black and olive ridley turtles that nest here. The Hotel de Mayto has rooms at modest prices and offers massage; next door, the friendly folks of El Rinconcito have a small store and a few rooms to rent as well as four-wheelers and horses (200 pesos per hour for either). **Facilities:** ATVs, horseback riding, kayaking; food concessions, camping. **Best for:** solitude; walking; sunset. ⊠ *South of Puerto Vallarta, Selva El Tuito.*

FAMILY **Tehuamixtle.** Just over 2 km (1 mile) from Mayto, Tehuamixtle is a sheltered cove with a few basic rooms to rent. The area is known for its oysters, which you can sample fresh from the sea at an open-air restaurant facing the fishing fleet. The surf here is very gentle and lacks currents, making it popular with local children. The pristine beach invites snorkeling and diving (bring your own equipment). Fishing boats bob at one end, below the restaurant; from here, the beach curves along in a sandy brown arch to a large green headland at the other end of the cove. Tehua, as locals call it, is about the same size as Mayto: 100 people. This fishing village has only had electricity since the turn of the 21st century. There's a beach road that connects Tehua with Cruz de Loreto, about 1½ hours to the south; otherwise go out through El Tuito. **Facilities:** fishing; food concessions. **Best for:** swimming; surfing. ⊠ *South of Puerto Vallarta, Tehuamixtle.*

Villa del Mar. Four kilometers (2½ miles) beyond Tehuamixtle, Villa del Mar is a beautiful virgin beach on a broad sweep of bay. Several miles long, flat and sandy, it's great for long walks; turtles nest here in late summer and fall. At the south end of the beach, a huge estuary surrounded by coconut palms invites kayaking. The sandy streets in and around town and the beach are great for mountain biking, and local people will rent horses for a ride on the beach or into the countryside. **Facilities:** Horseback riding. ⊠ *South of Puerto Vallarta.*

COSTALEGRE

Most people come to the Costalegre—dubbed "The Happy Coast" by Jalisco's tourism authorities—to stay at luxury accommodations on lovely, clean beaches: Las Alamandas, El Careyes, and El Tamarindo. Indeed, some of the nicest beaches with services are now the private domain of *gran turismo* (government-rated five-star-plus) hotels.

Other people head to southern Jalisco State without reservations to explore the coast at their leisure. There are still some delightful, pristine, and mainly isolated beaches along the Costalegre, most with few services aside from the ubiquitous seafood *enramadas* serving fish fillets and fresh ceviche. For lodging there are private homes to rent, condos, and unassuming hotels on or near the beach.

> ### SNORKELING SANCTUARY
>
> **Los Arcos.** Protected area Los Arcos is an offshore group of giant rocks rising some 65 feet above the water, making the area great for snorkeling and diving. For reasonable fees, local men along the road to Mismaloya Beach run diving, snorkeling, fishing, and boat trips here and as far north as Punta Mita and Las Marietas or the beach villages of Cabo Corrientes. Recommended for all of these trips is Mismaloya Divers, with 23-foot skiffs and new, 75-horsepower, four-stroke motors. Restaurants and fishermen at Playa Mismaloya can also set you up. ⊠ *South of Puerto Vallarta* ☎ *322/224–1175.*

Whether you kick back at an elegant resort or explore the wild side, the area between Cabo Corrientes and Barra de Navidad, the latter at the southern extreme of Jalisco State, will undoubtedly delight.

GETTING HERE AND AROUND

It's optimum to explore the beaches of southern Jalisco by car, SUV, or camper. Fill up with gas at every opportunity, as gas stations are few. (If you do get into a bind, ask locals about any small stores that sell gas.) If you're in a rental car, reset the odometer and look for the kilometer signs at the side of the road. If you're driving a car marked in miles, not kilometers, the road signs are still useful, as many addresses are simply "Carretera 200" or "Carretera a Barra de Navidad" along with the marker number.

Playa Chalacatepec. A sylvan beach with no services lies down a rutted dirt road about 82 km (50 miles) south of El Tuito and 115 km (70

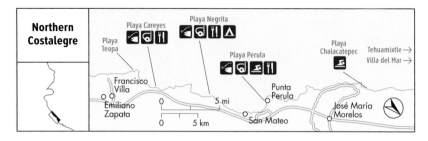

miles) south of PV. The road is negotiable only by high-clearance passenger cars and smallish RVs. The reward for 8 km (5 miles) of bone-
jarring travel is a beautiful rocky point, Punta Chalacatepec, with a
sweep of protected white-sand beach to the north that's perfect for
swimming and bodysurfing. There's a fish camp here, so you may find
some rather scraggly-looking dudes on this isolated beach. Admire the
tidal pools at the point during low tide. Take a walk along the open-
ocean beach south of the point, where waves crash more dramatically
and discourage swimming. To get here, turn toward the beach at the
town of José María Morelos (at Km 88). Just after 8 km (5 miles),
leave the main road (which bears right) and head to the beach over a
smaller track. From here it's less than 1½ km (1 mile) to the beach. At
this writing, an airport was being built near the county seat, Tomatlán,
and the beach was slated for hotels not yet named. **Facilities:** none. **Best
for:** swimming; surfing; walking. ⊠ *Costalegre, Talpa.*

Playa Perula. The handful of islands just off lovely Bahía de Chamela,
about 131 km (81 miles) south of PV, protects the beaches from strong
surf. The best place on the bay for swimming is wide, flat **Playa Perula**
(turnoff at Km 76, then 3 km [2 miles] on dirt road), in the protective
embrace of a cove just below the Punta Perula headland. Fishermen
there take visitors out to snorkel around the islands (about $45 for up
to 10 people) or to hunt for dorado, tuna, and mackerel (about $23
per hour for one to four people); restaurants on the soft beige sand sell
the same as fresh fillets and ceviche. **Facilities:** fishing, snorkeling; food
concessions. **Best for:** swimming; snorkeling. ⊠ *Costalegre, Chamela.*

Playa Negrita. Also on Bahía de Chamela, this lovely beach is fringed in
lanky coconut palms and backed by blue foothills. There are camping
and RV accommodations and plenty of opportunities for shore fishing,
swimming, and snorkeling. Almost every pretty beach in Mexico has
its own humble restaurant; this one is no exception. **Facilities:** fishing,
snorkeling; camping facilities, food concessions. **Best for:** swimming;
snorkeling; walking. ⊠ *Costalegre, Chamela.*

Playa Careyes. About 11 km (6½ miles) south of Bahía Chamela, this
beach is named for the *careyes* (hawksbill) turtles that lay eggs here.
It's a lovely soft-sand beach framed by headlands. When the water's not
too rough, snorkeling is good around the rocks, where you can also
fish. There's a small restaurant at the north end of the beach, and often
you can arrange to go out with a local fisherman (about $25 per hour).
Water-loving birds can be spotted around the lagoon that forms at the

south end of the bay. **Facilities:** birding, fishing, snorkeling; food concessions. **Best for:** swimming; snorkeling. ✉ *Costalegre, Costa Careyes.*

Playa Teopa. Here, you can walk south from Playa Careyes along the dunes, although guards protect sea turtle nests by barring visitors during the summer and fall nesting seasons. A road from the highway at Km 49.5 gains access to Playa Teopa by car; ask the guard for permission to enter this way, as you'll need to pass through private property to gain access to the beach. **Facilities:** none. **Best for:** swimming; walking. ✉ *Costalegre, Careyes.*

Playa Tenacatita. Named for the bay on which it lies, Tenacatita is a lovely beach of soft sand about 34 km (20 miles) north of San Patricio–Melaque and 172 km (106 miles) south of PV. Dozens of identical seafood shacks line the shore; birds cruise the miles of beach, searching for their own fish. Waves crash against clumps of jagged rocks at the north end of the beach, which curves gracefully around to a headland. The water is sparkling blue. There's camping for RVs and tents at Punta Hermanos, where the water is calm and good for snorkeling, and local men offer fishing excursions ($50–$60 for one to four people) and tours of the mangroves ($27). Of the string of restaurants on the beach, we recommend La Fiesta Mexicana. **Facilities:** fishing, snorkeling; camping facilities, food concessions. **Best for:** swimming; snorkeling; walking. ✉ *Costalegre, Tenacatita.*

Playa Mora. Near the north end of Playa Tenacatita, this pretty stretch of sand has a coral reef close to the beach, making it an excellent place to snorkel. Local fishermen take interested parties out on their boats, either fishing for tuna, dorado, or bonita or searching for wildlife such as dolphins and turtles. **Facilities:** fishing, snorkeling; food concessions. **Best for:** snorkeling; swimming; walking. ✉ *Costalegre, Tenacatita.*

Playa Boca de Iguanas. South of Playa Mora on Tenacatita Bay, this beach (whose name means "Mouth of the Iguanas") of fine gray-blond sand is wide and flat, and it stretches for several kilometers. Gentle waves make it great for swimming, boogie boarding, and snorkeling, but beware the undertow. Some enthusiasts fish from shore. It's a great place for jogging or walking on the beach, as there's no slope. There are a couple of beach restaurants and an RV park here. The entrance is at Km 17. The place goes completely bananas every year during one weekend in August when the International Beach Festival Boca de Iguanas takes place. **Facilities:** snorkeling; camping facilities, restrooms, showers, food concessions. **Best for:** swimming; snorkeling; surfing. ✉ *Costalegre, Manzanillo.*

FAMILY **Playa la Manzanilla.** This beautiful, 2-km-long (1-mile-long) beach is little more than a kilometer (half a mile) in from the highway, near the southern edge of Bahía de Tenacatita, 193 km (120 miles) south of PV and 25 km (15½ miles) north of Barra de Navidad (at Km 14). Informal hotels and restaurants are interspersed with small businesses and modest houses along the town's main street. Rocks dot the gray-gold sands and edge both ends of the wide beach; facing the sand are attractive, unpretentious vacation homes favoring a Venetian palate of ocher and brick red. The bay is calm. At the beach road's north end, gigantic, rubbery-looking crocodiles lie heaped together just out of harm's way in a mangrove swamp. The fishing here is excellent; boat owners on the beach can take you out for snapper, sea bass, and other *pescado* for $20–$25 an hour. **Facilities:** fishing; food concessions. **Best for:** swimming; walking; sunset. ⊠ *Costalegre, La Manzanilla.*

Playa Melaque. Twenty-one kilometers (13 miles) south of La Manzanilla, Bahía de Navidad represents the end of the Costalegre at the border with Colima State. First up (from north to south) is **San Patricio– Melaque,** the coast's most populous town, with about 12,000 people. (It's actually two towns that have now met in the middle.) While parts of town look dilapidated or abandoned, its long, coarse-white-sand beach is beautiful and has gentle waves. Restaurants, small hotels, homes, and tall palms line the beach, which slopes down to the water. About 5 km (3½ miles) east of Barra de Navidad, which shares Navidad Bay, Melaque's beach curves around for several kilometers to end in a series of jagged rocks poking from the water. If you plop down in a seat under a shade umbrella its owner will soon show up. Pay about $5 and stay as long as you like. Fishermen here will take anglers out in search of dorado, tuna, wahoo, swordfish, mackerel, and others. ■TIP→ The best swimming and boogie boarding are about half the length of town, in front of El Dorado restaurant. **Facilities:** banana-boat rides, boogie boarding, fishing, Jet Skis, kayaking, snorkeling, beach umbrellas. **Best for:** surfing; swimming; snorkeling. ⊠ *Costalegre, Barra de Navidad.*

Playa Principal (Barra de Navidad). Usually called just "Barra," this laid-back little town has sandy streets and a live-and-let-live demeanor. At any time but high tide you can walk between San Patricio and Barra, a distance of about 5 km (3½ miles). It's about 4½ km (3 miles) on the highway from one town to the other. Most of Barra is composed of two streets on a long sandbar. Calle Veracruz faces the vast lagoon and **Isla Navidad,** now home to the posh Gran Bay resort. Water taxis take folks to the Gran Bay's golf course or marina, or to the seafood restaurants of **Colimilla,** on the lagoon's opposite shore. Avenida Miguel de Legazpi faces Barra's sloping brown-sand beach and the ocean. These and connecting streets have small shops, simple but charming restaurants, and—like everywhere along Mexico's Pacific coast—a host of friendly townspeople. ■TIP→ Surfers look for swells near the jetty, where the sea enters the lagoon. **Facilities:** boating, fishing; food concessions. **Best for:** swimming; partiers; sunset. ⊠ *Costalegre, Barra de Navidad.*

WHERE TO EAT

PUERTO VALLARTA'S BEST STREET FOOD AND SNACKS

In New York you go for a slice; in Puerto Vallarta, you stop for a taco. Snacking at street stands and informal eateries might just be one of the most enjoyable ways to get yourself fed here—and doing so is an indisputably authentic Mexican experience.

Read on to discover unknown (and famous) places to enjoy savory and hygienic *antojitos*—snacks like tacos, burritos, gorditas, and quesadillas—that Mexicans enjoy as a sort of comfort food on the go. Many are fried and fattening, but other items are griddle-cooked with a minimum of oil, and quesadillas and burritos aren't fried at all. Mexican desserts and sweet breads can be insipidly similar; read on for the skinny on some of the best desserts and sweet snacks around, with a few options for snacking on the run. But cheap snacks don't have to mean a meal lacking presentation.

Picnic Time

Grab a box lunch starting at 6 am at Marina Vallarta's **The Coffee Cup** (⊠ *Condominios Puesto del Sol, Local 14–A, at the marina* ☎ *322/221–2517*). At **A Page in the Sun** (⊠ *Calle Olas Altas 399, Col. E. Zapata* ☎ *322/222–3608*), stop in for American-style comfort food to go, like a turkey and avocado sandwich. At Puerto Vallarta's Los Muertos Beach and bayside at Rincón de Guayabitos, look for beach vendors selling coconut bread, fish on a stick, and giant pieces of fruit.

PV's Best Street Food and Snacks

Nothing says "Pacific Coast Mexico" like a shrimp taco or a fish burrito, but other "street foods" are equally popular. Step up to these taco carts or tiny storefronts to get a taste of authentic Puerto Vallarta.

In downtown Vallarta, locals love the quesadillas, shredded beef burritos, and tacos at **Tutifruti** (⊠ *Allende 200, Centro* ☎ *322/222–1068* ⊙ *closed Sun.*), where you can also get a sandwich, burger, or fruit smoothie.

In the Zona Romántica, **Salud Super Foods** (⊠ *Olas Altas 534-A* ☎ *322/139–9398*) offers healthy and nutritious food with lots of flavor, which has crowds coming here every morning for breakfast. There is no guarantee that there will be space for you to sit at any time in particular, but there's always takeaway to be eaten at the boardwalk. Don't miss the smoothies!

In Marina Vallarta, an upscale place to go for snacks and beer is **La Barra Cerveceria** (⊠ *Av. Paseo de la Marina Sur s/n, across from Hotel Mayan Palace* ☎ *322/209–0909*), which sells pizza as well.

North of Banderas Bay, in little San Pancho (aka San Francisco), the multitudes rave about the fish and shrimp tacos at **Baja Takeria** (⊠ *Av. Tercer Mundo 70*).

Bucerías's **Tacos Linda** (⊠ *Av. Lázaro Cárdenas s/n at Abasolo, Bucerías*) occupies a small patio surrounded by hurricane fencing. Watch a telenovela on the overhead TV as you wait for

savory meat tacos and other snacks on huge, just-made tortillas.

SWEET STUFF

The locally owned bakery **Los Chatos** (⊠ *Francisco Villa 359, Col. Olímpico* ☎ *322/223–0485* ⊕ *www.loschatos. com*) sells cakes, tarts, and house-made gelato.

For a fresh-fruit water, frozen fruit bar, or ice cream cone, stop in at a **Michoacán** or **Holanda** ice cream shop.

In El Centro at **Paris Café** (⊠ *Pino Suarez 158, Col. E. Zapata* ☎ *322/222–8472*), a gruff and eccentric Frenchman who bakes bare-chested is PV's version of Seinfeld's "soup Nazi."

For European-style chocolates, succumb to **Xocodiva** (⊠ *Calle Rodolfo Gómez 118* ☎ *322/113–0352*), near the Zona Romántica.

In Sayulita, **Panino's** (⊠ *Delfines 1* ☎ *322/ 103–3723*) produces good brownies, croissants, and other baked goods.

If you're in Bucerías, grab a mini-cheesecake, crunchy chocolate cookie, or soft-center brownie at **Pie in the Sky** (⊠ *Heroe de Nacozari 202* ☎ *322/223–8183* ⊕ *www.pieinthesky.com.mx*). On Bucerías's South Side, a dedicated following snaps up the cinnamon rolls at **Sweet Things Bake Shop** (⊠ *Lázaro Cárdenas 64* ☎ *322/278–6960*).

Updated by Federico Arrizabalaga

First-time travelers come for the sun and sea, but it's PV's wonderful restaurants that create legions of long-term fans. You can pay L.A. prices for perfectly decorated plates but also get fresh-caught fish and hot-off-the-griddle tortillas for scandalously little dough. Enjoy a 300-degree bay view from a cliff-top aerie or bury your toes in the sand. Dress up or go completely casual. It's the destination's great variety of venues and cuisine that keeps returning foodies blissfully content.

During the past 30 years, immigrant chefs have expanded the culinary horizons beyond seafood and Mexican fare. You'll find everything from haute cuisine to fish kebabs. Some of the most rewarding culinary experiences are found outside of fancy restaurants and familiar chain eateries at the street-side tacos stalls and neighborhood *fondas,* humble spots serving bowls of chili-laced pozole and seafood-heavy Mexican comfort food.

The trend of the day is restaurant-lounges. Ten years ago, DeSantos (co-owned by the drummer of the Mexican rock band Maná) was the first to combine dining and dancing in a hip new way, with its noisy ground-floor bar-restaurant and pulsing dance club above. Today DeSantos, Mandala, and other lounges provide places to party with the locals beyond the cool and chill dining rooms.

For those who prefer dining alfresco (and wearing flip-flops) over the glamour scene, almost every popular beach has a *palapa* shanty or two selling fish fillets and snacks, sodas, and beer. Some offer the Pacific Coast specialty *pescado sarandeado* (butterflied red snapper rubbed with salt and spices and grilled over a wood fire) or the devilishly simple (and fiery hot) dish *aguachile,* which is a ceviche salad. The catch of the day may vary, but the white plastic tables and chairs in the sand are permanent fixtures.

PLANNING

EATING OUT STRATEGY

Where should we eat? With hundreds of PV-area eateries competing for your attention, it may seem like a daunting question. But fret not—we've eaten our way around town on your behalf. The selections here represent the best this destination has to offer—from tacos at street-side stands to five-star haute cuisine. Search "Best Bets" for top recommendations by price, cuisine, and experience. Or find a review quickly in the alphabetical listings.

MEALTIMES

Upon rising, locals start with coffee and *pan dulce* (sweet breads) or *chilaquiles* (broken fried tortillas in chili sauce) for *desayuno* (breakfast) at the area's coffee shops and small restaurants. Schedule permitting, Mexicans love to eat a hearty *almuerzo*, or full breakfast, at about 10. The day's main meal, *comida*, is typically between 2 and 5 pm and consists of soup and/or salad, bread or tortillas, a main dish, side dishes, and dessert. *Cena* (dinner) is lighter; many people just have milk or hot chocolate and a sweet roll or tamales between 8 and 9 pm.

That said, PV is tourist-friendly, and most eateries accommodate travelers by serving breakfast until noon and main meals from noon until late in the evening. Restaurants have long hours in PV, though seafood shacks on the beach may close by late afternoon or sunset. Outside the resort areas, restaurants may close at 7 or 8 pm. Nayarit State is on Mountain Standard Time (an hour earlier than PV), but since 2011 restaurants from Punta de Mita south officially follow Central Time (as in PV). Unless otherwise noted, restaurants in this guide are open daily for lunch and dinner.

PRICES

Avoid paying for water; instead ask for *un vaso con agua* or *agua de garrafón*—either should net you a glass of purified water from the jugs used for cooking and rinsing vegetables. Most restaurants offer lunch deals with special menus at great prices though at more traditional restaurants, the lunch menu may not be available before 1 or 1:30 pm. Some small or casual restaurants accept only cash.

WHAT IT COSTS IN U.S. DOLLARS AND PESOS			
	$	$$	$$$	$$$$
Restaurants in Dollars	under $12	$12–$19	$20–$25	over $25
Restaurants in Pesos	under M$160	M$160–M$250	M$251–M$330	over M$330

Prices are the average cost of a main course at dinner, or if dinner is not served, at lunch.

BEST BETS FOR PUERTO VALLARTA DINING

With hundreds of restaurants to choose from, how will you decide where to eat? Fodor's writers and editors have selected their favorite restaurants by price, cuisine, and experience in the Best Bets lists *below.* You can also search by neighborhood—just peruse the following pages to find specific details about a restaurant in the full reviews later in the chapter.

Fodor'sChoice ★

Café des Artistes Bistro Gourmet, p. 86
Casa Triskell, p. 97
ChocoBanana, p. 103
Daiquiri Dick's, p. 83
Eddie's Place, p. 95
El Arrayán, p. 87
El Brujo, p. 97
Frascati, p. 99
La Ola Rica, p. 101
Mar Etxea, p. 96
Sonora al Sur, p. 96
Tacos on the Street, p. 100
Trio, p. 91
Vallarta Food Tours, p. 92
Vista Grill, p. 85

Best by Price

$

Casa Triskell, p. 97
ChocoBanana, p. 103
The Coffee Cup, p. 93
Eddie's Place, p. 95
El Arrayán, p. 87
El Brujo, p. 97

Fredy's Tucan, p. 83
La Ola Rica, p. 101
La Piazzetta, p. 84
La Playa, p. 102
Mamá Rosa, p. 90
Mar Etxea, p. 96
Mariscos 8 Tostadas, p. 92
Sonora al Sur, p. 96
Tacos on the Street, p. 100
Trio, p. 91

$$

Archie's Wok, p. 81
Café des Artistes del Mar, p. 100
Daiquiri Dick's, p. 83
Vista Grill, p. 85

$$$

Café des Artistes Bistro Gourmet, p. 86
Frascati, p. 99
Mark's Bar & Grill, p. 97

$$$$

Barcelona Tapas, p. 86
Porto Bello, p. 93

Best by Cuisine

AMERICAN

ChocoBanana, p. 103
The Coffee Cup, p. 93

CLASSIC MEXICAN

El Arrayán, p. 87

INTERNATIONAL

Café des Artistes Bistro Gourmet, p. 86
Daiquiri Dick's, p. 83
Trio, p. 91

ITALIAN

Dolce Vita, p. 95
Frascati, p. 99
La Piazzetta, p. 84

SEAFOOD

El Brujo, p. 97
Langostino's, p. 85
Mariscos 8 Tostadas, p. 92

Best by Experience

BRUNCH

Mamá Rosa, p. 90

CHILD-FRIENDLY

ChocoBanana, p. 103
La Playa, p. 102
Memo's Pancake House, p. 85
Mr Cream, p. 96

GREAT VIEW

Hacienda San Angel Gourmet, p. 89
Vista Grill, p. 85

LIVE MUSIC WITH DINNER

Eddie's Place, p. 95
La Palapa, p. 84

MOST ROMANTIC

Café des Artistes del Mar, p. 100
Café des Artistes Bistro Gourmet, p. 86
Hacienda San Angel Gourmet, p. 89

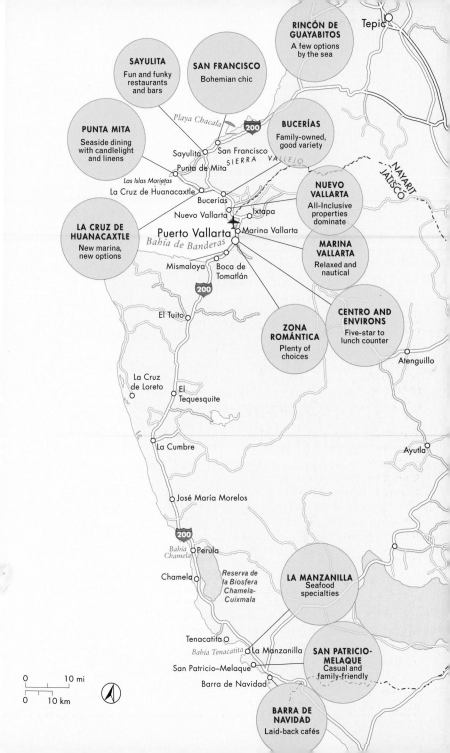

RINCÓN DE GUAYABITOS
A few options by the sea

Tepic

SAYULITA
Fun and funky restaurants and bars

SAN FRANCISCO
Bohemian chic

Playa Chacala

200

BUCERÍAS
Family-owned, good variety

PUNTA MITA
Seaside dining with candlelight and linens

Sayulita

San Francisco

SIERRA   *VALLEJO*

Punta de Mita

Las Islas Marietas

La Cruz de Huanacaxtle

Bucerías

NAYARIT
JALISCO

NUEVO VALLARTA
All-Inclusive properties dominate

Nuevo Vallarta

Ixtapa

LA CRUZ DE HUANACAXTLE
New marina, new options

Puerto Vallarta

Marina Vallarta

Bahía de Banderas

MARINA VALLARTA
Relaxed and nautical

Mismaloya   Boca de Tomatlán

200

El Tuito

ZONA ROMÁNTICA
Plenty of choices

CENTRO AND ENVIRONS
Five-star to lunch counter

Atenguillo

La Cruz de Loreto

El Tequesquite

La Cumbre

Ayutla

José María Morelos

200

Bahía Chamela   Perula

Chamela

Reserva de la Biosfera Chamela-Cuixmala

LA MANZANILLA
Seafood specialties

Tenacatita

Bahía Tenacatita   La Manzanilla

San Patricio–Melaque

SAN PATRICIO-MELAQUE
Casual and family-friendly

Barra de Navidad

BARRA DE NAVIDAD
Laid-back cafés

0   10 mi

0   10 km

CHILDREN

Though it's unusual to see children in the dining rooms of Puerto Vallarta's upscale restaurants, dining with youngsters here does not have to mean culinary exile. Many of the restaurants reviewed in this chapter are excellent choices for families.

RESERVATIONS

It's possible to get a same-day reservation if your timing's flexible. With a bit of luck it's possible to just show up for dinner, even at the nicest places; go early (6 pm) or late (after 9 pm) and politely inquire about any last-minute vacancies or cancellations. Occasionally, an eatery may ask you to call the day before your scheduled meal to reconfirm; don't forget, or you could lose out. You'll find that with the exception of small mom-and-pop establishments, many places provide valet parking at dinner for reasonable rates (often around $2–$3, plus tip).

TIPPING AND TAXES

In most restaurants, tip the waiter 10–15%. (To figure out a 10% tip, move the decimal point one place to the left on your total; add half that for 15%.) Some restaurants include a service charge, so only tip more if service has been exceptional. Tip at least $1 per drink at the bar. Never tip the maître d' unless you're out to impress your guests or expect to pay another visit soon. Even in the tonier restaurants, tax is typically already factored in to the cost of individual menu items.

WHAT TO WEAR

Dining out in Puerto Vallarta tends to be a casual affair—even at some of the more expensive restaurants you're likely to see customers in dressy shorts or jeans. It's extremely rare for PV restaurants to actually require a jacket and tie, but all of the city's more formal establishments appreciate a gentleman who dons a jacket. Let your good judgment be your guide.

BEER AND SPIRITS

Jalisco is far and away Mexico's most important tequila-producing state, and its green-agave cousin, *raicilla*, is gaining in popularity (though still hard to find). Mexican beers range from light like Corona and Sol to medium-bodied and golden like Pacífico and Bohemia; great darks include Negra Modelo and Indio.

GOURMET FESTIVAL

Gourmet Festival. Puerto Vallarta's annual gourmet festival has brought international attention since 1994. During the 10-day food fling each November, chefs from around the world bring new twists on timeless classics. Events include classes and seminars, and restaurants and guest chefs create special menus with wine pairings. Attendees can sample food from otherwise inaccessible restaurants of all-inclusive hotels, all of them at better-than-usual rates. ⊕ *www.festivalgourmet.com.*

SMOKING

The law forbids smoking in enclosed areas, including bars. However, smoking might still be allowed, especially if there is an outdoor patio. Call ahead to find out a restaurant's policy.

PUERTO VALLARTA

While there are several good hotel-based restaurants in Puerto Vallarta, most of the city's top spots are independent and can be found in El Centro or Zona Romántica, but there are also several good spots in Marina Vallarta and north along the Riviera Nayarit.

ZONA ROMÁNTICA

Many excellent restaurants are packed into this tourist-heavy neighborhood. As throughout Vallarta, they are mainly casual places where a sundress or a pair of slacks is about as dressed up as most people get. Seafood and Mexican fare are the specialties at taco stands and at the restaurants facing Los Muertos beach. Pizza joints and Italian eateries are also popular, and there are plenty of places for dessert and coffee, too.

$ ✕ **Andale.** Although many have been drinking, rather than eating, at
AMERICAN this local hangout for years, the restaurant serves fajitas, dependable burgers (of beef, chicken, or fish) with large portions of fries, black-bean soup, jumbo shrimp, and herb-garlic bread along with daily lunch and nightly drink specials at the chummy bar. The interior is cool, dark, and informal; two rows of mini-tables line the sidewalk outside. Service is generally attentive, although that doesn't mean the food will arrive promptly. This spot is party-hearty later in the evening, by 10 pm or so. Plus-size patrons should beware of the munchkin-size toilet stalls. ⑤ *Average main: 110 MP ⊠ Av. Olas Altas 425, El Centro, Puerto Vallarta, Jalisco* ☎ *322/222–1054* ⊕ *www.andales.com.* ✛ *1:C2*

$$ ✕ **Archie's Wok.** Dishes at this extremely popular pan-Asian restaurant
ASIAN include Thai garlic shrimp, *pancit* (Filipino stir-fry with pasta), and Singapore-style (lightly battered) crispy fish. There are also several vegetarian dishes. The spinach and watercress salad with feta, pecans, and a hibiscus dressing is healthy, refreshing, and perfect for a late lunch (the restaurant opens only after 2 pm). Ceilings are high, and the decor is Asian tropical: dark wood, lacy potted palms, and Indonesian étagères. Thursday through Saturday from 7:30 to 10:30 pm, the soothing harp music of well-known local musician D'Rachel is the perfect accompaniment to your meal. ⑤ *Average main: 200 MP ⊠ Calle Francisca Rodríguez 130, Zona Romántica* ☎ *322/222–0411* ⚏ *Reservations not accepted* ⊗ *Closed Sun. and Sept.* ✛ *1:C2.*

$ ✕ **Café de Olla.** Repeat visitors swear by the enchiladas and carne asa-
MEXICAN das at this earthy restaurant. It's also one of the few places in town where you can get a margarita made of *raicilla* (green-agave firewater as opposed to tequila, which comes from the blue agave) when available. A large tree extends from the dining-room floor through the roof, local artwork adorns the walls, and salsa music often plays in the background. Note that as soon as Café de Olla opens for the season, it fills up and seems to stay full: You may need to wait for a table, especially at breakfast and dinner. If you give up waiting, the taco shop next door is very good. ⑤ *Average main: 115 MP ⊠ Calle Basilio Badillo 168–A, Zona Romántica* ☎ *322/223–1626* ⊕ *www.cafedeollavallarta.*

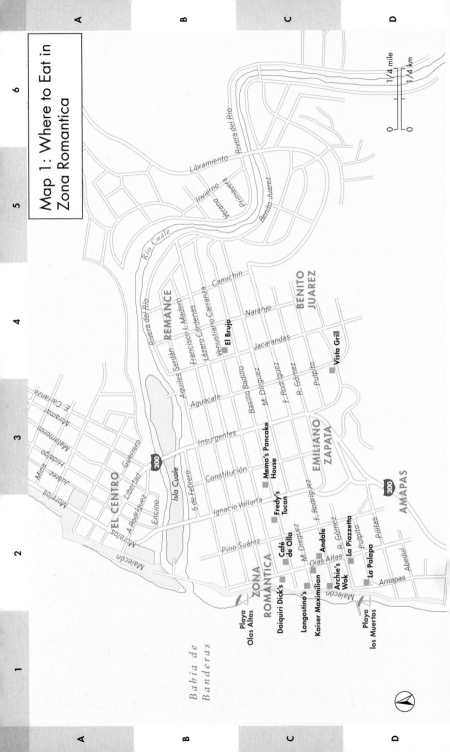

Map 1: Where to Eat in Zona Romantica

EL CENTRO

REMANCE

El Brujo

BENITO JUAREZ

Vista Grill

EMILIANO ZAPATA

Memo's Pancake House

Fredy's Tucan

ZONA ROMANTICA

Daiquiri Dick's

Café de Olla

Langostino's

Kaiser Maximilian

Archie's Wok

Andale

La Piazzetta

La Palapa

AMAPAS

Playa Olas Altas

Playa los Muertos

Bahía de Banderas

Río Cuale

Isla Cuale

1/4 mile
1/4 km

com 🍴 *Reservations not accepted* 🚫 *No credit cards* ⊘ *Closed Tues. and Sept. 15–Oct. 15* ✛ *1:C2.*

$$
INTERNATIONAL
Fodor's Choice
★

✕ **Daiquiri Dick's.** Locals come repeatedly for breakfast (the homemade orange-almond granola is great), visitors for the good service and consistent Mexican and world cuisine. The lunch-dinner menu has fabulous appetizers, including superb lobster or shrimp tacos with a drizzle of béchamel sauce and perfect, tangy jumbo-shrimp wontons. On the menu since the restaurant opened almost 30 years ago is Pescado Vallarta, or grilled fish on a stick. The tortilla soup is popular, too. Start with a signature daiquiri; move on to the extensive wine list. The open patio dining room frames a view of Playa Los Muertos, creating a beautiful, simple scene to enjoy while you sip that drink. ⑤ *Average main: 220 MP* ✉ *Av. Olas Altas 314, Zona Romántica* ☎ *322/222–0566* ⊕ *www.ddpv.com* ⊘ *Closed Sept. and Tues. May–Aug.* ✛ *1:C2.*

$
MEXICAN

✕ **El Brujo.** It's on a noisy street corner, but the seriously good food and generous portions mean that this is still an expat favorite. The *molcajete*—a sizzling black pot of tender flank steak, grilled green onion, and soft white cheese in a delicious homemade sauce of dried red peppers—is served with a big plate of guacamole, refried beans, and made-at-the-moment corn or flour tortillas. Try the breaded scallops, stuffed fish with shrimp and creamy *huitlacoche* (black corn fungus) sauce, or a grilled skirt steak with mushrooms and bell peppers bathed in tomato sauce. If you're into simpler fare, the unadorned grilled fish fillet is fresh and delicious, too. ⑤ *Average main: 120 MP* ✉ *Venustiano Carranza 510, at Naranjo, Zona Romántica* ☎ *322/223–2036* 🍴 *Reservations not accepted* ⊘ *Closed 2 wks in late Sept.–early Oct.* ✛ *1:B4.*

$
CAFÉ

✕ **Fredy's Tucan.** Even in low season, Fredy's, next door to the Hotel de Roger, is packed full of Mexican families, gringo friends, and local business people. Your mug of coffee will be refilled without having to beg; service is brisk, professional, and friendly. Breakfast is the meal of choice, with pancakes and waffles, Mexican specialties, omelets, and eggs Benedict with thick slices of ham. The lunch menu is abbreviated but offers plenty of choices for those who enjoy soups, salads, burgers, nachos, and quesadillas. Eat on the pretty covered patio or inside, where big plate-glass windows let you keep an eye on busy Calle Basilio Badillo. You can get a fruit smoothie or a stiff drink from the bar. It closes just before 3 pm. ⑤ *Average main: 80 MP* ✉ *Calle Basilio Badillo 245, Zona Romántica* ☎ *322/223–0778* ⊕ *fredystucan.com* 🍴 *Reservations not accepted* 🚫 *No credit cards* ⊘ *No dinner* ✛ *1:C2.*

$$$
EUROPEAN

✕ **Kaiser Maximilian.** Viennese entrées dominate the menu, which is modified each year when the restaurant participates in PV's culinary festival. One favorite is herb-crusted rack of lamb served with horseradish and pureed vegetables au gratin; another is venison medallions in chestnut sauce served with braised white cabbage and steamed vegetables. The adjacent café (open 8 am–midnight) has sandwiches, excellent desserts, and 20 specialty coffees—all of which are also available at the main restaurant. To avoid the stream of street peddlers off the patio, eat in the charming, European-style dining room, where handsome black-and-white-clad servers look right at home amid dark-wood framed mirrors, brightly polished brass, and lace café curtains. ⑤ *Average main: 300*

FOOD GLOSSARY

Here are some of the dishes you're likely to find on area menus or in the reviews below. *Buen provecho!*

arrachera: skirt steak.

carne asada: thin cut of flank or tenderloin, grilled or broiled and usually served with grilled onions, beans, rice, and guacamole.

carnitas: bites of steamed or fried pork served with tortillas and a variety of condiments.

chilaquiles: pieces of corn tortillas fried and served with red or green sauce; good ones are crispy, not soggy, and topped with chopped onions and *queso cotija*, a crumbly white cheese.

chile en nogada: a green poblano chili stuffed with a semisweet meat mixture and topped with walnut sauce and pomegranate seeds. As Mexico's national dish—the green chili, white sauce, and red seeds reflect the nation's flag—it is often served in September in honor of Independence Day.

chile relleno: batter-fried green chili (usually mild) stuffed with cheese, seafood, or a sweet meat mixture; served in a mild red sauce. Some health-conscious restaurants make them without batter.

menudo: tripe stew.

pozole: a rich pork- or chicken-based soup studded with hominy (corn kernels) and served alongside a plate of condiments including raw onions, chilies, radishes, cilantro, oregano, sliced cabbage, and tostadas.

tostada: a crispy fried tortilla topped with beans and/or meat, cheese, and finely chopped lettuce or cabbage. May also describe the corn tortilla, which is served with foods like ceviche and pozole.

MP ⊠ *Av. Olas Altas 380, Zona Romántica* ☎ *220/223–0760* ⊕ *www. kaisermaximilian.com* ☉ *Closed Sun.* ✛ *1:C2.*

$$$
INTERNATIONAL
✕ **La Palapa.** This large, welcoming, thatched-roof eatery is open to the breezes of Playa Los Muertos and filled with wicker-covered chandeliers, art-glass fixtures, and lazily rotating ceiling fans. The menu meanders among international dishes with modern presentation: roasted stuffed chicken breast, pork loin, seared yellowfin tuna drizzled in cacao sauce. The seafood enchilada plate is divine. It's pricey, but the beachfront location and, in the evening, the low lights and Latin jazz combo (8 to 11 pm nightly), keep people coming back. Breakfast here (daily after 8 am) is popular with locals as well as visitors. This is the sister property to Vista Grill, which has great views of the bay from the hills above town. Ⓢ *Average main: 300 MP* ⊠ *Calle Púlpito 103, Playa Los Muertos, Zona Romántica* ☎ *322/222–5225* ⊕ *www.lapalapapv. com* ✛ *1:D2.*

$
ITALIAN
✕ **La Piazzetta.** Locals come for the Naples-style pizza, cooked in a brick oven and with a crust that's not too thick, not too thin. There's also great pasta and a good variety of entrées, like salmon with caviar, and lemon and broccoli with fettuccine in cream sauce served piping hot. For appetizers try the tomato-topped bruschetta toasts or steamed mussels with lemon, parsley, and butter. Most folks sit on the large patio;

there's also an intimate dining room. The personal attention of the owner, Mimmo Lorusso, guarantees repeat business. It's open 4 pm to midnight. A new location has opened in the residential district behind Costco and the northern hotel zone. ⓢ *Average main: 115 MP* ⊠ *Calle Rodolfo Gómez 143, at Av. Olas Altas, Zona Romántica* ☎ *322/222–0650* ⊕ *www.lapiazzettapv.com* ⊗ *Closed Sun. No lunch* ✣ *1:D2.*

$

SEAFOOD

✕ **Langostino's.** Right on the beach just north of the pier at Playa Los Muertos, Langostino's is a great place to start the day with a heaping helping of Mexican rock, cranked up to a respectable volume. For lunch or dinner, the house favorite at this professional and pleasant place is surf and turf (called *mar y tierra*), and the three seafood combos are a good value. The kids can play on the beach while you linger over coffee. ⓢ *Average main: 100 MP* ⊠ *Calle Manuel M. Dieguez, at Los Muertos Beach, Zona Romántica* ☎ *322/222–0894* ▭ *No credit cards* ⊗ *Closed Aug. 20 through Sept.* ✣ *1:C2.*

$

AMERICAN
FAMILY

✕ **Memo's Pancake House.** Your child will most certainly find something he or she likes on this Pancake House menu. There are 12 kinds of pancakes—including the "Oh Henry," with chocolate bits and peanut butter—and eight kinds of waffles. Other breakfast items include *machaca* (shredded beef) burritos, *chilaquiles*, and eggs Florentine, but these tend to be perfunctory; pancakes and waffles are your best bet. The large dining room bursts with local families on weekends and homesick travelers. It can get noisy, and service tends to slip when Memo is out of town. The draped back patio is pretty, but it's like a greenhouse when the day heats up. The restaurant shuts down at 2 pm. ⓢ *Average main: 150 MP* ⊠ *Calle Basilio Badillo 289, Zona Romántica* ☎ *322/222–6272* ⌂ *Reservations not accepted* ▭ *No credit cards* ⊗ *No dinner* ✣ *1:C3.*

$$

INTERNATIONAL
Fodor'sChoice
★

✕ **Vista Grill.** Sensational views of the sunset and sparkling city-light panoramas after dark make this one of the best restaurants in PV for a celebratory toast—of life, love, or the perfect vacation. Dedicated observers can spot whales spouting offshore almost any day during the winter months. An army of attentive waiters brings baskets of delicious, buttery rolls and whisks away plates. Try the stellar crab-and-sea-bass cakes, lobster tacos, or sashimi with truffle-and-soy vinaigrette and avocado coulis. The chef adds new dishes every few weeks; the barman stocks top-of-the-line spirits; and there is a large wine cellar representing several continents. ⓢ *Average main: 230 MP* ⊠ *Calle Púlpito 377, near Calle Aguacate, El Centro* ☎ *322/222–3570* ⊕ *www.vistagrill.com* ⊗ *No lunch* ✣ *1:C4.*

EL CENTRO

Comprising the *malecón* (seawalk) and the half-dozen blocks behind it, El Centro has mostly moderately priced hotels—but plenty of upscale restaurants. Parking is limited mainly to streetside; many of the better restaurants offer valet parking. Café des Artistes, Trio, Vitea, Los Xitomates, and others offer a variety of cuisines and elegant yet casual dining, which is what Puerto Vallarta diners demand. At the other end of the spectrum, downtown PV has a great assortment of bargain eateries, including those offering tacos (in street stands and sit-down restaurants) and diners catering to locals with excellent prices on changing daily specials.

$$$$
SPANISH

✕ **Barcelona Tapas.** One of the few places in town with both good food and an excellent bay view, Barcelona Tapas has traditional Spanish tapas like garlicky roasted potatoes, spicy garlic shrimp, and grilled mushrooms. In addition to traditional paella, there's also a seafood-only version. To start you off, attentive waiters bring a free appetizer and delicious homemade

> **NATURAL THIRST-BUSTER**
>
> The guy on the malecón with a giant gourd and a handful of plastic cups is selling *agua de tuba*, a refreshing, pleasant, yet innocuous drink made from the heart of the coconut palm. It's stored in a gourd container called a *huaje* and served garnished with chopped walnuts and apples.

bread. The "chef's surprise" six-course tasting menu lets you try soup, salad, and dessert as well as hot and cold tapas. The restaurant is air-conditioned in summer; the rest of the year the windows are taken off to let the breeze in. You pay for that patio view by having to walk up a few dozen stairs. $ *Average main: 350 MP* ✉ *Calle Matamoros at 31 de Octubre, El Centro* ☎ *322/222–0510* ⊕ *www.barcelonatapas.net* ⌂ *Reservations essential* ✛ *2:C4.*

$$$
INTERNATIONAL
Fodor's Choice
★

✕ **Café des Artistes Bistro Gourmet.** Several sleek dining spaces make up the original, downtown restaurant Café des Artistes; the most beautiful and romantic is the courtyard garden with modern sculpture. The main restaurant achieves a contemporary Casablanca feel with glass raindrops and tranquil music. In either area, choose an appetizer, entrée, and dessert from the three-course bistro menu. Try the creamy soup of smoked chipotle chilies followed by a fresh fillet of fish cooked in one of several Mexican styles, and finishing with the crème brûlée. Also within these walls, Thierry Blouet's Cocina de Autor (closed Sunday and in September) is a limited-seating restaurant pairing four- to six-course tasting menus with or without wines. Decor is restrained, with a waterfall garden behind plate glass taking center stage. In these restaurants, drinks add significantly to the price of the meal. Many diners end the night at the clubby cigar bar or Constantini Wine Bar, which offers some 50 vintages by the glass as well as distilled spirits, appetizers, and live music most nights of the week. $ *Average main: 300 MP* ✉ *Av. Guadalupe Sánchez 740, El Centro* ☎ *322/222–3229* ⊕ *www.cafedesartistes.com* ☾ *No lunch* ✛ *2:C4.*

$
MEXICAN

✕ **Chez Elena.** Frequented in its heyday by Hollywood luminaries and the who's who of PV, this downtown restaurant still has a loyal following. The casual patio ambience is simple, but the wholesome food is satisfying, and the portions are generous. House specialties include fajitas and Yucatan-style pork. Elena's is also known for an eclectic signature dish, the Indonesian *sate mixto*, skewers of meat and chicken spiced with peanut sauce, as well as its killer handcrafted margaritas and its flaming coffee drinks. $ *Average main: 145 MP* ✉ *Calle Matamoros 520, El Centro* ☎ *322/222–0161* ⊕ *http://www.chezelena.com* ☾ *Closed June–Sept. No lunch* ✛ *2:B5.*

$ ✕ **Comedor de Sra. Heladia.** Here you can glimpse the real Old Vallarta.
MEXICAN   A short but steep walk up from the malecón is this neighborhood dining room, which serves construction workers and locals. It's in a typical
one-story Vallarta house of whitewashed brick with a red-tile roof and a
burnished-cement floor. The lady of the house serves breakfast from 8 to
11 am and a limited later meal of two or three entrées, served between
1 and 5 pm. Choices like meatballs in tomato sauce, pork chops, and
pig's feet are usually accompanied by rice, beans, homemade salsa,
and a basket of hot tortillas. There's no menu, and you'll need to communicate in basic Spanish. ⑤ *Average main: 90 MP* ⊠ *Calle Aldama,
El Centro* ☎ *322/223–9612* ⌲ *Reservations not accepted* ⊟ *No credit
cards* ⊘ *Closed Sun. No dinner* ✛ *2:B5.*

$ ✕ **Cueto's.** Teams of engaging waiters, all family members, squeeze past
SEAFOOD   the trio that croons romantic tunes throughout the day to refill beer
glasses, remove empty plates, and deliver fresh tostadas and hot, crusty
garlic bread. But don't fill up on nonessentials, as the casseroles—with
crab, clams, fish, shrimp, or mixed seafood—are so delicious you won't
want to waste even one bite. We particularly recommend the cream-
based casseroles. Enjoy a complimentary margarita with dinner or a free
digestif later on. Cueto's is a few blocks behind the Unidad Deportiva
complex of soccer fields and baseball diamonds. ⑤ *Average main: 85
MP* ⊠ *Calle Brasilia 469, El Centro* ☎ *322/223–0363* ⊕ *http://www.
mariscoscuetospv.com.* 🍴 *2:C1*

$$ ✕ **El Andariego.** A few blocks past the north end of the malecón is this
MODERN   lively Mexican restaurant. Paintings of the city brighten the walls; at
MEXICAN   night the lighting is subdued and the mood is family-oriented. Many
of the traditional breakfasts are the stick-to-your ribs variety. Lunch
and dinner menus are different, but the cost is about the same. Expect
numerous salads, pasta dishes, a good variety of chicken and beef
dishes, and seafood and lobster prepared to your taste. Enjoy live
music (electric guitar versions of "Proud Mary," or mariachi music)
nightly, usually between 6 and 10 pm. There's free wireless Internet in
both restaurant and bar. ⑤ *Average main: 200 MP* ⊠ *Av. México 1358,
at El Salvador, El Centro* ☎ *322/222–0916, 322/223–2100* ⊕ *www.
elandariego.com.mx* ✛ *2:C2.*

$ ✕ **El Arrayán.** The oilcloth table covers, enameled tin plates, exposed raf-
MEXICAN   ters, and red roof tiles of this patio-restaurant conjure up nostalgia for
Fodor's Choice   the quaint Mexican home of less frenetic times. Here you can find the
★   things *Abuelita* (Grandma) still loves to cook, with a few subtle varia-
tions. Highlights of classic Mexican dishes from around the country are
rib-eye steak served with traditional cactus-pad salad, duck *carnitas* in
a glaze of smoky chili and orange, and *cochinita pibil,* a dish from the
Yucatan Peninsula of tender pork cooked in a banana leaf and served
with black beans and fried plantain. For dessert try caramel flan or a
light tamarind-flavored ice. It's a bit pricey for Mexican comfort food,
but it has a very dedicated fan club. ⑤ *Average main: 150 MP* ⊠ *Calle
Allende 344, at Calle Miramar, El Centro* ☎ *322/222–7195* ⊕ *www.
elarrayan.com.mx* ⊘ *Closed Tues. No lunch. Closed Aug 16–Sep 18*
✛ *2:C4.*

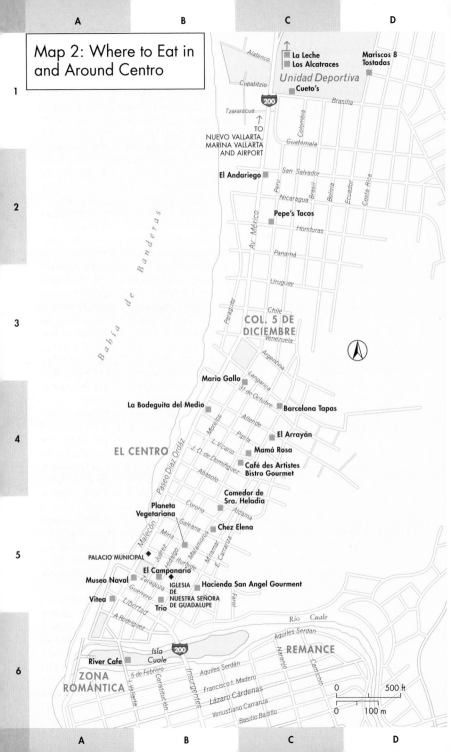

Map 2: Where to Eat in and Around Centro

A B C D

1

La Leche
Los Alcatraces

Mariscos 8
Tostadas

Alatenco

Cupatitzio

200

Unidad Deportiva

Cueto's

Tzararacua

Brasilia

↑
TO
NUEVO VALLARTA,
MARINA VALLARTA
AND AIRPORT

Guatemala

San Salvador

El Andariego

Colombia

Peru

Brasil

Bolivia

Ecuador

Costa Rica

2

Nicaragua

Pepe's Tacos

Honduras

Av. México

Panamá

Uruguay

B a h í a   d e   B a n d e r a s

Paraguay

Chile

3

COL. 5 DE
DICIEMBRE

Venezuela

Argentina

Maria Gallo

Langarica

31 de Octubre

Barcelona Tapas

La Bodeguita del Medio

Allende

El Arrayán

Morelos

Pipila

L. Vicario

EL CENTRO

Paseo Díaz Ordaz

J.O. de Domínguez

Mamá Rosa

Café des Artistes
Bistro Gourmet

4

Abasolo

Comedor de
Sra. Heladia

Corona

Planeta
Vegetariana

Galeana

Chez Elena

Aldama

Mina

Malecón

Juárez

Hidalgo

Iturbide

Matamoros

Miramar

E. Carranza

5

PALACIO MUNICIPAL ◆

El Campanario

Museo Naval

Zaragoza

IGLESIA
DE
NUESTRA SEÑORA
DE GUADALUPE

Hacienda San Angel Gourmet

Guerrero

Farol

Vitea

Libertad

Trio

A. Rodríguez

Río Cuale

*Isla
Cuale*

200

Aquiles Serdán

REMANCE

Naranjo

River Cafe

ZONA
ROMÁNTICA

5 de Febrero

I. Vallarta

Constitución

Aquiles Serdán

Insurgentes

Francisco I. Madero

Lázaro Cárdenas

Camichín

0   500 ft

0   100 m

6

Venustiano Carranza

Basilio Badillo

$ ╳ **El Campanario.** Fans swirl in the air, doors are open to the street, and
MEXICAN cheerful oilcloths cover wooden tables at this no-frills spot across from
the cathedral. Egg dishes and chilaquiles are served 9 am to 11 am, and
an inexpensive daily lunch menu is served 2 pm to 5 pm. For around
$5, you get soup, a main dish, a drink, homemade tortillas, and dessert.
Office workers come in for takeout or drift in between 6 pm and 10
pm for tacos, *tortas* (Mexican-style sandwiches on crispy white rolls),
or pozole. A recipe for the last is given—along with a positive dining
review—in a framed *Los Angeles Times* article from the 1980s. $ *Average main: 95 MP* ⊠ *Calle Hidalgo 339, El Centro* ☎ *322/223–1509*
▭ *No credit cards* ⊘ *Closed Sun. and 5–6 pm* ✛ *2:B5.*

$$$$ ╳ **Hacienda San Angel Gourmet.** Even non-mariachi fans are bewitched
INTERNATIONAL by the harmonious musical meanderings of the 12-piece, stunningly
uniformed, brass-and-string band that serenades diners most nights
from the second-floor terrace overlooking Banderas Bay and the velvet
hills of Puerto Vallarta. Ivy climbs blond, hacienda-style columns, and
chandeliers bathe in a romantic light the second-floor dining room
of this stunningly restored boutique hotel-restaurant. The chef has a
restrained hand when it comes to salt and spices; recipes are straightforward yet not bland or boring. Recommended is the red snapper with
polenta, tender filet mignon, or *cabrería* (a choice cut of beef on the
bone) served on a bed of mashed potatoes and sautéed spinach. You
might start with delicately battered and fried calamari served in a cone
of crisp nori; for dessert indulge in an ice cream sundae, coconut crème
brûlée, or peach crepes. $ *Average main: 400 MP* ⊠ *Calle Miramar 336,
El Centro* ☎ *322/222–2692* ⊕ *www.haciendasanangel.com* ⌂ *Reservations essential* ⊘ *No lunch* ✛ *2:B5.*

$ ╳ **La Bodeguita del Medio.** Near the malecón's north end, this world-
CARIBBEAN famous franchise restaurant with a fun-loving atmosphere has a bit of
a sea view from its second-floor dining room and a Caribbean flavor.
Specials vary by season; seek out the roast pork, the Cuban-style paella,
or the pork loin in tamarind sauce, and order rice, salad, or fried plantains separately. Like its Havana namesake, La Bodeguita sells Cuban
rum and cigars, and the music (canned during the day, live at night)—
like the cuisine—is pure *cubano*. During the day comrades lunch over
their laptops to use the free Wi-Fi; it opens at 9 am and is open most
nights until past midnight. Try the mojito, a signature Havana drink of
lime juice, sugar, white rum, and muddled fresh mint leaves. Offering
two-for-one beers at twice the normal restaurant price is bogus, however. $ *Average main: 120 MP* ⊠ *Paseo Díaz Ordáz 858, El Centro*
☎ *322/223–1584.* ✛ *2:B4*

$$$ ╳ **La Leche.** If chef Alfonso Cadena weren't so cool (he looks like a
INTERNATIONAL refined, former rock star because he is one!), then La Leche's main din-
ing room, an all-white rotunda lined with shelves of milk cans, could
come off as gimmicky. But each night as Cadena personally presents
a different menu on a chalkboard, his "blank canvas" dining space
becomes the perfect backdrop for a unique meal. For instance, a delicate
seafood bisque, unveiled in whimsical ceramic tureens, might precede
an exquisite mahimahi in a citrus reduction that provides the perfect
balance of sweet and sour, rich and refreshing. Servers are attentive and

friendly, but there is ample time between courses, so be prepared for an enjoyable but lengthy evening. Reservations aren't required but are a good idea. ⑤ *Average main: 300 MP* ⊠ *Blvd. Francisco M. Ascencio, Km 2.5, next to Hotel Fiesta Americana, Zona Hotelera* ☏ *322/293–0900* ⊕ *www.lalecherestaurant.com* ⊘ *No lunch* ✛ *2:C1.*

$

MODERN
MEXICAN

✕ **Mamá Rosa.** Locals return over and over for the expansive breakfast buffet (served until 2 pm, but freshest before noon) and, in the evening, for budget gourmet meals. Recommended main dishes include the nut-crusted salmon served on a bed of asparagus and thin sliced potatoes, shrimp medallions in pineapple and chipotle chili sauce, lamb meatballs in red wine sauce, and Mamá Rosa special chicken, stuffed with chorizo and spinach on a bed of beans. Ingredients are reassuringly recognizable but uniquely combined. Presentation is also a work of art, proving that a beautifully designed dish isn't the sole province of restaurants with high prices and small portions. The setting is pleasant but not fancy; upper and lower patios are surrounded by plenty of plants. ⑤ *Average main: 95 MP* ⊠ *Calle Leona Vicario 269, El Centro* ☏ *322/222–4010* ⊕ *www.mamarosavallarta.com* ⊘ *Closed Mon. No lunch, no dinner May–mid-Oct.* ✛ *2:C4.*

$

MEXICAN

✕ **Maria Gallo.** By day it offers nifty *comida corrida*: set-priced, three-course menus that change daily. For about five bucks you get a pitcher of freshly made *agua fresca*, a starter (usually soup or salad), and a choice of half a dozen main courses. Chef-owner Memo Wulff studied at San Francisco's California Culinary Institute, and although his dishes are Mexican, they are not quite business as usual. Recent dishes included calamari in a spicy red sauce (*a la diabla,* which means "to the devil"), char-grilled *carne asada,* and pork shank burritos, most served with rice, a puddle of refried black beans, and your choice of rolls or tortillas. After 7 pm the menu switches to *antojitos*: tacos, tostadas, flautas, and other snacking dishes. The ambience is casual, the music is lively and Latino, and the walls are decorated with handmade art projects. ⑤ *Average main: 70 MP* ⊠ *Calle Morelos 558, El Centro* ☏ *322/223–1193* ⊟ *No credit cards* ⊘ *Closed Sun.* ✛ *2:C3.*

$

CAFÉ

✕ **Museo Naval.** Overlooking the bay and boardwalk, Vallarta's snug little maritime museum café is across the way from the main plaza. The coffee bar at the back produces great coffee, and from the kitchen come fresh-squeezed orange juice, enchiladas, tortas (sandwiches), and other typical Mexican dishes. Brushed-metal tables, ceiling fans, and purse racks make this second-story snack shop a pleasant way to start off the day. The Mexican sailors who wait tables look a bit shy, almost like they'd rather be swabbing the deck than play-acting as waiters, but they certainly look sweet in their crisp white uniforms and sailor caps. Hours are 9 am to 7:40 pm Tuesday through Friday, opening an hour later on weekends. ⑤ *Average main: 100 MP* ⊠ *Calle Zaragoza 4, at the malecón, El Centro* ☏ *322/223–5357* ⊘ *Closed Mon.* ✛ *2:B5*

$

MEXICAN

✕ **Pepe's Tacos.** No longer the best in PV, Pepe's still can't be beat at 5 am, when most sensible taco-makers are asleep. It's an open-door dive across from the Pemex station at the north end of Old Vallarta. Expect plastic tablecloths, sports on several TVs, and 11 different types of quesadillas—from standard cheese in a flour tortilla to the "Japanese" version, with beef, sausage, pineapple, and mushrooms. You can order tacos by the set or individually (choose your meat grilled or barbecued over charcoal). One PV friend says she wakes up thinking about the tacos de chuleta con queso (pork and cheese tacos). The bar is serviceable with all the basics: rum, tequila, and beer. ⑤ *Average main: 55 MP* ⊠ *Honduras 173, between Avs. Peru and Mexico, El Centro* ☎ *322/223–1703* ▭ *No credit cards* ⊙ *Closed Mon. No lunch.* ⊕ *2:C2*

$

VEGETARIAN
FAMILY

✕**Planeta Vegetariano.** Those who stumble upon this hogless heaven can "pig out" on tasty, meatless *carne asada* and a selection of main dishes that changes daily. Choose from at least three healthful main dishes, plus beans, several types of rice, and a soup at this casual buffet-only place. A healthful fruit drink, coffee, or tea, and dessert are included in the reasonable price. ⑤ *Average main: 85 MP* ⊠ *Iturbide 270, El Centro* ☎ *322/222–3073* ▭ *No credit cards* ⊕ *2:B5.*

$$

INTERNATIONAL

✕**River Cafe.** At night, candles flicker at white-skirted tables with comfortable cushioned chairs, and tiny white lights sparkle in palm trees surrounding the multilevel terrace. This riverside restaurant is recommended for breakfast and for the evening ambience. Attentive waiters serve such international dishes as seafood fettuccine and vegetarian crepes; the wild-mushroom soup and fried calamari with aioli sauce are especially recommended. If you're not into a romantic dinner, belly up to the intimate bar for a drink and—Friday and Saturday evenings—live jazz. (In high season there's live music of various genres nightly.) Breakfast is served daily after 8 am. ⑤ *Average main: 170 MP* ⊠ *Isla Río Cuale, Local 4, El Centro* ☎ *322/223–0788* ⊕ *www.rivercafe.com. mx* ⊕ *2:A6.*

$

INTERNATIONAL
Fodor's Choice
★

✕**Trio.** Conviviality, hominess, and dedication on the parts of chef-owners Bernhard Güth and Ulf Henriksson have made Trio one of Puerto Vallarta's best restaurants—hands down. Fans marvel at the kitchen's ability to deliver perfect meal after perfect meal, mostly Mediterranean food. Popular demand guarantees rack of lamb with fresh mint and, for dessert, the warm chocolate cake. The kitchen often stays open until nearly midnight, and during high season the restaurant opens the back patio, second floor, and rooftop terrace. Waiters are professional yet unpretentious; either the sommelier or the maître d' can help you with the wine. But the main reason to dine here is the consistently fabulous food, which is also a great value. ⑤ *Average main: 150 MP* ⊠ *Calle Guerrero 264, El Centro* ☎ *322/222–2196* ⊕ *http://www.triopv.com* ⊙ *No lunch* ⊕ *2:B5.*

TACO PRIMER

In this region's informal eateries, a taco is generally a diminutive corn tortilla heated on an oiled grill filled with meat, shrimp, or batter-fried fish. If your server asks "*¿Preparadita?*" he or she is asking if you want it with cilantro and onions. Add-your-own condiments are *salsa mexicana* (chopped raw onions, tomatoes, and green chilies), liquidy guacamole made with green *tomatillos* (small green tomatoes), and pickled jalapeño peppers. Some restaurants also feature garnishes of chopped nopal cactus.

4

Fodor'sChoice **Vallarta Food Tours.** Not sure where to start? Why not sample a bit of
★ everything? These three-hour food tasting and walking tours of Puerto
Vallarta, away from the typical tourist spots, will educate you on
the ingredients and origins of each meal. Expect to mingle and laugh
with locals—they love to meet people who venture out of their hotels!
✉ *1193-A Av. Mexico, Colonia 5 de Deciembre, El Centro* ☎ *322/181–
7196* ⊕ *vallartafoodtours.com.*

$ ✕ **Vitea.** When chefs Bernhard Güth and Ulf Henriksson, of Trio, needed
SEAFOOD a challenge, they cooked up this delightful seaside bistro. So what if
your legs bump your partner's at the small tables? This will only make
it easier to sneak bites from her plate. The decor of the open, casual
venue is as fresh as the food. Appetizers include the smoked salmon
roll with crème fraîche, or choose from the selection of "small plates"
like the spicy shrimp tempura or the garlic-chili manicotti. Alternately,
make a meal of the bistro's soups, sandwiches, and salads. It's a nice
place for breakfast overlooking the malecón. ⑤ *Average main: 110
MP* ✉ *Libertad 2, north of Cuale River on the malecón, El Centro*
☎ *322/222–8703, 322/222–8695* ⊕ *www.viteapv.com* ⊘ *Closed 1 wk
in late Sept.* ✛ *2:A5.*

ZONA HOTELERA

$ ✕ **El Coleguita.** Just what you needed in the middle of the day: free
MEXICAN tequila shots. Waiters at this super-popular family- and businessperson-
oriented restaurant bring a generous serving of tequila to your table
soon after you arrive, along with a small bowl of shrimp broth to
open the appetite and a basket of crispy tostadas with a few types of
fresh salsas. But what really impresses the crowds are the enormous
platters of shrimp (breaded, spicy, or sautéed in garlic) served with a
small salad and a big scoop of rice. You can order a whole red snapper
or a generous fish fillet as well. The ambience at this patio restaurant
facing the boats and the marina is casual and festive; the crowd hums
with contentment while other restaurants nearby seemingly have been
drained of clientele. It's open from 1 pm to 8 pm. ⑤ *Average main: 115
MP* ✉ *Carretera Vallarta-Tepic, Zona Hotelera* ☎ *322/108–9726* ▭ *No
credit cards* ⊘ *Closed Tues.* ✛ *3:B1.*

$ ✕ **Los Alcatraces.** For a breakfast of chilaquiles that are crisp, not soggy,
MEXICAN come to "The Calla Lilies." *Café de olla,* real Mexican coffee simmered with cinnamon and *panela* (unrefined brown sugar), is served
in a keep-warm carafe; crumbly white cheese is delivered from a ranch
in the nearby hills. All meals are economical, especially the combo
plate: a quesadilla, chiles rellenos, skirt steak, rice, beans, and a taco.
Weekdays, a fixed-price lunch for under $5 consists of soup, main dish,
beans, and a fruit drink. This is a good, authentic-Mexican option for
people staying in the Hotel Zone, though not particularly picturesque
and with somewhat slow service. ⑤ *Average main: 100 MP* ✉ *Blvd.
Francisco M. Ascencio 1808, Zona Hotelera* ☎ *322/222–1182* ⊘ *No
dinner weekends* ✛ *2:C1.*

$ ✕ **Mariscos 8 Tostadas.** The original Mariscos 8 Tostadas (there are a
SEAFOOD few others in the bay) is located behind Blockbuster Video in the Hotel

Zone. It features full seafood plates alongside its ceviches, tacos, and appetizers. The odd menu translations at these restaurants are a clear indication that the clientele is local. For instance, the tuna sashimi appears as *atún fresco con salsa rasurada*, or "tuna cut thick with shaved sauce." The tuna *is* thicker than that in U.S. sushi houses and is served in a shallow dish with soy sauce, micro-thin cucumber slices, sesame seeds, green onions, chili powder, and lime. The ceviche couldn't be fresher, and portions are more than generous. ⑤ *Average main: 100 MP* ⊠ *Calle Río Guayaquil 413, at Calle Ecuador, Zona Hotelera* ☎ *322/222–7691* ▭ *No credit cards* ⊘ *Closed 2 wks in Sept. No dinner* ✛ *2:D1.*

MARINA VALLARTA

Many of Marina Vallarta's restaurants face the boats at this area's main attraction: the yacht harbor. Interspersed with shops and storefronts selling fishing charters and canopy tours, the restaurant scene is easy to negotiate, with no busy boulevards or rushing traffic. After their meals, diners can take a spin around the marina or look at the shops here or at Plaza Neptuno, which abuts it. It's also an easy walk to the Hotel Zone facing the beach, where international brand-name hotels offer their own fine-dining opportunities.

$ ✕ **The Coffee Cup.** Early risers and those heading off on fishing charters
CAFÉ will appreciate the daily 5 am opening time, and closing time isn't until 10 pm. The café, which is filled with wonderful art for sale, has fruit smoothies, coffee in many manifestations, and tasty frappes with Oreo cookie bits or frosting-topped carrot cake. Have a breakfast bagel (served all day), a wrap, or a generously filled deli sandwich on a kaiser roll (perhaps the roast beef with horseradish, the honey-roasted turkey, or pastrami). Box lunches to-go include sandwich, chips, two soft drinks or waters, dessert, and a trail-mix bar. Restaurant patrons can use the inexpensive Internet phone to call the United States or Canada, check email at one of three computers, or sit all day with their laptops to take advantage of the free Wi-Fi. ⑤ *Average main: 65 MP* ⊠ *Condominios Puesto del Sol, Local 14–A, at the marina, Marina Vallarta* ☎ *322/221–2517* ⊕ *www.coffeecuppv.com* ✛ *3:B4.*

$ ✕ **La Barra Cerveceria.** In Marina Vallarta, an upscale place to go for
FAST FOOD snacks and beer is La Barra Cerveceria, which sells pizza as well. ⑤ *Average main: 100 MP* ⊠ *Av. Paseo de la Marina Sur s/n, across from Hotel Mayan Palace, Marina Vallarta* ☎ *322/209–0909* ⊕ *labarracerveceria.com.* ✛ *3:B4*

$$$$ ✕ **Porto Bello.** Yachties, locals, and other return visitors attest that every-
ITALIAN thing on the menu here is good—start with mixed antipasto or fried calamari, and then move on to the signature fusilli with artichokes, olives, and lemons or the sautéed fresh fish with spinach and arugula sauce. And if you're not satisfied, the kitchen will give you something else without quibbling. Undoubtedly that's what makes Marina Vallarta's veteran restaurant one of its most popular. The dining room is diminutive and air-conditioned; the patio overlooking the marina is more elegant, with a chiffon ceiling drape and white ceiling fans. Since there are no lunch specials and the Italian menu is the same at dinner,

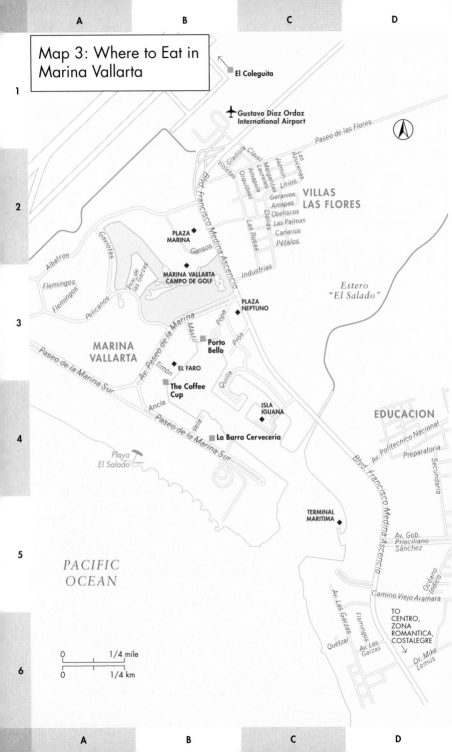

Map 3: Where to Eat in Marina Vallarta

El Coleguita

✈ Gustavo Díaz Ordaz
International Airport

Paseo de las Flores

VILLAS
LAS FLORES

Gladiola
Clavel
Margaritas
Laureles
Jazmín
Lirios
Violetas
Amapola
Orquídeas
Geranios
Amapas
Dalias
Obeliscos
Las Palmas
Canarios
Pétalos
Las Rosas

Las Azucenas

Blvd. Francisco Medina Ascencio

PLAZA
MARINA

Gansos

Industrias

MARINA VALLARTA
CAMPO DE GOLF

*Estero
"El Salado"*

Gaviotas

Albatros

Flemingos

Flemingos

Pelicanos

Paseo de las Garzas

PLAZA
NEPTUNO

Popa

Mástil

Proa

Porto
Bello

MARINA
VALLARTA

Av. Paseo de la Marina

Timón

EL FARO

Quilla

The Coffee
Cup

ISLA
IGUANA

EDUCACION

Paseo de la Marina Sur

Ancla

Vela

La Barra Cerveceria

Av. Politecnico Nacional

Preparatoria

Secundaria

Paseo de la Marina Sur

Playa
El Salado

TERMINAL
MARITIMA

Av. Gob.
Prisciliano
Sánchez

Océano Indico

PACIFIC
OCEAN

Camino Viejo Aramara

Av. Las Garzas

Flamingos

TO
CENTRO,
ZONA
ROMANTICA,
COSTALEGRE
↓

Av. Las
Garzas

Quetzal

Dr. Mike
Lemus

0 — 1/4 mile

0 — 1/4 km

most folks come in the evening. $ *Average main: 500 MP* ⊠ *Condominiums Marina del Sol, Local 7, Marina Vallarta* ☎ *322/221–0003* ⊕ *www.portobellovallarta.com* ✛ *3:B3.*

OLAS ALTAS

South of the Zona Romántica, condos, private homes, and hotels line the coast road or perch above the beach. Accessible by boat, beach towns like Las Animas, Quimixto, and Yelapa attract mainly day-trippers who enjoy the tropical beach scene and accept the limited and unoriginal menus of fish, ceviche, or grilled chicken or steak. Yelapa, with its dedicated cadre of seasonal (late fall–winter–early spring) foreign residents, has a broader selection of restaurants above the beach.

$ ✕ **La Playita de Lindo Mar.** Open to the ocean air, the wood-and-palm-front restaurant looks right at home on Conchas Chinas Beach. And there are wonderful views of waves crashing on or lapping at the shore at its bar El Set. Enjoy breakfast or an expansive, inexpensive weekend brunch buffet (it runs 8 am to 1 pm; come before 11 in the morning for the freshest food). Select from crepes, frittatas, omelets, and *huevos Felix* (eggs scrambled with fried corn tortillas, served with a grilled cactus pad, beans, and grilled serrano chilies). Lunch and dinner choices include crispy crab tacos, grilled burgers and chicken, shrimp enchiladas with spinach, and much, much more. If you're driving, look for the sign for Hotel Lindo Mar on the coast highway; you can park in the small lot near the beach or in the hotel lot and take the elevator down to the beach. $ *Average main: 50 MP* ⊠ *Carretera a Barra de Navidad, Km 2.5, Playa Conchas Chinas, at Hotel Lindo Mar, Olas Altas* ☎ *322/221–5511* ⊕ *www.hotelconchaschinas.com* ✛ *4:C5.*

INTERNATIONAL

NUEVO VALLARTA

$$ ✕ **Dolce Vita.** Fine Italian food is to be found at any of the two locations of this well-known local business. Pizzas are thin-crusted and baked in a traditional mud oven, the plate of seafood pasta never seems to be enough, and the salads are great for getting things started. Casual attire is expected, with the location in Nuevo Vallarta being somewhat fancier and ideal for either romantic dinners or family reunions. $ *Average main: 165 MP* ⊠ *Av. Paseo las Palmas #2, Nuevo Vallarta* ☎ *322/297–0403* ⊕ *www.dolcevitavallarta.com.*

ITALIAN

$ ✕ **Eddie's Place.** This restaurant is an institution among locals and visitors who know that in Nuevo Vallarta there's more than just all-inclusive hotels. Eddie and his staff serve ample and succulent breakfasts that include local specialties like chilaquiles as well as gringo favorites like omelets and sausages. Once the sun sets drop by for an even better dinner, with coconut shrimp with mango sauce or fulfilling kebabs as some of the most popular options, all while listening to smooth live music (not guaranteed) and Eddie's interest in meeting patrons (guaranteed). $ *Average main: 135 MP* ⊠ *Blvd. Nayarit 70 Local 1–3, Nuevo Vallarta* ☎ *322/297–4568* ⊕ *www.eddiesplacenuevovallarta.com.*

MEXICAN FUSION
Fodor'sChoice
★

$
TAPAS
Fodor's Choice
★

✕ **Mar Etxea.** If it's Spanish tapas and food you're after, this new restaurant (spring 2014) in Nuevo Vallarta will not disappoint. Sample *tortilla Española*, *chorizo a la sidra*, or some good ol´ Serrano ham, or simply let the chef make suggestions for the day. Oh, and they have several types of delicious paella as well. ⑤ *Average main: 85 MP* ⊠ *Paseo de la Marina 1 Local 16, Nuevo Vallarta* ☎ *322/297–1436* ⊕ *www.mar etxea.com.*

$
INTERNATIONAL
FAMILY

✕ **Mr Cream.** Chilaquiles, pancakes, waffles, baked goods, omelets whatever you want for breakfast, they have it. This brand new restaurant in Nuevo Vallarta has been a total success and a great excuse to leave your nearby hotel to eat good food any given morning. This said, it tends to be full on Sundays, so reservations may be a good idea. ⑤ *Average main: 115 MP* ⊠ *Av. Paseo de las Palmas #5, Nuevo Vallarta* ☎ *322/221–0868* ☉ *No dinner.*

$$$
ARGENTINE

✕ **Rincón de Buenos Aires.** Restaurants are a hard sell in all-inclusive-dominated Nuevo Vallarta. This one has managed to survive (it was formerly called La Porteña). The setting, an L-shaped covered patio with kids' play equipment in the center, is Mexican, but the food is pure Argentine flavor. Every cut of meat is grilled over mesquite, from the steaks to Angus prime rib. The adventurous yet tasty *chinculinas* (tender tripe appetizers) and chorizo turnovers certainly are authentic. Rice, veggies, and other sides must be ordered separately. Italian dishes and a few non-Argentine things like salmon and chicken dishes are also available. Come for a late lunch (it opens only after 2 pm) or dinner. ⑤ *Average main: 285 MP* ⊠ *Blvd. Nayarit 25, between highway to Bucerías and El Tigre golf course, Nuevo Vallarta* ☎ *322/297–4950* ☉ *Closed Mon.*

$
BARBECUE
Fodor's Choice
★

✕ **Sonora al Sur.** Throw in prime cuts from Mexico's finest meat producing state, Sonora, a chef that has found the secret to grilling perfect BBQ, and very affordable rates and you'll get a successful restaurant like this one, which sprouted out of the blue to become a favorite of diners who don't want to over-spend. Oh, the all-you-can-eat buffet for less than $6 is an added bonus. ⑤ *Average main: 100 MP* ⊠ *Blvd. Nuevo Vallarta No. 64, Nuevo Vallarta* ☎ *322/297–0376* ▭ *No credit cards.*

RIVIERA NAYARIT

AROUND BANDERAS BAY

Nuevo Vallarta is an all-inclusive destination and therefore has few dining options outside the hotels. To the north, Bucerías has many fine restaurants—some sophisticated, others family-friendly and inexpensive—as well as a few good Italian and French bistros. On the north side of town, a string of beach-facing restaurants offer fresh seafood in a variety of presentations, from regional dishes like *pescado sarandeado* (salt-and-herb-rubbed whole fish cooked over a wood fire) to fresh fillet of fish grilled with plenty of garlic. With its new marina, La Cruz de Huanacaxtle has a small but growing number of good restaurants. At the northern tip of the bay, Punta de Mita offers seafood restaurants facing the sand along with fine dining at the Four Seasons and St. Regis hotels, where reservations for nonguests are strictly required.

BUCERÍAS

$ ✕ **The Bar Above.** This little place above Tapas del Mundo defies cat-
CAFÉ egorization. It's a martini bar without a bar that also serves varied desserts—the owners prefer a setting that encourages people to come converse with friends rather than hang out like barflies. Order from the day's offerings, maybe molten chocolate soufflé (the signature dish), the cardamom-laced bread pudding, or a charred pineapple bourbon shortcake. Lights are dim, the music is romantic, and there's an eagle's view of the ocean from the rooftop nest. $ *Average main: 115 MP* ⊠ *Corner of Av. Mexico and Av. Hidalgo, 2 blocks north of central plaza, Bucerías* ☎ *329/298–1194* ▭ *No credit cards* ⊘ *Closed Sun. and June–Oct. No lunch* ✛ *4:C3.*

$ ✕ **Casa Triskell.** This midsize enclave is sure to satisfy anyone with a
CAFÉ sweet tooth, particularly those fond of well-crafted French crepes. Try
FAMILY the orange-flavored "Suzette" or, if you're a chocolate fan, the full-on
Fodor'sChoice "Tahitian" with ice cream, chocolate, and whipped cream. They also
★ have savory crepes and occasionaly hold a "moules et frites" (muscles and french fries) night for seafood-lovers. $ *Average main: 45 MP* ⊠ *Miguel Hidalgo 12, Riviera Nayarit, Bucerías* ☎ *322/120–5041* ▭ *No credit cards* ✛ *4:C3.*

$ ✕ **El Brujo.** This newer Bucerías branch of El Brujo is located right on
MEXICAN the beach but with the same food and generous portions of the origi-
Fodor'sChoice nal location in Puerto Vallarta. The *molcajete*—a sizzling black pot
★ of tender flank steak, grilled green onion, and soft white cheese in a delicious homemade sauce of dried red peppers—is served with a big plate of guacamole, refried beans, and made-at-the-moment corn or flour tortillas. Try the breaded scallops, stuffed fish with shrimp and creamy *huitlacoche* (black corn fungus) sauce, or a grilled skirt steak with mushrooms and bell peppers bathed in tomato sauce. If you're into simpler fare, the unadorned grilled fish fillet is fresh and delicious, too. $ *Average main: 150 MP* ⊠ *Av. del Pacífico 202-A, Bucerías* ☎ *329/298–0406* ⌕ *Reservations not accepted* ⊘ *Closed 2 wks late Sept.–early Oct.* ✛ *4:C3.*

$$$ ✕ **Mark's Bar & Grill.** You can dine alone at the polished black-granite
INTERNATIONAL bar without feeling too lonely, or catch an important ball game. But seemingly a world away from the bar and (muted) TV is the charming restaurant known for its delightful decor and international cuisine. Both can be appreciated on the back patio, open to the stars, or in the softly lit dining room. Menu standouts include the homemade pizza, the salads, and the macadamia-crusted fresh fish fillets with Thai curry. The lamb is flown in from New Zealand; shrimp comes from San Blas; and the black Angus beef is from Monterrey. Mixed organic lettuces, chives, and basil come from the lady down the street. The restaurant is elegant yet warm and inviting, with a golden glow over everything and, sometimes, roving musicians. More than a dozen wines are offered by the glass. $ *Average main: 280 MP* ⊠ *Lázaro Cárdenas 56, Bucerías* ☎ *329/298–0406* ⊕ *www.marksbucerias.com* ⊘ *No lunch* ✛ *4:C3.*

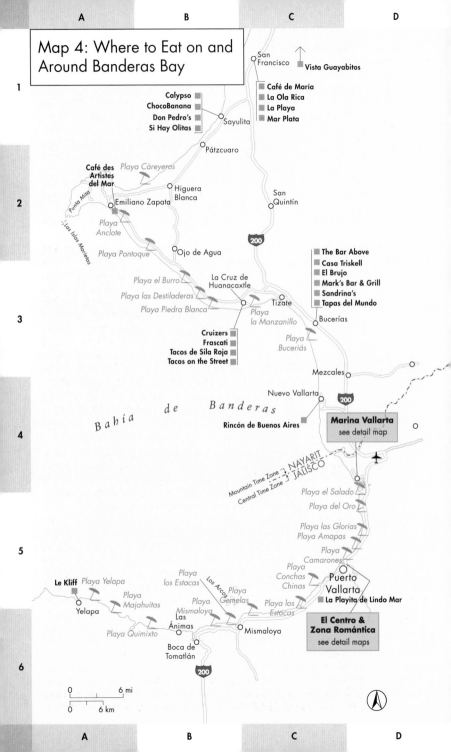

Map 4: Where to Eat on and Around Banderas Bay

San Francisco

Vista Guayabitos

Café de María
La Ola Rica
La Playa
Mar Plata

Calypso
ChocoBanana
Don Pedro's
Si Hay Olitas

Sayulita

Pátzcuaro

Playa Càreyeros

Café des Artistes del Mar

Higuera Blanca

San Quintín

Emiliano Zapata

Punta Mita

Playa Anclote

Las Islas Marietas

Playa Pontoque

Ojo de Agua

200

La Cruz de Huanacaxtle

Playa el Burro

Playa las Destiladeras

Playa Piedra Blanca

Tizate

The Bar Above
Casa Triskell
El Brujo
Mark's Bar & Grill
Sandrina's
Tapas del Mundo

Playa la Manzanillo

Bucerías

Playa Bucerías

Cruizers
Frascati
Tacos de Sila Roja
Tacos on the Street

Mezcales

Nuevo Vallarta

Bahía de Banderas

Rincón de Buenos Aires

Marina Vallarta
see detail map

Mountain Time Zone
Central Time Zone

NAYARIT
JALISCO

Playa el Salado

Playa del Oro

Playa las Glorias
Playa Amapas

Playa Camarones

Le Kliff

Playa Yelapa

Playa los Estacas

Los Arcos

Playa Conchas Chinas

Playa Gemelas

Puerto Vallarta

Playa Majahuitas

Playa Mismaloya

Playa los Estacas

La Playita de Lindo Mar

Yelapa

Las Ánimas

El Centro & Zona Romántica
see detail maps

Playa Quimixto

Boca de Tomatlán

Mismaloya

200

0   6 mi
0   6 km

$$
MEDITERRANEAN
FAMILY

✕ **Sandrina's.** The walls of this veteran, Canadian-owned restaurant and locals' favorite are covered in colorful paintings: portraits and tropical scenes and still lifes. Columns are adorned with bright broken-tile mosaics. The restaurant opens after 3 pm; it's very pleasant to dine on the back patio at night amid dozens of candles and tiny lights. The menu varies in accomplishment as well as cuisine: On our last visit we sampled tasty lentil soup and a nicely grilled hamburger as well as dry hummus and uninspired tzatziki. There are plenty of other choices, including pizza, salads, pasta dishes, and such Mediterranean fare as chicken souvlaki and Greek-style chicken. Order a liqueur-laced coffee or dessert from the bakery counter. The café at the front has great espresso but is open in high season only, usually December through Easter. ⑤ *Average main: 195 MP* ✉ *Av. Lázaro Cárdenas 33, Bucerías* ☎ *329/298–0273* ⊕ *www.sandrinas.com* ☽ *No lunch. Closed Tues. and 2 wks in Sept.* ✦ *4:C3.*

$
INTERNATIONAL

✕ **Tapas del Mundo.** Here, worldly recipes of this and that are served in small plates perfect for sharing. Sit at the long, U-shaped bar around the open kitchen or at a second table behind it. The cooks produce wonderful daily special dishes with ingredients found fresh that day, as well as the restaurant's standards, like shrimp with guajillo chilies served with homemade tortillas, goat cheese with herbs, Anaheim chilies stuffed with goat cheese, or stir-fried beef strips. Better order a second dish of the delightful breaded green olives—you'll be fighting over them. The owner's one-man stand-up routine can be entertaining or a bit overbearing, depending on your mood. The Bar Above, upstairs, serves coffee, desserts, and mixed drinks. ⑤ *Average main: 80 MP* ✉ *Corner of Av. Mexico and Av. Hidalgo, 2 blocks north of central plaza, Bucerías* ☎ *329/298–1194* ▭ *No credit cards* ☽ *Closed June–Sept. No lunch* ✦ *4:C3.*

LA CRUZ DE HUANACAXTLE

$
MEXICAN

✕ **Cruz'ers.** A view of the Nayarit mountains backing the yacht harbor is best from the newly named Cruz'ers, at La Cruz's new Marina Riviera Nayarit. Here you'll find both traditional Mexican as well as the usual standard fare. ⑤ *Average main: 160 MP* ✉ *Calle Marlín 39–A, Riviera Nayarit, La Cruz de Huanacaxtle* ☎ *329/295–5526.* ✦ *4:C3*

$$$
ITALIAN
Fodor'sChoice
★

✕ **Frascati.** La Cruz is slowly becoming more sophisticated (okay, *gentrified*), and Frascati combines the Old World and the New: It's friendly and intimate while simultaneously sophisticated. The ambience is mellow and earthy yet upscale. Wicker-basket light fixtures provide a moody feeling; you get a small but powerful light with which to read the menu. Background music slides between house, electronic, and aerobics-class boom-boom. Choose your pasta (several are house-made) and then one of 12 toppings, including traditionals (such as Bolognese, pesto, four cheeses, and pomodoro) or something chef-inspired like the Arturito, a sauce of fresh tomatoes, cream, chicken, and basil. The mixed seafood combo, served in an oversize martini glass, is delish. In addition to lightly battered and deep-fried denizens of the deep, the appetizer comes with batter-fried julienne zucchini and crispy fried parsley. ⑤ *Average main: 300 MP* ✉ *Av. Langosta 10, at Av. Coral, La Cruz de Huanacaxtle* ☎ *329/295–6185* ⊕ *www.frascatilacruz.com* ☽ *Aug.*

18th–1st week October, Closed Sun. May–June ✦ *4:C3.*

$
MEXICAN

✕ **Tacos la Silla Roja.** Aptly named the Red Chair (because of its Coca Cola chairs), this small and simple shack in La Cruz serves great Mexican food at even better prices. Tacos, pozole, gringas, quesadillas there are places like this everywhere, but the flavor here beats most of them. ⑤ *Average main: 50 MP* ✉ *Call Delfin 17, Riviera Nayarit, La Cruz de Huanacaxtle* ✆ *Closed Mon.–Wed.* ✦ *4:C3*

$
MEXICAN
FAMILY
Fodor'sChoice
★

✕ **Tacos on the Street.** This small no-frills restaurant offers what many claim to be the best tacos in all of Banderas Bay, but also the most expensive. The tender rib-eye meat that melts in your mouth is the secret to its success. ⑤ *Average main: 95 MP* ✉ *Huachinango St. 9, La Cruz de Huanacaxtle* ☎ *329/295–5056* ▭ *No credit cards* ✆ *Closed Mon.–Wed.* ✦ *4:C3*

PUNTA DE MITA

$$
INTERNATIONAL

✕ **Café des Artistes del Mar.** A more casual and beachy interpretation of the downtown Puerto Vallarta brand faces the water at the north end of Playa El Anclote. If you sit on the dark-stained deck, you'll have the best view of the ocean, Marietas Islands, and the left arm of Banderas Bay. Portions are petite, but the five-course tasting menu still manages to stuff one silly. Representative courses include a delicious beet-and-goat-cheese appetizer; spinach salad with poached pear and Gorgonzola cheese; salmon carpaccio with lemony scallops tartare; a deliciously tender short rib with pineapple chutney; and, for dessert, vanilla ice cream with mango foam. The soundtrack is sexy Brazilian and other ethnic-tinted jazz, the waitstaff is attentive, and the views are divine. It is attached to the condo-hotel Hotel Cinco, although separately owned and managed. ⑤ *Average main: 250 MP* ✉ *Av. El Anclote 5, Punta Mita* ☎ *329/291–5415* ⊕ *www.cafedesartistes.com* ✆ *Closed Mon.* ✦ *4:A2.*

NORTH OF BANDERAS BAY

As developers, vacationers, and retirees flock to the area north of Banderas Bay, its restaurants grow in number and sophistication. The exception is Rincón de Guayabitos, designed more for national tourism, where restaurants compete in number if not variety of cuisine or sophistication. Small San Francisco (aka San Pancho) has a number of stylish restaurants as well as a handful of excellent taco and burrito joints. Just a few minutes south, beachy Sayulita caters to surfers on a budget with lots of economical eateries, but also offers enough moderately priced restaurants serving international food to keep its multinational visitors happy.

RINCON DE GUAYABITOS

$ ✕ **Vista Guayabitos.** Portions are
MEXICAN large, and the cooking seems to have improved with time, although the main reason to visit is the lovely views of a solitary beach, uninhabited Coral Island, and the beaches of Rincón de Guayabitos. The hawk's-eye ocean view is especially wonderful around sunset. Order a full Mexican meal or just a shrimp or fish taco and a beer or cocktail. Changing daily specials like ribs, mashed potatoes, and corn on the cob, with a glass of wine or beer, are filling if unimaginative. Shrimp is prepared in a handful of ways; for kids there are hamburgers (or

> ### TIME IS OF THE ESSENCE
>
> Nayarit State (Nuevo Vallarta and points north, such as la Riviera Nayarit) is in the Mountain Standard Time zone, while Jalisco (Marina Vallarta to Barra de Navidad) is on Central Standard Time. But because tourism in Bucerías and Nuevo Vallarta has always been linked to that of Puerto Vallarta, Nayarit businesses now run on Jalisco time. When making dinner reservations or checking restaurant hours north of Punta Mita, ask whether the place runs on *hora de Jalisco* (Jalisco time) or *hora de Nayarit*.

4

shrimp burgers) and fries or quesadillas. Food service begins at noon, although the stated opening time is 11:30 am. ⑤ *Average main: 100 MP* ⊠ *Carretera a Los Ayala, Km 1.5, Rincón de Guayabitos* ☎ *327/274–2589* ⊕ *www.vistaguayabitos.com* ✛ *4:C1.*

SAN FRANCISCO

$ ✕ **Café de María.** There are three distinct menus for breakfast, lunch,
CAFÉ and dinner. In the morning order one of an army of different omelets, a smoothie, or an attractively presented fruit bowl with yogurt. The lunch menu lunges among the classics: BLTs and burgers, roast beef sandwiches, spaghetti, and four different salads. Coffee and a scoop of excellent Blue Bell ice cream or slice of carrot cake are also options. For dinner, choose among a reasonably priced rib-eye steak, shrimp in mango or chipotle chili sauce, or a fish fillet. Bathrooms are clean and pleasant. The two rooms of this renovated former home overlook the street just a few blocks from the beach. ⑤ *Average main: 95 MP* ⊠ *Av. Tercer Mundo at Calle América Latina, San Francisco* ☎ *311/258–4439* ⊟ *No credit cards* ⊗ *Closed Wed., no dinner Tues. (all year); closed Sept.–mid-Oct. No dinner June–Aug.* ✛ *4:C1.*

$ ✕ **La Ola Rica.** One of San Pancho's first upscale restaurants, "The Deli-
INTERNATIONAL cious Wave," has still got it goin'. Small, medium-crust, wood-fired
Fodor'sChoice pizzas are just right for an appetizer (we recommend the Brie pizza with
★ caramelized onions) or, with a soup or salad, as a delicious dinner for one. Another good appetizer is the fresh white cheese round served with warm tomato sauce and fresh basil. The margaritas are lovely, and wine by the glass is a generous portion. All of the doe-eyed, wasp-waisted waitresses are relatives of the locally born and raised co-owner, Triny. Eat to the beat of a jazz-dominated sound track: overlooking the street on the covered patio or inside the home-cum-restaurant, artfully decorated with eclectic paintings, photographs of Old Mexico, and saints

La Ola Rica has a delightfully homey feel.

in niches. Summer hours vary each season, depending on tourist traffic; it's best to call during the off-season to double-check days and hours open. ⑤ *Average main: 95 MP* ⊠ *Av. Tercer Mundo s/n, San Francisco, Nayarit* ☎ *311/258–4123* ⊗ *Closed Sun. No lunch. Closed Sat.–Wed. June–July. Closed Aug.–Oct.* ✛ *4:C1.*

$ ✕ **La Playa.** The owners of La Ola Rica, just up the street, have opened
MEXICAN this more casual lunch spot right on the sand of San Pancho's beach,
FAMILY squeezed between twin headlands. Sit at a table near the full bar (which specializes in mojitos) or settle into a chaise longue closer to the water's edge. Choose a roast beef or chipotle chicken sandwich, fish-and-chips (with crunchy wedge-cut fries and fresh mahimahi), a couple of fish tacos, or a shrimp tostada. Lively tropical tunes and lacy coconut palms complete the idyllic picture. You can walk off your meal along the beach or sleep it off on your plastic, umbrella-shaded chaise. Behind the restaurant are several snug, second-story bungalows with kitchenettes for rent. ⑤ *Average main: 90 MP* ⊠ *On San Pancho Beach, San Francisco* ☎ *311/258–4381* ▭ *No credit cards* ⊗ *Closed Mon. No dinner* ✛ *4:C1.*

$$$$ ✕ **Mar Plata.** Decor is nonchalant yet sophisticated and so, come to think
EUROPEAN of it, is the waitstaff. Impressive second-story digs have views of the sea as well as a celestial seasoning of stars on the ceiling in the form of tin lamps from Guadalajara. Dark-blue and deep terra-cotta walls juxtapose nicely; the huge space is saved from looking industrial by innovative installations and fixtures. Heavy old wood doors are transformed to tabletops, chairs are mismatched, and floors are poured of untreated cement. Co-owner and chef Amadine Darmstaedter's recipes wed traditional Argentine meats with updated Continental cuisine in a happy transcontinental marriage. Portions are smallish, and entrées exclude

sides. There's live music Sunday and occasional flamenco shows or tango classes. $ *Average main: 500 MP* ⊠ *Calle de Palmas 130, Col. Costa Azul, San Francisco* ☎ *311/258–4424, 311/258–4425* ⊘ *Closed Mon. and June–Sept. No lunch* ✛ *4:C1.*

DAILY SPECIALS

To save money, look for the fixed-menu lunch called either *comida corrida* or *menú del día*, served from about 1 to 5 pm in restaurants throughout Mexico, especially those geared to working-class folks.

SAYULITA

$$
ECLECTIC

✕ **Calypso.** This second-story restaurant overlooks the town plaza from beneath an enormous palapa roof. Locals rave about the deep-fried calamari served with spicy cocktail and tangy tartar sauces; it's an appetizer that's large enough for several people to share. Portions in general are very generous. There are good pasta dishes, including the house special with basil and sun-dried tomatoes. The Cobb salad has tons of blue cheese; the Caesar and Chinese-chicken salads are also highly recommended. Really you can get everything from a burger and fries to fajitas, enchiladas, or shrimp scampi with fettuccini. The menu is varied and the food reasonably priced. You can pay by credit card only if the bill totals 250 pesos or more. $ *Average main: 115 MP* ⊠ *Av. Revolución 44, across from plaza, Sayulita* ☎ *329/291–3704* ⊘ *No lunch* ✛ *4:B1.*

$
AMERICAN
FAMILY
Fodor's Choice
★

✕ **ChocoBanana.** One of Sayulita's pioneer restaurants has really gotten spiffy, adding tile mosaic accents and generally beautifying its terrace restaurant. The Wi-Fi doesn't hurt, either. BLTs and burgers, omelets and bagels, chicken with rice, and chai tea are some of what you'll find here. They also have a good selection of vegetarian dishes. Service isn't fast, in keeping with laid-back Sayulita's surfer attitude. This perennial favorite kitty-corner from the main square is almost always full of people eating and loafing; there's a kids' menu for the truly young. It closes at 6 pm (2 pm on Sunday). $ *Average main: 125 MP* ⊠ *Calle Revolución at Calle Delfín, on plaza, Sayulita* ☎ *329/291–3051* ▭ *No credit cards* ⊘ *No dinner Sun.* ✛ *4:B1.*

$
INTERNATIONAL
FAMILY

✕ **Don Pedro's.** Sayulita institution Don Pedro's has wonderful pizzas baked in a wood-fire oven, prepared by European-trained chef and co-owner Nicholas Parrillo. Also on the menu are consistently reliable seafood dishes, yummy Niçoise salad, and tapenade. The mesquite-grilled filet mignon is just about the best around; it comes with baby vegetables, mashed potatoes, and pita bread. The pretty second-floor dining room, with the better view, is open when the bottom floor fills up, usually during the high season (November to May). During high season they also have dance classes and dancing to Latin tunes, currently on Monday, and live flamenco guitar on Thursday. This is a good spot for breakfast, too, after 8 am. $ *Average main: 95 MP* ⊠ *Calle Marlin 2, at the beach, Sayulita* ☎ *329/291–3090* ⊕ *www.donpedros.com* ⊘ *Closed Sept.* ✛ *4:B1.*

$
MEXICAN
FAMILY

✕ **Si Hay Olitas.** This simply decorated, open-front restaurant near tiny Sayulita's main plaza is the one most often recommended by locals for dependable Mexican and American fare. Order a giant burrito, vegetarian platter, burger, grilled chicken, or a seafood combo. There's a little of everything to choose from, and it's open for breakfast. The setting is casual, and the menu has plenty of things that children will like. $ *Average main: 85 MP* ⊠ *Av. Revolución 33, Sayulita* 📞 *329/291–3203* ☗ *No credit cards* ✛ *4:B1.*

SOUTH OF PUERTO VALLARTA

YELAPA

The small fishing villages and quaint towns south of Puerto Vallarta like Yelapa are known for their delicious no-fuss seafood and rustic, beachfront palapa bars and restaurants. Eating out here is very informal and laid-back, and if you're not looking for a full meal, just grab a beach chair by the water and kick back with a cold drink and a light snack.

> **KNOW YOUR TORTILLAS**
>
> In Mexico, most tortillas are made of milled cornmeal. They are flattened into thin disks, griddle cooked, and served with just about every dish. Flour tortillas are a specialty of northern Mexico and are typically offered only with certain dishes, like *queso fundido* (cheese fondue).

$$$ ✕ **Le Kliff.** You'll find the best views
MEXICAN   at a series of open-air patios under a huge palapa roof at Le Kliff, south of PV. $ *Average main: 400 MP* ⊠ *Carretera a Barra, Km 17.5, South of Puerto Vallarta, Yelapa* 📞 *322/228–0666* ⊕ *www.lekliff.com.* ✛ *4:A5*

COSTALEGRE

BARRA DE NAVIDAD

Barra de Navidad is a funky little town catering to lovers of casual Mexico. Its restaurants are similarly informal, offering smoothies and homemade muffins and banana bread or other generally healthful, unsophisticated fare. Beach- and lagoon-facing restaurants offer up similar menus featuring grilled mahimahi served with rice and veggies. Across its lagoon, seaside shanties are the place to go for an afternoon idyll of sand, sea, ceviche, and cold beer.

SAN PATRICIO–MELAQUE

Like neighboring Barra de Navidad, San Patricio–Melaque faces Christmas Bay (Bahía de Navidad) and has plenty of seafood eateries facing the sand. (Those who want to burn a few calories can walk along the beach to eat at Barra's restaurants, or vice versa.) Surrounding the square are informal taco and sandwich shops as well as storefronts selling ice cream and groceries, which could be purchased for a picnic under one of the palm-thatch shade umbrellas for rent on the beach. A few more sophisticated and international restaurants, such as Canadian-owned Maya, enliven the dining scene during the winter season.

$ ✕ **El Dorado.** This is the best place in town for seafood; the ocean view
SEAFOOD   from under the tall, peaked palapa roof isn't bad either. In addition to the garlic-and-oil fish fillets and breaded shrimp, there's grilled chicken with baked potato, beef tips with rice and beans, soups, quesadillas, steak, great guacamole, and fries. It's open all day (8 am until 10 pm) and serves everyone from white-collar business types to families and friends meeting for lunch to tourists cleaned up for an evening out. Popular with local families, business people, and travelers, it's a simple and unadorned but large restaurant facing Christmas Bay. After your meal, kick your shoes off and take a walk on the beach. ⑤ *Average main: 92 MP* ✉ *Calle Gómez Farias 1, San Patricio–Melaque* ☎ *315/355–5239.*

$ ✕ **Maya.** Two Canadian women have teamed up to bring sophistication
INTERNATIONAL   to San Patricio–Melaque's dining scene. East meets West in contemporary dishes such as tequila-lime prawns and corn, and Gouda-cheese fritters with a smoked jalapeño aioli. Favorite entrées include Szechuan prawns and prosciutto-wrapped chicken. The hours of operation are complex and subject to change; it's best to check the website or confirm by phone. There's often live music including jazz or blues. ⑤ *Average main: 130 MP* ✉ *Calle Alvaro Obregón 1, Villa Obregón, San Patricio–Melaque* ☎ *315/102–0775 cell* ⊕ *www.restaurantmaya.com* ☐ *No credit cards* ☉ *Closed Sun.–Mon. and mid-May–Oct. No lunch.*

WHERE TO STAY

Updated by Federico Arrizabalaga

Centered in the middle of a large bay, Bahía de Banderas, Puerto Vallarta is the traditional hub for area beach hotels. Look for smaller budget hotels downtown, and ocean-front high-rise hotels to the north in the Hotel Zone (Zona Hotelera), Marina Vallarta, and Nuevo Vallarta. Even farther north, Riviera Nayarit is where to go for unique B&Bs, boutique hotels, and some truly luxurious villas.

Having reached critical mass, Puerto Vallarta's hotel scene is more about upgrading than building new properties. In the Centro and Zona Romántica neighborhoods, expect refurbished budget and moderately priced hotels (with the exception of luxury property Hacienda San Angel). Continue north into Zona Hotelera for condos, time-shares, and high-rises.

Areas directly to the north and south of the city continue to add vacation properties. Just north of town in Nuevo Vallarta, look for the new condo-hotel Taheima Wellness Resort & Spa. South of town in Costalegre, the boutique ecoluxe oasis Hotelito Desconocido was renovated with an extensive new holistic spa.

The most development is occurring in Riviera Nayarit, where the 161 km (100 miles) of coastline between San Blas and Nuevo Vallarta are experiencing a building boom. Once the private playground of surfers and beachgoers seeking waves and long stretches of solitary sand, many popular beaches are now becoming resort destinations. Playa Destiladeras, between La Cruz de Huanacaxtle and Punta Mita, is home to the new Fairmont Rancho Banderas—an upscale family-focused resort of one-, two-, and three-bedroom villas. The area is also home to the 2,100-acre Litubú development that is set to have two golf courses, the new La Tranquila resort, private homes, a beach club, and public shopping and dining options.

No matter what you're looking for—from cliff-side condos with beach access to small inns with trails leading into the jungle, from enormous pools with swim-up bars to private plunge pools—almost any hospitality wish can be fulfilled here.

PLANNING

LODGING STRATEGY

Where should I stay? With hundreds of hotels in Puerto Vallarta, it may seem like a daunting question. But fret not—most of the legwork has been done for you. The selections here represent the best this city has to offer—from the best budget digs to the sleekest designer resorts. Scan "Best Bets" on the following pages for top recommendations by price and experience. Or find a review quickly in the listings—search by neighborhood, then alphabetically. Happy hunting!

NEED A RESERVATION?

Hotel reservations are an absolute necessity when planning your trip to Puerto Vallarta—although rooms are easier to come by these days. Competition for clients also means properties undergo frequent improvements, especially late September through mid-November, so when booking ask about any renovations, lest you get a room within earshot of construction, or find your hotel is temporarily without commonplace amenities such as swimming pool or spa.

⚠ **Overbooking is a common practice, so get confirmation in writing via fax or email.**

SERVICES

Most resort hotels have air-conditioning, cable TV, one or more restaurants, room service, and in-room irons and ironing boards. Many have voice mail, coffeemakers, and hair dryers. Ethernet or Wi-Fi Internet service is common in guest rooms; if not, there's likely a guest computer or three in a common area. Most hotels above the budget or moderate price level have fitness facilities; alternatively, visit a nearby sports club or gym (there are many). Some hotels are entirely smoke-free, meaning even smoking outdoors is frowned upon or prohibited.

CAN I DRINK THE WATER?

Most of the fancier hotels have reverse osmosis or other water filtration systems. It's fine for brushing your teeth, but play it safe by drinking bottled water (there might be leaks that let groundwater in). Note that the bottled water might cost extra, although there's usually a notice if it's not free. Buy a few bottles at the corner grocery instead.

STAYING WITH KIDS

Puerto Vallarta is a popular destination for both foreign families and nationals, and in general its hotels have adopted a family-friendly attitude. Some properties provide in-room video games, playgrounds, game rooms, children's swimming pools, and other diversions; others have suites with kitchenettes and fold-out sofa beds to accommodate the family's needs. Most full-service Puerto Vallarta hotels provide roll-away beds and babysitting, but make arrangements when booking the room, not when you arrive. Beach resorts often have kids' clubs to allow their parents quality adult time.

CHAIN HOTELS

Tried-and-true chains may have excellent rates and can be good last-minute options. There are hotels from the Holiday Inn/InterContinental Group, Marriott, Sheraton, and various Starwood chains, including Westin and St. Regis.

BOUTIQUE HOTELS

Small boutique hotels are another option in Puerto Vallarta, especially in the Zona Romántica and El Centro. Some of these are simple, some luxurious, but they all offer hospitality and comfort on a more intimate scale.

APARTMENTS AND VILLAS

When shared by two couples, a spacious villa can save you a bundle on upscale lodging and on meals. Villas often come with stereo systems, DVD players, a pool, maid service, and air-conditioning. Prices range from $100 to $1,000 per night, with 20% to 40% discounts off-season.

PRICING

We list high-season prices, before meals or other amenities. Low-season rates usually drop 20%–30%. Less expensive hotels include tax in the quote. Most higher-priced resorts add 18% tax on top of the quoted rate; some add a 5%–10% service charge. Moderately priced hotels swing both ways. Tax and/or tips are often included with all-inclusive plans.

An all-inclusive (AI) might make you reluctant to spend money elsewhere. So you don't miss out on area restaurants and activities, stay at more modest digs for part of your trip, and go AI for a day or two. Some AI hotels also have day passes ($60–$90).

WHAT IT COSTS IN U.S. DOLLARS AND PESOS			
$	**$$**	**$$$**	**$$$$**
Hotels in Dollars	under $120	$120–$180	$181–$250	over $250
Hotels in Pesos	under M$1600	M$1600–M$2400	M$2401–M$3300	over M$3300

Prices are the lowest rate for a standard room in high season, generally excluding taxes and service charges.

WHERE SHOULD I STAY?

	NEIGHBORHOOD VIBE	PROS	CONS
Zona Romántica	Older, modest hotels with low price and proximity to the beach. Varied restaurants, cafés, and gay bars buzz well into the night.	Action central; walking distance to bars, shops, restaurants, and beaches north and south. Buses to other zones.	Few hotels offer parking; mostly modest hotels only with few amenities; many older hotels could use renovation.
El Centro	Colorful Old Vallarta, with a few interesting hotels in the hills with excellent bay views. More shops and restaurants than hotels.	Central location. Plenty of nightlife, buses, and taxis. Cruising the boardwalk is fun day or night.	Noisy traffic from old buses squeezing through narrow streets. Dearth of parking spaces. Less lively at night than Zona Romántica.
Zona Hotelera	The greatest concentration of hotels is on the stretch along the Francisco Medina Ascencio Avenue from the Puerto Vallarta Maritime Terminal to the Sheraton Buganvilias Resort.	All beachfront with spectacular views of the ocean; great jogging route.	Most of the hotels are not brand-new; lots of big sky-scrapers lack local charm.
Olas Altas	There are a few hotels on the southern board of Puerto Vallarta, just behind the famous Los Muertos Beach.	Great panoramic ocean views; upscale residential area.	Not near other hotels; the beaches in this area don't have amenities.
Marina Vallarta	Luxury high-rise hotels near the marina, facing the beach. Good for walking, casual biking, and jogging, but no city scene.	Close to a yacht harbor with boats, restaurant-bars, and shops. Near airport and golf courses.	Pricey hotels only; cab ride to most everywhere except marina; lacks local character; narrow to non-existent beach in front of many hotels.
Nuevo Vallarta	Away from more touristy Vallarta, but near enough for excursions are all-inclusive-focused Nuevo Vallarta, easy-going Bucerías, rustic La Cruz, and luxurious Punta Mita.	Less hustle and hype than Puerto Vallarta; small-town vibe (Nuevo Vallarta excepted); good for walking; safe and friendly; excellent beaches.	Expensive cab and long bus rides from Vallarta; fewer nightlife, restaurant, and shopping options; each town has a narrow range of accommodations.
Riviera Nayarit	Beachy, pleasant, youth- and family-oriented, these Riviera Nayarit towns attract self-sufficient travelers looking for R&R by the sea.	Pretty beaches; expanding tourist infrastructure; moderately priced lodgings and restaurants; easy-going appeal for laid-back singles, couples, and families.	Long way from airport; fairly long walk to main highway; carless travelers must rely on taxis (expensive when used routinely) or less-than-pristine local buses.

5

WHERE SHOULD I STAY?

	NEIGHBORHOOD VIBE	PROS	CONS
South of Puerto Vallarta	Smaller resorts and condos nestled in hills of towering tropical vegetation; most overlook the sea and are some distance apart. Friendly gay scene.	Beautiful views; close proximity to Zona Romántica, Mismaloya, and attractions to the south. Uncrowded villages; perfect for a tranquil escape.	Isolated from immediate action; proximity to nearest bars and restaurants varies depending on hotel location. Carless guests have long walks ahead of them.
Costalegre	Mix of deluxe hideaways for the rich and famous with small beach towns sporting basic lodgings, vacation rentals, and miles of glorious beaches.	Uncrowded, long, flat, sandy, palm-fringed beaches, fewer beach vendors, unadorned Mexico (except for the luxury spots); plenty of local color.	Fewer amenities; low-key to nonexistent nightlife. The area is challenging to explore without a car as it's far from transportation hubs.

PUERTO VALLARTA

ZONA ROMÁNTICA

The Romantic Zone, aka Colonia Emiliano Zapata, is PV's party central. Gay and straight bars are interspersed with diminutive boutiques and restaurants. Los Muertos and Amapas beaches face the fray, a convenient place to party, eat, and drink. Moderately priced hotels overlook the sand, with budget options a few blocks away. New parking structures provide parking, as most hotels here do not. Taxis and buses make exploring surrounding areas a snap.

$$$ **Casa Cúpula.** This popular, up-to-date boutique hotel is located a
HOTEL 10-minute walk from the beach and the Zona Romántica, catering largely to a gay and lesbian clientele. **Pros:** airport transfers via Cadillac Escalade; concierge service; free Wi-Fi; oh-so-comfy beds and pillows. **Cons:** challenging location up a hill, though not a far walk to attractions. ⑤ *Rooms from: 2950 MP* ⊠ *Callejón de la Igualdad 129, Zona Romántica* ☎ *322/223–2484, 866/352–2511* ⊕ *www.casacupula.com* ⟲ *14 rooms, 6 suites* ◎| *Breakfast* ✛ *4:C5.*

$$ **Hacienda Alemana Frankfurt.** Rooms here have king-size beds, 32-inch
·•RENTAL TVs, and double-pane windows to keep out noise. **Pros:** excellent on-
Fodor's Choice site German restaurant; free access to gym, sauna, and steam room (off-
★ site); DVDs and iPod stations upon request; great for couples. **Cons:** no real reception staff, so no one around when restaurant closed; possible noise from *biergarten.* ⑤ *Rooms from: $145* ⊠ *Calle Basilio Badillo 378, Centro* ☎ *322/222–2071* ⊕ *www.haciendaalemana.com* ⟲ *8 rooms, 2 suites* ◎| *Breakfast* ✛ *1:C3.*

$ **Hotel Eloísa.** A block from the beach and overlooking Lázaro Cárde-
HOTEL nas Park, this hotel has more of a downtown feel rather than a beachy one. **Pros:** snug studios overlook park; large pool on roof. **Cons:** no parking; mainly older a/c units. ⑤ *Rooms from: 1200 MP* ⊠ *Lázaro*

BEST BETS FOR PUERTO VALLARTA LODGING

Fodor's offers a selective listing of lodging experiences at every price range. Here, we've compiled our top recommendations by price and experience. The very best properties are designated in the listings with the Fodor's Choice logo.

Fodor's Choice ★

Casa Obelisco, p. 129

Garza Blanca Preserve Resort and Spa, p. 130

Hacienda Alemana Frankfurt, p. 112

Hotel Cinco, p. 126

Hotel St. Regis Punta Mita, p. 127

Playa Los Arcos Beach Resort & Spa, p. 115

Quinta Maria Cortez, p. 121

By Price

$

Casa Dulce Vida, p. 117

Hotel Eloísa, p. 112

Hotel Posada de Roger, p. 115

Hotel Sarabi, p. 134

Los Cuatro Vientos, p. 118

Marco's Place Suites & Villas, p. 125

Playa Los Arcos Beach Resort & Spa, p. 115

$$

Hacienda Alemana Frankfurt, p. 112

$$$

Buenaventura Grand Hotel & Spa, p. 121

Casa Cúpula, p. 112

Casa Obelisco, p. 129

Villa Amor, p. 129

$$$$

CasaMagna Marriott Puerto Vallarta Resort & Spa, p. 119

Four Seasons Resort Punta Mita, p. 126

Garza Blanca Preserve Resort and Spa, p. 130

Hotel Cinco, p. 126

Hotel St. Regis Punta Mita, p. 127

Punta Serena Villas & Spa, p. 134

Quinta Maria Cortez, p. 121

By Experience

BEST BEACH

Hotel Cinco, p. 126

Playa los Arcos Beach Resort & Spa, p. 115

Quinta Maria Cortez, p. 121

BEST SPA

CasaMagna Marriott Puerto Vallarta Resort & Spa, p. 119

Four Seasons Resort Punta Mita, p. 126

Paradise Village Beach Resort & Spa, p. 123

GREEN FOCUS

Four Seasons Resort Punta Mita, p. 126

Haramara Retreat, p. 129

Hotelito Desconocido Sanctuary Reserve & Spa, p. 131

House of Wind and Water, p. 119

MOST KID-FRIENDLY

Four Seasons Resort Punta Mita, p. 126

Meliá Puerto Vallarta All Inclusive Beach Resort, p. 121

Paradise Village Beach Resort & Spa, p. 123

BEST FOR SUNSETS

Hacienda San Angel, p. 117

Hotel Cinco, p. 126

Hotel St. Regis Punta Mita, p. 127

Punta Serena Villas & Spa, p. 134

5

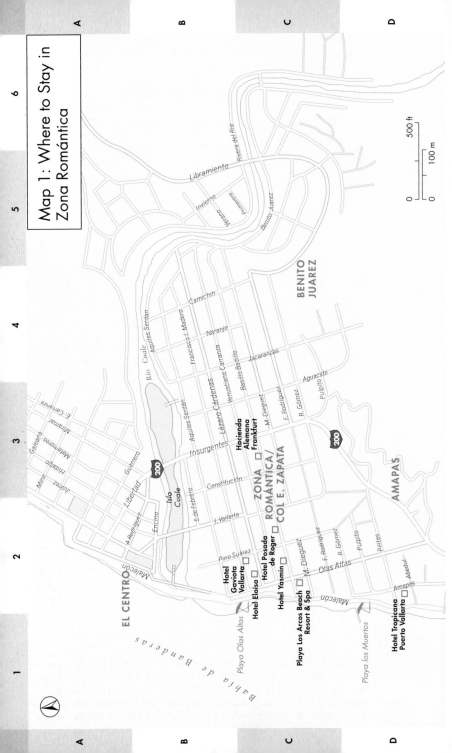

Map 1: Where to Stay in Zona Romántica

EL CENTRO

ZONA ROMÁNTICA/
COL E. ZAPATA

BENITO JUAREZ

AMAPAS

Hotel
Gaviota
Vallarta

Hotel Eloísa

Hotel Posada
de Roger

Hotel Yasmín

Hacienda
Alemana
Frankfurt

Playa Los Arcos Beach
Resort & Spa

Hotel Tropicana
Puerto Vallarta

Bahía de Banderas

Playa Olas Altas

Playa los Muertos

Río Cuale

Isla
Cuale

500 ft
100 m
0
0

Mina
Juárez
Hidalgo
Galeana
Matamoros
Miramar
E. Carranza

A. Rodríguez
Encino
Guerrero
Libertad
Aquiles Serdán
Insurgentes
Constitución
5 de Febrero
I. Vallarta
Pino Suárez
Olas Altas

Lázaro Cárdenas
Francisco I. Madero
Venustiano Carranza
Basilio Badillo
M. Dieguez
F. Rodríguez
R. Gómez

Camichín
Naranjo
Jacarandas
Aguacate
Pulpito

M. Dieguez
F. Rodríguez
R. Gómez
Pulpito
Pilitas

Malecón

Amapas
Abedul

Libramiento
Invierno
Primavera
Verano
Benito Juárez
Rivera del Río

Cárdenas 179, Centro ☎ *322/222–6465, 322/222–0286* ⊕ *www. hoteleloisa.com* ⤳ *63 rooms, 6 studios, 8 suites* ⫶◯⫶ *No meals* ✛ *1:C2.*

$ ⬚ **Hotel Gaviota Vallarta.** Simple rooms in this six-story low-rise have
HOTEL somewhat battered colonial-style furnishings; some have tiny balconies but only a few on the top floors have a partial ocean view. **Pros:** moderately priced rooms a block from the beach; choice of a/c or not; 5% cash discount; salsa club next door. **Cons:** poor pool placement; unattractive furnishings; no Internet; very small parking lot not open during high season. ⑤ *Rooms from: 850 MP* ⊠ *Francisco I. Madero 176, Centro* ☎ *322/222–1500, 322/222–5518* ⊕ *www.hotelgaviota. com* ⤳ *59 rooms, 25 suites* ⫶◯⫶ *No meals* ✛ *1:C2.*

$ ⬚ **Hotel Posada de Roger.** If you hang around the pool or the small shared
HOTEL balcony overlooking the street and the bay beyond, it's not hard to get to know the other guests—many of them savvy budget travelers from Europe and Canada. **Pros:** great location; tinkling fountain and quiet courtyard; good bar-restaurant; free Wi-Fi. **Cons:** no in-room safes; cramped rooms; get-what-you-pay-for beds. ⑤ *Rooms from: $70* ⊠ *Calle Basilio Badillo 237, Zona Romántica* ☎ *322/222–0836, 322/222–0639* ⊕ *www.hotelposadaderoger.com* ⤳ *47 rooms* ⫶◯⫶ *No meals* ✛ *1:C2.*

$ ⬚ **Hotel Tropicana Puerto Vallarta.** This is a reasonably priced, well-land-
HOTEL scaped, bright white hotel at the south end of Playa Los Muertos. **Pros:** good beach access; great Zona Romántica location; nice pool and landscaping. **Cons:** no bathtubs; no Internet access; wristbands required for all guests; furnishings and paint need upgrading. ⑤ *Rooms from: $73* ⊠ *Calle Amapas 214, Zona Romántica* ☎ *322/222–0912* ⊕ *www. tropicanavallarta.com* ⤳ *137 rooms, 29 suites* ⫶◯⫶ *No meals* ✛ *1:D2.*

$ ⬚ **Hotel Yasmín.** Two-story and L-shaped, this budget baby has no pool,
HOTEL but it's just a block from the beach and joined at the hip to Café de Olla, a popular Mexican restaurant. **Pros:** very inexpensive; close to Zona Romántica action; pleasant courtyard garden with café, tables, and chaise longues. **Cons:** dark rooms; low ceilings; no pool. ⑤ *Rooms from: $57* ⊠ *Amapas No. 214, Zona Romántica* ☎ *322/222–0087* ⤳ *27 rooms* ▭ *No credit cards* ⫶◯⫶ *No meals* ✛ *1:C2.*

$ ⬚ **Playa Los Arcos Beach Resort & Spa.** This hotel is recommended for its
RESORT location: right on the beach and in the midst of Zona Romántica's res-
FAMILY taurants, bars, and shops. **Pros:** great Zona Romántica location; nightly
Fodor's Choice entertainment with theme-cuisine buffet. **Cons:** small bathrooms; some
★ rooms have tired furnishings; tour-group noise in high season. ⑤ *Rooms from: $116* ⊠ *Av. Olas Altas 380, Zona Romántica* ☎ *322/222–0583, 800/648–2403 in U.S., 888/729–9590 in Canada, 01800/327–7700 toll-free in Mexico* ⊕ *www.playalosarcos.com* ⤳ *158 rooms, 13 suites* ⫶◯⫶ *Multiple meal plans* ✛ *1:C2.*

EL CENTRO

At the north end of downtown, moderately priced and four- to five-star hotels stretch north from the boardwalk along a manicured (and seasonally rocky) beach. A sunset stroll on the malecón is easily accessible from these hotels, as are bustling downtown's activities, galleries, shops, and restaurants. North of the Cuale River, El Centro has fewer hotels

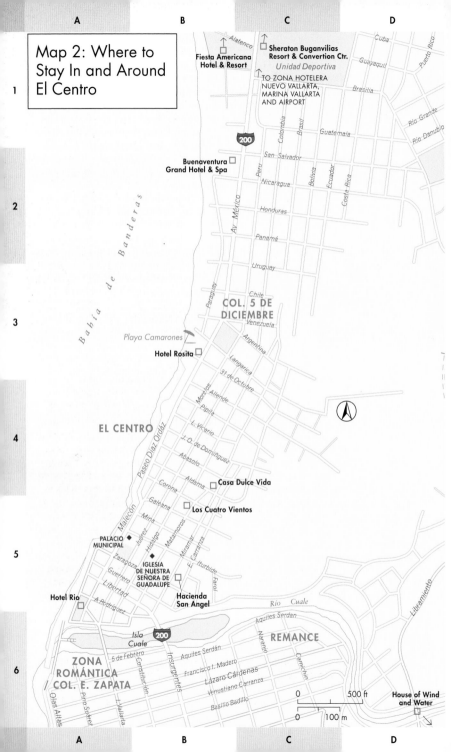

Map 2: Where to Stay In and Around El Centro

Alatenco

Fiesta Americana Hotel & Resort

Sheraton Buganvilias Resort & Convertion Ctr.

Unidad Deportiva

TO ZONA HOTELERA NUEVO VALLARTA, MARINA VALLARTA AND AIRPORT

Cuba

Guayaquil

Puerto Rico

Brasilia

Rio Grande

Rio Danubio

200

Columbia

Brasil

Guatemala

San Salvador

Peru

Nicaragua

Bolivia

Ecuador

Costa Rica

Buenaventura Grand Hotel & Spa

Av. México

Honduras

Panamá

Uruguay

Paraguay

Chile

COL. 5 DE DICIEMBRE

Venezuela

Bahía de Banderas

Playa Camarones

Hotel Rosita

Argentina

Langarica

31 de Octubre

Jo. Allende

Pipila

L. Vicario

J. O. de Dominguez

Abasolo

Aldama

Casa Dulce Vida

Corona

Galeana

Los Cuatro Vientos

Paseo Díaz Ordaz

EL CENTRO

Malecón

Mina

Juárez

Hidalgo

Matamoros

Miramar

E. Carranza

PALACIO MUNICIPAL

Zaragoza

Guerrero

IGLESIA DE NUESTRA SEÑORA DE GUADALUPE

E. Iturbide

Farol

Libertad

Hotel Rio

A. Rodríguez

Hacienda San Angel

Rio Cuale

Aquiles Serdan

Isla Cuale

200

ZONA ROMÁNTICA / COL. E. ZAPATA

5 de Febrero

Constitución

Insurgentes

Aquiles Serdán

Naranjo

REMANCE

Camichin

Libramiento

Francisco I. Madero

Lázaro Cárdenas

Venustiano Carranza

Basilio Badillo

Olas Altas

Pino Suárez

I. Vallarta

0   500 ft

0   100 m

House of Wind and Water

At Hacienda Alemana, guests can choose to dine alfresco.

than the Zona Romántica, which is just across the bridge and within easy walking distance. The area does have the city center's only luxury hotel, Hacienda San Angel, which is situated just far enough away from Zona Romántica for the walk to be notable (but still not prohibitive).

$ **RENTAL** ⛩ **Casa Dulce Vida.** Hidden four blocks off the busy malecón, this '60s-era villa has apartments of various sizes filled with modern Mexican art and comfortable, if well-worn, furniture. **Pros:** home-away-from-home feel; great value; lush landscaping and ocean breezes; friendly staff helps book tours; solid Wi-Fi in all rooms. **Cons:** booked for weeks and months at a time in high season; some rooms better than others. $ *Rooms from: $80* ⊠ *Calle Aldama 295, El Centro* ☎ *322/222–1008* ⊕ *www.dulcevida.com* ⤳ *6 suites* ⊟ *No credit cards* ⚏ *No meals* ✛ *2:B4.*

$$$$ **HOTEL** ⛩ **Hacienda San Angel.** Each room is unique and elegant at this pricey boutique hotel in the hills five blocks above the malecón. **Pros:** the most elegant lodging in downtown Puerto Vallarta; concierge service; excellent bay views; reasonably priced airport transfers. **Cons:** short but steep walk from the malecón; 5% service fee (in addition to taxes) plus 10% fee for using a credit card; three-night minimum; fewer amenities than hotels of comparable price point. $ *Rooms from: $395* ⊠ *Calle Miramar 336, at Iturbide, Centro* ☎ *322/222–2692, 877/815–6594* ⊕ *www.haciendasanangel.com* ⤳ *21 rooms* ⚏ *Breakfast* ✛ *2:B5.*

$$ **HOTEL** ⛩ **Hotel Rio.** Located in downtown Puerto Vallarta and just a block from the beach, Hotel Rio offers quaint traditional accommodations as well as some modern rooms (income from high season allows for renovations each year). **Pros:** a block from the boardwalk; free Wi-Fi everywhere; on-site restaurants; close to shops, restaurants, and entertainment. **Cons:** some rooms need an upgrade; traffic noise may be a problem for some guests. $ *Rooms from: $125* ⊠ *Morelos 170, Centro* ☎ *322/222–0366* ⊕ *www.hotelrio.com.mx* ⌫ *42 rooms, 5 suites* ⦿| *No meals.* ✣ *2:A5*

$ ⛉ **Hotel Rosita.** What started as a sleepy 12-room hostelry—Puerto
HOTEL   Vallarta's very first—is now a busy 115-room downtown hotel. **Pros:** old-fashioned value near downtown; Sunday brunch buffet under $10. **Cons:** no bathtubs; older floors and furnishings; so-so beach; Wi-Fi in lobby only. $ *Rooms from: $50* ⊠ *Paseo Díaz Ordáz 901, Zona Hotelera* ☎ *322/223–2000* ⊕ *www.hotelrosita.com* ⌫ *115 rooms* ⦿| *No meals* ✣ *2:B3.*

$ ⛉ **Los Cuatro Vientos.** This Old Vallarta original opened in 1955, and
HOTEL   some folks have been coming here forever. **Pros:** downtown location overlooking the bay; deep, grottolike pool; free Wi-Fi. **Cons:** short but steep walk or drive from downtown; no lounge area around pool; no a/c; some rooms up multiple flights of stairs. $ *Rooms from: 987 MP* ⊠ *Calle Matamoros 520, El Centro* ☎ *322/222–0161* ⊕ *www. cuatrovientos.com* ⌫ *11 rooms, 3 suites* ⦿| *Breakfast* ✣ *2:B5.*

$$$$ ⛉ **Sheraton Buganvilias Resort & Convention Center.** Juan Carlos Name
RESORT   (pronounced NAH-may), a disciple of modern-minimalist Mexican architect Luis Barragán, designed this looming high-rise near the Hotel Zone's south end and within walking distance of downtown. **Pros:** excellent Sunday champagne brunch; concierge service; AAA and AARP discounts. **Cons:** slow elevators; so-so beach; faces busy and rather unattractive boulevard. $ *Rooms from: $360* ⊠ *Blvd. Francisco M. Ascencio 999, Zona Hotelera* ☎ *322/226–0404, 800/325–3535* ⊕ *www.sheratonvallarta.com* ⌫ *480 rooms, 120 suites* ⦿| *Multiple meal plans* ✣ *2:C1.*

ZONA HOTELERA

The creation of the Hotel Zone moved the tourist accommodations outside the downtown boundaries, which has kept the historic center relatively untouched. Although most of the hotels are not brand new, they are all beachfront with spectacular ocean views over Banderas Bay, which makes them highly popular among Vallarta visitors. The latest additions to the area are numerous skyscrapers with exclusive oceanfront condominiums that are often available for short-term vacation rentals.

$$ ⛉ **Fiesta Americana Hotel & Resort.** The dramatically designed terra-cotta
HOTEL   building rises above a deep-blue pool that flows beside palm oases; a seven-story palapa (which provides natural air-conditioning) covers the elegant lobby—paved in patterned tile and stone—and a large round bar. **Pros:** across from Plaza Caracol, with its shops, grocery store, and Cinemex; lots of on-site shops; 24-hour room service. **Cons:** no ocean view from the second and third floors; hotel is a cab or bus ride from most restaurants. $ *Rooms from: $165* ⊠ *Blvd. Francisco M. Ascencio, Km 2.5, Zona Hotelera* ☎ *322/226–2100, 800/343–7821 in*

U.S. ⊕ *www.fiestaamericana.com* ↩ *288 rooms, 3 suites* ✴ *Multiple meal plans* ⊕ *2:C1.*

MARINA VALLARTA

Although its newness relative to the rest of Puerto Vallarta makes it feel a little homogenous, this small enclave of luxury hotels gives off a quiet, subdued vibe that more than makes up for it. This is the closest of the PV subdivisions to the airport. The Marriott, Westin, and other brand names face a narrow beach that pales in comparison to the properties' sparkling swimming pools and high-end spas. Offering all-inclusive as well as EP accommodations, these high-rise hotels are near a beautiful if low-key private marina (faced with shops, bars, and eateries) and the Marina Vallarta Golf Course.

$$$$
RESORT

🏨 **Casa Velas Hotel Boutique & Ocean Club.** Silky sheets and cozy down duvets, multiple ceiling fans, and large flat-screen TVs are a few of the creature comforts that set Velas apart from the rest. **Pros:** large suites; yoga, Spanish classes and other activities; pillow menu; special deals allowing kids to stay free are sometimes available. **Cons:** small spa; not beachfront; zealous time-share salespeople; high price point. ⑤ *Rooms from: $523* ⊠ *Av. Costera s/n LH2, Marina Vallarta* ☎ *322/226–9500, 866/847–4609* ⊕ *www.velasvallarta.com* ↩ *339 suites* ✴ *All-inclusive* ⊕ *3:A3.*

$$$$
RESORT
FAMILY

🏨 **CasaMagna Marriott Puerto Vallarta Resort & Spa.** The CasaMagna is hushed and stately in some places, lively and casual in others. **Pros:** lovely spa; great concierge service; good Japanese restaurant; excellent buffet breakfast. **Cons:** unimpressive beach; no business center or Internet terminals for guests. ⑤ *Rooms from: $254* ⊠ *Paseo de la Marina 455, Marina Vallarta* ☎ *322/226–0000, 888/236–2427 in U.S. and Canada* ⊕ *www.casamagnapuertovallarta.com* ↩ *404 rooms, 29 suites* ✴ *No meals* ⊕ *3:B4.*

$$$
RESORT
ALL-INCLUSIVE
FAMILY

🏨 **Crown Paradise Club Vallarta.** At the nationally owned Crown Paradise Club Vallarta, family rooms here have kid-size bunk beds and trundle beds in their own area with a TV. **Pros:** One the beach, great for families with kids **Cons:** Not the ideal place if you want to chill out and relax ⑤ *Rooms from: 3085 MP* ⊠ *Av. de las Garzas S/N, Zona Hotelera* ☎ *322/22 668 68* ⊕ *www.crownparadise.com* ↩ *252* ✴ *All-inclusive* ⊕ *3:D5.*

$$
B&B/INN

🏨 **House of Wind and Water.** While this cozy B&B has some traditional elements like brick archways, tile floors, and fine woodwork, most of the design elements are the creations or acquisitions of the artist-owners: large format paintings, whimsical bathrooms with hand-painted sinks and exposed copper tubing, and estate-sale furnishings. **Pros:** in a real Mexican neighborhood by the Cuale River; gorgeous views of jungle-clad hillside; eco-conscious owners. **Cons:** at end of a long, rather steep dirt driveway; no air-conditioning; no shopping or nightlife in immediate area. ⑤ *Rooms from: $120* ⊠ *Calle Azucena 1109, Marina Vallarta* ☎ *322/140–4866 cell* ⊕ *www.houseofwindandwater.com* ↩ *5 rooms* ✴ *Breakfast* ⊕ *2:D6.*

5

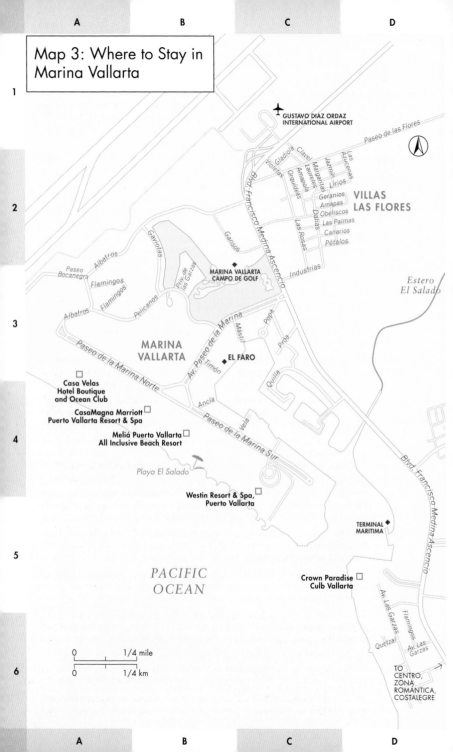

Map 3: Where to Stay in Marina Vallarta

A B C D

1

GUSTAVO DÍAZ ORDAZ
INTERNATIONAL AIRPORT

Paseo de las Flores

VILLAS
LAS FLORES

Gladiola
Clavel
Violetas
Margaritas
Laureles
Amapola
Orquideas
Jazmín
Lirios
Las Azucenas

Geranios
Amapas
Obeliscos
Dalias
Las Palmas
Las Rosas
Canarios
Pétalos

2

Paseo
Bocanegra
Albatros

Flamingos

Albatros
Flamingos
Pelicanos

Gaviotas

Gaviotas

Prol. de
las Garzas

Garsos

MARINA VALLARTA
CAMPO DE GOLF

Industrias

Estero
El Salado

3

Paseo de la Marina Norte

MARINA
VALLARTA

Av. Paseo de la Marina

Mastil

Proa

EL FARO

Poya

Quilla

Blvd. Francisco Medina Ascencio

□ Casa Velas
Hotel Boutique
and Ocean Club

Av. Timón

Ancia

Vela

4

CasaMagna Marriott □
Puerto Vallarta Resort & Spa

Meliá Puerto Vallarta □
All Inclusive Beach Resort

Paseo de la Marina Sur

Playa El Salado

Westin Resort & Spa, □
Puerto Vallarta

TERMINAL ◆
MARITIMA

Blvd. Francisco Medina Ascencio

5

PACIFIC
OCEAN

Crown Paradise □
Culb Vallarta

Av. Las Garzas

Flamingos
Av. Las Garzas

Quetzal

6

0   1/4 mile

0   1/4 km

TO
CENTRO,
ZONA
ROMÁNTICA,
COSTALEGRE

A B C D

$$$$
RESORT
ALL-INCLUSIVE
FAMILY

Meliá Puerto Vallarta All Inclusive Beach Resort. The sprawling, all-inclusive Meliá, on the beach and close to the golf course, is popular with families. **Pros:** lots of activities for small children; giant pool; concierge service; free Wi-Fi; two children under 5 free. **Cons:** small beach diminishes further at high tide; lots of children. $ *Rooms from: 3500 MP* ⊠ *Paseo de la Marina Sur 7, Marina Vallarta* ☎ *322/226–3000, 888/956–3542 in U.S.* ⊕ *www.solmelia.com* ⤳ *217 rooms, 4 suites* ⦾ *All-inclusive* ✛ *3:B4.*

$$$$
RESORT

Westin Resort & Spa, Puerto Vallarta. Hot pink! Electric yellow! Color aside, the Westin's buildings evoke ancient temples and are about as mammoth in size.**Pros:** fabulous beds and pillows; impressive architecture and landscaping; attentive but not overzealous staff; concierge service. **Cons:** small beach; no ocean views from lower floors. $ *Rooms from: $325* ⊠ *Paseo de la Marina Sur 205, Marina Vallarta* ☎ *322/226–1100, 800/228–3000 in U.S. and Canada* ⊕ *www.starwoodhotels.com* ⤳ *266 rooms, 14 suites* ⦾ *Breakfast* ✛ *3:C4.*

OLAS ALTAS

South of the Zona Romántica and above Los Muertos and Amapas beaches is a mix of gay hotels, pretty villas, and other vacation rentals (like individual homes and condo complexes). The continuous beach stretches all the way to Playa Conchas Chinas.

$$$
HOTEL
FAMILY

Buenaventura Grand Hotel & Spa. The location on downtown's northern edge is just a few blocks from the malecón, shops, hotels, and restaurants. **Pros:** great place to socialize; good breakfast buffet; concierge service; five-minute walk to the malecón and downtown. **Cons:** balconies are small, no parking; fee to use next-door gym. $ *Rooms from: 2841 MP* ⊠ *Av. México 1301, Olas Altas* ☎ *322/226–7000, 888/859–9439 in U.S. and Canada* ⊕ *www.hotelbuenaventura.com.mx* ⤳ *216 rooms, 18 suites* ⦾ *Multiple meal plans* ✛ *2:B2.*

$$$$
B&B/INN
Fodor's Choice
★

Quinta Maria Cortez. It takes a seven-levels ramble up a steep hill at Playa Conchas Chinas to reach this B&B, about a 20-minute walk along the sand to the Zona Romántica (or a short hop in a bus or taxi). **Pros:** intimate, personable digs; close to Puerto Vallarta; above lovely Conchas Chinas Beach. **Cons:** small property; frequently booked solid. $ *Rooms from: $300* ⊠ *Calle Sagitario 126, Olas Altas* ☎ *322/221–5317, 888/640–8100 reservations* ⊕ *www.quinta-maria.com* ⤳ *7 suites, 3 villas* ⦾ *Breakfast* ✛ *4:C5.*

NUEVO VALLARTA

The hotels in Nuevo Vallarta are located far enough away from the touristy hustle and bustle of El Centro to allow for a more relaxed and secluded feel, though this means longer bus and cab rides from Puerto Vallarta and less restaurant and nightlife choices.

$$$$
RESORT
ALL-INCLUSIVE
FAMILY

The Grand Mayan Nuevo Vallarta. This hugely impressive hotel is an excellent choice for both families with kids or couples looking for a place to get away from it all; just make sure you chose the appropriate hotel within the complex. **Pros:** good service; lots of facilities; great

STAYING WITH KIDS

Puerto Vallarta is an excellent destination for children. Miles of beaches keep kids busy in the sand and the sea, and activities like horseback riding, canopy tours, boating expeditions, and wildlife spotting keep tots and teens entertained. Area hotels also cater to kids. Most five-star beach resorts have children's pools and supervised programs that give adults the leisure time they crave. A good choice is the kids' club at The Grand Mayan Puerto Vallarta.

As for resorts, "upscale" sometimes translates as couples-oriented, but the Four Seasons Resort Punta Mita is all about families. Kids (and parents) love floating on the lazy river. The children's activity center is the envy of parents who sneak in to play foosball, table air hockey, or their favorite computer games, or attempt to keep up with the steps of the Dance Machine. Younger children dig the tree house and playground; a youthful concierge for teens organizes football games, bonfires on the beach, and dances, among other activities. Kids' club employees meet families at check-in with gift bags, and in-room amenities include bottle-warmers, strollers, and high chairs. There are also T-shirts and fun toiletries for children. These services carry no extra fee; babysitters are available at an hourly rate.

for kids; luxury available. **Cons:** the resort is huge don't forget anything in your room; time-share presentations are difficult to avoid and can be pushy; need transportation to get anywhere outside the hotel. ⑤ *Rooms from: 3429 MP* ⊠ *Av. Paseo de las Moras S/N, Nuevo Vallarta* ☎ *322/226–4000* ⊕ *www.mayanresorts.com* ⤳ *287 rooms, 502 suites* ⦾ *All-inclusive.* ✛ *4:C4.*

$$$$
RESORT
ALL-INCLUSIVE
⬚ **Grand Velas All Suites & Spa Resort.** In scale and majesty, the public areas of this property outshine all other Nuevo Vallarta all-inclusive resorts. **Pros:** exceptionally beautiful rooms and public spaces; lovely spa; extremely long beach great for walking. **Cons:** Nuevo Vallarta location is far from Puerto Vallarta if you're looking for shops and restaurants (but 10 minutes by car from Bucerías); at more than $600 per night, you think they'd kick in free Wi-Fi. ⑤ *Rooms from: $780* ⊠ *Paseo de los Cocoteros 98 Sur, Nuevo Vallarta* ☎ *322/226–8000, 888/261–8436 in U.S. and Canada* ⊕ *www.grandvelas.com* ⤳ *267 1-, 2-, and 3-bedroom suites* ⦾ *All-inclusive* ✛ *4:C4.*

$$
HOTEL
⬚ **Marina Banderas Suites Hotel Boutique.** The very large and well-appointed suites in this boutique hotel overlook the marina in Nuevo Vallarta and, if you're in the rooms facing west, you'll see spectacular sunsets, too. **Pros:** very clean and tasteful rooms; magnificent views; close to restaurants and the largest tour operator in Vallarta; five-minute walk to the beach. **Cons:** downtown Puerto Vallarta is a 20-minute drive away; no shops. ⑤ *Rooms from: $136* ⊠ *Paseo de la Marina y 16 de Septiembre #42, Nuevo Vallarta* ☎ *322/297–6056* ⊕ *www.marinabanderas.com.mx* ⤳ *16 suites* ⦾ *Breakfast* ✛ *4:C4.*

$$$$
RESORT
ALL-INCLUSIVE
⬚ **Marival Resort and Suites.** Come here if you're looking for an all-inclusive bargain that includes a wealth of activities. **Pros:** value-priced; immaculately kept grounds; premium booze brands. **Cons:** most rooms

Quinta Maria Cortez, just off Playa Conchas Chinas, has some of the most coveted palapas in town—not to mention tons of other amenities well worth the splurge.

have no tub or an uncomfortable square tub; musty smell in some rooms; cheap finishing touches like plastic chairs and fake plants. $ *Rooms from: $343* ✉ *Paseo Cocoteros s/n, at Blvd. Nuevo Vallarta, Nuevo Vallarta* ☎ *322/226–8200* ⊕ *www.gomarival.com* ⇗ *373 rooms, 122 suites* ⵑ◯ⵑ *All-inclusive* ✛ *4:C4.*

$$
RESORT
FAMILY

⛶ **Paradise Village Beach Resort & Spa.** This Nuevo Vallarta hotel and time-share property is perfect for families, with lots of activities geared to children. **Pros:** reasonably priced spa; can walk all the way to Bucerías on the beach; fully loaded kitchen in all suites; efficient air-conditioning units; wide range of accommodations. **Cons:** big cats caged in depressing zoo; Internet room for time-share guests only; time-share oriented; guests must bring cable for Internet access. $ *Rooms from: $134* ✉ *Paseo de los Cocoteros 1, Nuevo Vallarta* ☎ *322/226–6770, 866/334–6080* ⊕ *www.paradisevillage.com* ⇗ *702 suites* ⵑ◯ⵑ *Multiple meal plans* ✛ *4:C4.*

RIVIERA NAYARIT

AROUND BANDERAS BAY

Perfect for travelers who like to stay put, the Riviera Nayarit is adding five-star accommodations to previously undeveloped beaches like Litibú and Playa Destiladeras. In Bucerías, traffic-free streets and a gorgeous sandy beach lure older snowbirds. The same crowd tends toward less-built-up La Cruz, with its upscale marina but few hotels. At the

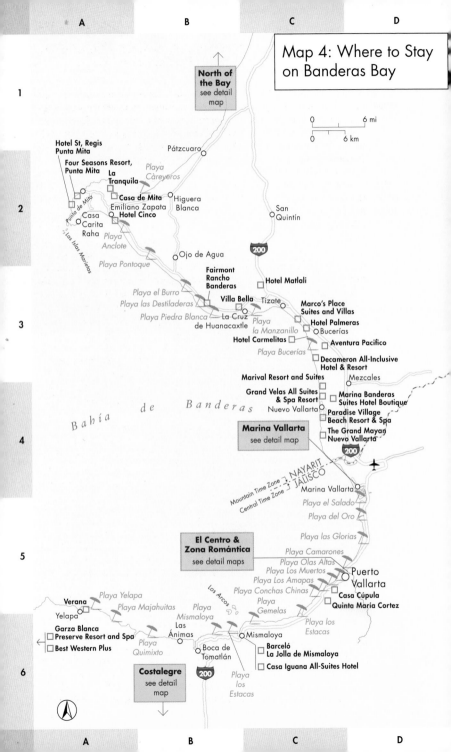

Map 4: Where to Stay on Banderas Bay

North of the Bay see detail map

0 — 6 mi
0 — 6 km

Hotel St, Regis Punta Mita
Four Seasons Resort, Punta Mita
La Tranquila
Casa de Mita
Emiliano Zapata
Hotel Cinco
Casa Carita Raha

Punta de Mita

Los Islas Marietas

Playa Cáreyeros
Pátzcuaro
Higuera Blanca
San Quintín

Playa Anclote
Playa Pontoque
Ojo de Agua

Fairmont Rancho Banderas
Hotel Matlali

Playa el Burro
Playa las Destiladeras
Villa Bella
Tízate
Marco's Place Suites and Villas

Playa Piedra Blanca
La Cruz de Huanacaxtle
Playa la Manzanillo
Bucerías
Hotel Palmeras

Hotel Carmelitas
Aventura Pacifico

Playa Bucerías
Decameron All-Inclusive Hotel & Resort

Marival Resort and Suites
Mezcales

Grand Velas All Suites & Spa Resort
Marina Banderas Suites Hotel Boutique
Nuevo Vallarta
Paradise Village Beach Resort & Spa

Bahía   de   Banderas

Marina Vallarta see detail map

The Grand Mayan Nuevo Vallarta

Mountain Time Zone NAYARIT
Central Time Zone JALISCO

Marina Vallarta
Playa el Salado
Playa del Oro

El Centro & Zona Romántica see detail maps

Playa las Glorias

Playa Camarones
Playa Olas Altas
Playa Los Muertos
Playa Los Amapas
Playa Conchas Chinas
Playa Gemelas

Puerto Vallarta

Casa Cúpula
Quinta María Cortez

Verana
Playa Yelapa
Playa Majahuitas
Yelapa
Playa Mismaloya
Las Ánimas

Los Arcos

Garza Blanca Preserve Resort and Spa
Best Western Plus
Playa Quimixto
Boca de Tomatlán
Mismaloya

Playa los Estacas

Barceló La Jolla de Mismaloya
Casa Iguana All-Suites Hotel

Costalegre see detail map

Playa los Estacas

northern end of Banderas Bay, exclusive Punta Mita has über-expensive villas and hotels as well as a few modest digs for avid surfers.

BUCERÍAS

$ · **Aventura Pacifico.** The condos at this boutique-style accommodation
RENTAL are a favorite among travellers and vacationers who return year after year. **Pros:** clean facilities; three-minute walk to the beach; close to restaurants; free Wi-Fi and VoiP. **Cons:** road leading to hotel isn't well paved. $ *Rooms from: $118* ⊠ *Calle Francisco I Madero 132, Riviera Nayarit* ☎ *329/298–2797* ⊕ *www.aventurapacifico.com* ⤳ *7 suites* ⍒ *No meals* ✢ *4:C3.*

$$$ · **Decameron All-Inclusive Hotel & Resort.** This high-volume hotel is at
RESORT the south end of long and lovely Bucerías Beach and has manicured
ALL-INCLUSIVE grounds and a pool for each of its six buildings. **Pros:** excellent deal for all-inclusive (room-only and air packages, too); long beach great for walking or jogging; Spanish classes, yoga classes, and dance lessons plus many other activities. **Cons:** only a few Internet stations for hundreds of guests; only one of six buildings has an elevator; loud entertainment music at night during high season. $ *Rooms from: $188* ⊠ *Calle Lázaro Cárdenas 150, Riviera Nayarit* ☎ *329/298–0226, 01800/011– 1111* ⊕ *www.decameron.com* ⤳ *620 rooms* ⍒ *All-inclusive* ✢ *4:C3.*

$ · **Hotel Carmelitas.** In the heart of Bucerías, this small budget hotel is
HOTEL as unassuming as can be, and well maintained. **Pros:** low price; close to beach; quiet residential neighborhood. **Cons:** no views; no amenities. $ *Rooms from: $26* ⊠ *Francisco I. Madero 19, Riviera Nayarit* ☎ *329/298–0024* ⤳ *12 rooms* ▬ *No credit cards* ⍒ *No meals* ✢ *4:C3.*

$ · **Hotel Palmeras.** A block from the beach, in an area with lots of good
HOTEL restaurants, "The Palms" has two floors of rooms surrounding a large, clean, rectangular pool. **Pros:** free Wi-Fi; inexpensive older rooms for bargain hunters; newer rooms have patios and ocean view; rooftop deck with views of red tile roofs, beach, and lacy palm trees; deals on weekly and monthly rentals. **Cons:** some rooms have odd layout; no parking. $ *Rooms from: $70* ⊠ *Lázaro Cárdenas 35, Riviera Nayarit* ☎ *329/298–1288, 647/722–4139 in U.S.* ⊕ *www.hotelpalmeras.com* ⤳ *21 rooms* ⍒ *No meals* ✢ *4:C3.*

$ · **Marco's Place Suites & Villas.** Despite its name, this property is a
HOTEL three-story motel. **Pros:** several different outdoor spaces for reading or relaxing; even least expensive room has kitchenette. **Cons:** uninspired decor; street parking only; cash only. $ *Rooms from: $48* ⊠ *Calle Juventino Espinoza 6–A, Riviera Nayarit* ☎ *329/298–0865* ⊕ *www. marcosplacevillas.com* ⤳ *15 rooms, 3 suites* ▬ *No credit cards* ⍒ *No meals* ✢ *4:C3.*

LA CRUZ DE HUANACAXTLE

$$$$ · **Hotel Matlali.** Perched on a hill overlooking La Cruz, this is a brand
RESORT new hotel and spa with 42 villas housing just as many suites, all tastefully decorated in Balinese style. **Pros:** brand new, elegant construction; good service; relaxed environment. **Cons:** limited Internet and phone reception; transportation needed to get anywhere. $ *Rooms from: $310* ⊠ *Carretera Punta Mita, Km 0.2, La Cruz de Huanacaxtle* ☎ *322/115– 7703* ⊕ *www.matlali.com* ⤳ *42 suites* ⍒ *Multiple meal plans* ✢ *4:C3.*

$ ⛱ **Villa Bella.** Tropical plants give character to this intimate property
HOTEL   where the owner gives her personal attention to guests. **Pros:** free airport pickup before 6 pm with at least three-night stay; lap pool; free
cocktail (or two) Monday through Saturday afternoons; large breakfast
with Mexican specialties. **Cons:** up a steep road (best for those with
a car); little nightlife in area; rooms have lots of knickknacks; three-
night minimum stay in high season. ⑤ *Rooms from: 1390 MP* ✉ *Calle
del Monte Calvario 12, La Cruz de Huanacaxtle* ☎ *329/295–5161,
329/295–5154, 877/273–6244 toll-free in U.S., 877/513–1662 toll-free
in Canada* ⊕ *www.villabella-lacruz.com* ⮡ *2 rooms, 4 suites* ❑ *Breakfast* ✛ *4:B3.*

PUNTA MITA

$$$$ ⛱ **Casa de Mita.** Architect-owner Marc Lindskog has created a nook
HOTEL   of nonchalant elegance, with updated country furnishings of wicker,
ALL-INCLUSIVE   leather, and wood; rock-floor showers without curtains or doors; and
cheerful Pacific Coast architectural details. **Pros:** delicious food; nearly
private beach; concierge service; free international phone calls. **Cons:**
little nightlife in vicinity; three-night minimum stay; strict cancellation policy. ⑤ *Rooms from: $700* ✉ *Playa Careyeros, Punta Mita*
☎ *329/298–4114, 866/740–7999* ⊕ *www.casademita.com* ⮡ *6 rooms,
2 suites* ❑ *All-inclusive* ✛ *4:A2.*

$$$$ ⛱ **Fairmont Rancho Banderas.** Located on a cliff above Destiladera Beach,
RESORT   Fairmont Rancho Banderas's rooms have ocean or garden views, and
the attractive pool spills down several levels to end above the sand,
where palm-thatch "umbrellas" shade chaise longues. **Pros:** well-
equipped kitchens; rooms have stereo, iPod dock, DVD player, and
plasma TV. **Cons:** 10 am checkout; one restaurant only; car, bus, or
taxi ride required from any restaurants and nightlife. ⑤ *Rooms from:
$718* ✉ *Carretera a Punta de Mita, Km 8.3, Punta Mita* ☎ *329/291–
7000* ⊕ *www.ranchobanderas.com* ⮡ *48 1-, 2-, and 3-bedroom suites,
1 penthouse villa* ❑ *No meals* ✛ *4:B3.*

$$$$ ⛱ **Four Seasons Resort, Punta Mita.** The hotel and its fabulous spa perch
RESORT   above a lovely beach at the northern extreme of Bahía de Banderas,
FAMILY   about 45 minutes from the Puerto Vallarta airport and an hour north
of downtown Puerto Vallarta. **Pros:** beautiful beach; concierge service;
yoga on the point; excellent spa; private yacht for charter. **Cons:** staff
trained to be overly solicitous (you'll be saying "hola" a lot); very
expensive spa treatments; not all rooms have ocean view. ⑤ *Rooms
from: $820* ✉ *Bahía de Banderas, Punta Mita* ☎ *329/291–6019,
800/819–5053 in U.S. and Canada* ⊕ *www.fshr.com/puntamita* ⮡ *141
rooms, 27 suites* ❑ *Multiple meal plans* ✛ *4:A2.*

$$$$ ⛱ **Hotel Cinco.** Located at the north end of Punta de Mita, this three-
RENTAL   story condo-hotel offers charming two- and three-bedroom apartments.
Fodor's Choice   **Pros:** lots of amenities for a small condo-hotel; 20 minutes from fun,
★   funky Sayulita; multiple air-conditioning units; great beach to paddle
surf. **Cons:** owner-decorated apartments leave design open to their
whims, though most have good taste. ⑤ *Rooms from: $340* ✉ *Av. El
Anclote 5, Punta Mita* ☎ *329/291–5005* ⊕ *cincopuntamita.com* ⮡ *12
2- and 3-bedroom suites* ❑ *Breakfast* ✛ *4:A2.*

Hotel Cinco

$$$$
HOTEL
Fodor's Choice
★

🏨 **Hotel St. Regis Punta Mita.** The first St. Regis in Mexico (there's now a lovely sister property in Mexico City), this Starwood group member boasts a nouveau Mexican architectural style combining geometric simplicity with the warmth of giant palapa roofs and other natural elements. **Pros:** 80% of rooms have at least partial beach views; personal butlers perform services for all guests; faces Las Marietas Islands; impressive guest-to-employee ratio. **Cons:** rocky beach means no kayaking, swimming, or other water sports; three-night minimum stay (seven nights in high season). ⓢ *Rooms from: $820* ⊠ *Carretara 200, Km. 19.5, Lote H4, Punta Mita* ☎ *329/291–5830* ⊕ *www.stregis.com/puntamita* 🛏 *99 rooms, 20 suites* ⑩ *No meals* ✦ *4:A2.*

NORTH OF BANDERAS BAY

Although distinctive in flavor, both San Francisco (aka San Pancho) and Sayulita attract youthful, laid-back travelers and offer mid-range and modest hotels, plus vacation rentals. San Francisco offers a real community feel, with wide gridlike streets, family homes with character, and a plain but pretty beach. Surfers head for smaller, hipper Sayulita, with a pretty bay and a variety of nearby beaches. On beautiful Jaltemba Bay, Rincón de Guayabitos caters to middle-class Mexican families (and snowbirds in the winter), with moderately priced hotels and small restaurants offering mainly Mexican dishes and seafood. Each town lies on the beach about a mile off the coast highway.

Map 5: Where to Stay North of the Bay

PACIFIC OCEAN

Platanitos

Ixtapan de le Concepción

Zacualpan

Chacala   Las Varas

200

Divisadero

Bahía de Jaltemba

La Peñita de Jaltemba   □ **Villas Buena Vida**
Los Ayala
Rincón de Guayabitos

200

Haramara Retreat □   Menteón
Costa Azul □
Casa Obelisco □   Lo de Marco

San Francisco

Mountain Time Zone
Central Time Zone

Villa Amor □

Sayulita

Patzcuarito

Las Palmas

Higuera Blanca   San Quintín   San Juan Abajo

Valle de Banderas

70

Punta de Mita
Punta de Mita   Tizate
Mezcales
El Ranchito

Emiliano Zapata   La Cruz de Huanacaxtle   Bucerías
San Vicente

Islas las Tres Marietas

Nuevo Vallarta   Ixtapa
Los Juntas

Bahía de Banderas

Marina Vallarta

0   9 mi
0   9 km

Puerto Vallarta

Los Arcos
Mismaloya

Boca de Tomatlán

Yelapa

Chimo

$$$ **Casa Obelisco.** The vibe is warm and romantic, the cozy-chic rooms—
B&B/INN   endowed with original paintings, folk art, and super-comfortable king
Fodor'sChoice   beds with pillow-top mattresses and mosquito nets—are perfect for
★   spooning and honeymooning. **Pros:** attentive hosts; bountiful, varied
breakfasts; newer construction. **Cons:** down long, bumpy cobblestone
road from town; street parking only. $ *Rooms from: $210* ⌧ *Calle Palmas 115, Fracc. Costa Azul, San Francisco* ☎ *311/258–4315* ⊕ *www.casaobelisco.com* ⇗ *4 rooms* ▭ *No credit cards* ⊙ *Closed July–Sept.*
⏀ *Breakfast* ⊹ *5:B3.*

$ **Costa Azul.** What makes this place attractive are the many activities
HOTEL   offered: horseback riding, kayaking, hiking, surfing (with lessons), and
FAMILY   excursions to the Marietas Islands or La Tobara mangroves near San
Blas. **Pros:** great place to bond with kids of all ages; lots of planned
outdoor activities and tours. **Cons:** mediocre food; some guests have
complained of disorganized and unhelpful staff members; stringent cancellation policy. $ *Rooms from: $120* ⌧ *Calle Amapas at Calle Las Palmas, Fracc. Costa Azul, San Francisco* ☎ *311/258–4000, 800/365–7613
toll-free in U.S.* ⊕ *www.costaazul.com* ⇗ *18 rooms, 5 suites, 3 villas*
⏀ *Multiple meal plans* ⊹ *5:B3.*

$$$$ **Haramara Retreat.** With stunning views and acres of trees, as well as
HOTEL   blissful breezes off the Pacific Ocean, Haramara Retreat is an oasis of
tranquility just south of Sayulita. **Pros:** wonderful views; tranquil setting on a huge, tree-studded property; gifted body workers and yoga
teachers. **Cons:** no Wi-Fi access; cab ride from Sayulita; limited cell
phone coverage. $ *Rooms from: $348* ⌧ *Sayulita* ⊹ *Off paved road
from Sayulita to Punta de Mita, about 2½ km (1½ miles) off Carretera
200* ☎ *329/291–3558* ⊕ *www.haramararetreat.com* ⇗ *15 bungalows,
1 dorm-style room* ⏀ *All meals* ⊹ *5:B3.*

$$$ **Villa Amor.** What began as a hilltop home has slowly become an amal-
HOTEL   gam of unusual, rustic, but luxurious suites with indoor and outdoor
living spaces. **Pros:** nice location across bay from Sayulita's main beach;
staff arranges tours, transportation, and tee times; charming and unique
lodgings at reasonable prices. **Cons:** tons of stairs; no phones or Wi-Fi
in guest rooms; open-to-the-elements rooms can have creepy crawlies.
$ *Rooms from: $250* ⌧ *Sayulita* ☎ *329/291–3010* ⊕ *www.villaamor.
com* ⇗ *33 villas* ⏀ *No meals* ⊹ *5:B4.*

$ **Villas Buena Vida.** On beautiful Rincón de Guayabitos Beach, this
HOTEL   property has three-story units, breeze-ruffled palms, and manicured
walkways. **Pros:** beautiful bay-side location; 5% cash discount. **Cons:**
uninspired furnishings; unreliable Internet access in rooms via Wi-Fi.
$ *Rooms from: 950 MP* ⌧ *Retorno Laureles 2, Rincón de Guayabitos*
☎ *327/274–0231* ⊕ *www.villasbuenavida.com* ⇗ *36 rooms, 9 suites*
⏀ *No meals* ⊹ *5:C3.*

SOUTH OF PUERTO VALLARTA

As the coast stretches south, more isolated beaches like Mismaloya
are home to small individual hotels as well as five-star beauties like
Dreams and the InterContinental. Although removed from the action

(and traffic) of PV's other hotel areas, these accommodations offer relatively easy access to Zona Romántica and El Centro via taxis and public buses.

$$$
RESORT
ALL-INCLUSIVE
FAMILY

☷ **Barceló Puerto Vallarta.** Guests consistently give this hotel high marks for the classy suites, each with a brown-and-taupe color scheme and an ample terrace with a table and four chairs. **Pros:** recently redecorated and remodeled; concierge service; lots of on-site dining and activity options. **Cons:** beach is small; least expensive rooms don't have ocean views; no bathtubs. ⑤ *Rooms from: $243* ⊠ *Carretera a Barra de Navidad, Km 11.5, Zona Hotelera Sur, Mismaloya* ☎ *322/226–0660, 800/227–2356* ⊕ *www.barcelo.com* ⇘ *317 suites* ❍❘ *All-inclusive* ✛ *4:C6.*

$$
RESORT

☷ **Best Western Plus.** This property has an enviable location above a beautiful aqua-toned cove. **Pros:** lovely bay great for swimming; 24-hour concierge and business center; resort package same price as what most upscale hotels charge for Wi-Fi alone, but with more privileges. **Cons:** small gym and spa. ⑤ *Rooms from: $124* ⊠ *Carretera a Barra de Navidad (Carratera 200), Km 8.6, Mismaloya* ☎ *322/228–0191, 888/424–6835* ⊕ *www.bestwestern.com* ⇘ *97 rooms, 23 suites* ❍❘ *Multiple meal plans* ✛ *4:A6.*

$
HOTEL

☷ **Casa Iguana All-Suites Hotel.** Palms and plants edge the walkways that line the swimming pool and goldfish ponds; balconies look down on this idyllic garden scene. **Pros:** experience village life not far from Puerto Vallarta's bars and restaurants; on-site grocery; FAP meals at gourmet restaurant. **Cons:** tiny gym; a cab or bus ride from nightlife, restaurants, and shops; not on beach. ⑤ *Rooms from: $55* ⊠ *Av. 5 de Mayo 455, Mismaloya* ☎ *322/228–0186* ⊕ *casaiguana.com.mx* ⇘ *49 2-bedroom suites, 3 3-bedroom suites* ❍❘ *Multiple meal plans* ✛ *4:C6.*

$$$$
RESORT
Fodor's Choice
★

☷ **Garza Blanca Preserve Resort and Spa.** Hollywood celebrities have stayed at this new and award-winning resort when visiting Puerto Vallarta for vacation—and it's no surprise why. **Pros:** elegant and sophisticated; great restaurants; immaculate facilities; spotless beach. **Cons:** pricey; need transportation to get to Puerto Vallarta. ⑤ *Rooms from: $462* ⊠ *Carretera a Barra de Navidad, Km 7.5, South of Puerto Vallarta, Chapala* ☎ *322/176–07000, 877/845–3791 in the U.S.* ⊕ *www.garzablancaresort.com* ⇘ *73 rooms* ❍❘ *Multiple meal plans.* ✛ *4:A6*

$$$
HOTEL

☷ **Verana.** Understated luxury and an open-to-nature building design describe this eight-suite boutique property located in a jungle about an hour south of Vallarta. **Pros:** simple luxury; no electronic distractions; Watsu massage and yoga classes; Wi-Fi keeps guests in reasonable contact with the world. **Cons:** accessible to Puerto Vallarta only by boat; five- to seven-night minimum depending on season; steep hike up from boat dock (ask for mule if needed). ⑤ *Rooms from: $200* ⊠ *Playa de Yelapa, Domicilio Conocido, Yelapa* ✛ *30-minute boat ride west from Boca de Tomatlan* ☎ *322/222–0878* ⊕ *www.verana.com* ⇘ *8 rooms* ☉ *Closed June 8–Oct.* ❍❘ *Multiple meal plans* ✛ *4:A5.*

COSTALEGRE

LA MANZANILLA AND POINTS NORTH

More developed for tourism than neighboring towns on gorgeous Tena-catita Bay, La Manzanilla springs to life in the winter months, when previously shuttered galleries and restaurants open. Mexican families visit in the rainy months for summer vacation. The vibe is earthy and organic; streets are sandy and traffic-free. Miles of gorgeous beaches beckon, and those travelers with a car or a penchant for bus travel can explore miles of similarly natural and charming Costalegre beaches even farther north toward San Mateo, Punta Perula, and beyond.

$$
B&B/INN

Coconuts by the Sea. A friendly couple of American expats own and run this charming cliff-top hideaway with a drop-dead-gorgeous view of the ocean and Boca de Iguana Beach below. **Pros:** homey apartments; great sea views; very nice beaches on Tenacatita Bay. **Cons:** its few rooms make last-minute reservations unlikely; long downhill walk to the beach; car is almost a must unless you're staying put; to pay by credit card, must use PayPal in advance. $ *Rooms from: $150 ⊠ Playa Boca de Iguanas, 6 Dolphin Way, Costalegre, Bahía Tenacatita ✛ 195 km (121 miles) south of Puerto Vallarta, 21 km (13 miles) north of Barra de Navidad ☎ 315/100–8899 cell, 949/945–7465 in U.S. or Canada ⊕ www.coconutsbythesea.com ⟳ 4 rooms ⦿ No meals ✛ 6:C5.*

$$$$
HOTEL

Hotelito Desconocido Sanctuary Reserve & Spa. A two-year renovation, during which time the resort was closed, has resulted in a more sedate, less whimsical decor that, like the original Hotelito, includes elements of hardwood, bamboo, and palm-thatch designed by a group of young *tapatios* (artisans from Guadalajara). **Pros:** isolated, unique, and charming; holistic spa with aromatherapy, yoga, and many other services; concierge service. **Cons:** rustic-chic it is, affordable it isn't; isolated. $ *Rooms from: $550 ⊠ Playón de Mismaloya s/n, Tenacatita ✛ 97 km (60 miles) south of Puerto Vallarta, 119 km (74 miles) north of Barra de Navidad ☎ 800/851–1143 ⊕ www. hotelito.com ⟳ 27 suites, 3 villas ⦿ Multiple meal plans ✛ 6:A1.*

$$$$
RESORT

Las Alamandas. Personal service and exclusivity lure movie stars and royalty to this low-key resort in a thorn-forest preserve about 1½ hours from both Puerto Vallarta and Manzanillo. **Pros:** star-gazing from rooftop bar; stunning yet cozy architecture; one-hour horseback ride and use of bicycles; boogie boards included; concierge service. **Cons:** high humidity; not close to any restaurants or nightlife;

TURTLE RESCUE

Releasing tiny turtles into the sea, done in the evening when there are fewer predators, is a real thrill for kids, and for many adults as well. The Westin, CasaMagna Marriott Puerto Vallarta, Fiesta Americana, Velas Vallarta, and Dreams Resort in Puerto Vallarta as well as Las Alamandas and El Tamarindo on the Costalegre coast have marine turtle conservation programs. They employ biologists to collect eggs from nests on nearby beaches, incubate them in protected sand pits, and help guests repatriate them into the wild blue sea.

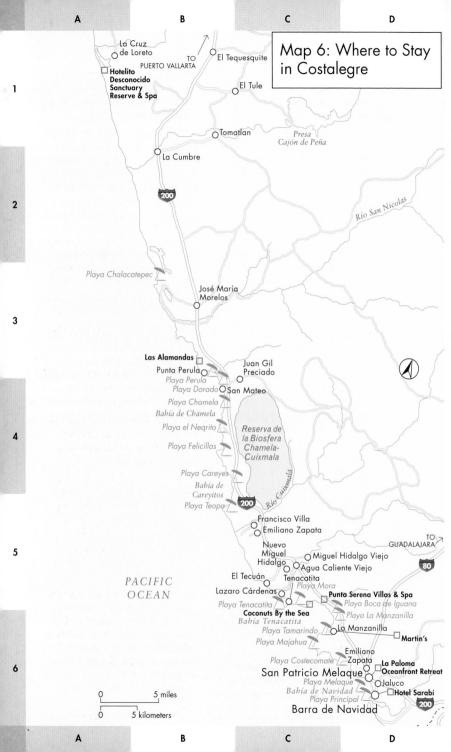

Buying a Time-Share

In Puerto Vallarta, time-share sales-people are as unavoidable as death and taxes, and almost as dreaded. Although a slim minority of people actually enjoy going to one- to four-hour time-share presentations to get the freebies that range from a bottle of $12 Kahlúa to rounds of golf, car rentals, meals, and shows, most folks find the experience incredibly annoying. For some it even casts a pall over their whole vacation.

The bottom line is, if the sharks smell interest, you're dead in the water. Time-share salespeople occupy tiny booths up and down main streets where tourists and cruise passengers walk. In general, while *vallartenses* are friendly, they don't accost you on the street to start a conversation. Those who do are selling something. Likewise, anyone calling you *amigo* is probably selling. The best solution is to walk by without responding, or say "No thanks" or "I'm not interested" as you continue walking. When they yell after you, don't feel compelled to explain yourself.

Some sly methods of avoidance that have worked for others are telling the tout that you're out of a job but dead interested in attending a presentation. They'll usually back off immediately. Or explaining confidentially that the person you're with is not your spouse. Time-share people are primarily interested in married couples—married to each other, that is! But our advice is still to practice the art of total detachment with a polite rejection and then ignore the salesperson altogether if he or she persists.

Even some very nice hotels allow salespeople in their lobbies disguised as the Welcome Wagon or information gurus. Ask the concierge for the scoop on area activities, and avoid the so-called "information desk."

Time-share salespeople often pressure guests to attend time-share presentations, guilt-tripping them ("My family relies on the commissions I get," for example) or offering discounts on the hotel room and services. The latter are sometimes difficult to redeem and cost more time than they're worth. And although it may be the salesperson's livelihood, remember that this is your vacation, and you have every right to use the time as you wish.

But if you do return to Puerto Vallarta frequently, a time-share might make sense. Here are some tips for navigating the treacherous waters:

■ Cruise the Internet before your vacation. Check out resale time-shares in the area, which makes it easier to determine the value of what's offered.

■ Worthwhile time-shares come with the option of trading for a room in another destination. Ask what other resorts are available.

■ Time-share salespeople get great commissions and are very good at their jobs. Be brave, be strong, and sign on the dotted line only if it's what you really want. Remember there are plenty of good vacation deals out there that require no long-term commitment.

■ Buyer's remorse? If you buy a time-share and want to back out, be aware that most contracts have a five-day "cooling-off period." Ask to see this in writing before you sign the contract; then you can get a full refund if you change your mind.

riptides. Ⓢ *Rooms from: $480* ⊠ *Carretera 200, Km 85, Tenacatita* ✛ *83 km (52 miles) south of Puerto Vallarta, 133 km (83 miles) north of Barra de Navidad* ☎ *322/285–5500, 888/882–9616* ⊕ *www. lasalamandas.com* ⊸ *14 suites* ⫶◉⫶ *Multiple meal plans* ✛ *6:C3.*

$$$
RESORT
ALL-INCLUSIVE

▦ **Punta Serena Villas & Spa.** Perched on a beautiful headland, "Point Serene" enjoys balmy breezes and life-changing views from the infinity hot tub. **Pros:** gorgeous views; intriguing spa treatments; complimentary horseback ride and mangrove cruise. **Cons:** isolated; limited menu; cobblestone walkways and hills make walking difficult for some folks. Ⓢ *Rooms from: $248* ⊠ *Carretera Barra de Navidad–Puerto Vallarta (Carretera 200), Km 20, Costalegre, Tenacatita, Jalisco* ✛ *196 km (122 miles) south of Puerto Vallarta, 20 km (12 miles) north of Barra de Navidad* ☎ *315/351–5020* ⊕ *www.puntaserena.com* ⊸ *12 rooms, 12 suites* ⫶◉⫶ *All-inclusive* ✛ *6:C5.*

SAN PATRICIO–MELAQUE

San Patricio–Melaque is actually two towns that have met in the middle. Slightly more bustling than nearby Barra, its tourist-related shops and restaurants are interspersed among those catering to the needs of its 12,000 residents. Visitors tend to be older and stay longer than those in Barra, which can be reached via a 5-km (3.5-mile) walk along the beach. Modest hotels and reasonably priced vacation rentals predominate.

$
HOTEL

▦ **La Paloma Oceanfront Retreat.** Rates are reasonable considering these small studio apartments have all the creature comforts of home: the spacious kitchens come with juicers, blenders, toasters, and coffeemakers in addition to stoves and refrigerators; microwaves are available upon request. **Pros:** beside a beautiful bay; long beach perfect for walking and jogging. **Cons:** one-week minimum stay in high season; pay cash, Paypal, or bank deposit only. Ⓢ *Rooms from: $119* ⊠ *Av. Las Cabañas 13, San Patricio–Melaque* ✛ *6 km (4 miles) north of Barra de Navidad* ☎ *315/355–5345* ⊕ *www.lapalomamexico.com* ⊸ *13 studio apartments* ▭ *No credit cards* ⊙ *Closed Sept. and Oct.* ⫶◉⫶ *Breakfast* ✛ *6:D6.*

BARRA DE NAVIDAD

With its two main sandy streets on a skinny sandbar separating Christmas Bay and the open ocean, this casual little town is about three hours south of Vallarta at the southern extreme of Jalisco state. Easy to navigate on foot, Barra is within striking distance of many beautiful beaches, which can be visited by car, taxi, or public bus. Hotels are mainly basic, with the exception of the luxurious and snooty Grand Bay Hotel, across the channel.

$
HOTEL

▦ **Hotel Sarabi.** These snug little rooms a block from the beach are indeed a bargain. **Pros:** owner managed; clean and tidy; close to the beach; well priced. **Cons:** no telephone; no Internet station; cash only. Ⓢ *Rooms from: $52* ⊠ *Av. Veracruz 196, Barra de Navidad* ☎ *315/355–8223* ⊕ *www.hotelsarabi.com* ⊸ *16 rooms, 5 bungalows* ▭ *No credit cards* ⫶◉⫶ *No meals* ✛ *6:D6.*

NIGHTLIFE AND PERFORMING ARTS

Updated by Luis Domínguez

Outdoorsy Vallarta switches gears after dark and rocks into the wee hours. When the beachgoers and sightseers have been showered and fed, Vallarta kicks up its heels and puts the baby to bed. Happy hour in martini lounges sets the stage for an evening that might include a show, live music, or just hobnobbing under the stars at a rooftop bar.

Many hotels have Mexican fiesta dinner shows, which can be lavish affairs with buffet dinners, folk dances, and even fireworks. Tour groups and individuals—mainly middle-age and older Americans and Canadians—make up the audience at the Saturday-night buffet dinner show at Playa Los Arcos and other hotels. *Vaqueros* (cowboys) do rope tricks and dancers perform Mexican regional or pseudo-Aztec dances. The late-late crowd gets down after midnight at dance clubs, some of which stay open until 6 am.

The scene mellows as you head north and south of Puerto Vallarta. In Punta Mita (aka Punta de Mita), Bucerías, Sayulita, and San Francisco (aka San Pancho), local restaurants provide live music; the owners usually scare up someone good once or twice a week in high season. Along the Costalegre, tranquility reigns. Most people head here for relaxation, and nightlife generally takes the form of stargazing, drink in hand. If you're visiting June through October (low season), attend live performances whenever offered, as they are few and far between.

Although there's definitely crossover, many Mexicans favor the upscale bars and clubs of the Hotel Zone and Marina Vallarta hotels, while foreigners tend to like the Mexican flavor of places downtown and on the south side (the Zona Romántica), where dress is decidedly more casual.

PUERTO VALLARTA

ZONA ROMÁNTICA

BARS, PUBS, AND LOUNGES

Like any resort destination worth its salt—the salt on the rim of the margarita glass, that is—PV has an enormous variety of watering holes. Bars on or overlooking the beach sell the view along with buckets of beer. Martini bars go to great lengths to impress with signature drinks, and sports bars serve up Canadian hockey and Monday-night football. Hotels have swim-up bars and lobby lounges, and these, as well as restaurant bars, are the main options in places like Nuevo Vallarta, Marina Vallarta, and most of the small towns to the north and south.

Andale. Most nights, crowds spill out onto the sidewalk as party-hearty men and women shimmy out of the narrow saloon, drinks in hand, to the strains of Chubby Checker and other vintage tunes. For a laugh, intoxicated or less inhibited patrons sometimes take a bumpy ride on the burro just outside Andale's door (a handler escorts the burro). Andale opens at 8 am. ⊠ *Av. Olas Altas 425, Zona Romántica* ☏ *322/222–1054* ⊕ *www.andales.com.*

Apaches. It's gay friendly, lesbian friendly, *people* friendly. Heck, owner Mariann and her partner, Endra, would probably welcome you and your pet python with open arms and give you both a squeeze. PV's original martini bar, Apaches is the landing zone for expats reconnoitering after a long day, and a warm-up for late-night types. When the outside tables get jam-packed in high season, the overflow heads into the narrow bar and the adjacent, equally narrow bistro. It opens at 4 pm; happy hour is 5 to 7. If you're alone, this is the place to make friends of all ages. ⊠ *Av. Olas Altas 439, Zona Romántica* ☏ *322/222–5235.*

Bar Bolero Vallarta. Looking for a small bar with an authentic taste of Puerto Vallarta? Bolero is just what you need—a cozy little bar with a pool table and not much more. No flashy design here, just good rock and pop music and interesting people of all ages and nationalities. It's open from 6 pm to 4 am. This is the kind of place you don't find in guidebooks oh wait! ⊠ *Ignacio L. Vallarta 229, Zona Romántica* ☏ *322/429–0643.*

Burro's Bar. Right on the sand across from Parque Lázaro Cárdenas, this restaurant-bar has bargain brewskis and equally inexpensive fruity margaritas by the pitcher. The seafood is less than inspired, but nachos and other munchies are good accompaniments to the drinks. Watch the waves and listen to Bob Marley and the Gypsy Kings among lots of gringo couples and a few middle-age Mexican vacationers. It opens daily from 9 am to 10 pm. ⊠ *Av. Olas Altas 208 at Calle Lázaro Cárdenas, Zona Romántica* ☏ *322/222–0122.*

Fodor'sChoice **Los Muertos Brewing Company.** If you love a good beer, Los Muertos
★ Brewing Company is for you. The first craft brewery in Puerto Vallarta offers a relaxed atmosphere and the best beer on tap in town. It's a mix between the typical cantina and the traditional sports bar and they have a selection of rock and pop both in English and Spanish. Young

gringos love it, and it's also getting attention from locals who come for the pizzas and stay for the beer. It's open every day from noon until midnight. ⊠ *Lazaro Cardenas 302, Zona Romántica* ☎ *322/222–0308* ⊕ *losmuertosbrewing.com.*

Roxy Rock House. Puerto Vallarta's only rock house is a very energetic club that features live music every night at 11 pm. Roxy is an institution in this town and one of the very few places that attracts all kind of visitors—you'll find nationals and foreigners of all ages on the premises, and they are not afraid to sing and dance. It's open from 9 pm to 6 am every day. And the music? Pure rock, baby! ⊠ *Ignacio L. Vallarta 217, Zona Romántica* ☎ *322/225–6901* ⊕ *www.roxyrockhouse.com.*

> **HANGOVER CURES**
>
> For a hangover, *menudo* (tripe stew) and pozole are recommended, both with the addition of chopped fresh onions and cilantro, a generous squeeze of lime, and as much chili as you can handle. Ceviche is another popular cure, with the same key ingredients: lime and chili.

Steve's Bar. With NASCAR on Sunday morning, NFL on Monday night, hockey, indispensable motocross, and welterweight fights, Steve's is a sports mecca. Five feeds and nine television sets guarantee simultaneous broadcasts of many sporting events from various continents. There are piles of board games, too, and the burgers and fries couldn't be better. ⊠ *Calle Basilio Badillo 286, Zona Romántica* ☎ *322/222–0256* ⊕ *www.stevesbarpv.com.*

GAY BARS

Blue Chairs. In addition to its famous beach scene, Blue Chairs, at the south end of Los Muertos Beach, has the popular **Blue Sunset Rooftop Bar,** which is the perfect place to watch the sunset. It has daily late-afternoon and evening entertainment, and is open to the public between 3 and 11 pm; after that, it's hotel guests only. ⊠ *Almendro 114 at the malecón, Zona Romántica* ☎ *322/222–5040* ⊕ *www.bluechairsresort.com.*

Frida. We've heard this place described as "the gay Cheers of Mexico." It's a friendly neighborhood cantina where you'll meet middle-aged to older queens, many Mexicans, a few foreigners, and maybe even some straights. Show up a few times for $1 beers (served daily between 1 pm and 2 am) and everyone is sure to know your name. It has moved around the corner from its original location and now serves daily lunch specials in the small second-story restaurant. ⊠ *Av. Insurgentes 301-A, Zona Romántica* ☎ *322/222–3668* ⊕ *barfrida.com.*

Garbo. This isn't necessarily the kind of place where you'll strike up a conversation with the guy on the next barstool; rather, it's an upscale place to go with friends for a sophisticated, air-conditioned drink or two. A musician plays piano or gentle jazz on weekend nights at 10:30 during high season, less often the rest of the year. Garbo, renowned for its martinis, is primarily a gay club, but is straight-friendly and is open nightly from 6 pm to 2 am. ⊠ *Púlpito 142 at Av. Olas Altas, Zona Romántica* ☎ *322/223–5753.*

La Noche. This charming martini lounge has red walls and a huge, eye-catching chandelier. Gringo-owned, it attracts a crowd of gay 20- to 40-year-old men (a mix of foreigners and Mexicans). Electronica and house music are the favorites. But, to get back to the martinis, the house makes excellent cocktails, and they're not too expensive, either. Make sure to visit the spectacular rooftop garden. Open from 7 pm to 4 am. ⊠ *Calle Lázaro Cárdenas 263, Zona Romántica* ☎ *322/222–3364.*

Sama Martini Bar. A nice, sophisticated martini bar in the heart of the Zona Romántica, Sama is a cozy little place with a lovely terrace just by the sidewalk—a great place to enjoy a night out with friends or with your partner. It's frequented mostly by gay foreigners, but you will also find the occasional Mexican. Happy hour is from 4 to 7 pm. ⊠ *Calle Olas Altas 510, Zona Romántica* ☎ *322/278–1475* ⊕ *www.facebook. com/sama.martinibar.*

COFFEEHOUSES

Café San Angel. It's moody and romantic, with tables along the sidewalk and comfortable couches and chairs inside, and is a favorite with locals and the gay crowd. The menu includes soups, sandwiches, salads, and a great frappuccino. ⊠ *Av. Olas Altas 449, at Calle Francisca Rodriguez, Zona Romántica* ☎ *322/223–1273.*

Pie in the Sky Vallarta. Come for the excellent coffee as well as *the* most scrumptious pies, cookies, and cakes. There's free Wi-Fi for those with their trusty laptops. A classic of the bakery scene in PV! ⊠ *Calle Aquiles Serdan 242, L-3, Zona Romántica* ☎ *322/223–8183* ⊕ *www. pieinthesky.com.mx.*

SHOWS

Fodor's Choice
★

Act II Entertainment. A breath of fresh air in the nightlife scene of Puerto Vallarta, Act II is a multigenre theater, cabaret, and sophisticated bar all in one. On the top floor of a little shopping center in Zona Romántica, it offers a great diversity of shows, both on the "Main Stage" and in the more intimate "Red Room," which recalls the good cabaret shows of old. In the intermission, you can also enjoy a drink at the Encore Piano & Wine Bar. Altogether, it's an excellent option for a different kind of night out in Puerto Vallarta. ⊠ *Calle Insurgentes 300 at Basilio Badillo, 2nd fl., Zona Romántica* ☎ *322/222–1512* ⊕ *actiientertainment.com.*

Playa Los Arcos. This place has a themed dinner show three nights a week and live music every night. The most popular theme night is Saturday's Mexico Night, with mariachis, rope tricks, and folkloric dance. Monday is Tex-Mex food and a pre-Hispanic show. The price—225 pesos (around $17)—includes a buffet and one cocktail. ⊠ *Av. Olas Altas 380, Zona Romántica* ☎ *322/226–7100* ⊕ *www.playalosarcos.com.*

EL CENTRO

Cervecería Unión. A favorite with the locals, this is a delightful place to have a quality beer and enjoy some of the best oysters in town. In fact, it's the only oyster bar on the malécon, and it offers a wide array of handcrafted beers, both Mexican and international. With a nice location, Cervecería Unión is a relaxing, large spot with full ocean views.

Take in a charrería, or Mexican rodeo performance, at Mundo Cuervo in Tequila.

It's open from 11 am to 3 am. ⊠ *Paseo Díaz Ordaz 610, El Centro* ☎ *322/223–0929.*

El patio de mi casa. The go-to place for the artistic community of PV, El patio de mia casa is advertised as a sandwich shop, pizza place, and vegetarian/vegan haven—and it's one of those few places that actually delivers what it offers. A cozy indoor/outdoor design ("patio" means backyard) fits perfectly with the laid-back vibe, with "Friends"-style sofas for socializing while sipping a good mescal and eating brick-oven pizza. Frequently scheduled jazz and reggae jam sessions, as well as guest DJs and regular movie screenings, make this so much more than a restaurant. It's open daily 6 pm to 2 am. ⊠ *Calle Guerrero 311 at Matamoros, El Centro* ☎ *322/222–0743* ⊕ *www.facebook.com/ elpatiodemicasavallarta.*

El Solar. This oceanfront bar is just the way a beach bar is supposed to be—small, hip, and laid-back—making it a real pleasure to enjoy a beer while watching the waves of Playa Camarones. There's live music on Friday night and a DJ on Saturday. There is always a good vibe in this place, and, if you feel like having a bite, you can always ask the waiter to bring you some food from the sister restaurant, Barracuda. ⊠ *Calle Paraguay 1290, El Centro* ☎ *322/222–4034.*

La Cantina. Although it isn't especially hip, La Cantina has a good view of Banderas Bay and the boardwalk from its second floor. It also has canned (and sometimes live) Mexican tunes, especially *ranchera, norteño, grupera,* and *cumbia.* ⊠ *Calle Morelos 709 at J.O. de Dominguez, El Centro* ☎ *322/222–1734.*

La Regadera. Talent at this karaoke spot varies; it's open Monday through Saturday (except during low season, when the schedule is less consistent) after 9 pm. Come practice your standard Beatles tunes or hip-hop before your next official recording session. ⌂ *Calle Morelos 666, El Centro* ☎ *322/110–0730* ⊕ *www.facebook.com/laregadera. puertovallarta.*

Party Lounge. This place, across from Parque Hidalgo, is open daily from noon to 6 am for stop-and-go drinks, mainly *litros (34-ounce tequila sunrises), Long Island ice teas, piña coladas, and the like.* The upstairs bar plays '70s, '80s, and lounge music, making it popular with an older set, foreign and domestic. ⌂ *Av. México 993, El Centro* ⊕ *www.facebook.com/partyloungepv.*

> ### DRINKS ON THE BEACH
>
> Playa Los Muertos is the destination of choice for a sunset cocktail and dinner on the beach. Strolling mariachi bands or trios playing romantic ballads serenade diners overlooking the sand. Candles and torches, along with the moon, light the scene. After dinner you can take a stroll, sit on the beach, or head to another restaurant-bar for a coffee or after-dinner digestive to the tunes of marimba, folk music, or jazz.

Party Lounge Nuevo Vallarta. This may be the only proper nightclub in all Nuevo Vallarta. Inaugurated in 2014 after traditional motorbike-rock club Choppers closed its doors, Party Lounge Nuevo Vallarta offers pretty much the same as its sister property in downtown Vallarta, minus the liter drinks. You will hear hits from the '70s, '80s, and '90s, mixed up with contemporary rock and house music. Popular among young locals, it features a couple of dance floors and on selected nights they have live music. Cover varies depending on the night of the week and the season of the year, but usually it won't be more than about 135 pesos ($10). ⌂ *Carretera a Tepic 995, Nuevo Vallarta* ☎ *322/157–4975.*

Peyote Lounge. Bon vivants should head for the latest offshoot of hotshot restaurant Café des Artistes. Peyote Lounge is a celebration of the Huichol, the indigenous people of the Jalisco/Nayarit region, and is named after the psychotropic cactus central to the Huichol vision of the world. Sophisticated and colorful, it's the perfect place to enjoy a cocktail or martini before heading to the theater or to a nightclub. ⌂ *Café des Artistes, Av. Guadalupe Sánchez 740, El Centro* ☎ *322/222–3229* ⊕ *www.cafedesartistes.com.*

Señor Frog's. What's called simply "Frog's" by the locals is a good old-fashioned free-for-all for the young and the restless. There are black lights on the walls, bar stools shaped like thong-clad women's butts, and a giant-screen TV above the dance floor. Expect foam parties; ladies'-night Fridays; or, in the high season, beach parties with bikini contests and other shenanigans. It's open from 11 am to 4 am. ⌂ *Calle Morelos 518, El Centro* ☎ *322/226–9260* ⊕ *www.senorfrogs.com.*

DANCE AND MUSIC CLUBS

You can dance salsa with the locals, groove to rock in English or *en español*, or even tango. Things slow down in the off-season, but during school vacations and the winter, clubs stay open until 3, 5, or even

6 am. Except those that double as restaurants, clubs don't open until 10 pm. ■TIP→ If you care about looking hip, don't show up at a club before midnight—it will most likely be dead. Arriving around 10 pm, however, could save you a cover charge.

Have a late and leisurely dinner, take a walk on the beach and get

> ## COCKTAILS TO GO
>
> Stop-and-go bars, where you get your drink in a cardboard cup, are mainly geared toward teens. But it can be fun to sip a cocktail while drinking in the sights along the malecón.

some coffee, and then stroll into the club cool as a cucumber at 12:30 am or so.

Most of Puerto Vallarta's live music is performed in restaurants and bars, often on or overlooking the beach. ■TIP→ Musical events happening anywhere in Vallarta are listed in Bay Vallarta (⊕ *www. bayvallarta.com*). This twice-monthly rag is an excellent source of detailed information for who's playing around El Centro, the Zona Hotelera Norte, Marina Vallarta, and even as far north as the Riviera Nayarit. More detail-oriented than most similar publications, *Bay Vallarta* lists showtimes, venues, genres, and cover charges. Live music is much less frequent in the smaller towns to the north and south of PV; to find out what's happening there, ask in tourist-oriented bars, restaurants, or hotels.

Bebotero. This upscale, second-story nightclub has live rock. Although it opens nightly after 7, music doesn't start until 10 or 11; closing time is 4 am. There's no cover charge. ⊠ *Paseo Díaz Ordaz 522, El Centro* ☎ *322/113–0099* ⊕ *www.bebotero.com.mx.*

La Bodeguita del Medio. People of all ages come to salsa and drink mojitos made with Cuban rum at this wonderful Cuban bar and restaurant with a friendly vibe. The small dance floor fills up as soon as the house sextet starts playing around 9:30 pm. There's no cover. ⊠ *Paseo Díaz Ordaz 858, El Centro* ☎ *322/223–1585* ⊕ *labodeguitadelmedio.com.mx.*

La Vaquita. La Vaquita is arguably the hippest of all El Centro clubs. A mostly young crowd packs the place every weekend, dancing to the rythms of house, techno, Latin, pop, and rock music. The location is outstanding, with great ocean views. Here it's customary to enjoy your favorite drink in a *litro*, a one-liter (a little more than 2 pints) Styrofoam cup, with a straw. It opens every day from 7 pm to 6 am. ⊠ *Paseo Diaz Ordaz 610, El Centro* ☎ *322/222–8281* ⊕ *www.lavaquitadisco.com.*

Mandala. If you were to choose just one of the malecón nightclubs, Mandala may be a good choice. It's the most stylish club all of El Centro, and throws some of the best parties, too. The music is mostly electronic, with lots of house and techno. Here you will find people from all ages and nationalities, and plenty of entertainers such as mimes and go-go dancers. The cover varies according to the night of the week and the season of the year, but it's in line with the rest of the nightclubs along the malecón. ⊠ *Paseo Diaz Ordaz, at Abasolo, El Centro* ☎ *322/121–5002* ⊕ *mandalanightclub.com.*

Sky Mandala. The sister nightclub of Mandala has its entrance just around the corner and it's on a gorgeous rooftop terrace with stunning views of the malecón and the Pacific Ocean. It's a bit more exclusive than Mandala and offers a more intimate kind of atmosphere, with a small dance floor and an open design that makes the most of its location. House, techno, and Latin beats will play out all night long. Sky, as it's known by the locals, attracts mostly locals and national visitors that range between 20 and 35 years old. ⊠ *Morelos 633, El Centro* ☎ *322/223–0977* ⊕ *www.facebook.com/Sky.Mandala.pv.*

Zoo Bar & Dance. Ready to party? Then head here for DJ-spun techno, Latin, reggae, and hip-hop. The adventurous can dance in the cage. It attracts a mixed crowd of mainly young locals and travelers, though after midnight the median age plunges. It's open until 6 am when things are hopping. The restaurant fills with cruise-ship passengers early in the evening. ⊠ *Paseo Díaz Ordaz 630, El Centro* ☎ *322/222–4945.*

MOVIES

Movie tickets here are less than half what they are in the United States and Canada. Many theaters have discounted prices on Wednesday. See theater websites or visit ⊕ *www.vallartaonline.com/cinema.*

Cinépolis. Until Cinemex showed up, this was PV's newest movie theater. Next to Soriana department stores at the south entrance to El Pitillal, it has 15 screens and shows movies in English and Spanish. Tickets are about 55 pesos ($4), less on Wednesday. ⊠ *Plaza Soriana, Av. Francisco Villa 1642–A, El Centro* ☎ *322/225–1251* ⊕ *www.cinepolis.com.mx.*

SHOWS

Most hotels have lounge music, and many hotels have buffet dinners with mariachis, folkloric dancers, and *charros* (elegantly dressed horsemen, who, in this case, perform mostly roping tricks, as horses are a bit too messy for the stage and most of their feats on horseback involve running at top speed in a specially designed arena called a *lienzo charro*). All-inclusive hotels generally include nightly entertainment in the room price. Drag shows are crowd pleasers—whether the crowd is straight or gay.

Teatro Vallarta. The biggest cultural center in Puerto Vallarta, Teatro Vallarta is in a modern building with an outstanding sound system that qualifies it to screen New York Met operas. It offers a bit of everything: national theater companies that are happy to include this beach town in their yearly circuit; sporadic international ballet performances or touring musicians; local conferences; dance contests; and all kinds of other events. ⊠ *Calle Uruguay 184, El Centro* ☎ *322/222–4525* ⊕ *teatrovallarta.com.*

ZONA HOTELERA

DANCE AND MUSIC CLUBS

BarraBar. A nightclub where the oldies rule! It's the typical posh Mexican *antro* (nightclub) where nobody actually dances, but everybody seems to be dancing (and singing) at their own tables. Frequented by not-so-young locals, BarraBar is a nice option when you are not looking for

Continued on page 152

CLOSE UP

Mexican Rhythms and Roots

Salsa, merengue, *cumbia*—do they leave you spinning before you even hit the dance floor? This primer is designed to help you wrap your mind around Latin beats popular in Pacific Mexico. Unfortunately, it can't cure two left feet, and these flat-footed styles of dancing can be difficult for anyone not accustomed to Latin beats. In Puerto Vallarta, the dance club J.B. is great for lessons.

Latin dance rhythms were born of African drumming. Dancing was vital to West African religious ceremonies; these rhythms spread with importation of slaves to the New World. Evolving regional tastes and additional instruments have produced today's Latin music.

From Colombia, wildly popular **cumbia** combines vocals, wind, and percussion instruments. With a marked rhythm (usually 4/4 time), the sensual music is relatively easy to dance to. Hip-hop and reggae influences have produced urban cumbia, with up-tempo, accordion-driven melodies. Popular artists include Kumbia Kings, La Onda, Control, and Big Circo.

Fast-paced and with short, precise rhythms, **merengue** originated in the Dominican Republic. Although the music sounds almost frantic, the feet aren't meant to keep pace with the melody. Check out Elvis Crespo's 2004 album *Saboréalo*.

Born in Cuba of Spanish and African antecedents, **son** is played on accordion, guitar, and drums. The folkloric music was translated to various dialects in different parts of Mexico. "La Bamba" is a good example of *son jarrocho* (from Veracruz).

American Prohibition sent high rollers sailing down Cuba way, and they came back swinging to son, mambo, and rumba played by full orchestras—think Desi Arnaz and his famous song "Babalou." In New York these styles morphed into **salsa**, popularized by such luminaries as Tito Puente and Celia Cruz and carried on today by superstars like Marc Anthony.

Mexicans love these African-inspired beats but are especially proud of homegrown genres, like **música norteña**, which has its roots in rural, northern Mexico (in Texas, it's called *conjunto*). The traditional instruments are the *bajo sexto* (a 12-string guitar), bass, and accordion; modern groups add the trap drums for a distinctive rhythmic pulse. It's danced like a very lively polka, which is one of its main influences.

A subset of música norteña is the **corrido**, popularized during the Mexican Revolution. Corridos informed isolated Mexican communities of the adventures of Emiliano Zapata, Pancho Villa, and their compatriots.

But the quintessential Mexican music is **mariachi**, a marriage of European instruments and native sensibilities born right here in Jalisco, Mexico. Guitars, violins, and trumpets are accompanied by the *vihuela* (a small, round-backed guitar) and the larger, deep-throated *guitarrón*. Professional mariachis perform at birthdays and funerals, engagements, anniversaries, and life's other milestones. ⇨ *For more about mariachi, see "Mariachi: Born in Jalisco" in Chapter 9.*

TEQUILA AND MEZCAL—¡SALUD!

If God were Mexican, tequila and mezcal would surely be our heavenly reward, flowing in lieu of milk and honey. Before throwing back your first drink, propose a toast in true Mexican style and wave your glass accordingly— *"¡Arriba, abajo, al centro, pa' dentro!"* ("Above, below, center, inside!")

Historians maintain that, following Spanish conquest and the introduction of the distillation process, tequila was adapted from the ancient Aztec drink *pulque*. Whatever the true origin, Mexico's national drink long predated the Spanish, and is considered North America's oldest spirit.

When you think about tequila, what might come to mind are spaghetti-Western-style bar brawls or late-night teary-eyed confessions. But tequila is more complex and worldly than many presume. By some accounts it's a digestive that reduces cho-lesterol and stress. Shots of the finest tequilas can cost upward of $100 each, and are meant to be savored as ardently as fine cognacs or single-malt scotches.

Just one of several agave-derived drinks fermented and bottled in Mexico, tequila rose to fame during the Mexican Revolution when it became synonymous with national heritage and pride. Since the 1990s tequila has enjoyed a soaring popularity around the globe, and people the world over are starting to realize that tequila is more than a one-way ticket to (and doesn't necessitate) a hangover.

Harvesting agave in Jalisco.

TEQUILA AND MEZCAL 101

Harvesting blue agave to make tequila.

WHICH CAME FIRST, TEQUILA OR MEZCAL?

Mezcal is tequila's older cousin. Essentially, all tequila is mezcal but only some mezcal is tequila. The only difference between tequila and mezcal is that the tequila meets two requirements: 1) it's made only from blue agave (but some non-agave sugar can be added) and 2) it must be distilled in a specific region in Jalisco or certain parts of neighboring Guanajuato, Michoacán, Nayarit, and Tamaulipas. Unlike tequila, all mezcal must be made from 100 percent agave and must be bottled in Mexico.

CHOOSE YOUR LIQUOR WISELY

Your first decision with tequila is whether to have a *puro* or a *mixto*. You'll know if a bottle is *puro* because it will say so prominently on the label; if the words "100% de agave" don't appear, you can be sure you're getting mixto. Don't be fooled by bottles that say, "Made from agave azul," because all tequila is made from agave azul; that doesn't mean that cane sugar hasn't been added. Popular wisdom holds that puro causes less of a hangover than mixto, but we'll leave that to your own experimentation.

Even among *puros*, there's a wide range of quality and taste, and every fan has his or her favorite. For sipping straight (*derecho*), most people prefer *reposado*, *añejo*, or extra *añejo*. For mixed drinks you'll probably want either a *blanco* or a *reposado*.

Herradura

TEQUILA TIMELINE

Pre-Columbian	Aztecs brew pulque for thousands of years; both priests and the sacrificial victims consume it during religious rituals.
1600	The first commercial distillery in New Spain is founded by Pedro Sanches de Tagle, the father of tequila, on his hacienda near the village of Tequila.
1740	*Mezcal de Tequila* earns an enthusiastic following and King Philip V of Spain grants José Antonio Cuervo the first royal license for a mezcal distillery.

Aztec ritual human sacrifice as portrayed on the Codex Magliabechiano.

THE MAKING OF MEZCAL

1 To make both mezcal and tequila, the agave may be cultivated for as long as ten years, depending on growing conditions and the variety of plant.

2 When the agave is ripe, the leaves, or *pencas*, are removed and the heavy core (called a *piña*, Spanish for "pineapple," because of its resemblance to that fruit) is dug up, **3** cut into large chunks, and cooked to convert its starches into sugars.

4 The *piñas* are then crushed and their juice collected in tanks; yeast is added and the liquid ferments for several days.

After the fermentation, the resulting *mosto* generally measures between 4 and 7 percent alcohol. **5** Finally it's distilled (usually twice for tequila, once for mezcal). This process of heating and condensing serves to boost the alcohol content. **6** And finally, the alcohol is aged in barrels.

While the process is the same, there are a few critical differences between tequila and mezcal: mezcal is made in smaller distilleries and still retains more of an artisanal quality; mezcal magueys are grown over a wider area with more diverse soil composition and microclimate, giving mezcals more individuality than tequila; and lastly, the *piñas* for mezcal are more likely to be baked in stone pits, which imparts a distinctive smoky flavor.

The World's Columbian Fair in Chicago, 1893.

1800s	As the thirst for mezcal grows, wood (used to fire the stills) becomes scarce and distilleries shift to more efficient steam ovens.
1873	Cenobio Sauza exports mezcal to the United States via a new railroad to El Paso, Texas.
1893	*Mezcal de Tequila* (now simply called tequila) receives an award at Chicago's Columbian Exposition.

TEQUILA COCKTAILS

Margarita: The original proportions at Rancho La Gloria were reportedly 3 parts tequila, 2 parts Triple Sec, and 1 part lime juice, though today recipes vary widely. In Mexico an orange liqueur called Controy is often substituted for the Triple Sec. The best margaritas are a little tart and are made from fresh ingredients, not a mix. Besides deciding whether you want yours strained, on the rocks, or frozen, you have dozens of variations to choose from, many incorporating fruits such as strawberry, raspberry, mango, passion fruit, and peach. To salt the rim or not to salt is yet another question.

Sangrita: The name meaning "little blood," this is a very Mexican accompaniment, a spicy mixture of tomato and orange juice that's sipped between swallows of straight tequila (or mezcal).

Tequila refresca: Also very popular in Mexico, this is tequila mixed with citrus soft drinks like Fresca, or Squirt. Generally served in a tall glass over ice.

Tequila Sunrise: Invented in the 1950s, this is a distant runner-up to the margarita, concocted from tequila, orange juice, and grenadine syrup. The grenadine sinks to the bottom, and after a few refills you might agree that the resulting layers resemble a Mexican sky at dawn.

Bloody Maria: One to try with brunch, this is a bloody Mary with you-know-what instead of vodka.

DID YOU KNOW?

Aging mezcal and Tequila imparts a smoothness and an oaky flavor, but over-aging can strip the drink of its characteristic agave taste.

TEQUILA TIMELINE

Mexican revolutionaries

1910–1920	During the Mexican Revolution, homegrown tequila becomes a source of national pride, associated with the hard-riding, hard-drinking rebels.
1930s	Federal land reforms break up the great haciendas and Mexico's agave production slumps by two thirds. To make up for the shortfall, the government allows distillers to begin mixing non-agave sugars into their tequila. This blander drink, called mixto, is better suited to American tastes and sales surge.

TEQUILA AND MEZCAL VOCABULARY

pulque: an alcoholic drink made by the Aztecs

mexcalmetl: Nahuatl word for agave

mixto: a type of tequila that is mixed with non-agave sugars

puro: tequila made with no non-agave sugars

reposado: aged between two months and a year

añejo: aged between one and three years

extra añejo: aged longer than three years

blanco: tequila that is aged less than two months

joven: young tequila, usually a mixto with colorings and flavors

caballito: tall shot glass

pechuga: mezcal flavored with raw chicken breast

cremas: flavored mezcal

aguamiel: agave juice

piña: the agave core

salmiana: a type of agave

pencas: agave leaves

mosto: fermented agave before it is distilled

gusano: the larva found in mescal bottles

WHAT'S WITH THE WORM?

Some mezcals (never tequila) are bottled with a worm (*gusano*), the larva of one of the moths that live on agave plants. Rumor has it that the worm was introduced to ensure a high alcohol content (because the alcohol preserves the creature), but the truth is that the practice started in the 1940s as a marketing gimmick. The worm is ugly but harmless and the best mezcals are not bottled *con gusano*.

Agave

6

Early 1940s	The history of mixology was forever altered when Carlos Herrera invented the margarita for American starlet Marjorie King.
2004	The agave fields around Tequila become a UNESCO World Heritage Site.
2006	A one-liter bottle of limited-edition premium tequila sold for $225,000. The most expensive bottle ever sold according to The Guiness World Records.

CHOOSING A BOTTLE

Reposado (rested) Silver Añejo (mature)

Corralejo

BUYING TEQUILA

There are hundreds of brands of tequila, but here are a baker's half dozen of quality *puros* to get you started; generally these distillers offer blanco, reposado, añejo, and extra añejo.

Corralejo—An award winner from the state of Guanajuato, made on the historic hacienda once owned by Pedro Sanchez de Tagle, "the father of tequila" and birthplace of Miguel Hidalgo, the father of Mexican independence.

Corzo—Triple distilled, these tequilas are notably smooth and elegant.

Don Julio—This award-winning tequila, one of the most popular in Mexico, is known for its rich, smooth flavor; the *blanco* is especially esteemed.

Espolón—A relative newcomer founded only in 1998, this distiller has already won several international awards.

Herradura—This is a venerable, popular brand known for its smoky, full body.

Patrón—Founded in 1989, this distiller produces award-winning tequilas. The *añejo* is especially noteworthy for its complex earthiness.

Siete Leguas—Taking their name ("Seven Leagues") from the horse of Pancho Villa, a general in the Mexican Revolution, these quality tequilas are known for their big, full flavor.

TYPES OF TEQUILA AND MEZCAL

Three basic types of tequila and mezcal are determined by how long they've been aged in oak barrels.

Blanco (white) is also known as *plata* or silver. It's been aged for less than two months.

Reposado ("rested") is aged between two months and a year.

añejo ("mature") is kept in barrels for at least a year and perhaps as long as three. Some producers also offer an extra *añejo* that is aged even longer.

Herradura

Don Julio

Gusano Rojo

BUYING MEZCAL

As for enjoying mezcal, it can be substituted in any recipe calling for tequila. But more often it's drunk neat, to savor its unique flavor. Like tequila, straight mezcal is generally served at room temperature in a tall shot glass called a *caballito*.

Some producers now add flavorings to their mezcals. Perhaps the most famous is *pechuga*, which has a raw chicken breast added to the still, supposedly imparting a smoothness and subtle flavor. (Don't worry, the heat and alcohol kill everything.) Citrus is also a popular add-in, and *cremas* contain flavorings such as peaches, mint, raisins, or guava, along with a sweetener such as honey or *aguamiel* (the juice of the agave).

Part of the fun of mezcal is stumbling on smaller, less commercial brands, but here are a few recognized, quality producers. Most make *blancos, reposados,* and *añejos,* and some offer extra *añejos,* flavored mezcals, and *cremas* as well.

El Señorio—Produced in Oaxaca the traditional way, with stone ovens and a stone wheel to crush the *piñas*.

El Zacatecano—Founded in 1910 in the northern state of Zacatecas; in a recent competitive tasting, their añejo was judged the best in its category.

Gusano Rojo—This venerable Oaxaca distillery makes the number-one-selling mezcal in Mexico. Yes, there's a worm in the bottle.

Jaral de Berrio—From Guanajuato, this distiller uses the *salmiana* agave. Their *blanco* recently garnered a silver medal.

Real de Magueyes—From the state of San Luis Potosí, these fine mezcals are also made from the local *salmiana* agave. Try the flavorful añejo.

Scorpion—More award-winning mezcals from Oaxaca. Instead of a worm, there's a scorpion in the bottle.

something too extreme. It's open Wednesday to Saturday from 10 pm to 6 am. ⊠ *Plaza Peninsula, 2nd fl., Zona Hotelera* ☎ *322/183–9777* ⊕ *barrabar.net.*

Blanco y Negro. Here's a wonderful place for a quiet drink. The intimate café-bar is comfortable yet rustic, with *equipale* (leather-and-wood) love seats and traditional round cocktail tables. At around 10:30, *trova* (think Mexican Cat Stevens) by Latino legends Silvio Rodríguez and Pablo Milanés begins; songs composed and sung by the owner liven up the atmosphere. There's never a cover. It opens after 8 pm every night but Sunday (closed Sunday and Monday in low season). ⊠ *Calle Lucerna at Calle Niza, behind Blockbuster Video store, Zona Hotelera* ☎ *322/293–2556.*

J&B Dance Club. People call it "Hota Bay" (it's how you pronounce the letters "j" and "b" in Spanish), and it's the best club in town for salsa. The crowd varies, but tends toward the thirties to forties age group and because J&B is serious about dancing, it feels young at heart. There's usually a band Friday and Saturday nights and DJs the rest of the week. Those with *dos patas zurdas* (two left feet) can attend salsa lessons Thursday and Friday 8 to 9 pm (50 pesos) or take tango lessons for the same price on Monday at 8 pm. The dance club's cover is about 110 pesos ($8) when there's live music, otherwise about 55 pesos ($4) and free on Monday and Tuesday. ⊠ *Bd. Francisco M. Ascencio 2043, Zona Hotelera* ☎ *322/224–4616* ⊕ *zamittizj8.wix.com/jbdancingclub.*

La Santa. The most recent addition to Puerto Vallarta's nightlife scene, and the trendiest club in town at the time of writing this review, has quickly become a favorite of locals and foreigners alike. It's a huge place with two different dance floors, one playing electronic and house music and the other mixing a variety of pop and rock in English and Spanish. There is a stylish swimming pool in the second room (where things can sometimes get a bit out of control). It has some great parties, but can get a bit too crowded at times. Ladies Night is on Thursday. ⊠ *Francisco Medina Ascencio 2468, at Fluvial Vallarta, Zona Hotelera* ☎ *322/150–5451.*

Fodor's Choice ★ **Strana.** This stylish nightclub seems to be a bit small, but it features an enormous dance floor. The lights and sound systems are state-of-the-art, which is highly appreciated by the world-famous DJs that come here to mix it up. They play mostly Electronic Dance Music (EDM), but, as the night goes on, you'll also hear some '80s and '90s pop-rock hits. The place attracts the hippest locals, and it's a must for visitors, nationals, and foreigners alike. It's open from Thursday to Saturday after 10 pm. ⊠ *Francisco Medina Ascencio 2125, Zona Hotelera* ☎ *322/224–7793* ⊕ *strana.mx.*

MUSIC ALFRESCO

The outdoor Los Arcos amphitheater has some sort of live entertainment almost every evening, and also in the afternoon on weekends. It's as likely to be mimes or magicians as musicians but it's always worth stopping by for the camaraderie with local people.

Xtine. The spectacular light shows here are set to bass-thumping music that ranges from techno and house to disco, rock, and Mexican pop. Most people (young boomers and Gen-Xers) come for the duration (it doesn't close until 6 am), as this is a classic in PV's nightlife scene. A favorite of locals, it's also filled with American and Canadian youngsters during the Spring Break season. Don't miss its new lounge bar, Xtine Garden. ✉ *Av. de las Aguilas s/n, Zona Hotelera* ☎ *322/105–8437.*

MOVIES

Cinemex Plaza Caracol. This easy-to-access movie theater is in the heart of the Hotel Zone, on the second floor at the south end of the Plaza Caracol mall. The latest movies are shown on its 10 screens. Tickets are around 50 pesos (less than $4), with a 25% Wednesday discount. ✉ *Plaza Caracol, Av. de los Tules 178, Zona Hotelera* ☎ *01800/710– 8888* ⊕ *cinemex.com.*

MARINA VALLARTA

BARS, PUBS, AND LOUNGES

El Faro. Here you can admire the bay and marina from atop a 110-foot lighthouse. It's mainly a baby-boomer crowd (think yachters) and open daily after 6 pm. During high season, especially on weekends, there's mellow music (including Mexican folk, or trova) after 10 pm. ✉ *Royal Pacific Yacht Club, Paseo de la Marina 245, Marina Vallarta* ☎ *322/221–0541.*

MOVIES

Cinemex Galerías Vallarta. Across from the cruise-ship pier in the Liverpool shopping complex is the newest of Puerto Vallarta's movie theaters. It has 10 screens and 55 peso ($4) tickets. The nearly PV-wide Wednesday discount of 25% means prohibitively large crowds at this particular theater; we suggest coming on a full-price day. ✉ *Galerías Vallarta, Bd. Francisco M. Ascencio 2920, L-234, Zona Hotelera* ☎ *01800/710– 8888* ⊕ *cinemex.com.*

NUEVO VALLARTA

BARS, PUBS, AND LOUNGES

Party Lounge Nuevo Vallarta. This may be the only proper nightclub in all Nuevo Vallarta. Inaugurated in 2014 after traditional motorbike-rock club Choppers closed its doors, Party Lounge Nuevo Vallarta offers pretty much the same as its sister property in downtown Vallarta, minus the liter drinks. You will hear hits from the '70s, '80s, and '90s, mixed up with contemporary rock and house music. Popular among young locals, it features a couple of dance floors and on selected nights they have live music. Cover varies depending on the night of the week and the season of the year, but usually it won't be more than about 135 pesos ($10). ✉ *Carretera a Tepic 995, Nuevo Vallarta* ☎ *322/157–4975.*

Puerto Fish Bar & Seafood. Locals, mostly in their 20s, frequent this small bar with a comfortable second floor equipped with sofas and a nice balcony. Lounge and house music fills the airwaves, and there are large TV screens all over the place showing every major sports event. Its kitchen is a bit more sophisticated than that of their competitors across the parking lot, with a wide menu offering seafood specialties and a few other snacks. It's open daily until 3 am. ⊠ *Av. Tepic Sur 1508, L-15 at Plaza Parabien, Nuevo Vallarta* ☎ *322/297–1462* ⊕ *www.puertofish.com.*

Wing's Army Nuevo Vallarta. This unpretentious place came to fill a bar void in Nuevo Vallarta. Large TV screens show every major sporting event, and the second floor has a pool table. The bar fills with young locals, especially on Thursday when there is live music (mostly rock). A variety of chicken wings and other snacks is available, along with a wide array of beers, both national and international. It's open daily from 1 pm to 3 am. ⊠ *Av. Tepic Sur 1508, L-2 at Plaza Parabien, Nuevo Vallarta* ☎ *322/297–4929.*

MOVIES

Cinepolis Lago Real. In the new shopping mall of Nuevo Vallarta, Cinepolis Lago Real is a modern, well-designed complex and also the cheapest option to catch a movie in the whole Banderas Bay region. On Wednesdays prices are even lower! ⊠ *Plaza Lago Real, Av. Tepic 430 Ote, Nuevo Vallarta* ☎ *322/297–6175.*

SPORTS AND
THE OUTDOORS

Updated
by Federico
Arrizabalaga

For the sheer variety of activities, Puerto Vallarta is one of the best adventure-vacation destinations on Mexico's Pacific coast. The water is warm and swimmable year-round, even downright bathlike July through November. The big blue bay attracts sea turtles, humpback whales, dolphins, and a growing number of snorkelers and divers. The fishing is excellent—from deep-sea angling for marlin and sailfish to trolling near shore for roosters and red snapper.

Banderas Bay and the beaches to the north and south have some surfable waves as well as plenty of calm bays and inlets for swimming and paddleboarding. Party boats and private yachts are great for accessing gorgeous and hard-to-reach beaches, primarily south of Vallarta along Cabo Corrientes.

The subtropical foothills are laced with streams and rivers that rush and tumble over rocks in the rainy season and dwindle but still impress at other times. Trails challenge mountain bikers and thrill dune-buggy and ATV aficionados. Many family-owned ranches have horse-riding tours at reasonable prices—lasting from an hour or two to overnight forays into the Sierra Madre.

Most of the well-established tour operators are in Puerto Vallarta. North and south of town, activities are often arranged through hotels, though there are companies springing up to meet an increasing demand. Operators generally provide transportation from strategic pickup points, usually in downtown Puerto Vallarta, Marina Vallarta, Nuevo Vallarta, and sometimes in Conchas Chinas. To save traveling from one end of the bay to the other, try to choose an outfitter near your neck of the woods.

MULTISPORT TOURS

Ecotours. A PV–based operator (with the main office at Marina Vallarta) whose offerings include hiking, diving, snorkeling, kayaking, bird-watching, whale-watching, and turtle tours. ⊠ *Proa 20, Marina Vallarta* ☎ *322/209-2195* ⊕ *www.ecotoursvallarta.com.*

Puerto Vallarta Tours. This company offers tours that are available from other area operators, but we recommend it for its all-in-one website, English-speaking operators and crew, and the convenience factor: through this one operator, you can book everything from canopy tours, ATVs, deep-sea fishing, and mountain biking to cruise tours, cultural tours, and bullfighting. ⊠ *Centro* ☎ *322/222–4935, 866/217–9704 toll-free in U.S., 866/464–6205 toll-free in Canada* ⊕ *www. puertovallartatours.net.*

Sociedad Cooperativa Corral del Risco. Local fishermen at Punta Mita (aka Punta de Mita) have formed this cooperative, which offers reasonably priced fishing trips, surfing, whale-watching excursions, diving and snorkeling outings. ⊠ *Riviera Nayarit, Punta Mita* ☎ *329/291–6298* ⊕ *www.puntamitacharters.com.*

Tours Soltero. Canadian expat Ray Calhoun and his wife Eva rent mountain bikes, snorkeling equipment, and boogie boards ($10 per day) and lead active tours from their base in San Patricio Melaque, a town next to Barra de Navidad south of PV. Typical excursions are snorkeling in Tenacatita with boogie boarding at Boca de Iguana, from 10 to 5 ($32), and a day trip to the state capital, Colima, which includes lunch and a stop at a typical hacienda-cum-museum ($60). ⊠ *South of Puerto Vallarta, San Patricio–Melaque* ☎ *315/355–6777* ✎ *raystoursmelaque@ yahoo.com.*

Fodor'sChoice ★ **Wildlife Connection.** Based in Puerto Vallarta's marina, this Mexican-owned company does what its name implies: it connects you with wildlife (specifically birds, turtles, dolphins, and whales) on seasonal trips. It also leads snorkeling and photography outings as well as cultural tours. Without a doubt the most popular tour is the one where you can swim with wild dolphins in the bay. Oh, and unlike in most other tours, most of these are led by real biologists. ⊠ *Paseo de la Marina Sur #214, Marina Vallarta* ☎ *322/225–3621, 322/227–1645* ⊕ *www. wildlifeconnection.com.*

CRUISES

Daytime bay cruises generally begin with a quick jaunt to Los Arcos Underwater Preserve, off Mismaloya Beach. There's about a half hour for snorkeling or swimming—sometimes with legions of little jellyfish in addition to the turtles that feed on them. Cruises then proceed to Yelapa, Quimixto, or Playa las Animas, or to Islas Marietas for whale-watching (in winter), snorkeling, swimming, and lunch. Horseback riding is usually available at an additional cost (about $15).

There are plenty of tours available; our list contains some of the most popular and professional.

LOGISTICS

Buy your ticket from licensed vendors along the boardwalk at Los Muertos Beach, online, or through area tour operators. Prices are fluid; like car salespeople, the ticket sellers give discounts or jack up the price as the market allows. Full-day booze cruises cost about $40–$55 per person, including open bar, Continental breakfast, snacks, and snorkeling and/or kayaks. Three-hour sunset cruises with access to an open bar cost about $85 per person. Dinner cruises start at $85.

OUTFITTERS

Boana Hot Springs. Boana Hot Springs offers a twice-weekly romantic hot-spring tour ($75). Included are transportation, a candlelit dinner, and open bar. In high season tours operate Tuesday and Friday, leaving at 4:45 pm and returning to PV at midnight. To hold a spot, make a deposit in person at Boana's office in Boana Torre Malibu, behind Blue Chairs on Highway 200 just south of the Romantic Zone. ⊠ *Boana Torre Malibu Condo-Hotel, Calle Amapas 325, Col. E. Zapata, Zona Romántica* ☎ *322/222–0999* ⊕ *www.boana.net.*

Diana's Gay Cruise. Diana's Gay Cruise is a booze-and-beach cruise (Thursdays and most Fridays in high season) popular with lesbians and gays. Straights are also welcome, but minors are not. Go for the swimming, snorkeling, and lunch on the beach at Las Animas or another area beach, or for the unlimited national-brand beers and mixed drinks. Most of the time is spent on the boat. It's easiest to reserve tickets ($80) online using PayPal. Private tours are also available. ☎ *322/222–1510 in PV, 866/514–7969 in U.S. for reservations* ⊕ *www.dianastours.com.*

FAMILY **Marigalante.** A true sailing vessel that has circumnavigated the world more than once, the *Marigalante* has a pirate crew that keeps things hopping for kids and teens with games, snorkeling, kayaking, or banana-boat rides during a seven-hour day cruise. The five-hour dinner cruise, with open bar, snacks, and pre-Hispanic show, is for adults only and has some bawdy pirate humor. Women who don't want to be "kidnapped" may prefer the day cruise or another operator. Both tours cost $85 for adults and about half that for kids under 12. Buy tickets online at a discount or from licensed vendors in town. The boat embarks from Terminal Marítima, across from Sam's Club on Boulevard Francisco M. Ascencio, in Marina Vallarta. ⊠ *Av. Politecnico Nacional 78 Int 304, Marina Vallarta* ☎ *322/223–0309, 322/223–0875, 866/915–0361 from the U.S., 866/954–5984 from Canada* ⊕ *www.barcopiratavallarta.com.*

LAND SPORTS

ATV AND DUNE-BUGGY TOURS

Increasingly, ATV, dune buggy, and jeep tours are heading for the hills around Puerto Vallarta. Most rides are to small communities, ranches, and rivers north, south, and east of town. Sharing a vehicle with a partner means significant savings.

Stereotypical "tourist" activity? Maybe. But riding an ATV down a beach is a good way to see more of the area than walking allows, and it's some serious fun.

LOGISTICS

You need a valid driver's license and a major credit card. Wear lightweight long pants, sturdy shoes, a bandanna (some operators provide one as a keepsake), and/or tight-fitting hat, sunglasses, and both sunscreen and mosquito repellent. In rainy season (July–October) it's hot and wet—ideal for splashing through puddles and streams; the rest of the year is cooler and dustier. In either season, prepare to get dirty. Three- to four-hour tours run $80–$120; full-day trips to San Sebastián cost about $165 for one rider or $175 for two.

■TIP→ **If you plan to gulp rather than sip on a tequila-tasting tour, please strongly consider riding two per ATV and designating one person as the day's driver.** Doubling up is usually also the bargain rental option.

OUTFITTERS

Adventure ATV Jungle Treks. This company leads daily ATV tours ($75 to $165) that head into the hills behind Vallarta, Sayulita or beyond. Those that stop at Rancho Las Pilas include a brief tequila-making tour and tasting, but lunch there is optional and not included in the price. A four-hour tour combines this ATV trek with a canopy tour through River Canopy, along the Cuale River ($135 for one rider, $190 for two). Dune buggies and Polaris RZR tours are also available, and now there is also a convenient branch in Bucerías if you're based in Nuevo Vallarta or Bucerías itself. ⊠ *Calle Basilio Badillo 400, Zona Romántica* ☎ *322/222–8944* ⊕ *www.wildtreksadventures.com.*

BIRD WATCHING

Although there aren't many dedicated birding operators here, this region is perfect for the pastime. Vallarta has more than 350 species in a wide variety of habitats, including shoreline, rivers, marshes, lagoons, mangroves, and tropical and evergreen forests. In the mangroves, standouts are the great blue heron, mangrove cuckoo, and vireo. Ocean and shorebirds include brown and blue-footed boobies and red-billed tropic birds. Military macaws patrol the thorn forests, and songbirds of all stripes serenade the pine-oak forests at higher elevations.

LOGISTICS

Most people come on trips through birding clubs or organizations or hire a private birding guide. Outfitters charge $50–$60 for half-day tours and $100–$125 for full-day tours.

OUTFITTERS

Wings. A Tucson, Arizona–based operator leads at least one weeklong tour each year to the mangroves and tropical forest around San Blas, Jalisco, and Colima. ☎ 520/320–9868, 888/293–6443 in U.S. and Canada ⊕ www.wingsbirds.com.

CANOPY TOURS

Canopy tours are high-octane thrill rides during which you "fly" from treetop to treetop, securely fastened to a zip line. Despite the inherent danger of dangling from a cable hundreds of feet off the ground, the operators we list have excellent safety records. If you're brave, bring your camera to take photos while zipping along; just be sure the neck strap is long enough to leave your hands free (some tours may not allow photography because they provide their own photos—at a price).

LOGISTICS

Check with each operator regarding maximum weight (usually 250 pounds) and minimum ages for kids. ■TIP➔ Don't take a tour when rain threatens. A thunderstorm isn't the time to hang out near trees attached to metal cables, and rain makes the activity scary to say the least. During the rainy season, you can usually count on generally sunny weather in the mornings and *early* afternoons.

OUTFITTERS

Canopy El Edén. The daily trips to the spirited Mismaloya River and an adjacent restaurant are 3½-hour adventures ($81) that depart from the downtown office. You zip along 10 lines through the trees and above the river. To take full advantage of the lovely setting and good restaurant, take the first tour (departures are weekdays at 9, 10, 11, noon, 1:30, and 2:30—sometimes less frequently in low season), and bring your swimsuit. The schedule includes about an hour to spend at the river, spa, or restaurant. If you wish to stay longer and there's room, you can return to Vallarta with a later group; otherwise take a taxi or ask the restaurant staff for a lift to the highway, where buses frequently pass. ⊠ Office: Plaza Romy, Calle I. Vallarta 228, Interior 1, Zona Romántica ☎ 322/222–2516 ⊕ www.puertovallartatours.net/el-eden-canopy-tour.htm.

Both the young and the young at heart can zip through the nearby jungle on a tour with Canopy El Edén.

Canopy Tour de Los Veranos. Los Veranos was the first canopy tour company to establish itself here and has extended the number of services it offers, now including ATV and city tours as combos. After the descent you may want to enjoy its restaurant, sip some tequila or go on a fantastic nature hike. Canopy tours start at $67 (web) and the post-tour trek along Freddy's trail is free. ⊠ *Office: Calle Francisca Rodríguez 336, Zona Romántica* ☎ *322/223–0504, 619/955–6993 from U.S., 877/563–4113 toll-free in U.S. and Canada* ⊕ *www.canopytours-vallarta.com.*

Rancho Mi Chaparrita. On his family ranch, Luis Verdin runs a 13-zip-line tour ($79) and horseback-riding trips ($30 per hour), or combine the two, accessing the ranch on Señor Verdin's lively, healthy horses via the beach and backcountry for a complete adventure ($100). The company rents boogie boards, surfboards, and paddleboards, gives surfing lessons, offers snorkeling, sportfishing and whale- or wildlife-watching excursions around the Marietas Islands. ⊠ *Manuel Rodriguez Sanchez 14, Riviera Nayarit, Sayulita* ☎ *329/291–3112* ⊕ *www.michaparrita.com.*

Fodor's Choice
★

Vallarta Adventures. Possibly Vallarta's most famous and popular adventure tour operator, Vallarta Adventures has something exciting for everyone: adrenaline-pumping canopy tours in the jungle, spectacular whale-watching in winter, romantic sunset sailing tours for adults, themed dinner shows for families, and many more. Safety is taken very seriously, and all tours are guided in English and Spanish (when necessary) by a very friendly and entertaining staff. ⊠ *Av. Las Palmas, 39, Nuevo Vallarta* ☎ *322/297–1212 in Nuevo Vallarta, 322/221–1477*

The Puerto Vallarta area has some of the best golf options in Mexico, like the beautiful course at the Four Seasons Punta Mita.

in Marina Vallarta, 888/526–2238 from U.S. and Canada ⊕ www. vallarta-adventures.com.

GOLF

"Not a bad mango in the bunch" is how one golf aficionado described Puerto Vallarta's courses. From the two courses at Four Seasons Punta Mita (prohibitively expensive for those not staying at the hotel) to the Gran Bay at Barra de Navidad, the region is a close second to Los Cabos in variety of play at a range of prices. Well-known designers are represented, including Jack Nicklaus and Tim Weiskopf.

LOGISTICS

Most of these courses offer first-class services including driving ranges and putting greens, lessons, clinics, pro shops, and clubhouses.

COURSES

PUERTO VALLARTA

Marina Vallarta. Joe Finger designed this 18-hole course; the $135 greens fee includes practice balls, tax, and a shared cart. It's the area's second-oldest course and is closest and most convenient for golfers staying in the Hotel Zone, downtown Puerto Vallarta, and Marina Vallarta. Although it's very flat, it's far more challenging than it looks, with lots of water hazards. Speaking of hazards, the alligators have a way of blending into the scenery. They might surprise you, but they supposedly don't bite. Go to the course's website to find hotels participating in their "Stay and Play" golf packages. ⊠ *Paseo de la Marina s/n, Marina*

Vallarta ☎ *322/221–0545, 322/221–0073* ⊕ *www.clubcorp.com/Clubs/ Marina-Vallarta-Club-de-Golf.*

Vista Vallarta. Some of the best views in the area belong to the aptly named Vista Vallarta. There are 18 holes designed by Jack Nicklaus and another 18 by Tom Weiskopf. The greens fee for the course, which is a few miles northwest of the Marina Vallarta area, is $204. A shared cart and tax are included. ⊠ *Circuito Universidad 653, Centro* ☎ *322/290– 0030* ⊕ *www.vistavallartagolf.com.*

NUEVO VALLARTA TO BUCERÍAS

El Tigre. This 18-hole course with 12 water features is at the Paradise Village hotel and condo complex. The greens fee of $180 includes a shared cart, bottled water, practice balls, and cold towels. After 2 pm it's $116. Don't be surprised if you see a guy driving around with tiger cubs in his truck: the course's namesake animals, tigers, are a passion of the club's director, Phil Woodrum. ⊠ *Paseo las Garzas, Nuevo Vallarta* ☎ *322/226–8190, 866/843–5951 from U.S., 800/214–7758 from Canada* ⊕ *www.eltigregolf.com.*

Four Seasons Punta Mita. Nonguests are permitted to play the 195-acre, par-72, Jack Nicklaus–designed Pacífico course; however, they must pay the hotel's day use fee of 50% of the room rate (approximately $300 plus 28% tax and service charge), which covers use of a guest room and hotel facilities until dark. Reservations are essential. The greens fee is $240, including tax and the golf cart. The club's claim to fame is that it has perhaps the only natural island green in golf. Drive your cart to it at low tide; otherwise hop aboard a special amphibious vessel (weather permitting) to cross the water. There are seven other oceanfront links. Opened in 2009, the Bahía is another stunning 18-hole course. It has more undulating fairways and greens than the first course, but similarly spectacular ocean views—and a high price tag. ⊠ *Punta Mita* ☎ *329/291–6000* ⊕ *www.fourseasons.com/es/puntamita/golf.*

Los Flamingos Country Club. Designed by Percy Clifford in 1978, PV's original course has been totally renovated. The 18-hole course in Los Flamingos development, at the northern extremity of Nuevo Vallarta, has new irrigation and sprinkler systems to maintain the rejuvenated greens. The high-season greens fee is $149, including a shared cart, tax, a bottle of water, and a bucket of balls. ⊠ *Carretera 200, Km 145, 12 km (8 miles) north of airportNuevo Vallarta* ☎ *329/296–5006* ⊕ *www. flamingosgolf.com.mx.*

Nayar Golf Course at Mayan Palace. This par 70, nearly 7,000-yard course is a natural and technical masterpiece. The course features conditions to fit every player, and was recently redesigned by the celebrated group Nicklaus Design. It's challenging because of the constant, strong crosswinds coming off the ocean. Spotting iguanas is part of the fun and you can keep an eye on the crocodiles sunning in a neighboring sanctuary. The full 18-hole course runs $195. The fee includes cart rental, taxes, use of the practice range, and return transportation to your hotel. Twilight fees (after 1 pm) cost $145. ⊠ *Paseo de las Moras s/n, Fracc. Náutico Turístico, Nuevo Vallarta* ☎ *322/226–4000* ⊕ *www. vidantagolf.com/nuevo-vallarta.*

COSTALEGRE

El Tamarindo. About two hours south of Vallarta on the Costalegre is one of the area's best courses. At least six of the holes play along the ocean; some are cliff-side holes with fabulous views, while others go right down to the beach. On a slow day, golfers are encouraged at tee time to have a swim or a picnic on the beach during their round, or to play a hole a second time if they wish. Designed by David Fleming, the breathtaking course is the playground of birds, deer, and other wildlife. It's an awesome feeling to nail the course's most challenging hole, the 9th: a par 3 with a small green surrounded by bunkers. The greens fee is $240, including cart and tax. Resort guests get priority for tee times; call up to a week ahead to check availability. ⊠ *Carretera Melaque–Puerto Vallarta, Carretera 200, Km 7.5, Costalegre, Cihuatlán* ☎ *315/351–5032* .

HIKING

The coastal fringe and the hills behind Vallarta—with streams and rivers heading down from the mountains—are beautiful areas for exploring, but few tour operators have hiking and walking trips. If you plan an impromptu exploration, it's best to take along a local familiar with the area.

LOGISTICS

Some of the biking tour operators *(⇨ Mountain Biking, above)* will lead hiking outings as well, if you ask.

OUTFITTERS

Ecotours. The three-hour hike around El Nogalito River ($60) includes a pit stop at a rocky, waterfall-fed pool for a dip. En route you'll see a small number of birds, butterflies, and tropical plants. ⊠ *Ignacio L. Vallarta 243, Zona Romántica* ☎ *322/223–3130, 322/222–6606* ⊕ *www. ecotoursvallarta.com.*

HORSEBACK RIDING

Most of the horseback-riding outfits are based on family ranches in the foothill towns of the Sierra Madre, such as Las Palmas. Horses are permitted on the beach in smaller towns like Sayulita and San Francisco, but not in Vallarta proper, so expect to ride into the hills.

LOGISTICS

Outfitters pick you up either from the hotel or strategic locations north and south of town and return you to your hotel or to the pickup point. Short rides depart morning and afternoon, while longer rides are generally in the morning only, at least in winter, when the sun sets earlier.

Ask at the beachfront restaurants of tiny towns like Yelapa, Quimixto, and Las Animas, south of PV, to hook up with horses for treks into the jungle. Horses are generally well cared for; some are exceptionally fit and frolicky.

Cabalgatas, or horseback rides, are a wonderful way to get out into the countryside. These visitors are touring with guide company Rancho El Charro.

OUTFITTERS

Boana Tours. Three-hour, $45 horseback adventures with Boana Tours include one-way transportation to a ranch outside the city, a little more than an hour on a horse, a snack, and two drinks. You can take a swim in the river before returning on your own to PV. Daily tours at 9:15 am and 2:15 pm. ⊠ *Torre Malibu, Carretera a Mismaloya, Zona Romántica* ☎ *322/222–0999* ⊕ *www.boana.net.*

Club de Polo Costa Careyes. Though the trail rides here are expensive at $100 for 45 minutes, you know you're getting an exceptional mount. Trips leave in early morning or around sunset. ⊠ *Carretera 200, Km 53.5, Carretera a Barra de Navidad, Careyes* ☎ *315/351–0320.*

Rancho El Charro. Rancho Charro provides transportation to and from your hotel for rides to rivers and waterfalls. Choices include three-hour ($62), five-hour ($82), and all-day rides ($120). There are two different trails for average or experienced riders. ⊠ *Calle Vicente Guerrero 99, Centro* ☎ *322/224–0114* ⊕ *www.ranchoelcharro.com.*

Rancho Manolo. The friendly folks at this family-owned property take you into the mountains they know so well. The usual tour is to El Edén, the restaurant-and-river property where the movie *Predator* was filmed. The three-hour trip includes about an hour each way on horseback, with an additional hour for a meal, which is not included, or for splashing in the river. The cost is just $30—definitely a good deal. ⊠ *Carretera 200, Km 12, at Mismaloya Bridge, South of Puerto Vallarta* ☎ *322/228–0018.*

MOUNTAIN BIKING

Although the tropical climate makes it hot for biking, the Puerto Vallarta area is lovely and has challenging and varied terrain. Aim for the relatively cooler months of November through mid-April. A few operators lead rides up river valleys to Yelapa and from the old mining town of San Sebastián (reached via plane; included in price), high in the Sierra, back to Vallarta. It's about 45 km (28 miles) of twisty downhill. Should this be too tough you may want to rent a bike and participate on the Wednesday night rides instead, when the main road is closed to cars and even full families can enjoy the cooler night safely.

In the rainy season, showers are mainly in the late afternoon and evening, so bike tours can take place year-round. In summer and fall rivers and waterfalls are voluptuous and breathtaking. A popular ending point for rides into the foothills, they offer a place to rest, rinse off (there's lots of mud), and have a snack or meal. In dry season, it's relatively cooler and less humid. The very best months for biking are December through February: the weather is coolest, and the vegetation, rivers, and waterfalls are still reasonably lush after the end of the rainy season in October.

LOGISTICS

Four- to five-hour rides average $35 to $45; trips to Yelapa cost $110 and up. The ride down from San Sebastián goes for around $150. Rides of more than a half-day include lunch, and all include helmets, gloves, and bikes.

OUTFITTERS

Eco Ride. A few streets behind Vallarta's cathedral, Eco Ride caters to intermediate and expert cyclists. Most rides start at the shop and go up the Río Cuale, passing some hamlets along single tracks and dirt roads. A few rides include time at local swimming holes; the Yelapa ride ($115) starts in El Tuito, about an hour south of PV (you get there by vehicle), and enjoys some magnificent scenery—with two 10-km (6-mile) uphills and a 20-km (12-mile) downhill—and returns by boat after lunch on the beach. If cycling is not your thing, no worries: they now also offer hiking tours. ⊠ *Calle Miramar 382, Centro* ☎ *322/222–7912* ⊕ *www. ecoridemex.com.*

SKYDIVING

Skydiving is an excellent adrenaline-pumping activity in Puerto Vallarta that is available for both new and experienced divers. There are beautiful aerial views from the plane, but the best part of the experience is landing on the gorgeous sands of the Nuevo Vallarta beaches.

Skydive Vallarta. During the winter season particularly, but also year-round, you'll frequently see skydivers landing at the beach in Nuevo Vallarta. Thrill-seekers at Skydive Vallarta will take off at the airport in Puerto Vallarta and fly for about 25 minutes before jumping in tandem at around 9,000 ft, with three jumping schedules to choose from. ⊠ *Calle Mirlo 109 Int2, Zona Hotelera* ☎ *322/189–3909* ⊕ *skydivevallarta.mx.*

TURTLE-WATCHING AND REPATRIATION

Mexico has seven of the world's eight sea-turtle species. Three of those species live in and around Banderas Bay. The fastest growing and earliest to mature of the Pacific Coast turtles are the olive ridley, or *golfina*, which are more numerous than the Careyes and the even less frequently sighted leatherback. Researchers estimate there are 1 to 10 leatherbacks for every 1,000 olive ridleys in the Puerto Vallarta area.

After the female turtle creates a nest in the sand, the eggs incubate for approximately 60 days. The babies must bust out of eggs and earth on their own, and with luck they will head for the ocean under cover of night. Birds, crabs, and other wild animals are relentless predators. For every 1,000 baby turtles born, only 1 survives to adulthood. Fortunately the average nest holds several hundred eggs.

LOGISTICS

Tours run from summer through late fall. Wear shoes or sandals that are comfortable for walking in the sand. Bring a sweatshirt or light jacket, and plan to stay out late in the evening for most turtle repatriation programs, as that's when predators are less active. Most tours cost $46–$50 per person, last three to four hours, and combine educational programs with hands-on activities; for a quicker and cheaper hands-on experience, contact the Marriott Hotel in Puerto Vallarta, which offers free turtle release experiences during the season.

OUTFITTERS

Ecotours. Three-hour turtle tours August through mid-December cost $48. Depending on the time of year, you may walk the beach searching for females depositing their eggs in the sand and help remove these eggs for safekeeping. Whether or not you find egg-laying females, there are always little turtles for releasing to the wild at the end of the evening. Tours are Monday through Saturday. ⊠ *Ignacio L. Vallarta 243, Zona Romántica* ☎ *322/223–3130, 322/222–6606* ⊕ *www.ecotoursvallarta.com.*

WATER SPORTS

DOLPHIN ENCOUNTERS

Many folks find the idea of captive dolphins disturbing; others cherish the opportunity to interact with these intelligent creatures that communicate through body language as well as an audible code we humans have yet to decipher. Decide whether you support the idea of captive-dolphin encounters, and act accordingly. Listed below are operators with captive dolphin programs as well as one that has an open-ocean encounter. As these gregarious mammals are fond of bow-surfing, many bay-tripping boats will encounter dolphins as they motor along, providing more opportunities to see dolphins as well as leaping manta rays and other sea life.

LOGISTICS

Dolphins are abundant in the bay year-round, though not 24/7. Dolphin encounters limit the number of humans per encounter and usually allow just two visits a day. Call before you arrive or early in your stay to book.

OUTFITTERS

FAMILY **Aquaventuras Park.** Kids can plummet down one of 10 enormous waterslides, play on playground equipment, and indulge in junk food at the obligatory snack shops while their parents swim or relax around the pool. On the property are the dolphin and sea-lion discovery adventures. ✉ *Carretera a Tepic, Km 155, Nuevo Vallarta* ☎ *322/297–0724* ⚑ *$18* ☿ *Tues.– Sun. 10–5.*

Dolphin and Sea Lion Discovery. For both the Dolphin Encounter ($79)

ART ADVENTURE

The owners of **Galeria Arte 550** (⇨ *Chapter 8;* ☎ *322/222-7365* ⊕ *www.yourcreativeawakening. com*) offer unique tours combining art and adventure. Visits to the mountains and the botanical gardens, whale-watching trips, or other activities provide a springboard for journal drawing and artistic expression in clay, tile-decorating, or other media. Students can arrange their own accommodations or book a package at the new B&B **House of Wind and Water** (⇨ *Chapter 6*): lovely lodgings in a neighborhood most tourists never see, along the Cuale River on the east side of Highway 200.

and the Dolphin Swim ($99) at Dolphin Discovery in the Sea Life Park you spend about 30 of the 45-minute experience in the water interacting with dolphins. In the Royal Dolphin Swim ($149), you still get only 30 minutes in the pool, but, with a higher ratio of cetaceans to humans, you get more face time. It's an expensive outing, and the memento photos really jack up the price (you're not allowed to take your own snaps, and they photograph each family member individually). To get the most bang for your buck, plan to spend the day at the water park. The entrance fee of $18/$14 for adults/kids to Aquaventuras Park is included with the dolphin program. ✉ *Aquaventuras Park, Carretera a Tepic, Km 155, Nuevo Vallarta* ☎ *322/297–0724, 866/393–5158 in U.S., 866/793–1905 in Canada* ⊕ *www.aquaventuras.com.*

Wildlife Connection. This Mexican-owned company uses two-motor skiffs equipped with listening equipment to find pods of dolphins in the wild blue sea. You can then jump in the water to swim with these beautiful creatures in their own environment. The most common destination is around the Marietas Islands. The cost is $76 per person for a three- to four-hour tour; tours are conducted April through December only. There's no guarantee, however, that the dolphins will stick around for the fun. There's also a combined tour ($80 per person) searching for both whales and dolphins between December and March only. ✉ *Calle Francia 140, Dpto. 7, Marina Vallarta* ☎ *322/225–3621.*

Participating in a turtle-hatching tour (held from summer to late fall) will likely put you face to face with the adorable Lepidochelys olivacea, or olive ridley turtle, the smallest sea turtle species in the world.

FISHING

Sportfishing is excellent off Puerto Vallarta, and fisherfolk have landed monster marlin well over 500 pounds. Surf-casting from shore nets snook, roosters, and jack crevalles. Hire a *panga* (skiff) to hunt for Spanish mackerel, sea bass, amberjack, snapper, bonito, and rooster-fish on full- or half-day trips within the bay. Pangas can be hired in the traditional fishing villages of Mismaloya and Boca de Tomatlán, just south of town; in the Costalegre towns of La Manzanilla and Barra de Navidad; and in the north, at El Anclote and Nuevo Corral del Risco, Punta Mita.

Yachts are best for big-game fishing: yellowfin tuna; blue, striped, and black marlin; and dorado. Hire them for four to ten hours, or over-night. Catch-and-release of billfish is encouraged. If you don't want to charter a boat, you can also join a party boat. Most sport-fishing yachts are based at Marina Vallarta; only a few call the marina at Paradise Village, in Nuevo Vallarta, home. The resort hotels of Costalegre and Punta Mita arrange fishing excursions for their guests. Bass fishing at Cajón de Peña, about 1½ hours south of Vallarta, nets 10-pounders on a good day.

LOGISTICS

Most captains and crews are thoroughly bilingual, at least when it comes to boating and fishing.

DID YOU KNOW?

Many travelers choose to skip captive dolphin swims due to the practice's ethical implications. In Puerto Vallarta, alternative options include wild dolphin swims and boat-based dolphin-watching tours—low impact on the dolphins and high impact on the participant.

LICENSES

Licenses are required; however, a new set of regulations requires anglers to buy their fishing licenses ahead of time via a confusing online bank-deposit system. Since boat owners are the ones (heavily) fined if there are unlicensed anglers aboard, you can leave it to the captain to make the necessary arrangements.

PRICES

Prices generally hover around $600–$650 for six hours, $600–$800 for eight hours, and $1,000–$1,200 for a 10-hour trip. A longer trip is recommended for chasing the big guys, as you can go to prime fishing grounds like El Banco and Corbeteña. Pangas usually accommodate up to six clients and yachts hold four to ten people. Party boats start at $140 per person for an eight-hour day. Drinking water is generally included in the price. Box lunches and beer or soda may be sold separately or included; sometimes it's BYOB. Pangas and superpangas, the latter with shade and a head of some sort, charge $200–$300 for four hours. You'll obviously save lots of money by going with the local guys in their often fast, but not luxurious, pangas.

> **CAUTION**
>
> Several organizations, including Greenpeace, the Humane Society (U.S.), and the Whale and Dolphin Conservation Society, have spoken out against captive dolphin encounters, asserting that some water parks get dolphins from restricted areas and that the confined conditions at some parks put the dolphins' health at risk. Consider putting the $100-plus fee toward a snorkeling, whale-watching, or noncaptive dolphin encounter, where you can see marine life in its natural environment.

OUTFITTERS

CharterDreams. Although most fisherfolk choose to leave around dawn, you set your own itinerary with this company. Excursions range from trips with one to three people for bass fishing to cruises with up to 12 people aboard luxury yachts. CharterDreams also offers whale-watching and private sailing, sightseeing, or snorkeling tours. ✉ *Marina Las Palmas II, Locales 1, Marina Vallarta* ☎ *322/221–0690* ⊕ *www.charterdreams.com.*

Fishing with Carolina. This Canadian expat has been sending out anglers for 25 years. Fishing tours last 4 to 8 hours and they recently upgraded their boat to a newer and better 30-ft powerboat. Whale-watching and snorkeling tours are also available. ✉ *Terminal Marítima, Los Peines Pier, Marina Vallarta* ☎ *322/109–4094* ⊕ *www.fishingwith carolina.com.*

Gerardo Kosonoy. For fishing excursions in and around Barra de Navidad, at the southern end of the Costalegre, contact Sr. Kosonoy. He speaks excellent English and has low hourly rates. Alternatively, you can round up another fisherman with a panga from one of the two large fishing co-ops on the lagoon side of town. There's usually at least one representative hoping for clients at the water-taxi dock. Gerardo and his compadres charge 500 pesos (just shy of $30 at this writing) per hour for one to four passengers or 3,000 pesos for 7 hours. There's a three-hour minimum. For fishing close to the shore, the price can be split among up to six anglers. ⊠ *Barra de Navidad* ☎ *315/355–5739, 315/354–2251 cell* ✆ *hakunakosonoy@yahoo.com.*

Mismaloya Divers. Do you remember the seductive-looking divers in *Night of the Iguana?* Well, their progeny might be among the local staffers at this outfitting company. Panga trips here go for $200 for four hours, a bit more for longer trips, and can include anything from whale-watching to fishing to night-diving. ⊠ *Av Paseo del Rio 125, Mismaloya* ☎ *322/228–0020* ⊕ *www.mismaloyadivers.blogspot. com.*

Vallarta Tour and Travel. Captain Peter Vines can accommodate eight fisherfolk with top-of-the-line equipment, including the latest electronics, sonar, radar, and two radios. Rates are reasonable (four hours $400, six hours $500, eight hours $600, 12 hours $800). Transportation from your hotel is included in the full-day bass-fishing expedition to Cajón de Peña; clients should call a couple weeks ahead to schedule this trip to make sure the bass are running. ⊠ *Marina Las Palmas II, Local 4, in front of Dock B, Marina Vallarta* ☎ *322/294–6240 cell, 877/301–2058 from U.S. and Canada.*

SEASONAL CATCHES

Sailfish and dorado are abundant practically year-round (though dorado drop out a bit in early summer and sailfish dip slightly in spring).

Winter: bonito, dorado, jack crevalle, sailfish, striped marlin, wahoo

Spring: amberjack, jack crevalle, grouper, mackerel, red snapper

Summer: grouper, roosterfish, yellowfin tuna

Fall: black marlin, blue marlin, sailfish, striped marlin, yellowfin tuna, wahoo

KAYAKING

Except on calm, glassy days, the open ocean is really too rough for enjoyable kayaking unless you're based in the southern end of the bay, and the few kayaking outfitters there mainly offer this activity in combination with snorkeling, dolphin-watching, or boating excursions to area beaches. The best places for kayaking-and-birding combos are the mangroves, estuaries, large bays, and islands off the Costalegre coast, south of Puerto Vallarta.

LOGISTICS

Many of the larger beachfront hotels rent or loan sea kayaks to their guests. Double kayaks are easier on the arms than single kayaks. Since the wind usually picks up in the afternoon, morning is generally the best time to paddle. Stick to coves if you want to avoid energy-draining chop and big waves. Kayaks range from $10 to $15 an hour or $27 to $35 per day. All-inclusive hotels like Dreams, just south of Puerto Vallarta, usually don't charge their guests for kayaks.

ANNUAL SPORTING EVENTS

MARCH

Banderas Bay Regatta. The winter season brings foreign vessels and lots of racing and boating activities, including the five-day Banderas Bay Regatta that usually takes place in March. There are cocktail parties, charity events, receptions, seminars, additional races, and boat parades as well as competitive races among boats designed for coastal and offshore cruising. ✉ *Marina Vallarta* ☎ *322/297–2222* ⊕ *www. banderasbayregatta.com.*

MAY

International Sports Classic. The seven-day Annual Sports Classic that takes place in May invites amateurs, pros, and semipros to compete in basketball, soccer, and bowling; some years they also offer events in tennis and beach volleyball. Most events take place at the Agustín Flores Contreras Stadium, Los Arcos Amphitheater, or the beach in front of the Holiday Inn. ✉ *Zona Hotelera* ☎ *322/226–0404 [Veronica Alarcon at Sheraton Buganvilias]* ⊕ *www. puertovallarta.net/sportsclassic/ index.php.*

NOVEMBER

International Puerto Vallarta Marlin & Sailfish Tournament. The International Puerto Vallarta Marlin & Sailfish Tournament celebrated its 59th anniversary in 2014. The entry fee is nearly $4,000 per boat (up to four fishermen), but the prizes and prestige of winning are great. Categories are dorado (mahimahi), tuna, marlin, and sailfish—the last one is catch-and-release. ✉ *Marina Vallarta* ☎ *322/225–5467* ⊕ *www. fishvallarta.com.*

Puerto Vallarta International Half Marathon. The Puerto Vallarta International Half Marathon, held in mid-November, gets bigger each year. There's a 5K run, too, and a big pasta dinner on the beach the day before the race. ✉ *12 de Octubre 688-A, Centro* ☎ *322/299–1839* ⊕ *www.maratonvallarta.com.*

7

SAILING

Although large Bahía de Banderas and towns to the north and south have lots of beautiful beaches to explore and wildlife to see, there are few sailing adventures for the public. Most boating companies don't want to rely on the wind to get to area beaches for the day's activities.

LOGISTICS

For insurance reasons, companies or individuals here don't rent bareboat (uncrewed) yachts even to seasoned sailors. Those who want to crew the ship themselves can do semi-bareboat charters, where the captain comes along but allows the clients to sail the boat.

SCUBA DIVING AND SNORKELING

The Pacific waters here aren't nearly as clear as those in the Caribbean, but they are warm and nutrient-rich, which means they attract a variety of sea creatures. Many of the resorts rent or loan snorkeling equipment and have introductory dive courses at their pools.

The underwater preserve surrounding Los Arcos, a rock formation off Playa Mismaloya, is a popular spot for diving and snorkeling. The rocky bay at Quimixto, about 32 km (20 miles) south of PV and accessible only by boat, is a good snorkeling spot. *Pangeros* based in Boca, Mismaloya, Yelapa, and elsewhere can take you to spots off the tourist trail.

On the north side, Punta Mita has the Marietas Islands, with lava tubes and caves and at least 10 good places to snorkel and dive, including spots for advanced divers. El Morro Islands, with their big fish lurking in the underwater pinnacles and caves, are also suitable for experienced divers.

LOGISTICS

Although it's fine all year long, winter is the very best time for snorkeling and diving. You can spot gigantic manta rays, several species of eel and sea turtles, and many species of colorful fish. During the rainy summer months, while the water is at its warmest, visibility is not the best because of runoff from the rivers. In winter's colder conditions, some luck will yield orca and humpback-whale sightings.

OUTFITTERS

Chico's Dive Shop. This shop arranges PADI or NAUI certification, equipment rentals, and one- or two-tank dives. Trips to Los Arcos accommodate snorkelers ($40 per person) as well as those who want a one- or two-tank dive ($70 and $79, respectively). Book several days ahead for a night dive ($60 for one tank). You can also book tours with Vallarta Adventures from them. ⊠ *Paseo Díaz Ordáz 772, Centro* ☎ *322/222–1895, 805/617–0121* ⊕ *www.chicos-diveshop.com.*

Vallarta Undersea. This operation offers PADI dive courses; runs dive trips; and sells, rents, and repairs dive equipment. On Monday, Wednesday, Friday and Sunday tours are to Los Arcos National Park and another dive spot to Majahuitas, Colomitos or Mismaloya. Tuesday, Thursday and Saturday they visit Marietas Island National Park. Rates are $125 for certified divers, and snorkelers can tag along for $69. ⊠ *Calle Proa, Local 22, Marina Vallarta* ☎ *322/209–0025, 956/287–3832* ⊕ *www.vallartaundersea.com.*

SURFING

The main surfing areas are in the north, in Nayarit State, and include Sayulita and Punta Mita, where there are nearly a dozen offshore breaks for intermediate and advanced surfers, some best accessed by boat. The best spots for beginners are shore breaks like those at El Anclote and Sayulita; in the south, Barra de Navidad is also appropriate for beginners.

LOGISTICS

SEASONS

Waves are largest and most consistent between June and December; the water is also warmest during the rainy season (late June–October), averaging nearly 80°F (27°C) July through September.

Surf quality in Puerto Vallarta ranges from beginner-friendly to challenging.

PRICES

Surfboard rentals start at $4 an hour or $18 a day. Surfing trips run around $45 per hour, usually with a three- or four-hour minimum. Shops sell rash guards (you usually don't need a full wet suit here), boogie boards, wax, and other necessities. For good info and links, check out ⊕ *www.surf-mexico.com.*

OUTFITTERS

Accion Tropical. All surfers in the area know that the best waves are found in the beaches of Punta Mita on the northernmost tip of the bay. Accion Tropical is one of the most established surf businesses in the area and can hook you up with surf and SUP lessons, snorkeling tours, whale-watching, and more. All staff members are bilingual and will make sure you enjoy the sport of kings! ⊠ *Av. Anclote 16, Riviera Nayarit, Punta Mita* ☎ *329/291–6633, 329/295–5087, 322/131–6586* ⊕ *www.acciontropical.com.mx.*

Captain Pablo. At this outfitter on the beach at Sayulita you can rent equipment or take surfing lessons with Patricia: $30 should get you to your feet (board included). Surf tours, gear included, cost $180 for four hours (up to four surfers). ⊠ *Calle Las Gaviotas at beach, Riviera Nayarit, Sayulita* ☎ *329/291–2070 early morning and evenings only* ✉ *pandpsouthworth@hotmail.com.*

Sininen. Sininen rents surfboards ($5 per hour, $18 for the day) and paddleboards ($8 per hour, $33 all day), gives lessons on both pieces of equipment, and sells surfboards and surf paraphernalia. Rent from the shop or head straight to its outpost a block away on the beach. ⊠ *Calle Delfín 4–S, Riviera Nayarit, Sayulita* ☎ *329/291–3186.*

Wildmex. Located right on the beach in Sayulita, Wildmex rents surfboards (as well as bicycles and kayaks) and gives surf lessons either at Sayulita or elsewhere around the bay, depending on conditions. It offers four- and six-day surf packages and a week-long surf camp; the latter includes accommodations, some meals, and airport transfer. The company also arranges horseback riding, fishing,

> **WHEN TO CATCH A WAVE**
>
> Locals have lots of folk wisdom about when to catch the best waves. Some say it's best right before a good rain, while others believe it's when the tide is moving toward an extreme high or low.

yoga classes, and other activities. ⊠ *The beach at Sayulita, Riviera Nayarit, Sayulita* ☎ *329/291–3726 cell, 877/904–3974 from U.S.A* ⊕ *www.wildmex.com.*

WHALE-WATCHING

Most of the boats on the bay, whether fishing boats or tour boats, also run whale-watching tours (December–mid-March). Some boats are equipped with hydrophones for listening to the whales' songs and carry trained marine biologists; others use the usual crew and simply look for signs of cetaceans. The species you're most likely to see are humpback and killer whales (a gray whale occasionally); false killer whales; and bottlenose, spinner, and pantropic spotted dolphins.

LOGISTICS

Whale-watching is only available December through March. Prime breeding grounds are around the Marietas Islands. The larger boats leave from Marina Vallarta, but you can hire fishermen in villages like Corral del Risco, Anclote, Mismaloya, Boca de Tomatlán, Yelapa, Las Animas, Barra de Navidad, and Tenacatita for less formal, more intimate trips. The larger boats are more likely to have radio equipment useful for communicating with others about the location of whale pods. Some outfitters offer a discount if you sign up online.

OUTFITTERS

Ecotours. After a brief lecture about cetacean ecosystems, you'll board a boat equipped with hydrophones at Punta Mita for a three-hour whale-watching tour. Tours are daily in season (mid-December to mid-March) and cost $75. ⊠ *Ignacio L. Vallarta 243, Col. E. Zapata* ☎ *322/223–3130, 322/222–6606* ⊕ *www.ecotoursvallarta.com.*

SHOPPING

Updated
by Luis
Domínguez

It's hard to decide which is more satisfying: shopping in Puerto Vallarta, or feasting at its glorious restaurants. There are enough of both to keep a bon vivant busy for weeks. But while gourmands return home with enlarged waistlines, gluttonous shoppers need an extra suitcase for the material booty they bring home.

Puerto Vallarta's highest concentration of shops and restaurants shares the same prime real estate: El Centro. But as construction of hotels, time-shares, condos, and private mansions marches implacably north up the bay, new specialty stores and gourmet groceries follow the gravy train. To the south, the Costalegre is made up primarily of modest seaside towns and self-contained luxury resorts, and shopping opportunities are rare.

More than a half-dozen malls line "the airport road," Boulevard Francisco M. Ascencio, which connects downtown with the Hotel Zone and Marina Vallarta. There you'll find folk art, resort clothing, and home furnishing stores amid supermarkets, and in some cases bars and banks. Galerías Vallarta is the largest of these shopping malls and by far the most sophisticated. Here you will find some of the most exclusive boutiques in town, an ultra-modern gym, stylish beauty salon, a casino, a food court, and a movie theater complex.

A 15% value-added tax (locally called IVA, officially the *impuesto al valor agregado*) is levied on most larger purchases. (Note that it's often included in the price, and it's usually disregarded entirely by market vendors.) As a foreign visitor, you can reclaim this 15% by filling out paperwork at a kiosk in the Puerto Vallarta airport and other major airports around the country. That said, most visitors find the system tedious and unrewarding and avoid it altogether. You must make purchases at approved stores and businesses, and your merchandise must total $115 or more. Even if you plan to pay with cash or a debit card, you must present a credit card at the time of purchase and obtain a receipt and an official refund form from the merchant. Tax paid on meals and lodgings won't be refunded.

SMART SOUVENIRS

ARTS AND CRAFTS

Puerto Vallarta is an arts and crafts paradise, particularly if you're fond of ceramics, masks, fine art, and Huichol folk art. Indeed, there are several shops in and around Puerto Vallarta that specialize in or carry a good selection of Huichol works, including Galería Tanana, Peyote People, and Hikuri. A few shops sell stunning pieces of Huichol beaded jewelry. You'll also find stylish clothing and better-than-average bathing suits; vivid handwoven and embroidered textiles from Oaxaca and Chiapas; and comfortable, family-size hammocks from Yucatán State. Handmade or silk-screened blank greeting cards make inexpensive and lovely framed prints.

GLASS AND PEWTER

Glassblowing and pewter were introduced by the Spanish. A wide range of decorative and utilitarian pewter items are produced in the area. The glassware selection includes distinctive deep-blue goblets and chunky, emerald-green-rimmed drinking glasses. All are excellent buys, although breakable and heavy to ship.

JEWELRY

Many PV shop owners travel extensively during the summer months to procure silver jewelry from Taxco, north of Acapulco *(⇨ see "One Man's Metal" below for more information).*

POTTERY

After Guadalajara and its satellite towns Tlaquepaque and Tonalá—which produce ceramics made using patterns and colors hundreds of years old—Puerto Vallarta is the best place in the region to buy pottery, and at reasonable prices. PV shops also sell Talavera (regular or tin-glazed majolica) pottery from Puebla and Tlaxcala.

UNUSUAL GIFTS

For less-than-obvious souvenirs, go traditional and consider a *molinillo,* a carved wooden beater for frothing hot chocolate; you can find these at street vendors or traditional markets for about $1.50. A set of 10 or so *tiras de papel* (string of colored tissue-paper flags) in a gift shop will set you back only about $2. Handmade *huaraches,* or traditional sandals, are hard to break in (get them wet and let them dry on your feet), but they last for years.

TIPS AND TRICKS

Better deals are often given to cash customers—even though credit cards are nearly always accepted—because stores must pay a commission to the credit-card companies. You may have to pay an additional 5% or more on credit-card purchases. U.S. dollars are almost universally accepted, although most shops pay a lower exchange rate than a bank (or ATM) or *casa de cambio* (money exchange).

Bargaining is expected in markets and by beach vendors, who may ask as much as two or three times their bottom line. Occasionally an itinerant vendor will ask for the real value of the item, putting the energetic haggler into the awkward position of offering far too little. One vendor says he asks *norteamericanos* "for twice the asking price, since they always want to haggle." The trick is to know an item's true worth by comparison shopping. It's not common to bargain for already inexpensive trinkets like key chains or quartz-and-bead necklaces or bracelets.

Shop early. Though prices in shops are fixed, smaller shops may be willing to bargain if they're really keen to make a sale. Anyone even slightly superstitious considers the first sale of the day to be good luck, an auspicious start to the day. If your purchase would get the seller's day started on the right foot, you might just get a super deal.

WALKING AND GAWKING

On Wednesday evening during high season (November–April), the PV art community hosts Old Town artWalk (⇨ *Chapter 1*). Participating galleries welcome lookie-loos as well as serious browsers between 6 and 10 pm; most provide at least a cocktail. Look for signs in the windows of participating galleries, or pick up a map at any of them ahead of time. There's a smaller version in Bucerías on Thursday evening at a few galleries on Avenida Lázaro Cárdenas near Calle Galeana.

HOURS OF OPERATION

Most stores are open daily 10–8 or even later in high season. A few close for siesta at 1 pm or 2 pm, then reopen at 4 pm. Fewer than half of PV's shops close on Sunday; those that do usually close up by 2 or 3 on Saturday afternoon as well. Many shops close altogether during the low season (August or September through mid-October). This is noted in the review whenever possible; however, some shops simply close up for several weeks if things get excruciatingly slow. In any case, low-season hours are usually reduced, so call ahead during that time of year.

WATCH OUT

Watch that your credit card goes through the machine only once, so that no duplicates of your slip are made. If there's an error and a new slip needs to be drawn up, make sure the original is destroyed. Another scam is to ask you to wait while the clerk runs next door ostensibly to use another business's phone or to verify your number—but really to make extra copies. Don't let your card leave a store without you. While these scams aren't common in Puerto Vallarta and we don't advocate excessive mistrust, taking certain precautions doesn't hurt.

Don't buy items made from tortoiseshell or any sea turtle products—it's illegal (Mexico's turtle species are endangered or threatened, and these items aren't allowed into the United States, Canada, or the United Kingdom anyway). Cowboy boots, hats, and sandals made from the leather of endangered species such as crocodiles may also be taken from you at customs, as will birds (such as squawking parrots) or stuffed iguanas. Both the U.S. and Mexican governments also have strict laws and guidelines about the import-export of antiquities. Check with customs beforehand if you plan to buy anything unusual or particularly valuable.

SHOPPING IN SPANISH

bakery: *panadería*	**ice cream parlor:** *heladería*
bookseller: *librería*	**jewelry store:** *joyería*
butcher shop: *carnicería*	**market:** *mercado*
candy store: *dulcería* (often sells piñatas)	**notions store:** *mercería*
florist: *florería*	**shoe store:** *zapatería*
furniture store: *mueblería*	**stationery store:** *papelería*
grocery store: *abarrotes*	**tobacconist:** *tabaquería*
hardware store: *ferretería*	**toy store:** *juguetería*
health-food store: *tienda naturista*	**undergarment store:** *bonetería*

Although Cuban cigars are readily available, American visitors aren't allowed to bring them into the United States and will have to enjoy them while in Mexico. However, Mexico produces some fine cigars from tobacco grown in Veracruz. Mexican cigars without the correct Mexican seals on the individual cigars and on the box may be confiscated.

PUERTO VALLARTA

8

ZONA ROMÁNTICA

ART

Pepe Cerroblanco. This contemporary gallery features fine pieces of jewelry, clothing, painting, and sculpture. Every artwork is from a renowned artist, such as Italian Alessandro Alpiani or Mexican Rodrigo Lara. ⊠ *Basilio Badillo 274, Zona Romántica* ☎ *322/222–4169* ⊕ *www. facebook.com/cerroblancogallery.*

Fodor's Choice
★
Galleria Dante. Classical, contemporary, and abstract works are displayed and sold in this 6,000-square-foot gallery—PV's largest—and sculpture garden. Check out the marvelous large-format paintings of indigenous people in regional costumes by Juana Cortez Salazar, whimsical statues by Guillermo Gómez, and the work of nearly 60 other talented artists. A classic in the art scene of Puerto Vallarta. ⊠ *Calle Basilio Badillo 269, Zona Romántica* ☎ *322/222–2477* ⊕ *www.galleriadante.com.*

BOOKS AND PERIODICALS

A Page in the Sun. Folks read books they've bought or traded at this outdoor café by the Hotel Eloisa, and there are almost always people playing chess. The large selection of tomes is organized according to genre and then alphabetized by author. ⊠ *L. Cardenas 179, Zona Romántica* ☎ *322/222–3608* ⊕ *apageinthesun.com.*

CANDY

Fodor's Choice ★ **Xocodiva.** Exquisite truffles and molded chocolates are all stylishly arranged on immaculate glass shelves at this classic Canadian chocolatier. The chocolate itself is European; among the different mousse fillings are some New World ingredients, including lime, coconut, cinnamon, Kahlúa, espresso, and a few dozen more. Stop by after dinner for a fab dessert; it's open until 10 pm. During holidays, out come the molded Santas or Day of the Dead skulls, some packaged as pretty gifts. Don't miss their new ice cream store just next door called Lix by Xocodiva; they have very unusual flavors and interesting original creations. ⊠ *Calle Basilio Badillo 168B, Zona Romántica* ☎ *322/113–0352* ⊕ *www.xocodiva.com* ☉ *Daily 10–10.*

CERAMICS, POTTERY, AND TILE

Mundo de Azulejos. Buy machine- or hand-made tiles starting at about 13 pesos ($1) each at this large shop. You can get mosaic tile scenes (or order your own design), a place setting for eight, hand-painted sinks, or any number of soap dishes, cups, saucers, plates, or doodads. Around the corner and run by family members, Mundo de Cristal *(⇨ below)* has more plates and tableware in the same style. ⊠ *Av. Venustiano Carranza 374, Zona Romántica* ☎ *322/222–2675* ⊕ *www.talavera-tile.com.*

Talavera Etc. Here you can buy reproductions of tiles from Puebla churches and small gift items or choose made-to-order pieces from the catalog. Note that hours are limited. ⊠ *Av. Ignacio L. Vallarta 266, Zona Romántica* ☎ *322/222–4100* ⊕ *www.talaveraetc.com* ☉ *Mon.–Sat. 10–3 (closed for lunch and for two weeks in Sept.).*

CLOTHING

Etnica Boutique. This shop has a well-edited collection of cotton and linen dresses, shawls, purses, hats, sandals, and jewelry. A few items from Indonesia are mixed in with things from different regions of Mexico and Central America. ⊠ *Av. Olas Altas 388, Zona Romántica* ☎ *322/222–6763.*

La Bohemia. Some of the elegant clothing sold here was designed by the equally elegant owner, Toody. You'll find unique jewelry, accessories, and the San Miguel shoe—the elegant yet comfortable footwear designed for walking on cobblestone streets like those of San Miguel and Puerto Vallarta. ⊠ *Calle Constitución at Calle Basilio Badillo, Zona Romántica* ☎ *322/222–3164* ☉ *Closed Sun.*

FAMILY **Myskova Beachwear Boutique.** This boutique has its own extensive line of sexy bikinis, plus cover-ups, yoga pants, and some items for children (sunglasses, bathing suits, flip-flops). There's a small line of jewelry, and Brazilian flip-flops for adults in a rainbow of colors. The shop is open daily until 11 pm. ⊠ *Calle Basilio Badillo 278, Zona Romántica* ☎ *322/222–6091* ⊕ *www.myskova.com.mx* ⊠ *Paseo Diaz Ordaz 542, El Centro* ☎ *322/222–6059.*

Rebeca's. You can browse the large selection of beachwear here daily until late. Look for shorts, pseudo-Speedos, and swimming trunks for men, and sandals, fashionable flip-flops, attractive tankinis, lots of bikinis, and a few one-piece suits for women. Most of the goods

CLOSE UP

One Man's Metal

In less than a decade after William Spratling arrived in the mining town of Taxco—275 km (170 miles) north of Acapulco—he had transformed it into a flourishing silver center, the likes of which had not been seen since colonial times. In 1929 the writer-architect from New Orleans settled in the then-sleepy, dusty village because it was inexpensive and close to the pre-Hispanic Mexcala culture that he was studying in Guerrero Valley.

In Taxco—Mexico's premier "Silver City"—marvelously preserved white-stucco, red-tile-roof colonial buildings hug cobblestone streets that wind up and down the foothills of the Sierra Madre. Taxco (pronounced "TAHS-ko") is a living work of art. For centuries its silver mines drew foreign mining companies. In 1928 the government made it a national monument.

For hundreds of years Taxco's silver was made into bars and exported overseas. No one even considered developing a local jewelry industry. Journeying to a nearby town, Spratling hired a couple of goldsmiths and commissioned them to create jewelry, flatware, trays, and goblets from his own designs.

Ever the artist, with a keen mind for drawing, design, and aesthetics, Spratling decided to experiment with silver using his designs. Shortly afterward, he set up his own workshop and began producing highly innovative pieces. By the 1940s Spratling's designs were gracing the necks of celebrities and being sold in high-end stores abroad.

Spratling also started a program to train local silversmiths; they were soon joined by foreigners interested in learning the craft. It wasn't long before there were thousands of silversmiths in the town, and Spratling was its wealthiest resident. He moved freely in Mexico's lively art scene, befriending muralists Diego Rivera (Rivera's wife, Frida Kahlo, wore Spratling necklaces) and David Alfaro Siqueiros as well as architect Miguel Covarrubios.

The U.S. ambassador to Mexico at the time, Dwight Morrow, father of Anne Morrow, who married Charles Lindbergh, hired Spratling to help with the architectural details of his house in Cuernavaca. American movie stars were frequent guests at Spratling's home; once, he even designed furniture for Marilyn Monroe. Indeed, when his business failed in 1946, relief came in the form of an offer from the U.S. Department of the Interior: Spratling was asked to create a program of native crafts for Alaska. This work influenced his later designs.

Although he never regained the wealth he once had, he operated the workshop at his ranch and trained apprentices until he died in a car accident in 1969. A friend, Italian engineer Alberto Ulrich, took over the business and replicated Spratling's designs using his original molds. Ulrich died in 2002, and his children now operate the business.

Each summer PV shop owners travel to Taxco to procure silver jewelry.

8

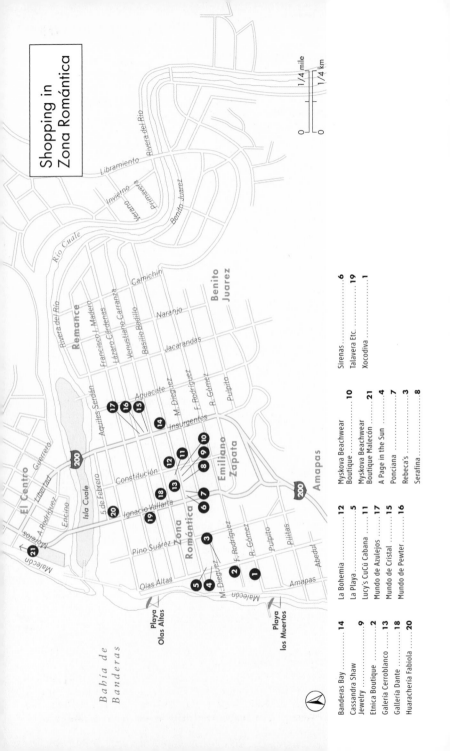

Shopping in Zona Romántica

Bahía de Banderas

Playa Olas Altas

Playa los Muertos

El Centro

Remance

Benito Juarez

Amapas

Zona Romántica

Emiliano Zapata

1/4 mile
1/4 km

are manufactured in Mexico. ⊠ *Olas Altas 403, Zona Romántica* ☎ *322/222–2320.*

Serafina. This is the place to go for over-the-top ethnic clothing; stamped leather purses from Guadalajara; belt buckles from San Miguel; and clunky necklaces and bracelets of quartz, amber, and turquoise. It also sells wonderful tchotchkes. ⊠ *Calle Basilio Badillo 260, Zona Romántica* ☎ *322/223–4594* ⊙ *Mon.–Sat. 9–9.*

Sirenas. Affiliated with Serafina and geared to women with eclectic tastes, this shop sells chic, unusual, and exuberant fantasy jewelry made by creative sisters from Tamaulipas State; innovative and colorful clutches and makeup bags from Mexico City, made from recycled packaging; and an assortment of ethnically inspired yet edgy and contemporary blouses and skirts from Indonesia and elsewhere. ⊠ *Calle Basilio Badillo 252B, Zona Romántica* ☎ *322/223–1925* ⊙ *Closed Sun.*

> ### TRUE MEXICAN TALAVERA
>
> Talavera ceramics are named for the Spanish town where the style originated; indigenous artisans in the New World added rust, green, black, and ocher to the original blue-and-white palate. Authentic Mexican Talavera is produced in Puebla and parts of Tlaxcala and Guanajuato. The glazing process follows centuries-old "recipes." Look on the back or bottom of the piece for the factory name and state of origin. Manufacturers throughout Mexico produce Talavera-style pieces, which should sell for much less.

FOLK ART AND CRAFTS

Lucy's CuCú Cabana. At this very small shop you can buy inexpensive, one-of-a-kind folk art from Guerrero, Michoacán, Oaxaca, and elsewhere. Note that Lucy closes during lunch. ⊠ *Calle Basilio Badillo 295, Zona Romántica* ☎ *322/222–1220* ⊙ *Closed Sun. and Sept.–mid-Oct.*

Mundo de Cristal. Come for the glassware from Jalisco and Guanajuato states, in sets or individual pieces. Also available are Talavera place settings and platters, pitchers, and decorative pieces. Look in the back of the store for high-quality ceramics with realistic portrayals of fruits and flowers. You can have your purchase packed and shipped. ⊠ *Av. Insurgentes 333 at Calle Basilio Badillo, Zona Romántica* ☎ *322/222–4157* ⊕ *mundodecristal.com.mx* ⊙ *Mon.–Sat. (closed Sat. afternoon).*

Mundo de Pewter. Relatives of the owners of Mundo de Cristal and Mundo de Azulejos (⇨ *see above*) own this shop. Attractive, lead-free items in modern and traditional designs are sold here at reasonable prices. The practical, tarnish-free pieces can go from stovetop or oven to the dining table and be no worse for wear. ⊠ *Av. Venustiano Carranza 358, Zona Romántica* ☎ *322/222–8503.*

HOME FURNISHINGS

Ponciana. You can find things here that you won't find at other stores, like porcelain replicas of antique dolls or an old reliquary transformed into wall art. Leaving room for creative license means that some "antiques" here may only have a few original parts (say, a cupboard that only has original doors). Also look for tablecloths and place mats from Michoacán, place settings, arty statuettes, matchboxes decorated with Frida

Beaded figurines decorated with colorful Huichol symbols are practically de rigueur on any first-timer's shopping list.

Kahlo and Mexican movie themes, and other decorative items. ⊠ *Calle Basilio Badillo 252–A, Zona Romántica* ☎ *322/222–2988.*

JEWELRY

Cassandra Shaw Jewelry. It's hard to ignore the huge, chunky rings, brace-lets, and necklaces here. In the back of the shop are more delicate items of pure silver set with various stones in artful ways. All are unusual. ⊠ *Calle Basilio Badillo 276, Zona Romántica* ☎ *322/223–9734.*

LEATHER, SHOES, AND HANDBAGS

Huarachería Fabiola. Longtime visitors to Puerto Vallarta will remember this shop. Buy huaraches off the rack or order custom sandals for men or women. Most styles can be made in one to three days. There are lim-ited hours (roughly 10–3) on Sunday, and credit cards aren't accepted. ⊠ *Av. Ignacio L. Vallarta 145 at Calle A. Serdán, Zona Romántica* ☎ *322/222–9154.*

EL CENTRO

ART

Art Gallery Millan. A breath of fresh air in the gallery scene, Millan has cheeky oils by Eduardo Eguía, sculpture by Benito Arciniegas, and affordable, fun ceramic cyclist statuettes created by Rodo Padilla. ⊠ *Amapas 129, El Centro* ☎ *322/137–3519.*

ARTE 550. Wonderful ceramic pieces and sculptures are found at this shop a few blocks in from the malecón. Co-owner/artist Patricia Gawle digs her own clay outside El Tuito. Her monotypes are color-ful, cheerful, and tropical-themed. You can browse through the catalog of hand-painted tile work to order pieces for a kitchen or bathroom mural. Business partner Kathleen Carrillo paints equally cheerful acrylics, and the two also lead tours combining whale-watching, snorkeling, or other activities with journaling and other types of artistic expression. ⊠ *Calle Hidalgo at Corona, El Centro* ☎ *322/222–6719* ⊕ *www.yourcreativeawakening.com* ⊗ *Tues.–Sat.*

Galería Pacífico. Open since 1987, Pacífico features the sculpture of Ramiz Barquet, who created the bronze *Nostalgia* piece on the malecón. Brewster Brockmann paints contemporary abstracts; Marco Alvarez, Alejandro Mondria, and Alfredo Langarica are other featured artists. During the summer months the gallery can be visited only by appointment. ⊠ *Calle Aldama 174, 2nd fl., El Centro* ☎ *322/222–1982* ⊕ *www.galeriapacifico.com.*

Sergio Bustamante. Internationally known Sergio Bustamante—the creator of life-size brass, copper, and ceramic animals, mermaids, suns, and moons—has a team of artisans to execute his never-ending pantheon of creative and quirky objets d'art, such as pots shaped like human torsos that sell for more than $1,000. Paintings, purses, shoes, and jewelry are sold here as well. It's across the street from the statue by the same artist, on the malecón. ⊠ *Av. Juárez 275 at Calle Corona, El Centro* ☎ *322/223–1405* ⊕ *www.sergiobustamante.com.mx.*

CERAMICS, POTTERY, AND TILE

Alfarería Tlaquepaque. This is a large store with a ton of red-clay items traditional to the area—in fact, their predecessors were crafted before the 1st century AD. Rustic pottery and glazed ceramic pieces come in traditional styles at reasonable prices. ⊠ *Av. México 1100, El Centro* ☎ *322/223–2121.*

Galería de Ollas. The 300 or so potters from the village of Juan Mata Ortiz add their touches to the intensely—sometimes hypnotically—geometric designs of their ancestors from Paquimé. At this shop pieces range from about $60 to $10,000, with an average of about $400. Stop in during artWalk, or have a look at its great website. ⊠ *Calle Corona 176, El Centro* ☎ *322/223–1045* ⊕ *www.galeriadeollas.com* ⊗ *Mon.–Sat. (closes lunchtime on Sat.).*

∎**TIP**➔ **Before you buy rustic ceramic plates, bowls, and cups, ask if there's lead in the glaze ("¿hay plomo en el vidriado?"), unless you plan to use them for decoration only and not for food service.**

CIGARS

La Casa del Habano. The Cuban cigars for sale here start at around 55 pesos ($4) each and top out at about 2,700 pesos ($200) for a Cohiba Siglo VI (by order only; they don't keep them in stock). The owner claims that 95% of the cigars sold in Vallarta are fake Cubans, but

> **EXPAT HUMOR**
>
> The co-owner of Lucy's CuCú Cabana is Gil Gevens, who pens quirky epistles, often at his own expense or the expense of other expats, about life in Puerto Vallarta. Gil writes regularly for the weekly English-language paper *Puerto Vallarta Tribune*, and you can buy his tongue-in-cheek books around town or at Lucy's.

8

his are the genuine article. You can smoke your stogie downstairs in the casual lounge while sipping coffee or enjoying a shot of Cuban rum. ✉ *Aldama 170, El Centro* ☎ *322/ 223–2758* ⏱ *Weekdays noon–9, shorter hours Sat.*

■ TIP→ **If you're bringing any Mexican cigars back to the United States, make sure they have the correct Mexican seals on both the individual cigars and on the box. Otherwise, they may be confiscated.**

CLOTHING

Curvas Peligrosas. Here it's all about beachwear, particularly nice bathing suits. The emphasis is on plus

sizes, but you can find some items that are as small as size 12. Choose from Jantzen, Longitude, Miracle Suits, and other quality brands. The shop also has cute cover-ups and skirts. ✉ *Av. Juárez 178, El Centro* ☎ *322/223–5978* ⊕ *www.curvaspeligrosaspv.com* ⏱ *Weekdays 11–5 (may change seasonally).*

D'Paola. The large and somewhat unusual selection here includes pashminas, purses, and shawls as well as lots of muslin clothing. You'll find 32 different lines and plenty of plus sizes. We'd guess that any woman patient enough to search the massive inventory (the main shop has the most) will find something to her taste—there's that much variety. Complement your clothing purchases with a signature piece of jewelry, perhaps a chunky necklace with giant stones or one made of strands of tiny beads. The Paradise Plaza branch has sexy resort wear and halter dresses from Gecko Batik and other designers, but the best experience on the whole is at the main branch, where the owners' warm friendliness is contagious. ✉ *Calle Agustín Rodríguez 289, El Centro* ☎ *322/222–1120* ⏱ *Mon.–Sat.* ✉ *Paradise Plaza, Local 11–A, Nuevo Vallarta* ☎ *322/297–1030.*

FAMILY **La Surtidora.** At first glance the items in this long-established shop seem mainly matronly, but plowing through the racks will unearth fashionable cocktail dresses, trendy tops, and T-shirts, plus men's guayaberas and slacks. The location near the bridge in Colonia E. Zapata has the larger selection; it also has shoes (high heels to flip-flops) and children's clothing. ✉ *Calle Morelos 256 at Guerrero, El Centro* ☎ *322/222–1439.*

DEPARTMENT STORE

FAMILY **LANS.** At this multilevel department store for men, women, and children, look for Perry Ellis khakis and Levi's, Lee, and Dockers shirts, pants, and jeans. The store also sells housewares; purses and Swatch watches; Samsonite luggage; ladies' perfume and makeup (Chanel, Gucci, Estée Lauder); and men's underwear. Both locations offer parking, which is especially nice in crowded downtown Vallarta. ✉ *Calle Juárez 867 at Pípila, El Centro* ☎ *322/226–9100* ✉ *Plaza Caracol,*

Bd. Francisco M. Ascencio 2216, near Soriana supermarket, Zona Hotelera ☎ *322/226–0204* ⊕ *www. lans.com.mx.*

FOLK ART AND CRAFTS

Alas de Aguila. In addition to pewter there's a wide selection of Talavera-style objects—from soap holders and liquid-soap dispensers to pitchers, platters, and picture frames—in a variety of patterns. Quality is middle-of-the-road; prices are excellent. ⊠ *Av. Juárez 547 at Calle Corona, El Centro* ☎ *322/222–4039* ⊗ *Closed Sun.*

WORD OF MOUTH

"ArtWalk on Wednesday night was fantastic and never ending. Though the prices for the art and jewelry were steep, it was more than worth our time just to experience such a large variety of styles and media." —Ohrowver

Galería Indígena. The assortment of handicrafts here is huge: Huichol yarn paintings and beaded bowls and statuettes, real Talavera ceramics from Puebla, decorative pieces in painted wood, and many other items. The owner likes offering customers a drink of water or other refreshment, no strings attached. ⊠ *Av. Juárez 628, El Centro* ☎ *322/223–0800* ⊗ *Mon.–Sat. (closes lunchtime on Sat.).*

JEWELRY

Caballito de Mar. Lynn Auch and Carol Simonton own and operate this small store. At the heart of the collection of vintage and antique silver jewelry are pieces acquired by their mother over 40 years of collecting, beginning in the 1940s. The sisters continue to add select, handmade jewelry to their small but stellar collection, and they offer a small selection of folk art as well. ⊠ *Calle Aldama 162, El Centro* ☎ *322/113–0363* ⊕ *galeriacaballitodemar.com* ⊗ *Oct.–July, Tues.–Sat.*

LEATHER, SHOES, AND HANDBAGS

Rolling Stone. This place is good for custom-made boots, sandals, and shoes in a wide variety of leathers, but the help is often unhelpful, letting customers wait while they attend to other duties—real or imagined. ⊠ *Paseo Diaz Ordaz 802, El Centro* ☎ *322/223–1769* ⊗ *Daily 10–10.*

MALL

Plaza Caracol. This shopping mall is lively and full on weekends and evenings, even when others are dead. Its anchors are the Soriana (formerly Gigante) supermarket and the adjacent LANS department store. Surrounding these are tiny stores dispensing electronics, ice cream, fresh flowers, and more. This is also a good place for manicures and haircuts. Adding to the commercial center's appeal is the six-screen Cinemex movie theater. ⊠ *Bd. Francisco M. Ascencio, Km 2.5, Zona Hotelera* ☎ *322/224–3444* ⊕ *plazacaracol.mx.*

MARKETS

Mercado de Artesanías. Flowers, piñatas, produce, and plastics share space in indoor and outdoor stands with souvenirs and lesser-quality crafts. Upstairs, locals eat at long-established, family-run restaurants. ⊠ *Calle Agustín Rodríguez, between calles Matamoros and Miramar, at base of bridge, El Centro.*

8

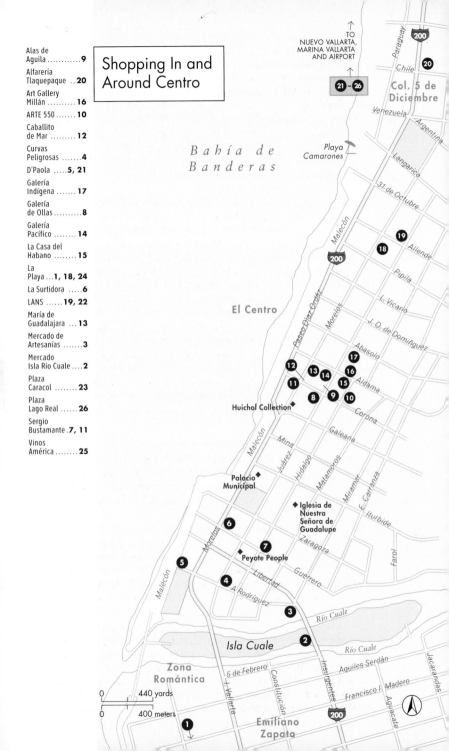

Shopping In and Around Centro

Mercado Isla Río Cuale. Small shops and outdoor stands sell an interesting mix of wares at this informal and fun market that divides El Centro from Colonia E. Zapata. Harley-Davidson kerchiefs, Che paintings on velvet, and Madonna icons compete with the usual synthetic lace tablecloths, shell and quartz necklaces, and silver jewelry amid postcards and key chains. The market is partially shaded by enormous fig and rubber trees and serenaded by the rushing river; a half-dozen cafés and restaurants provide sustenance. ⊠ *Access at Calle Morelos, Calle I. Vallarta, Calle Matamoros, Calle Constitución, Calle Libertad, Av. Insurgentes, and the malecón, El Centro.*

WINE, BEER, AND SPIRITS

La Playa. Yes, it has tequila, but it also has wines from Chile, California (Gallo), and Spain; imported vodka and other spirits; and the cheapest beer around. You'll find it across from IMSS (Mexican Social Security Agency). ⊠ *Bd. Francisco M. Ascencio, Km 1.5, Zona Hotelera* ☎ *322/224–7130* ⊕ *superlaplaya.com* ⊠ *Calle Morelos at Calle Pípila, El Centro* ☎ *322/223–1818* ⊕ *superlaplaya.com* ⊠ *Olas Altas 246 at Calle Basilio Badillo, Zona Romántica* ☎ *322/222–5304.*

Vinos América. A huge and excellent inventory of wine from Germany, Spain, France, Argentina, Chile, California, Australia, and elsewhere makes this a natural stop for lovers of the grape. The shop sells champagne and other sparkling vintages, sherry, port, and two Napa Valley non-alcoholic wines. There's no shortage of Mexican wines, of course, as well as tequila, *raicilla* (green agave liquor), *Agavero* (Damiana liqueur with tequila), and other hard liquor. ⊠ *Av. de las Américas 433, El Centro* ☎ *322/223–3334* ⊕ *vinosamerica.com.mx.*

MARINA VALLARTA

ART

Galería Em. This shop sells art glass, stained glass, and glass sculpture and also has a small selection of eccentric jewelry made by local artists. The shop offers fully insured international shipping, too. ⊠ *Marina Las Palmas II, Local 17, Marina Vallarta* ☎ *322/221–2228* ☉ *Mon.–Sat. 9–3 and 6–8*

CLOTHING

María de Guadalajara. It's DIY chic here. You choose the colorful, cotton, triangular sash of your liking, miraculously transforming pretty but baggy dresses into flattering and stylish frocks. The color palette is truly inspired, although the selection for men is limited. ⊠ *Morelos 552, El Centro* ☎ *322/222–2387* ⊕ *www.mariadeguadalajara.com.*

DEPARTMENT STORE

Galerías Vallarta. This is the main shopping mall in the whole Puerto Vallarta–Riviera Nayarit area, offering 73,000 square feet of shopping distributed on two floors and a magnificent view of the arriving cruise ships. This mall and the surrounding shops are mainly visited by cruise-ship passengers and Mexican out-of-towners looking for everything from sporting goods to clothing to housewares. Galerías Vallarta has two escalators; restaurants; parking; a 12-theater cinema; and a fast-food

Continued on page 197

8

DID YOU KNOW?

Huichol is pronounced wee-CHOL; the people's name for themselves, however, is Wi-rarika (we-RAH-ri-ka), which means "healer."

THE ART OF THE HUICHOL

Updated by
Georgia de Katona

The intricately woven and beaded designs of the Huichols' art are as vibrant and fascinating as the traditions of its people, best known as the "Peyote People" for their traditional and ceremonial use of the hallucinogenic drug. Peyote-inspired visions are thought to be messages from God and are reflected in the art.

Like the Lacandon Maya, the Huichol resisted assimilation by Spanish invaders, fleeing to inhospitable mountains and remote valleys. There they retained their pantheistic religion in which shamans lead the community in spiritual matters and the use of peyote facilitates communication directly with God.

Roads didn't reach larger Huichol communities until the mid-20th century, bringing electricity and other modern distractions. The collision with the outside world has had pros and cons, but art lovers have only benefited from their increased access to intricately patterned woven and beaded goods. Today the traditional souls that remain on the land—a significant population of perhaps 6,000 to 8,000—still create votive bowls, prayer arrows, jewelry, and bags, and sell them to finance elaborate religious ceremonies. The pieces go for as little as $5 or as much as $5,000, depending on the skill and fame of the artist and quality of materials.

(left) Huichol yarn painting, National Museum of Anthropology, (top) Huichol art, Puerto Vallarta

UNDERSTANDING THE HUICHOL

When Spanish conquistadors arrived in the early 16th century, the Huichol, unwilling to work as slaves on the haciendas of the Spanish or to adopt their religion, fled to the Sierra Madre. They lived there, disconnected from society, for nearly 500 years. Beginning in the 1970s, roads and electricity made their way to tiny Huichol towns. Today, about half of the population of perhaps 12,000 continues to live in ancestral villages and *rancheritas* (tiny individual farms).

THE POWER OF PRAYER

They believe that without their prayers and offerings the sun wouldn't rise, the earth would cease spinning. It is hard, then, for them to reconcile their poverty with the relative easy living of "free-riders" (Huichol term for non-spiritual freeloaders) who enjoy fine cars and expensive houses thanks to the Huichols efforts to sustain the planet. But rather than hold our reckless materialism against us, the Huichol add us to their prayers.

THE PEYOTE PEOPLE

Visions inspired by the hallucinogenic peyote plant are considered by the Huichol to be messages from God and to help in solving personal and communal problems. Indirectly, they provide inspiration for their almost psychedelic art. Just a generation or two ago, annual peyote-gathering pilgrimages

were done on foot. Today the journey is still a man's chief obligation, but they now drive to the holy site at Wiricuta, in San Luis Potosi State.

SHAMANISM

A Huichol man has a lifelong calling as a shaman. There are two shamanic paths: the path of the wolf, which is more aggressive, demanding, and powerful (wolf shamans profess the ability to morph into wolves); and the path of the deer, which is playful. A shaman chooses his own path.

BEADED ITEMS

The smaller the beads, the more delicate and expensive the piece.

Items made with iridescent beads from Japan are the priciest. Look for good-quality glass beads, definition, symmetry, and artful use of color.

Beads should fit together tightly in straight lines, with no gaps.

YARN PAINTINGS

Symmetry is not necessary, although there should be an overall sense of unity. Thinner thread results in finer, more costly work. Look for tightness, with no visible gaps or broken threads. Paintings should have a stamp of authenticity on the back, including artist's name and tribal affiliation.

PRAYER ARROWS

Collectors and purists should look for the traditionally made arrows of brazilwood inserted into a bamboo shaft. The most interesting ones contain embroidery work, or tiny carved icons, or are painted with copal symbols indicative of their original intended purpose, for example protecting a child or ensuring a successful corn crop.

Huichol bird, Jalisco

HOW TO READ THE SYMBOLS

Spiders that come out at dawn are thought to welcome the rising sun.

The deer is the animal manifestation of the god Kahumari, who intercedes in heaven on earthlings' behalf.

Anything with horns or antlers symbolizes communion and oneness with God.

Yarn painting

■ The trilogy of corn, peyote, and deer represents three aspects of God. According to Huichol mythology, peyote sprang up in the footprints of the deer. Depicted like stylized flowers, peyote represents communication with God. Corn, the Huichol's staple

Corn symbol

food, symbolizes health and prosperity. An image drawn inside the root ball depicts the essence of God within it.

■ The double-headed eagle is the emblem of the omnipresent sky god.

Peyote

■ A nierika is a portal between the spirit world and our own. Often in the form of a yarn painting, a nierika can be round or square.

■ Salamanders and turtles are associated with rain; the former provoke the clouds. Turtles maintain underground springs and purify water.

■ A scorpion is the soldier of the sun.

Scorpion

■ The Huichol depict raindrops as tiny snakes; in yarn paintings they descend to enrich the fields.

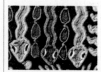

Snakes

Jose Beníctez Sánchez, (1938—) may be the elder statesman of yarn painters and has shown in Japan, Spain, the U.S., and at the Museum of Modern Art in Mexico City. His paintings sell for upward of $3,000 a piece.

TRADITION TRANSFORMED

The art of the Huichol was, for centuries, made from undyed wool, shells, stones, and other natural materials. It was not until the 1970s that the Huichol began incorporating bright, zingy colors, without sacrificing the intricate patterns and symbols used for centuries. The result is strenuously colorful, yet dignified.

YARN PAINTINGS
Dramatic and vivid yarn paintings are highly symbolic, stylized visions of life.

MASKS AND ANIMAL STATUETTES
Bead-covered wooden or ceramic masks and animal statuettes are other adaptations made for outsiders.

PRAYER ARROWS
Made for every ceremony, prayer arrows send petitions winging to God.

VOTIVE BOWLS
Ceremonial votive bowls, made from gourds, are decorated with bright, stylized beadwork.

WOVEN SHOULDER BAGS
Carried by men, the bags are decorated with traditional Huichol icons.

For years, Huichol men as well as women wore BEADED BRACELETS; today earrings and necklaces are also made.

Diamond-shape GOD'S EYES of sticks and yarn protect children from harm.

court with the ubiquitous McDonald's, Dominos Pizza, Chili's, and Starbucks (it also has the most slippery polished-stone flooring known to man). ⊠ *Av. Francisco M. Ascencio 2920, Marina Vallarta* ☎ *01800/288–0888* ⊕ *www. galerias.com/galerias Vallarta.*

SPAS

Ohtli Spa. The modern Ohtli spa and its high-tech gym offer 22,000 square feet of elegant pampering. You can relax before or between treatments in the lounge with a

glass of water infused with love in the form of pink quartz crystals and amorous messages in foreign languages. Come early to load up on this liquid love and to enjoy the cold pool, steam, sauna, and other elements of the separate men's and women's spa facilities. Inspiration for this tasteful, soothing spa came from indigenous cultures. Treatment rooms are adorned with Huichol art and interior gardens to maintain a spiritual and nature-oriented mood. Many of the treatments—like the hydrating tequila-coconut body treatment—use local ingredients. The signature exfoliation treatment contains agave essence and sea salt. ⊠ *CasaMagna Marriott Puerto Vallarta, Paseo de la Marina 435 Norte, Marina Vallarta* ☎ *322/226–0079* ⊕ *www.marriott.com.*

Terra Noble. Your cares begin to melt away as soon as you enter the rustic, garden-surrounded property of this day-spa aerie overlooking Banderas Bay. Familiar and unpretentious, Terra Noble is more accessible price-wise than some of the area's more elegant spas. After-treatment teas are served on an outdoor patio with a great sea view. There's the full-body clay for sunburned skin, chardonnay-grape-seed therapy for maximum hydration, and a full-body coconut scrub and chocolate mask for a pre-party body refresher. Two-hour temazcal sweat-lodge rituals cleanse on three levels: physically, mentally, and spiritually. Groups can take advantage of the clay and painting classes. Note that although credit cards aren't accepted, you can pay online in advance using PayPal. ⊠ *Col. 5 de Diciembre, Av. Tulipanes 595, at Fracc. Lomas de Terra Noble, Centro* ☎ *322/223–0308* ⊕ *www.terranoble.com.*

MALLS

Plaza Marina. One long block north of Plaza Neptuno, this mall has several banks with ATMs, a dry cleaner, a photo-developing shop, a pharmacy, a café, an Internet café, and several bars and shops. The whole place is anchored by the Comercial Mexicana supermarket, a McDonald's, and the best tacos *al pastor* in town at Valapanza. ⊠ *Carretera al Aeropuerto, Km 8, Marina Vallarta* ☎ *322/221–0490* ⊕ *plaza marina.com.*

Plaza Neptuno. This small mall in the heart of the marina district is home to a number of fine-home-furnishing shops, several classy clothing

8

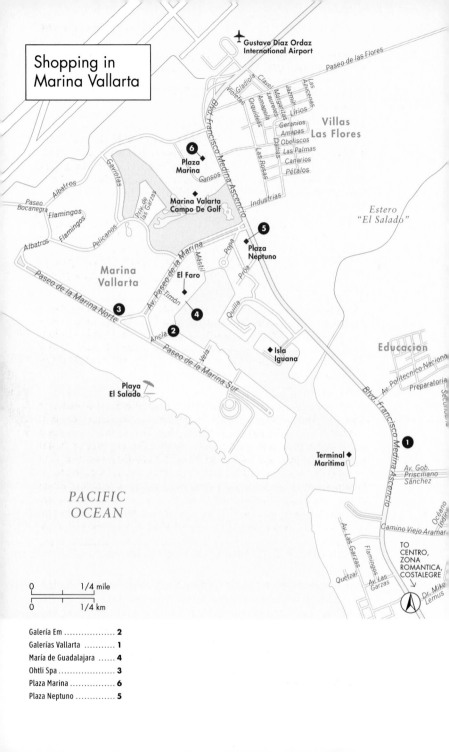

Shopping in Marina Vallarta

✈ Gustavo Díaz Ordaz
International Airport

Paseo de las Flores

Villas
Las Flores

6 Plaza Marina

Gansos

Marina Valarta
Campo De Golf

Estero
"El Salado"

5
Plaza
Neptuno

El Faro

3
Marina
Vallarta

4

2 Ancla

Vela

♦ Isla
Iguana

Educación

Playa
El Salado

Terminal ♦
Maritima

1

PACIFIC
OCEAN

Camino Viejo Aramara

TO
CENTRO,
ZONA
ROMANTICA,
COSTALEGRE
↓

Dr. Mike Lemus

0	1/4 mile
0	1/4 km

boutiques, and, just behind it, a few good, casual restaurants. ⊠ *Carretera al Aeropuerto, Km 7.5, Marina Vallarta.*

NUEVO VALLARTA

BOOKS

NV Bookstore. It may be small, but this bookstore has the area's best-distilled selection of English-language books. There are guidebooks; books about Mexican culture, history, and arts; and best-selling titles to read around the pool. ⊠ *Paradise Plaza, 2nd fl., Nuevo Vallarta* ☎ *322/297–2274.*

MALL

Paradise Plaza. It's the most comprehensive plaza in the Nuevo Vallarta Hotel Zone, with a food court, grocery store, several coffee and juice shops, an Internet café, a Starbucks, clothing and handicraft boutiques, and a bank. You will also find in here Riviera Nayarit's Conventions & Visitors Bureau in the second floor. ⊠ *Paseo de los Cocoteros 85 Sur, Nuevo Vallarta.*

Plaza Lago Real. Nuevo Vallarta was in dire need of a proper, non-tourist-oriented shopping center, and that's exactly what Lago Real is—an unpretentious mall featuring a wide array of shops and services including Wal-mart, Cinepolis, Telcel, a food court, and several banks. ⊠ *Carretera Tepic 430 Ote, Valle Dorado, Nuevo Vallarta* ☎ *322/297–6175* ⊕ *www.lagoreal.mx.*

SPAS

Grand Velas Spa. The spa at Nuevo Vallarta's most elegant all-inclusive resort has dramatic architectural lines and plenty of marble, stone, teak, and tile. The 16,500-square-foot facility has 20 treatment rooms and ample steam, sauna, and whirlpools. Lounge in the comfortable chaises near the "plunge lagoon" (with warm and cold pools) between or after treatments. Highlights of the extensive treatment menu are the chocolate, gold, or avocado wrap; Thai massage; cinnamon-sage foot scrub; and the challenging buttocks sculpt-lift. There's even a kids' spa menu. Adjoining the spa is an impressive fitness facility. ⊠ *Av. de los Cocoteros 98 Sur, Nuevo Vallarta* ☎ *322/226–8000* ⊕ *www.grandvelas.com.*

RIVIERA NAYARIT

FLAMINGOS

GROCERIES

Mega Comercial Nuevo Vallarta. The area's first large supermarket, just south of Flamingos Country Club, is almost as convenient for people in Bucerías as for those in Nuevo Vallarta. It has the full range of grocery, liquor, deli items, and more. ⊠ *Hwy. 200, Fracc. Flamingos, Bucerías* ☎ *322/222–7709.*

BUCERÍAS

FOLK ART

Jan Marie's Boutique. The gift items here include small housewares and tin frames sporting Botero-style fat ladies. The classy selection of Talavera pottery is both decorative and utilitarian. An extension half a block down the street has an even larger inventory, and the merchandise is larger, too, including classy leather settees, lamps, desks, and other furnishings as well as decorative and utilitarian pieces from various parts of Mexico. Neither shop is for bargain hunters, but prices are reasonable given the high quality of the merchandise. ⊠ *Av. Lázaro Cárdenas 56 and 58, Riviera Nayarit, Bucerías* ☎ *329/298–0303.*

SAYULITA

FOLK ART

Banannie Jewelry. With more than 17 years in Sayulita, Annie Banannie has become one of the most beloved residents in town. She's the shop owner, manager, and jewelry artist, working strictly in silver (no gold) and semiprecious exotic stones from all over the world. You will find great pieces with emeralds, sapphires, and rubies, among many other stones. ⊠ *Calle Pelicanos 50D, Riviera Nayarit, Sayulita* ☎ *329/291–3769.*

Fodor'sChoice ★ **Galería Tanana.** The beauty of its glistening glass-bead (Czech) jewelry in iridescent and earth colors may leave you weak at the knees. Sometimes a Huichol artisan at the front of the store works on traditional yarn paintings, pressing the fine filaments into a base of beeswax and pine resin to create colorful and symbolic pictures. Money from sales supports the owner's nonprofit organization to promote cultural sustainability for the Huichol people. ⊠ *Av. Revolucion 22, Riviera Nayarit, Sayulita* ☎ *329/291–3889* ⊕ *www.thehuicholcenter.org.*

La Hamaca. The inventory of folk art and utilitarian handicrafts is large, and each piece is unique. Scoop up masks and pottery from Michoacán, textiles and shawls from Guatemala, hammocks from the Yucatán, and lacquered boxes from Olinalá. ⊠ *Calle Revolución 110, Riviera Nayarit, Sayulita* ☎ *329/291–3039* ☉ *Daily 9–9.*

LA CRUZ DE HUANACAXTLE

FARMERS' MARKET

Fodor'sChoice ★ **La Cruz de Huanacaxtle Farmers' Market.** This is arguably the best farmers' market in the whole Puerto Vallarta/Riviera Nayarit region. It offers a balanced combination of good quality Mexican handicrafts and jewelry, as well as clothes, lamps, hammocks, cigars, organic products, and lots of delicious food. Everything is in a delightful environment with stunning views of the Marina Riviera Nayarit and Banderas Bay, and there's live music in the background. It makes for a great way to spend a Sunday morning. ⊠ *Marina, Riviera Nayarit, La Cruz de Huanacaxtle* ⊕ *www.mercadohuanacaxtle.com* ☉ *Nov.–Apr., Sun. 10–2.*

SIDE TRIPS

SIDE TRIPS FROM PUERTO VALLARTA

TOP REASONS TO GO

★ **Alchemic atmosphere:**
San Blas's basic but charismatic attractions—beaches, markets, churches, and boat trips—combine like magic for a destination that's greater than the sum of its parts.

★ **Highland rambles:**
Drop-dead-gorgeous hills and river valleys from Talpa de Allende to San Sebastián get you out into nature and away from coastal humidity.

★ **Amazing photography:**
In the mountain towns like San Sebastián, Mascota, and Talpa, even amateurs can capture excellent small-town and nature photos.

★ **Palpable history:** Soak up Mexican history and culture in Guadalajara's churches, museums, and political murals.

★ **Getting the goods:**
Guadalajara has excellent housewares and handicrafts at great prices for sale in its megamalls as well as in nearby pre-Hispanic townships.

1 San Blas. Change happens slowly in San Blas, which has yet to experience a tourism boom. Cruise wide dirt streets on one-speed bikes, read books in the shade, dig your toes in the sand, and just enjoy life—one lazy day at a time. Blue mountains and green hills provide a beautiful backdrop.

2 The Mountain Towns.
The former mining and supply towns within the Sierra Madre—Talpa de Allende, Mascota, and tiny San Sebastián—were isolated for centuries by narrow roads and dangerous drop-offs and remain postcards of the past. Soak up the small-town atmosphere and alpine air.

3 Greater Guadalajara. Home to cherished archetypes like mariachi, *charrería* (elegant "rodeos"), and tequila, Guadalajara is often called "the Mexican's Mexico." The metropolitan area includes former farming community Zapopan and two districts known for crafts: Tlaquepaque and neighboring Tonalá. Outside the city are unique archaeological digs at Teuchitlán, lakeside retreat Chapala, artists' and expats' enclave Ajijic, and Tequila, famous for . . . do we even need to say it?

GETTING ORIENTED

About 156 km (95 miles) north of PV, mountain-backed San Blas has beaches and birding. Inland 340 km (211 miles) or so from PV, Jalisco capital Guadalajara (pop. 4 million) sits in the Atemajac Valley, circled by Sierra Madre peaks. Sleepy mountain towns Talpa de Allende, Mascota, and San Sebastián lie about halfway between PV and Guadalajara; each offers a glimpse of rural life from centuries long gone.

9

Updated by Luis Domínguez

Puerto Vallarta's location means lots of variety. You can explore little-visited beaches and miles of mangrove canals in San Blas. You can shop and "get culture" in historic Guadalajara. Or you can head to the mountains for a look at mining towns and long walks down country lanes.

Although San Blas is now the northern terminus of the so-called Riviera Nayarit (the new term for the stretch of coast from San Blas to the southern Nayarit State border at Nuevo Vallarta), thus far it's changed little. Things here are low-key and friendly—a nice change from bustling Vallarta and environs, where traffic sometimes snarls. There are no supermarkets; everyone shops at mom-and-pop groceries or the daily market for tropical fruits and vegetables, tortillas, and hot or cold snacks. Many of the restaurants around the plaza are relatively simple and inexpensive.

Founded by the Spanish but soon all but abandoned for busier ports, San Blas has several historic structures to visit, including the old customs and counting houses, and original churches. But more of a draw are its miles of sandy beaches and La Tobara, a serpentine series of mangrove-lined channels leading to a freshwater spring.

Even less sophisticated than San Blas are a handful of former silver-mining towns and supply centers in the hills behind Puerto Vallarta. Until a 21st-century road improvement, Mascota, Talpa de Allende, San Sebastián, and other villages en route to Guadalajara were accessible only by narrow, treacherous, snaky mountain road or small plane. Today sunny, unpolluted days and crisp nights lure people out of the fray and into a more relaxed milieu, where lingering over coffee or watching kids play in the town plaza are the activities of choice. If this sounds too tame, there's horseback riding, hiking, and fishing at Presa Coriches, among other activities.

Guadalajara—Mexico's second-largest city—makes an excellent add-on to a Vallarta beach vacation. You can shop in megamalls or in surrounding towns, where artisans were producing pottery centuries before the Spanish invasion. You can take in modern Russian ballet or Mexican folkloric dances; see a fast-paced *charrería*, with men and women on well-groomed Arabian horses; listen to a 12-piece mariachi band; or visit one of a dozen museums. Although at times overwhelming, this modern city provides an excellent overview of all Mexico has to offer. For a foray outside the metropolis, head for Lago de Chapala, Mexico's largest natural lake, or to Tequila, land of the blue agave, where the country's national drink is produced and bottled.

PLANNING

WHEN TO GO

Thanks to a springlike climate, Guadalajara is pleasant at most times of year, though May and June can be uncomfortably hot for some. Book well in advance to visit during the October Festival or other holidays. Roads can be dangerous during summer rains; June through October isn't the best time to visit the mountain towns by land.

San Blas and the coast begin to heat up in May; during the late June through October rainy season both the ambient and ocean temps are highest. In Guadalajara, rain tends to be limited to the late afternoon and evening.

FESTIVALS AND SPECIAL EVENTS

Guadalajara's major events include the International Mariachi Festival in September, the Tequila Festival in March, and a cultural festival in May. Also in Guadalajara, the entire month of October is given up to mariachis, *charreadas* (rodeos), soccer matches, and theater.

GETTING HERE AND AROUND

If you plan to visit both Puerto Vallarta and Guadalajara, consider flying into one and out of the other. Some open-jaw trips cost even less than a round-trip flight to/from PV. If you plan your trip right, travel between PV and Guadalajara by bus is $32–$37. One-way drop-off charges for rental cars are steep. Access to Mascota and Talpa from Guadalajara is more direct than from PV, although the latter road is now paved, with new bridges in place. Nonetheless, this windy mountain route is occasionally impassable in rainy season. Buses take you directly from PV to San Blas, or you can get off at nearby beaches. That said, a car is handier for exploring the coast. The mostly two-lane PV–San Blas road is curvy but otherwise fine.

■ TIP→ Most small towns that don't have official stations sell gas from a home or store. Ask around before heading out on the highway if you're low on gas.

PLANNING YOUR TIME

DAY TRIPS VERSUS EXTENDED STAYS

The San Blas area is best as an overnight unless you go with an organized tour, though you could easily drive to Platanitos, south of San Blas, for a day at the beach.

If busing or driving to the mountain towns, plan to overnight unless you take the day tour with Vallarta Adventures or another PV tour company. Alternatively, you can fly on your own with **Aerotaxis de la Bahía** (☎ 322/221–1990) for a day trip or an overnight stay.

Guadalajara is too far to go for the day from Vallarta or San Blas; we recommend at least three nights if you're doing a round-trip.

HOW MUCH CAN YOU DO?

What you can (physically) do and what you should do are very different things. To get the most out of your excursion from Puerto Vallarta, don't overdo it. It's a vacation—it's supposed to be relaxing! If you'll be in the Sayulita, San Francisco, and Chacala areas in Nayarit, it's easy to do an overnight jaunt up to San Blas, enjoying the myriad beaches and small towns as you travel up and back. Or make San Blas your base and explore from there.

You could also feasibly spend one night in San Blas and two in Guadalajara, about 4½ hours by rental car and 6 hours by bus. For lovers of the road less traveled, two to three nights gives you ample time to explore the mountain towns of San Sebastián, Mascota, and Talpa as well as the surrounding countryside. Or you could spend one night in the mountains and continue to Guadalajara the next day. To fully appreciate Guadalajara, plan to spend at least three nights as traveling there takes half a day.

DRIVING TIMES FROM PUERTO VALLARTA	
San Blas	3–3½ hours
San Sebastián	1½–2 hours
Mascota	2½–3 hours
Talpa de Allende	3–3½ hours
Guadalajara	4½–6 hours

TOUR COMPANIES

Charter Club Tours. The bilingual guides of Ajijic's Charter Club Tours lead tours of Guadalajara, shopping and factory trips in Tlaquepaque and Tonalá, Tequila, the Teuchitlán archaeological site, and treks to Jalisco's lesser-known towns. ⊠ *Carretera Oriente, 1 Local C Centro, Ajijic* ☎ *376/766–1777, 408/626–7479 in U.S.* ⊕ *www.charterclubtours. com.mx.*

Tequila Express Train. Contact the Cámara de Comercio de Guadalajara for information about the all-day tour aboard the Tequila Express Train. The cost is about $80, including lunch, a factory tour, mariachi serenades, and of course tequila. ⊠ *Chamber of Commerce Av., Vallarta 4095, Zona Minerva, Guadalajara* ☎ *33/3880–9090, 01800/503–9720 toll-free in Mexico* ⊕ *www.tequilaexpress.com.mx.*

Vallarta Adventures. Highly recommended Vallarta Adventures has daily, seven-hour jeep tours to San Sebastián ($92). ⊠ *Edifício Marina Golf, Local 13–C, Calle Mástil, Marina Vallarta, Puerto Vallarta* ☎ *322/297–1212, 888/526–2283 in U.S. and Canada* ⊕ *www.vallarta-adventures.com.*

ABOUT THE RESTAURANTS

The most popular international restaurants are scattered about west Guadalajara, but some of the best Mexican food is near the main attractions in downtown Guadalajara, Tlaquepaque, and Tonalá.

If sitting down to a meal before 8 pm, you may find you don't need reservations—and you might even have the restaurant to yourself. By around 10 pm, the locals will start filling up the place, and reservations become a must. Good food tends to be very low-priced compared to comparable food in the States, even at the best restaurants in town. A main course is $6 to $15, and alcoholic beverages start at $2. Some of the best food in the city can be found at smaller taco shops and stands, where you can come away full having spent under $5 for four tacos and a soda. It's important to be careful when eating food from street vendors, however; the best sign of a stand worth trying is a long line of locals waiting to order.

ABOUT THE HOTELS

Choosing a place to stay is a matter of location, price, and comfort. Tourists are often drawn to the Centro, where colonial-style hotels are convenient to the historical center and other sights. But hotels in the center tend to be a bit run down and don't offer the amenities available at those farther west. Businesspeople and those looking for more modern digs head for the area around Avenida López Mateos Sur, a 16-km (10-mile) strip extending from the Minerva Fountain to the Plaza del Sol shopping center, or Avenida Americas in Providencia where they can take advantage of newer facilities and four-star comforts. Several hotels, like the polished Hilton, are near the Expo Guadalajara convention center.

WHAT IT COSTS IN U.S. DOLLARS AND MEXICAN PESOS				
	$	$$	$$$	$$$$
Restaurants in Dollars	under $13	$13–$19	$20–$25	over $25
Restaurants in Pesos	under M$160	M$160–M$250	M$251–M$330	over M$330
Hotels in Dollars	under $120	$120–$180	$181–$250	over $250
Hotels in Pesos	under M$1600	tM$1600–M$2400	M$2401–M$3300	Over M$3300

Restaurant prices are for a median main course at dinner, excluding tax, drinks, and service. Hotel prices are for a standard room, generally excluding taxes and service charges.

Hotel reviews have been shortened. For full information, visit Fodors. com.

SAN BLAS AND ENVIRONS

The cool thing about San Blas and the surrounding beaches is that they're untouristy and authentic. Sure, there's an expat community, but it's minuscule compared to that of Puerto Vallarta. Parts of San Blas itself are deliciously disheveled or, should we say, ungentrified. The lively square is a nice place to polish off an ice-cream cone and watch the world. If you're looking for posh restaurants and perfect English speakers, this isn't the place for you.

Most people come to the San Blas area for basic R&R, to enjoy the long beaches and seafood shanties. The town's sights can be seen in a day, but stay for a few days at least to catch up on your reading, visit the beaches, and savor the town as it deserves. A La Tovara jungle cruise through the mangroves should not be missed.

SAN BLAS

Many travelers come here looking for Old Mexico, or the "real Mexico," or the Mexico they remember from the 1960s. New Spain's first official Pacific port has experienced a long, slow slide into obscurity since losing out to better-equipped ports in the late 19th century. But there's something to be said for being a bit player rather than a superstar. Industrious but not overworked, residents of this drowsy seaside city hit the beaches on weekends and celebrate their good fortune during numerous saints' days and civic festivals. You can, too.

GETTING HERE AND AROUND

If you want to head directly to San Blas from outside Mexico, fly to Mexico City and on to Tepic (69 km [43 miles] from San Blas), capital of the state of Nayarit, on Aeromar (affiliated with Mexicana de Aviación). To get to San Blas by road from Tepic, head north on Highway 15D, then west on Highway 11. Most visitors, however, make San Blas a road trip from PV.

The Puerto Vallarta bus station is less than 5 km (3 miles) north of the PV airport; there are usually four daily departures for San Blas ($10; three hours). These buses generally don't stop, and most don't have bathrooms. Departure times vary throughout the year, but at this writing, there were no departures after 4:30 pm. To get to Platanitos Beach, about an hour south of San Blas, take the Puerto Vallarta bus. ■ TIP➔ **Always check the return schedule with the driver when taking an out-of-town bus.** A taxi from Puerto Vallarta or from the airport costs about $100.

A car is handy for more extensive explorations of the coast between PV and around San Blas. Within San Blas, the streets are wide, traffic is almost nonexistent, and, with the exception of the streets immediately surrounding the main plaza, parking is easy. From Puerto Vallarta, abandon Highway 200 just past Las Varas in favor of the coast road. (Follow the sign toward Zacualpan, where you must go around the main plaza to continue on the unsigned road. Ask locals "San Blas?" and they'll point you in the right direction.) The distance of about 160 km (100 miles) takes 3 to 3½ hours.

From Guadalajara, you can take 15D (the toll road, about $40) to the Miramar turnoff to San Blas. It's actually much faster and less congested, however, to take Highway 15 at Tequepexpan and head west through Compostela on Highway 68 (toll about $5); merge with Highway 200 until Las Varas, and then head north on the coastal route (Highway 66) to San Blas.

To really go native, rent a bike from Wala Restaurant, a half block up from the plaza on Avenida Benito Juárez, and cruise to your heart's content. To get to the beaches south of town, to Matanchén Bay, and to the village of Santa Cruz, take a bus (they usually leave on the hour) from the bus station across the street from the church on the main plaza. To come back, just stand by the side of the road and flag down a passing bus.

EXPLORING

If you need a break from all-out relaxation, visit some of these locations. However, keep in mind that, like the town itself, the sites of San Blas are very low-key.

Old Aduana. The old Customs House has been partially restored and is now a cultural center with sporadic art or photography shows and theatrical productions. ⊠ *Calle Juárez, near Calle del Puerto.*

Cerro de San Basilio. For a bird's-eye view of the town and coast, hike or drive up Calle Juárez, the main drag, to Cerro de San Basilio.

 Contaduría. Cannons protect the ruined Counting House, built during colonial times when San Blas was New Spain's first official port. ⊠ *Cerro de San Basilio.*

Templo de la Virgen del Rosario. Continuing down the road from the Contaduría brings you to el Templo de la Virgen del Rosario. Note the new floor in the otherwise ruined structure; the governor's daughter didn't want to soil the hem of her gown when she married here in 2005. A bit farther on, San Blas's little cemetery is backed by the sea and the mountains. ⊠ *Calle Jose Ma. Mercado, at Echevarria.*

Templo de San Blas. Templo de San Blas, called *La Iglesia Vieja* ("the old church") by residents, is on the town's busy plaza. It's rarely open these days, but you can admire its diminutive beauty and look for the words to Henry Wadsworth Longfellow's poem "The Bells of San Blas," inscribed on a brass plaque. (The long-gone bells were actually at the church dedicated to the Virgin of the Rosary, on Cerro de San Basilio.)

9

WHERE TO EAT

$
SEAFOOD
✕ **La Isla.** Shell lamps; pictures made entirely of scallops, bivalves, and starfish; shell-drenched chandeliers—every inch of wall space is decorated in different denizens of the sea. Service isn't particularly brisk (pretty much par for the course in laid-back San Blas), but the seafood, filet mignon, and fajitas are all quite good. Afterward stroll over to the main plaza a few blocks away. $ *Average main: $10* ⊠ *Calle Mercado at Calle Paredes* ☎ *323/285–0407* ▭ *No credit cards* ⊗ *Closed Mon. except holidays* ✛ *B4.*

WHERE TO STAY

$
HOTEL
FAMILY
 Casa Mañana. Some of the pleasant rooms overlook the beach from a balcony or terrace, but most people stay here for easy access to the good burgers, guacamole, and seafood platter for two ($13) at the adjoining El Alebrije restaurant. **Pros:** good burgers; nice beachfront location. **Cons:** must take a bus or taxi to and from San Blas. $ *Rooms from: $36* ⊠ *South end of Playa Los Cocos, 13 km (8 miles) south of San Blas* ☎ *323/254–9070, 800/202–2079 in Mexico only* ⊕ *www.*

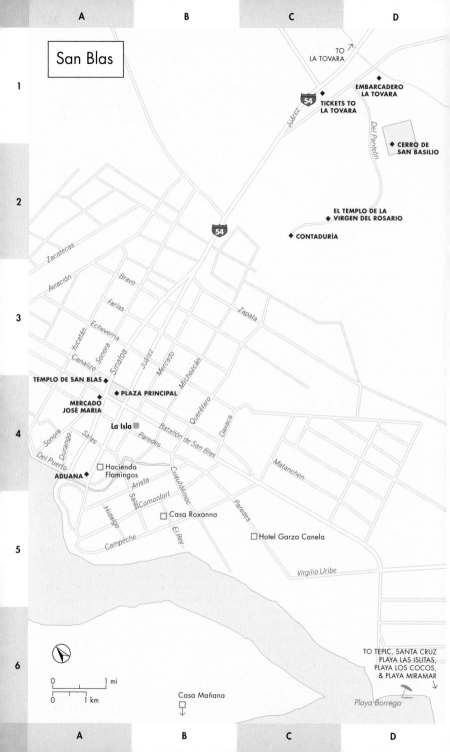

casa-manana.com 26 *rooms* *No meals* ✣ *A1.*

$ HOTEL **Casa Roxanna.** This is an attractive little enclave of cozy and clean (albeit basic) cottages with screened windows. **Pros:** personable staff; great lap pool. **Cons:** so-so a/c units; lackluster interior decor. *Rooms from: $55* ✉ *Callejón El Rey 1* ☎ *323/285–0573* 🌐 *www.casaroxanna.com* 6 *cottages* *No credit cards* *No meals* ✣ *B5.*

$ HOTEL **Hacienda Flamingos.** Built in 1882, this restored mansion-turned-hotel was once part of a large hacienda. **Pros:** lovely decor; close to town center. **Cons:** sometimes eerily devoid of other guests; staff can be chilly. *Rooms from: $82* ✉ *Calle Juárez 105* ☎ *323/285–0930, 669/985–1818 for information in English* 🌐 *www.sanblas.com.mx* 20 *rooms* *No meals* ✣ *A4.*

$ HOTEL **Hotel Garza Canela.** Opened decades ago by a family of dedicated birdwatchers, this meandering, three-story hotel with expansive grounds is the home base of choice for birding groups. **Pros:** very good French restaurant; suites have hot tub; babysitters. **Cons:** estuary location means there are some biting bugs. *Rooms from: $88* ✉ *Calle Paredes 106 Sur* ☎ *323/285–0112, 01800/713–2313 toll-free in Mexico* 🌐 *www.garzacanela.com* 44 *rooms, 6 suites* *No meals* ✣ *C5.*

BIRDER'S PARADISE

More than 500 species of birds settle in the San Blas area; 23 are endemic. Organize a birding tour through Hotel Garza Canela (⇨ *below).*

International Festival of Migratory Birds. In late January, you can attend the International Festival of Migratory Birds for birdwatching tours and conferences with experts and fellow enthusiasts. 🌐 *avessanblas.uan.mx.*

SPORTS AND THE OUTDOORS

FAMILY **La Tovara.** A series of narrow waterways winds through the mangroves to La Tovara, San Blas's most famous attraction. Turtles on logs, crocs that *look* like logs, birds, iguanas, and exotic orchids make this maze of mud-brown canals a magical place. Begin the tranquil ride ($8 per person; four-person minimum or $27 [360 pesos] total for fewer than four) at El Conchal Bridge, at the entrance-exit to San Blas, or the village of Matanchén. Boats depart when there are enough customers, which isn't usually a problem. Either way you'll end up, after a 45-minute boat ride, at the freshwater pool fed by a natural spring. Rest at the snack shop overlooking the water or jump in using the rope swing, keeping an eye out for the allegedly benign resident croc. There's an optional trip to a crocodile farm for a few dollars more, making it a three-hour instead of a two-hour tour. ✉ *Carr. Las Islitas s/n. Embarcadero principal, Matanchen* 🌐 *www.latovara.com* *$10* *Daily 8–6.*

ECOTOUR

Singayta. Singayta is a typical Nayarit village that is attempting to support itself through simple and ungimmicky ecotours. The basic tour includes a look around the town, where original adobe structures compete with more practical but less picturesque structures with corrugated tin roofs. Take a short guided hike through the surrounding jungle, and a boat ride around the estuary ($6 per person). This is primo birding

Take in the expansive landscape from San Blas Fort at Cerro de San Basilio.

territory. The townspeople are most geared up for tours on weekends and during school holidays and vacations: Christmas, Easter, and July and August. The easiest way to book a tour is to look for English-speaking Juan Bananas, who sells banana bread from a shop called Tumba de Yako (look for the sign on the unmarked road Avenida H. Batallón between calles Comonfort and Canalizo, en route to Playa Borrego). He can set up a visit and/or guide you there. Groups of five or more can call ahead to make a reservation with Juan (☎ 323/285–0462 ✎ ecomanglar@yahoo.com) or with Santos (☎ 323/100–4191); call at least a day ahead if you want to have a meal. ✉ 8 km (5 miles) from San Blas on road to Tepic.

BEACHES

Like San Blas itself, the surrounding beaches attract mostly local people and travelers fleeing glitzier resort scenes. Beaches here are almost uniformly long, flat, and walkable, with light brown sand, moderate waves, and seriously bothersome no-see-ums, especially around sunrise and sunset (and during the waxing and waning moons). Almost as ubiquitous as these biting bugs are simple *ramadas* (open-sided, palm-thatch-roof eateries) on the beach whose owners don't mind if you hang out all day, jumping in the ocean and then back into your shaded hammock to continue devouring John Grisham or leafing through magazines. Order a cold lemonade or a beer, or have a meal of fish fillets, ceviche, or chips and guacamole. Don't expect a full menu, rather what's fresh and available. All these beaches are accessible by bus from San Blas's centrally located bus station.

FAMILY **Playa Borrego.** You can walk or ride
Fodor$Choice a bike to long, lovely Playa Bor-
★ rego, 1 km (½ mile) south of town.
Rent a surfboard at Stoners' or Mar
y Sol restaurant to attack the year-
round (but sporadic) shore or jetty
breaks here, or stroll down to the
southern end to admire the lovely,
palm-fringed estuary. ⊠ *Turistico
Playa del Borrego.*

BEHIND THE MUSIC

If you're a fan of the rock group
Maná, it's interesting to note that
the song "Muelle de San Blas"
("San Blas's Wharf") refers to a
tiny dock and a few wooden posts
hosting friendly-looking pelicans,
just south of the Aduana.

Playa Las Islitas. About 6 km (4
miles) south of Playa Borrego, at the northern edge of Bahía de Matanchén, Playa Las Islitas used to be legendary among surfers for its long
wave, but this has diminished in recent years. The beach is now suitable
for swimming, bodysurfing, and boogie boarding.

Playa Los Cocos and Playa Miramar. At the south end of the Matanchén
Bay, Playa Los Cocos and Playa Miramar are both great for taking long
walks and for hanging out at ramadas.

Playa Platanitos. Beyond Matanchén Bay the road heads inland and
reemerges about 8 km (5 miles) later at Playa Platanitos, a lovely little
beach in a sheltered cove. Fishermen park their skiffs here and simple
shacks cook up the catch of the day.

Santa Cruz. Adjacent to Miramar Beach is the well-kept fishing village
of Santa Cruz. Take a walk on the beach or around the town; buy a
soft drink, find the bakery, and pick up some banana bread. Outdoor
dances are occasionally held on the diminutive central plaza.

THE MOUNTAIN TOWNS

9

A trip into the Sierra Madre is an excellent way to escape the coastal
heat and the hordes of vacationers. The Spanish arrived to extract ore
from these mountains at the end of the 16th century; after the Mexican
Revolution the mines were largely abandoned in favor of richer veins.
The isolation of these tiny towns has kept them old-fashioned.

The air is crisp and clean and scented of pine, the valley and mountain
views are spectacular, and the highland towns are earthy, unassuming,
and charming. Whitewashed adobe homes radiate from plazas where
old gents remember youthful exploits. Saturday night boys and girls
court each other alfresco while oompah bands entertain their parents
from the bandstand. Although most of the hotels in the region have
only basic amenities (construction of a massively improved road from
PV is encouraging entrepreneurs, however), the chill mountain air and
pounds of blankets can produce a delicious night's sleep.

GETTING HERE AND AROUND

For an effortless excursion, go on a tour through Vallarta Adventures. It
has excellent day trips ($80) to San Sebastián by bus or jeep, depending
on the number of passengers.

To have more flexibility or to spend the night in a cozy, no-frills hotel or a refurbished hacienda, charter a twin-engine Cessna through Aerotaxis de la Bahía in PV. For one to seven passengers the rate is about $700 split among them to San Sebastián, $750 to Mascota or Talpa de Allende. Add to these fares 15% sales tax and $20 per person for air travelers' tax. ■TIP→ The return flight is usually free if you fly back with the pilot within three hours of arrival.

> **CAUTION**
>
> The fierce biting *jejenes* (no-see-ums) of San Blas are legendary; luckily, early afternoon breezes keep them (relatively) at bay. They're worst during full and new moons, when the tide is highest.

ATM (Autotransportes Talpa–Mascota) buses depart from the bus station in PV three times a day around 9 am, 2:30 pm, and 6:30 pm, stopping at La Estancia (11 km [7 miles] from San Sebastián; 1½ hours), then Mascota (2 to 2½ hours) and Talpa (3 to 3½ hours). The cost is about $5 one way to San Sebastián (La Estancia); $9 to Mascota; and $10 to Talpa.

Buses also depart several times a day from Guadalajara's new bus station (Entronque Carretera Libre a Zapotlanejo, modules 3 and 4). Note that the bus doesn't enter San Sebastián; you'll be dropped at a small rest area, where taxis usually are available to transport you to town. The cost for the short drive is a bit steep at about $12. Share the cab with others on the bus to split the cost; or get a lift with a local and offer to pay (note that many will decline or ask just a small amount to help out with gas).

From Puerto Vallarta the road to San Sebastián is paved now, but those going to San Sebastián still have to get off the bus at La Estancia and take a taxi those last few miles. A suspension bridge was inaugurated in early 2007 to cover the last 8 km (5 miles) of the road to Mascota, which used to get washed out regularly in the rainy season. (Note that this road still may become dangerous or at least frightening during the rainy season, when landslides can occur.) Lago Juanacatlán is an hour from Mascota on a rough one-lane road of dirt and rock.

Taxis hang out near the main square in Talpa, Mascota, and San Sebastián.

VISITOR INFORMATION

Contacts Oficina de Turismo de Mascota ⊠ *La presidencia [town hall], Calle Ayuntamiento, at Calle Constitución, facing plaza, Mascota* ☎ *388/386–1179.* **Oficina de Turismo de San Sebastián** ⊠ *Calle López Mateos, around corner from la presidencia [town hall], San Sebastián* ☎ *322/2267863.* **Oficina de Turismo de Talpa** ⊠ *La presidencia [town hall], Calle Independencia s/n, 2 blocks north of plaza, Talpa de Allende* ☎ *388/385-0009, 388/385-0287.*

TOURS

Contacts Vallarta Adventures ☎ *322/297–1212, 888/526–2238* ⊕ *www. vallarta-adventures.com.*

Banco HSBC ⊠ *Calle Independencia, across from la presidencia [town hall], Talpa* ☎ *388/385–0223.* **Bancomer** ⊠ *Calz. Independencia Norte, Mascota* ☎ *33/3669 0229.*

SAN SEBASTIÁN

Physically, there are only about 80 km (50 miles) between Puerto Vallarta and San Sebastián, but metaphorically they're as far apart as the Earth and the moon. Sleepy San Sebastián is the Mayberry of Mexico, but a little less lively. It's the kind of place where you feel weird walking past people without saying hello, even though you don't know them from Adam. The miners who built the town have long gone, and more recently, younger folks are drifting away in search of opportunity. Most of the 800 or so people who have stayed seem perfectly content with life as it is, although rat-race dropouts and entrepreneurs are making their way here along improved roads.

> **BEST BEACH BITE**
>
> For a marvelous albeit simple barbecue fish feast, visit **Enramada Ruiz,** a sinfully sublime seafood shanty on Playa Platanitos.

EXPLORING

The most interesting thing to see in San Sebastián is the town itself. Walk the cobblestone streets and handsome brick sidewalks, admiring the white-faced adobe structures surrounding the plaza. Take any side street and wander at will. Enjoy the enormous walnut trees lining the road into town, and diminutive peach trees peaking over garden walls. The reason to go to this cozy, lazy, beautiful town at 5,250 feet above sea level is to look inward, reflecting on life, or outward, greeting or chatting as best you can with those you meet. Look anywhere, in fact, except at a laptop or, if possible, a television screen. That's just missing the point.

San Sebastián has a few attractions, although none of them are the main reason to visit.

Casa Museo de Doña Conchita. You're welcome any time at the Casa Museo de Doña Conchita. The aged but affable lady loves to show visitors photos of her venerable family—which she traces back six generations. See bank notes from the mining days, bloomers, shirts made by hand by the lady for her many children, and other old memorabilia. If you speak Spanish, ask Doña Conchita to tell you about the ghosts that haunt her house, which is right on the square between the basketball court and *la presidencia,* or town hall. ⊠ *Calle Juárez 2* ☎ *322/297–2860* ⌦ *$1* ☉ *Mon.–Sat. 10:30–3 and 5–7, Sun. 12 pm–3.*

Iglesia de San Sebastián. Iglesia de San Sebastián is a typically restored 1800s-era church that comes to life in the days preceding its saint's day, January 20th.

9

GREAT ITINERARIES

If you're not joining an organized day tour, there are many possible itineraries, depending on whether you leave from PV or from Guadalajara, your tolerance for driving mountain roads, and your desire to explore (i.e., either to see lots or just relax and enjoy the tranquility, mountain-and-valley views, and quaint lifestyle).

From Puerto Vallarta, consider a two-day trip to the area beginning in San Sebastián and returning to PV (or Guadalajara) from Talpa de Allende. There are many ways to go, but avoid driving at night and try to enjoy the slow pace. Drive to San Sebastián, taking in the mountain scenery en route. After a look around the quaint old mining village and an early lunch, continue to Mascota, the area's largest town and a good

base. Spend the night in Mascota. The Sierra Lodge on Lake Juanacatlán, which serves excellent food, can be added as an overnight trip, but it doesn't take day-trippers. If you prefer, make a day trip from Mascota to Talpa de Allende, whose raison d'être is the tiny, beloved Virgin statue in the town's ornate basilica.

Each of the three towns has hills to climb for excellent vistas and photos. Otherwise, activities include wandering the streets, visiting small museums and Catholic churches, tasting regional food, and drinking in the mountain air and old-fashioned ambience. Make sure you get where you're going before dark, as mountain roads are unlighted and narrow and in many cases have sheer drop-offs.

WHERE TO EAT AND STAY

$

MEXICAN

✕**Fonda de Doña Lupita.** Typical food of the countryside—enchiladas, tamales, pozole, beefsteak with beans and tortillas, and so on—is served in an equally typical family home. The house has been enlarged to welcome guests, and the friendly owner does her part. Straw-bottom chairs are comfortable enough, and the oilcloths shiny and new. The small bar is at the back behind the large, open kitchen. It's open for breakfast, too. ⑤ *Average main: $6* ✉ *Calle Cuauhtemoc 89* ☎ *322/297–2803* ▭ *No credit cards.*

$$

HOTEL

⚄ **La Galerita de San Sebastián.** A pair of displaced *tapatíos* (Guadalajarans) have created a cluster of pretty cabins on their property about four blocks from the plaza. **Pros:** stylish; in-room fireplaces. **Cons:** pricey compared to other area digs; extra charge for each child. ⑤ *Rooms from: $145* ✉ *Camino a Las Galeritas 62, Barrio La Otra Banda* ☎ *322/297–3040* ⊕ *www.lagalerita.com.mx* ↵ *3 bungalows* ⚋⚊ *Breakfast.*

$

HOTEL

⚄ **Real de San Sebastián.** Small rooms are dominated by snug king beds in curtained alcoves in this interesting B&B. **Pros:** friendly, helpful hosts; good value. **Cons:** living room is dated; guest rooms are dominated by the bed and don't have phones; credit cards aren't accepted. ⑤ *Rooms from: $54* ✉ *Calle Lerdo de Tejada 16* ☎ *322/150–7457* ▭ *No credit cards* ↵ *6 rooms* ⚋⚊ *Breakfast.*

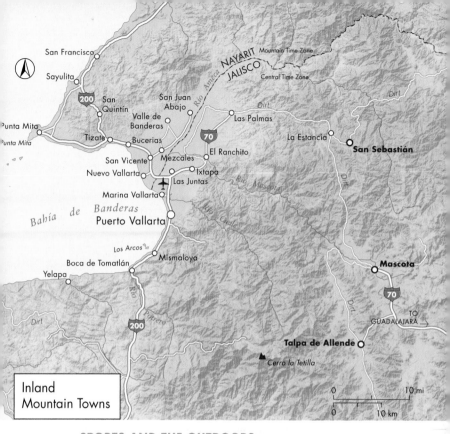

Inland
Mountain Towns

SPORTS AND THE OUTDOORS

La Bufa. Local men can be hired for a truck ride up to La Bufa, a half-dome visible from the town square. The truck will wait while you climb—about 15 minutes to the top—and enjoy the wonderful view of the town, surrounding valleys, and, on a clear day, Puerto Vallarta. San Sebastián was founded as a silver- and gold-mining town; ask the driver to stop for a quick visit to a mine en route. The excursion takes about three hours. Or you can hike both ways; it takes most folks two to two and a half hours to reach the top, and half to two-thirds that time to return.

Obed Dueñas. Obed Dueñas can be hired to take you up to La Bufa. He charges about $70 for the trip, whether for two or eight passengers. It's the same price if you return with him or hike back. ☎ 322/297–2864.

MASCOTA

Mascota's cool but sunny climate is perfect for growing citrus, avocados, nuts, wheat, corn, and other crops. Fed by the Mascota and Ameca rivers and many springs and year-round streams, the blue-green hills and valleys surrounding town are lusciously forested; beyond them rise indigo mountains to form a painterly tableau. This former mining town and municipal seat is home to some 13,000 people. Its banks, shops,

San Sebastián is beautiful at dusk; get to higher ground for the full effect.

and hospital serve surrounding villages. On its coat of arms are a pine tree, deer, and rattlesnake. The town's name derives from the Nahuatl words for "deer" and "snake."

EXPLORING

Cerro de la Cruz. The countryside just outside town is ideal for hikes and drives. From Mascota's plaza you can walk up Calle Morelos out of town to Cerro de la Cruz. The hike to the summit takes about a half hour and rewards with great valley views.

Iglesia de la Virgen de los Dolores. On one corner of the plaza is the town's white-spire Iglesia de la Virgen de los Dolores. The Virgin of Sorrow is feted on September 15, which segues into Mexican Independence Day on the 16th. ⊠ *Calle Ponciano Arriaga 110.*

La Iglesia de la Preciosa Sangre. Mascota's pride is La Iglesia de la Preciosa Sangre (Church of the Precious Blood), started in 1909 but unfinished due to the revolution and the ensuing Cristero Revolt. Weddings, concerts, and plays are sometimes held here under the ruins of Gothic arches. Note the 3-D blood squirting from Jesus's wound in the chapel—you could hardly miss it. ⊠ *Calle Rosa Davalos s/n.*

Lago Juanacatlán. Lago Juanacatlán is a lovely lake in a volcanic crater at 7,000 feet above sea level. Nestled in the Galope River valley, the pristine lake is surrounded by alpine woods, and the trip from Mascota past fields of flowers and self-sufficient *ranchos* is bucolic.

Palacio de Cultura y el Arte de Mascota. Around the corner from the Mascota Museum, the Palacio de Cultura y el Arte has rotating exhibits of photography and art. It's open 10–3 Monday through Saturday. ⊠ *Calle*

Independencia 47 ☎ *388/386–1679* ⊙ *Mon.–Sat. 10–3 pm.*

Plaza. Walk around the plaza, where old gents share stories and kids chase balloons. Couples dance the stately *danzón* on Thursday and Saturday evenings as the band plays in the wrought-iron bandstand. The town produces ceramics, saddles, and *raicilla*, a relative of tequila made from the green agave plant (tequila comes from the blue one).

Presa Corinches. Presa Corinches, a dam about 5 km (3 miles) south of town, has bass fishing, picnic spots (for cars and RVs), and a restaurant where locals go for fish feasts on holidays and weekend afternoons. To get to the dam, head east on Calle Juárez (a block south of the plaza) and follow the signs to the reservoir. Take a walk along the shore or set up a tent near the fringe of pine-oak forest coming down to meet the cool blue water, which is fine for swimming when the weather is warm.

WHERE TO EAT

$
CAFÉ
✕ **Café Napolés.** Originally a coffee-and-dessert stop and fashionable hangout for Mascotans, this snug little eatery serves big breakfasts and now main dishes at lunch and dinner, too. Sit on the small street-facing patio, in the diminutive dining room, or facing the glass case featuring fantastic-looking cakes, pies, and tarts. You can get wine and beer as well as pizza, barbecue, spaghetti, and other Italian food. ⑤ *Average main: $6* ⊠ *Calle Hidalgo 105, Centro* ☎ *388/386–0051* ▭ *No credit cards.*

$
MEXICAN
✕ **La Casa de Mi Abuelita.** Everyone and his mother likes "Grandma's House," which is conveniently open all day (and evening), every day, starting at around 8 am with breakfast. In addition to beans, rice, carne asada, and other recognizable Mexican food, there are backcountry recipes that are much less familiar to the average traveler. ⑤ *Average main: $7* ⊠ *Calle Corona, at Calle Zaragoza* ☎ *388/386–1975.*

$
MEXICAN
✕ **Navidad.** It's named for the small town 14 km (9 miles) from Mascota, not the Christmas holiday, which is the only day this restaurant closes. The cavernous space, lined in red brick, makes the restaurant look rather generic, but it's actually family-owned and run and oh-so-personable. Best yet, it's open 7 am to nearly midnight. Try the regional dishes like goat stew and enchiladas, pizza, or a daily special such as beef tongue or *jocoque* (strained yogurt). ⑤ *Average main: $4* ⊠ *Calle Juan Díaz de Sandi 28, Centro* ☎ *388/386–0469.*

WHERE TO STAY

$
HOTEL
▦ **Mesón de Santa Elena.** Beautiful rooms in this converted 19th-century house have lovely old tile floors, beige cotton drapes covering huge windows, rag-rolled walls, and wonderful tile floors and sinks. **Pros:** two blocks from the town square; feels like you're a guest in someone's home; Internet café about a block away. **Cons:** Internet intermittent

in some rooms; feels like you're a guest in someone's home. ⑤ *Rooms from: $65* ✉ *Hidalgo 155* ☎ *388/386-0313* ⊕ *www.mesonde santaelena.com* ↵ *10 rooms, 2 suites* ⑩ *Breakfast.*

$ ⊞ **Rancho La Esmeralda.** Catering
HOTEL   to small groups and father-and-son outings, this ranch-style lodging near the entrance to town also accepts individual travelers. **Pros:** newer construction; fireplaces and king-size beds; midweek discount. **Cons:** 10-minute drive from town center; bumpy cobblestone entry road. ⑤ *Rooms from: $50* ✉ *Calle Salvador Chavez 47* ☎ *388/386-0953* ⊕ *www.rancholaesmeralda.com. mx* ↵ *10 rooms, 7 cabins.*

$$$ ⊞ **Sierra Lago Resort & Spa.** An hour north of Mascota, this lodge of
HOTEL   knotty pine is a tranquil lakeside retreat. **Pros:** beautiful scenery and mountain air; activities included in all-inclusive room rate. **Cons:** no phone in room; no Internet access. ⑤ *Rooms from: $213* ✉ *Domicilio Conocido, Lago Juanacatlán* ☎ *855/704-7344 in U.S. and Canada, 01800/099-0362 toll-free in Mexico* ⊕ *www.sierralago.com* ↵ *24 suites* ⑩ *Multiple meal plans.*

SHOPPING

Stores in town sell homemade preserves, locally grown coffee, *raicilla* (an alcoholic drink made of green agave), and sweets.

> **HOLY CITY**
>
> During several major annual fiestas, the town swells with visitors. The Fiesta de la Candelaria culminates in Candlemass on February 2. The town's patron saint, St. Joseph, is honored on March 19. May 12, September 10, September 19, and October 7 mark rituals devoted to the Virgen del Rosario de Talpa.

TALPA DE ALLENDE

Another tranquil town surrounded by pine-oak forests, Talpa, as it's called, has just over 7,000 inhabitants but welcomes 4 million visitors a year. They come to pay homage or ask favors of the diminutive Virgen del Rosario de Talpa, one of Jalisco's most revered Virgins. Some people walk three days from Puerto Vallarta as penance or a sign of devotion; others come by car, horse, bicycle, or truck but return annually to show their faith.

EXPLORING

Basilica de Talpa. On the large plaza, the Basilica de Talpa is the main show in town. The twin-spire limestone temple is Gothic with neoclassic elements. After visiting the diminutive, royally clad Virgin in her side chapel, stroll around the surrounding square. Shops and stalls sell sweets, miniature icons of the Virgin in every possible presentation, T-shirts, and other souvenirs. *Chicle* (gum) is harvested in the area, and you'll find small keepsakes in the shapes of shoes, flowers, and animals made of the (nonsticky) raw material.

WHERE TO EAT AND STAY

$ ✕ **Casa Grande.** This steak house also serves grilled chicken and seafood.

STEAKHOUSE   Under a roof but open on all sides and with an incredible view, it's highly recommended by visitors and locals. In fact, it's a popular place for locals' reunions and family parties. ⑤ *Average main: $11* ⊠ *Calle Juárez 53* ☎ *388/385–0709* ◐ *Closed Tues.*

$ ✕ **El Herradero.** "The Blacksmith" will win no awards for cuisine or, for

MEXICAN   that matter, decoration. But it's often filled with families of pilgrims, and the locals recommend it, too. The menu offers mainly meat dishes, including burgers with fries, plus *antojitos, gorditas,* and *sopes* (all cornmeal-based, fried concoctions stuffed with meat or beans and, in the case of the latter, topped with beans and salsa), pozole, and quesadillas. The tortillas are made fresh at the back of the restaurant. Half orders are available, and there's a bar serving national booze and beer. ⑤ *Average main: $6* ⊠ *Calle 23 de Junio 8* ☎ *388/385–0376* ➡ *No credit cards.*

$ 🖼 **Renovación.** Basic yet comfortable rooms in this three-story hotel

HOTEL   (opened in 2007) have king-size beds with dark blue, hunting-theme spreads and desks of shiny lacquered wood. **Pros:** newer property; a couple of blocks from the main plaza. **Cons:** no elevator; no credit cards accepted. ⑤ *Rooms from: $27* ⊠ *Calle Independencia 45, Centro* ☎ *388/385–1412* ⤸ *18 rooms* ➡ *No credit cards.*

GUADALAJARA

Guadalajara rests on a mile-high plain of the Sierra Madre Occidental, surrounded on three sides by rugged hills and on the fourth by the spectacular Oblatos Canyon. Mexico's second-largest city has a population of 4 million and is the capital of Jalisco State. This cosmopolitan if traditional and quintessentially Mexican city offers a range of activities. Shop for handicrafts, housewares, and especially fine ceramics in smart shops or family-owned factories. Dress up for drinks, dinner, and dancing in smart Zona Minerva, in downtown Guadalajara, or put on your comfy walking shoes to visit satellite neighborhoods of indigenous origin. For shoppers and metropolis lovers, this is a great complement to a Puerto Vallarta vacation.

GETTING HERE AND AROUND

AIR TRAVEL   Many major airlines fly nonstop from the United States to Guadalajara. Aeropuerto Internacional Libertador Miguel Hidalgo is 16½ km (10 miles) south of the city, en route to Chapala. Autotransportaciones Aeropuerto operates a 24-hour taxi stand with service to any place in the Guadalajara area; buy tickets at the counters at the national and international exits. Some hotels also offer airport pickup shuttles; these need to be arranged in advance.

BUS AND SUB-   Flying from your hometown to Guadalajara, then back home from

WAY TRAVEL   PV can be a good deal; flying round-trip to Guadalajara from Puerto Vallarta is not. The bus is much cheaper, scenic, and efficient. Luxury buses between PV and Guadalajara take 4½ hours and cost $30–$35. With one wide seat on one side of the aisle and only two on the other, ETN is the most upscale line and has about nine trips a day to and

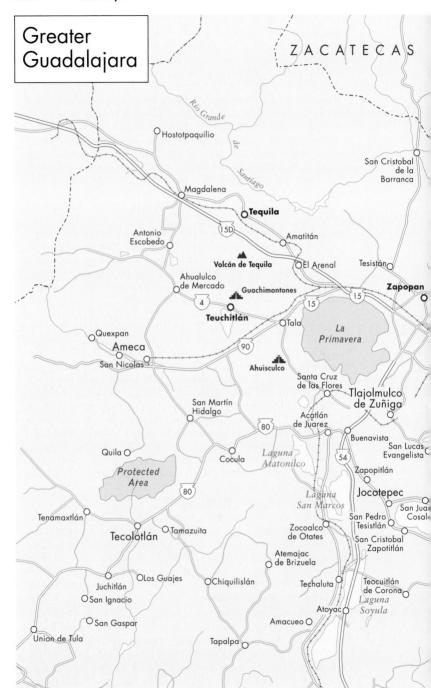

Greater Guadalajara

Z A C A T E C A S

Hostotpaquilio

Río Grande

de

Santiago

San Cristobal
de la
Barranca

Magdalena

15D **Tequila** Amatitán

Antonio
Escobedo

Tesistán

Volcán de Tequila El Arenal

Ahualulco
de Mercado Guachimontones 15 15 **Zapopan**

4 **Teuchitlán** Tala La
Primavera

Quexpan 90

Ameca

San Nicolas Ahuisculco

Santa Cruz
de las Flores Tlajolmulco
de Zuñiga

San Martín
Hidalgo Acatlán
de Juarez Buenavista

Quila 80 Cocula Laguna
Atotonilco 54 San Lucas
Evangelista

Zapopitlán

Laguna
San Marcos **Jocotepec**

San Juan
Cosala

Tenamaxtlán 80 San Pedro
Tesistlán

Zocoalco
de Otates San Cristobal
Zapotitlán

Tamazuita Atemajac
de Brizuela

Tecolotlán

Los Guajes Chiquilislán Techaluta Teocuitlán
de Corona

Juchitlán Laguna
Soyula

San Ignacio Atoyac

San Gaspar Amacueo

Union de Tula Tapalpa

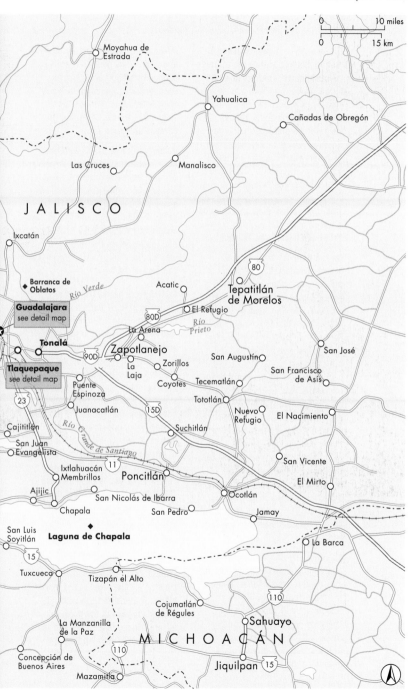

GUADALAJARA ITINERARY

The four primary municipalities of metropolitan Guadalajara are Guadalajara, Zapopan, Tlaquepaque, and Tonalá. Aside from Zapopan, areas of interest to visitors can be navigated on foot in a few hours, though each deserves at least half a day. Zapopan requires more time since it's a sprawling suburb with lots of shopping. Due west of Guadalajara's Centro Histórico, Zona Minerva is the place to go for great restaurants and after-dark action. Plan on a third day if you want to visit outlying areas like Lake Chapala and Teuchitlán.

On the morning of Day 1, visit historic Guadalajara, checking out the cathedral and other landmarks on the plazas. Mercado Libertad (aka Mercado San Juan de Dios) is several long blocks east of Plaza Fundadores; you can walk or take the subway two blocks south of the cathedral on Avenida Juárez. If it's Sunday, see a *charrería* (rodeo); otherwise head to Zapopan to see the basilica, the Huichol Museum, and the Art Museum of Zapopan, and spend 15 minutes at *la presidencia municipal* (city hall) to admire the mural inside. Check out the market, two blocks west at Calles Eva Briseño and Hidalgo, before grabbing a snack on Paseo Teopinztle, two blocks south. For dinner, dine in downtown Guadalajara or the Zona Minerva.

Spend the second day shopping and visiting churches and museums in the old towns of Tonalá and the more compact, walkable Tlaquepaque. If you're here on Thursday or Sunday, don't miss the Tonalá crafts market. El Parián in Tlaquepaque is a great place to enjoy a mariachi serenade and refreshments. Have lunch or dinner in one of Tlaquepaque's charming restaurants. If you don't want to shop, consider spending an afternoon listening to mariachi music, seeing a charrería, or visiting the gardens at Parque Azul.

If you have three days, you'll have time to visit Tequila or Lake Chapala and admire the relatively dry hills and valleys, noting the fields of blue agave that are Tequila's reason for being. Tequila is en route to San Blas and Puerto Vallarta. Lake Chapala and the towns on the shore work well as a day excursion, especially if you have a car.

LOGISTICS AND TIPS

You need at least three hours for the Centro Histórico, longer if you really want to enjoy the sculptures and street scene. Mornings are the least crowded time of day, although the light is particularly beautiful in the afternoon, when the jugglers, street musicians, and other informal entertainers emerge. Take advantage of free walking tours in the historical district. Accompanied by mariachis or other musicians, the two-hour tours meet most evenings around dusk in front of city hall. Show up at about 7 pm (an hour earlier during winter) to register.

Beware of heavy traffic and *topes* (speed bumps). Traffic circles are common at busy intersections.

Tonalá's crafts market and Mercado Libertad are the region's top marketplaces. El Trocadero is a weekly antiques market at the north end of Avenida Chapultepec. Feel free to drive a hard bargain at all three.

As with nearly all of Mexico, Guadalajara has no shortage of religious iconography in public spaces.

from PV, except Sunday, which has only one. Within Mexico, it accepts advance reservations with a credit card. Estrella Blanca is an umbrella of different bus lines, many of which head straight for Guadalajara. TAP (Transportes del Pacifico) is a first-class line that serves major Pacific Coast destinations between Ixtapa/Zihuatanejo and the U.S. border, including service to Guadalajara, Puerto Vallarta, and Tepic. ■ TIP→ Many bus lines do not accept credit cards. Guadalajara's Nueva Central Camionera (New Central Bus Station) is 10 km (6 miles) southeast of downtown.

Most city buses (45¢) run from every few minutes to every half hour between 6 am and 9 pm; some run until 11 pm. ⚠ The city's public transit buses are infamously fatal; drivers killed more than 100 pedestrians annually in the late 1990s before the government intervened. These poorly designed, noisy, noxious buses are still driven ruthlessly and cause at least a dozen deaths per year.

Large mint-green Tur and red Cardinal buses are the safest, quickest, and least crowded and go to Zapopan, Tlaquepaque, and Tonalá for around 10 pesos. Wait for these along Avenida 16 de Septiembre.

Autotransportes Guadalajara–Chapala serves the lakeside towns from Guadalajara's new bus station (Central Camionera Nueva) and from the old bus station (Antigua Central Camionera); the cost is around $4. It's 45 minutes to Chapala and another 15 minutes to Ajijic; there are departures every half hour from 6 am to 9:30 pm. Make sure you ask for the *directo* (direct) as opposed to the *segunda clase* (second-class) bus, which stops at every little pueblo en route.

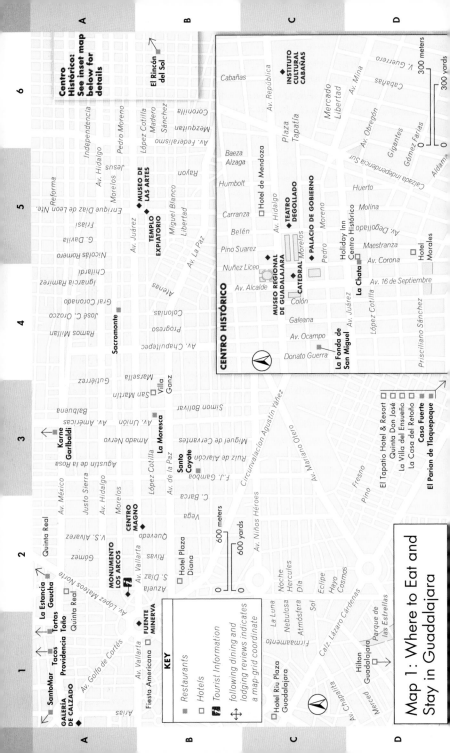

Map 1: Where to Eat and Stay in Guadalajara

KEY

- **Restaurants**
- ☐ **Hotels**
- 🛈 **Tourist Information**

↔ *following dining and lodging reviews indicates a map-grid coordinate*

CENTRO HISTÓRICO

Centro Histórico: See inset map below for details

Restaurants and Hotels (main map)

- SantoMar
- La Estancia Gaucha
- Tacos Providencia Toño
- Tortos Toño
- Quinta Real
- Quinta Real
- GALERÍA DE CALZADO
- MONUMENTO LOS ARCOS
- FUENTE MINERVA
- Fiesta Americana
- Karne Garibaldi
- Sacromonte
- La Moresca
- Santo Coyote
- CENTRO MAGNO
- TEMPLO EXPIATORIO
- MUSEO DE LAS ARTES
- El Rincón del Sol
- Hotel Plaza Diana
- Hotel Ríu Plaza Guadalajara
- Hilton Guadalajara

Centro Histórico inset

- MUSEO REGIONAL DE GUADALAJARA
- TEATRO DEGOLLADO
- PALACIO DE GOBIERNO
- CATEDRAL
- INSTITUTO CULTURAL CABAÑAS
- Plaza Tapatía
- Mercado Libertad
- Hotel de Mendoza
- Holiday Inn Centro Histórico
- Hotel Morales
- La Chata
- La Fonda de San Miguel

Bottom listing

- ☐ El Tapatío Hotel & Resort
- ☐ Quinta Don José
- ☐ La Villa del Ensueño
- ☐ La Casa del Retoño
- ■ Casa Fuerte
- ■ El Parián de Tlaquepaque

Scale

- 300 meters / 300 yards (inset)
- 600 meters / 600 yards (main map)

Guadalajara's underground *tren ligero* (light train) system is clean and efficient. Trains run every 10 minutes from 5 am to midnight; a token for one trip costs about 40¢.

CAR TRAVEL Metropolitan Guadalajara's traffic gets intense, especially at rush hour, and parking can be scarce. Streets shoot off at diagonals from round-abouts (called *glorietas*), and on main arteries, turns (including U-turns and left turns) are usually made from right-side lateral roads (called *laterales*), which can be confusing for drivers unfamiliar with big city traffic. ■TIP→ **Ubiquitous and inexpensive, taxis are the best way to go in Guadalajara.**

TAXI TRAVEL Taxis are easily hailed on the street in the Centro Histórico, Zapopan, Tlaquepaque, and most other areas of Guadalajara. All cabs are sup-posed to use meters (in Spanish, *taxímetro*)—you can insist the driver use it or else agree on a fixed price at the outset. Many hotels have rate sheets showing the fare to major destinations and parts of town.

Taxi is the best way to get to Tonalá or Tlaquepaque (about $7). To continue from Tlaquepaque to Tonalá, take a taxi from Avenida Río Nilo southeast directly into town at the intersection of Avenida de los Tonaltecas ($4–$6; 5–10 minutes depending on traffic).

VISITOR INFORMATION

Contacts Jalisco State Tourist Office ⊠ *Calle Morelos 102, Centro Histórico, Guadalajara, Jalisco* ☎ *33/3668–1600, 01800/363–2200 toll-free in Mexico* ⊕ *visita.jalisco.gob.mx.* **Tlaquepaque Municipal Tourist Office** ⊠ *Calle Morelos 288, top fl., Tlaquepaque, Jalisco* ☎ *33/1057–6212* ⊕ *www.tlaquepaque.gob. mx/turismo.* **Tonalá Municipal Tourist Office** ⊠ *Av. de los Tonaltecas Sur 140, Tonalá, Jalisco* ☎ *33/3284–3092, 33/3284–3093.*

EXPLORING

The Guadalajara region's must-see sights can be found in four major areas: Guadalajara city itself, Zapopan, Tlaquepaque, and Tonalá. Each can be navigated on foot in a few hours, hitting the major sites, though to get a good feel for these places one must devote at least a day to each, and more to Guadalajara city.

In Guadalajara city, the historic Zona Centro houses many of the city's key tourist attractions, but several of the surrounding neighborhoods are also worth a visit. You'll find modern hotels, boutique shops, and some of the city's best cafés, bars, and restaurants in Zona Minerva, due west of the Centro, Plaza del Sol to the southwest, and Providencia to the northwest. Sample the Zona Minerva district by strolling down the Avenida Juárez–Avenida Vallarta corridor; Avenida Vallarta is shut to vehicular traffic from 8 am to 2 pm every Sunday for Via Recreativa, where locals and tourists gather to walk or bike.

CENTRO HISTÓRICO

The downtown core is a mishmash of modern and old buildings con-nected by a series of large plazas, four of which were designed to form a cross when viewed from the sky, with the cathedral in the middle. Though some remain, many colonial-era structures were razed before authorities got serious about preserving them. Conservation laws,

however, merely prohibit such buildings from being altered or destroyed; there are no provisions on upkeep, as plenty of abandoned, crumbling buildings indicate.

Must-visit sights include the Palacio del Gobierno and the Instituto Cultural Cabañas; both have phenomenal murals by José Clemente Orozco. Even if you're not in the mood to shop, you should experience the bustling Mercado Libertad. Explore the district in the morning if you dislike crowds; otherwise, you'll get a more immediate sense of Mexico's vibrant culture if you wait for street performers and vendors to emerge around the huge Plaza Tapatía in the afternoon.

Allot at least three hours for the Centro, longer if you really want to absorb the main sights and stroll along the pedestrian streets.

> ## OPEN-AIR BUSES
>
> **Tapatío Tour.** The Tapatío Tour is an easy way to get an overview of the city and its history. The open-air, double-decker buses leave every 30 minutes from Rotunda de los Jalisciences Ilustres (to the left of the cathedral) and cost 90 pesos (less than $9) per person. The one-hour tour is narrated in six different languages via headphones. There's also a trip to Tlaquepaque; buses back leave every 30 min. ☒ *Av. Hidalgo, Rotonda de los Hombres Ilustres, Centro Histórico* ☎ *33/3613-0887, 33/3614-7430* ⊕ *www.tapatio tour.com.*

TOP ATTRACTIONS

FAMILY

Fodor'sChoice

★

Instituto Cultural Cabañas. Financed by Bishop Juan Ruiz de Cabañas and constructed by Spanish architect-sculptor Manuel Tolsá, this neo-classical-style cultural center, also known as Hospicio Cabañas, was originally opened in 1810 as a shelter for widows, orphans, and the elderly. The Instituto's 106 rooms and 23 flower-filled patios now house art exhibitions (ask for an English-speaking guide). The main chapel displays murals by José Clemente Orozco, including *The Man of Fire*, his masterpiece. In all, there are 57 murals by Orozco, plus many of his smaller paintings, cartoons, and drawings. Kids can wonder at the murals, some of which appear as optical illusions, and investigate the labyrinthine compound. The center, named a UNESCO World Heritage Site in 1997, is closed Monday. ☒ *Calle Cabañas 8, Centro Histórico* ☎ *33/3668-1645* ⊕ *hospiciocabanas.jalisco.gob.mx* ☑ *$7; free Tues.* ☉ *Tues.–Sun. 10–6.*

Fodor'sChoice

★

Museo del Premio Nacional de la Cerámica Pantaleon Panduro. The museum is named after Pantaleon Panduro, who's considered the father of modern ceramics in Jalisco. On display are prizewinning pieces from the museum's annual ceramics competition, held every June. It's possibly the best representation of modern Mexican pottery under a single roof. You can request an English-speaking guide. ☒ *Calle Donato Guerra 160, Centro Histórico* ☎ *33/3838-6556* ⊕ *www.premionacionaldelaceramica. com/museo-pantaleon-panduro* ☑ *Free* ☉ *Tues.–Sat. 10–6, Sun. 10–3.*

WORTH NOTING

Catedral. Begun in 1561 and consecrated in 1618, this downtown focal point is an intriguing mélange of baroque, Gothic, and other styles. Its emblematic twin towers replaced the originals, felled by the earthquake

9

of 1818. Ten of the silver-and-gold altars were gifts from King Fernando VII for Guadalajara's financial support of Spain during the Napoleonic Wars. Some of the world's most magnificent *retablos* (altarpieces) adorn the walls; above the sacristy (often closed to the public) is Bartolomé Esteban Murillo's priceless 17th-century painting *The Assumption of the Virgin*. In a loft above the main entrance is a magnificent 19th-century French organ. ⊠ *Av. 16 de Septiembre, between Av. Hidalgo and Calle Morelos, Centro Histórico* ☎ *33/3614–5504, 33/3614–3058* 🖙 *Free* ⊘ *Daily 8–8.*

Museo Regional de Guadalajara. Constructed as a seminary and public library in 1701, this has been the Guadalajara Regional Museum's home since 1918. First-floor galleries contain artifacts tracing western Mexico's history from prehistoric times through the Spanish conquest. Five 19th-century carriages, including one used by General Porfirio Díaz, are on the second-floor balcony. There's an impressive collection of European and Mexican paintings. ⊠ *Calle Liceo 60, Centro Histórico* ☎ *33/3614–9957* 🖙 *$3.50* ⊘ *Tues.–Sat. 9–5:30, Sun. 9–4:30.*

Palacio de Gobierno. The adobe structure of 1643 was replaced with this churrigueresque and neoclassical stone structure in the 18th century. Within are Jalisco's state offices and two of José Clemente Orozco's most passionate murals, both worth the visit alone. One just past the entrance depicts a gigantic Father Miguel Hidalgo looming amid figures representing oppression and slavery. Upstairs, the other mural (look for a door marked "Congreso") portrays Hidalgo, Juárez, and other Reform-era figures. ⊠ *Av. Corona 31, between Calle Morelos and Pedro Moreno, Centro Histórico, Guadalajara* ☎ *33/3614–4038* 🖙 *Free* ⊘ *Daily 10–6.*

Teatro Degollado. Inaugurated in 1866, this magnificent theater was modeled after Milan's La Scala. The refurbished theater preserves its traditional red-and-gold color scheme, and its balconies ascend to a multitier dome adorned with Gerardo Suárez's depiction of Dante's *Divine Comedy*. The theater is home to the Jalisco Philharmonic. ⊠ *Av. Degollado between Av. Hidalgo and Calle Morelos, Centro Histórico* ☎ *33/3614–4773* 🖙 *Free* ⊘ *Tues.–Fri. 12:30 pm–2 pm.*

ZONA MINERVA

Also known as Zona Rosa (Pink Zone), this district west of the Centro Histórico is arguably the pulse of the city. At night a seemingly endless strip of the region's trendiest restaurants and watering holes lights up Avenida Vallarta east of Avenida Enrique Díaz de León. Victorian mansions, art galleries, a striking church, and two emblematic monuments—the Fuente Minerva (Minerva Fountain) and the Monumento Los Arcos—are scattered throughout the tree-lined boulevards.

The best way to get here from the Centro is by cab. Museo de las Artes requires two hours when all its exhibits are open. Budget an hour for the Templo Expiatorio across the street.

Museo de las Artes. The University of Guadalajara's contemporary-art museum is in this exquisite early-20th-century building. The permanent collection includes several murals by Orozco. Revolving exhibits have contemporary works from Latin America, Europe, and the United

LIVE PERFORMANCE

Plaza de Armas. The State Band of Jalisco and the Municipal Band sometimes play at the bandstand on Tuesday around 6:30 pm. ☒ *Av. Corona between Calle Morelos and Pedro Moreno, across from Palacio de Gobierno, Centro Histórico.*

Small, triangular Plaza de los Mariachis, south of the Mercado Libertad, was once the ideal place to tip up a beer and experience mariachi, the most Mexican of music, at about $15 a pop. Now boxed in by a busy street, a market, and a run-down neighborhood, it's safest to visit in the day or late afternoon.

For about the same amount of money but a more tourist-friendly atmosphere, mariachis at El Parián, in Tlaquepaque, will treat you to a song or two as you sip margaritas at this enormous, partly covered conglomeration of 17 cantinas running diagonally from the town's main plaza. Once a marketplace dating from 1883, it has traditional *cazuela* drinks, which are made of fruit and tequila and served in ceramic pots.

Ballet Folclórico of the University of Guadalajara. After a brief stint at the newer Teatro Diana, the internationally acclaimed Ballet Folclórico of the University of Guadalajara has returned to perform its traditional Mexican folkloric dances and music in the Teatro Degollado most Sundays at 12:30 pm; tickets are $5–$25. ☒ *Calle Belén s/n, Guadalajara, Jalisco* ☎ *33/3614–4773* ⊕ *www.ballet.udg.mx.*

Orquesta Filarmónica de Jalisco. Though it's among Mexico's most poorly paid orchestras, the state-funded philharmonic manages remarkably good performances (usually pieces by Mexican composers mixed with standard orchestral fare). When in season (it varies), the OFJ performs Sunday afternoons and Wednesday and Friday evenings at Teatro Delgollado. On the facing plaza, they hold an annual outdoor performance that helps kick off September's Mariachi Festival. ☒ *Calle Belen at Morelos, Teatro Degollado, Guadalajara, Jalisco* ☎ *33/3030–9772* ⊕ *www.ofj.com.mx* ▭ *$8–$35.*

States. ☒ *Av. Juárez 975, Centro Histórico* ☎ *33/3134–1664* ⊕ *musa.udg.mx* ▭ *Free* ☉ *Tues.–Sun. 10–6.*

Templo Expiatorio. The striking neo-Gothic Church of Atonement is Guadalajara's most breathtaking church. Modeled after Italy's Orvieto Cathedral, it has phenomenal stained-glass windows—observe the rose window above the choir and pipe organ. ☒ *Calle Díaz de León 930, at Av. López Cotilla, Centro Histórico* ☎ *33/3825–3410* ▭ *Free* ☉ *Daily 6:30 am–10:30 pm.*

TLAQUEPAQUE

Local arts and handicrafts fill the showrooms and stores in this touristy town, where you'll find carved wood furniture, colorful ceramics, and hand-stitched clothing among other goods. Pedestrian malls and plazas are lined with more than 300 shops, many run by families with generations of experience. One of Guadalajara's most exceptional museums,

which draws gifted artists for its annual ceramics competition in June, is also here.

But there's more to Tlaquepaque than shopping. The downtown area has a pleasant square and many pedestrian-only streets, making this a good place to take a stroll, even if you're not interested in all the crafts for sale. There are several good restaurants, some with outdoor seating perfect for people-watching.

■TIP→ **Many tourists come to Tlaquepaque via the Tapatío Tour, an open-air bus that leaves from Guadalajara's historic center.**

Museo Regional de la Cerámica. The frequently changing exhibits at the Regional Museum of Ceramics are in the many rooms surrounding a central courtyard. Track the evolution of ceramic wares in the Atemajac Valley during the 20th century. The presentation isn't always strong, but the Spanish-language displays discuss six common processes used by local ceramics artisans, including *barro bruñido,* which involves polishing large urns with smoothed chunks of the mineral pyrite. Items in the gift shop are surprisingly uninteresting. ⊠ *Calle Independencia 237, at Calle Alfareros, Tlaquepaque,* ☎ *33/3635–5404* ⊕ *www.artesaniasjalisco.gob.mx* ⊠ *Free* ⊙ *Tues.–Sun. 10–6.*

ZAPOPAN

Mexico's former corn-producing capital is now a municipality of wealthy enclaves, modern hotels, and malls surrounded by hills of poor communities (as is much of metropolitan Guadalajara). Farther out, some farming communities remain. The central district, a good 25-minute cab ride from downtown Guadalajara, has two worthwhile museums, an aged church that's home to the city's most revered religious icon, and a pedestrian corridor punctuated by restaurants and watering holes popular with young Tapatíos.

WORTH NOTING

Basílica de Zapopan. This vast church with an ornate plateresque facade and *Mudejar* (Moorish) tile dome was consecrated in 1730. It's home to the Virgin (or Our Lady) of Zapopan: a 10-inch-high, corn-paste statue venerated as a source of many miracles. Every October 12 more than a million people crowd the streets around the basilica, where the Virgin is returned after a five-month tour of Jalisco's parish churches. It's an all-night fiesta capped by an early-morning procession. ⊠ *Av. Hidalgo at Matamoros, Zona Zapopan Norte* ☎ *33/3633–6614* ⊠ *Free* ⊙ *Daily 7 am–9 pm.*

Museo de Arte de Zapopan. Better known by its initials, MAZ, the large and modern Art Museum of Zapopan is Guadalajara's top contemporary-art gallery. The museum regularly holds expositions of distinguished Latin American painters, photographers, and sculptors, as well as occasional international shows. ⊠ *Andador 20 de Noviembre 166, at Calle 28 de Enero, Zona Zapopan* ☎ *33/3818–2575* ⊕ *www.mazmuseo.com* ⊠ *$1; free Tues.* ⊙ *Tues.–Sun. 10–6.*

Museo Huichol Wixarica de Zapopan. The Huichol Indians of northern Jalisco and neighboring states of Zacatecas and Nayarit are famed for their fierce independence and exquisite beadwork and yarn "paintings."

Continued on page 242

MARIACHI: BORN IN JALISCO

By Sean Mattson

It's 4 AM and you're sound asleep somewhere in Mexico. Suddenly you're jolted awake by trumpets blasting in rapid succession. Before you can mutter a groggy protest, ten men with booming voices break into song. Nearby, a woman stirs from her slumber. The man who brought her the serenade peeks at her window from behind the lead singer's sombrero, hoping his sign of devotion is appreciated— and doesn't launch his girlfriend's father into a shoe-throwing fury.

Left and top right: Mariachis in traditional attire. Above: Mariachi strumming the guitarrón.

At the heart of Mexican popular culture, mariachi is the music of love and heartache, of the daily travails of life, and nationalistic pride. This soundtrack of Mexican tradition was born in the same region as tequila, the Mexican hat dance, and *charrería* (Mexican rodeo), whose culture largely defines Mexican chivalry and machismo.

Today, mariachi bands are the life of the party. They perform at weddings, birthdays, public festivals, restaurants, and city plazas. The most famous bands perform across the globe. Guadalajara's annual mariachi festival draws mariachis from around the world.

WHY IS IT CALLED "MARIACHI"?

The origin of the word mariachi is a source of some controversy. The legend is that it evolved from the French word *mariage* (marriage), stemming from the French occupation in the mid-1800s. But leading mariachi historians now debunk that myth, citing evidence that the word has its origins in the Nahuatl language of the Coca Indians.

Flying mariachi skeleton formed out of paper, used to celebrate Day of the Dead.

THE RISE OF MARIACHI

Historians trace the roots of mariachi to Cocula, a small agricultural town south of Guadalajara. There, in the 17th century, Franciscan monks trained the local indigenous populations in the use of stringed instruments, teaching them the religious songs to help win their conversion.

The aristocracy, who preferred the more refined contemporary European music, held early mariachi groups in disdain. But by the late 19th century, mariachi had become enormously popular among peasants and indigenous people in Cocula, eventually spreading throughout southern Jalisco and into neighboring states.

MODERN MARIACHI INSTRUMENTS

Traditional mariachi groups consisted of two violins (the melody), and a vihuela and guitarrón (the harmony). Some long-gone groups used a *tambor* or drum, not used in modern mariachi. All members of the group shared singing responsibilities.

VIOLINS
Essential to any mariachi group

GUITARS
The round-backed vihuela is smaller and higher-pitched than the standard guitar

5-string Vihuela   6-string guitar

THE FOLK HARP
Longstanding mariachi instrument, used today by large ensembles and by some traditional troupes

TRUMPETS
Added to the traditional mariachi lineup in the 1930s when mariachis hit the big screen, at the insistence of a pioneer in Mexican radio and television

THE GUITARRÓN
A large-bellied bass guitar

In 1905, Mexican dictator Porfirio Díaz visited Cocula and was received with a performance of a mariachi group. Impressed, Diaz invited the group to Mexico City where, after a few years and a revolution, mariachi flourished. Over the next two decades, more groups followed to Mexico City. Mariachi groups gained more popularity by the 1930s, when Jorge Negrete and Pedro Infante began portraying mariachi musicians in their films. In 2011, UNESCO included mariachi on its List of Intangible Cultural Heritage of Humanity.

MARIACHI STYLE

The mariachi *traje* (suit) consists of matching vest, *chaleco* (short jacket), and form-fitting pants, and *moño* (large bow tie). Simple *trajes* have soutache trim or embroidery; finer versions have suede patterns on the jacket with metal buttons down the pants legs. Trajes come in all colors, but formal costumes are black.

Sombreros made from pressed rabbit fur are the highest quality.

The modern mariachi's dress is an adaptation of *charro*, or Mexican cowboy attire, first worn by the members of an early mariachi group led by Cirilo Marmolejo and adopted for Mexican movies of the 1930s–50s. A complete formal outfit can cost as much as US$3,000.

Botonaduras (decorative buttons on the pants legs) can be simple, or ornate, made of silver or gold. A brooch on the front of the jacket often matches the botonadura.

Black leather *botínes* (half-boots) are standard mariachi footwear.

IN FOCUS MARIACHI: BORN IN JALISCO

9

WHERE AND HOW TO HEAR MARIACHI

HIRE A MARIACHI GROUP

There may be no better way to thoroughly surprise (or embarrass) your significant other than with a mariachi serenade. Hiring a band is easy. Just go to Plaza de los Mariachis, beside Mercado Libertad in downtown Guadalajara. Negotiate price and either leave a deposit (ask for a business card and a receipt) and have the band meet you at a determined location, or, as Mexicans usually do, accompany the band to the unexpecting lady.

HIT THE INTERNATIONAL MARIACHI FESTIVAL

The last weekend of every August, some 700 mariachi groups from around the world descend upon Guadalajara for this event. Mexico's most famous mariachi groups—Mariachi Vargas de Tecalitlán, Mariachi los Camperos, and Mariachi de América—play huge concerts in the Degollado Theater, accompanied by the Jalisco Philharmonic Orchestra. The weeklong annual charro championship is held simultaneously, bringing together the nation's top cowboys and mariachis.

THE WORLD'S BEST MARIACHI BAND

At least, the world's most *famous* mariachi band, Mariachi Vargas de Tecalitlán was founded in 1897, when the norm was four-man groups with simple stringed instruments. Started by Gaspar Vargas in Tecalitlán, Jalisco, the mariachi troupe shot to fame in the 1930s after winning a regional mariachi contest, which earned them the favor of Mexican president Lázaro Cárdenas. The group quickly became an icon of Mexican cinema, performing in and recording music for films. Now in its fifth generation, Mariachi Vargas performs the world over and has recorded more than 50 albums, and music for more than 200 films.

The *gabán* (poncho) was worn traditionally for warmth.

CATCH YEAR-ROUND PERFORMANCES

If you miss Guadalajara's mariachi festival you can still get your fill of high-quality mariachi performances on street corners, in city plazas, and at many restaurants. An estimated 150 mariachi groups are currently active in the City of Roses.

Restaurants, most notably Guadalajara's Casa Bariachi chain, hire mariachi groups, whose performance is generally included with your table (though tips won't be refused). On occasion, mariachis perform free nighttime concerts in Guadalajara's Plaza de Armas. Another venue, the Plaza de Mariachi, beside Guadalajara's landmark Mercado Libertad, is a longstanding attraction, albeit during the day—at night it's better known for crime than mariachi.

Tlaquepaque's El Parián, a former market turned series of bars around a tree-filled central patio, is a fantastic intimate setting for mariachi music. Between free performances in the central kiosk, you can request serenades at about $15–18 per song or negotiate deals for longer performances for your table.

ALL ABOARD THE TEQUILA TRAIN!

To experience the Jalisco quartet of traditions—mariachi, charreria, folkloric dance, and tequila—in one adventure, take the Tequila Express. It includes a train ride from Guadalajara through fields of blue agave to a tequila-making hacienda, live mariachi music, all the food and drink you can handle, and a charro and folkloric dance performance.

WORKING HARD FOR THE MONEY

It is becoming harder for mariachi groups to make a living at the trade. The increasing cost of living has made nighttime serenades, once a staple of a mariachi's diet of work, expensive ($200 and up) and out of the reach of many locals. Performers generally work day jobs to make ends meet.

THE COWBOY CONNECTION

Mariachi and Mexican rodeo, or *charreada* (Mexico's official sport), go together like hot dogs and baseball. Both charreada and mariachi music evolved in the western Mexican countryside, where daily ranching chores like branding bulls eventually took on a competitive edge. The first of Mexico's 800 charro associations was founded in Guadalajara in 1920, and to this day holds a two-hour rodeo every Sunday. Throughout the competition, mariachi music is heard from the stands, but the key mariachi performance is at the end of a competition when female riders called *escaramuzas* perform synchronized moves, riding side-saddle in traditional ribboned and brightly colored western Mexican dresses.

IN FOCUS MARIACHI: BORN IN JALISCO

9

TONALÁ

Among the region's oldest pueblos is bustling Tonalá, a unique place filled with artisan workshops small and large. Although it's been swallowed by ever-expanding Guadalajara, Tonalá remains independent and industrious. More geared to business than pleasure, it doesn't have the folksy character of nearby Tlaquepaque. There's a concentration of stores on Avenida Tonalá and Avenida de los Tonaltecas, the main drag into town, and many more shops and factories can be found spread throughout Tonalá's narrow streets. ■TIP→ **The town has unusually long blocks, so wear your most comfortable shoes.**

While Tonalá and its shops may not be as quaint or as touristy as Tlaquepaque, this is where you'll find the best bargains since most local goods—from furniture to glassware and ceramics—are made here. Most stores are open daily 10–5. On Thursday and Sunday, bargain-price merchandise is sold at a street market (⊠ *Av. Tonaltecas at Calle Benito Juárez*) packed with vendors from 9 am to 5 pm. Vendors set up ceramics, carved wood sculptures, candles, glassware, furniture, metal crafts, and more. Look for *vajilla* (ceramic place settings), but note that the more high-end ceramic offerings are sold at more formal stores.

This small museum has rather hokey mannequins wearing the intricately embroidered clothing of both men and women. Bilingual placards explain the Huichol religion and worldview. The gift shop sells a small inventory of beaded items, prayer arrows, and god's eyes. ⊠ *Calle Eva Briseño 152, Zona Zapopan* ☎ *33/3636–4430* ⊕ *www.facebook. com/museodearte.wixarika* ≊ *2 pesos* ⊙ *Mon.–Sat. 9:30–1 and 3–6, Sun. 10–2.*

WHERE TO EAT

CENTRO HISTÓRICO

$ ╳ **La Chata.** At high meal times, travelers will find lines of locals and tourists alike extending out the door of this traditional Mexican restaurant in El Centro. While the decor is plain, the food is the best in the city. Items worth testing include the *queso fundido* (cheese fondue) and the enchiladas. If you're staying in West Guadalajara, there's a second restaurant at 405 Terranova in Providencia. $ *Average main: $10* ⊠ *Corona 126, between Avs. López Cotilla and Juárez, Centro Histórico* ☎ *33/3613–1315* ⊕ *www.lachata.com.mx* ⊟ *No credit cards* ✚ *1:D5.*

MEXICAN

Fodor'sChoice
★

$ ╳ **La Fonda de San Miguel.** La Fonda, in a former convent, is perhaps the Centro's most exceptional eatery. Innovative, high-end Mexican dishes are presented in a soaring courtyard, the middle of which is dominated by a stone fountain and hung with a spectacular array of shining tin stars and folk art from Tlaquepaque and Tonalá. Relish the freshly made tortillas with the *molcajete*, a steaming stew of chicken, seafood, or beef that comes in a three-legged volcanic stone bowl. *Camarones en mole* (shrimp) is another good dish. There's piano or saxophone music every evening except Monday. Piano music accompanies a

MEXICAN

Fodor'sChoice
★

breakfast buffet 8:30–noon on Saturday and Sunday. $ *Average main: $10* ✉ *Donato Guerra 25, Centro Histórico* ☎ *33/3613–0809* ⊕ *www. lafondadesanmiguel.com.mx* ⊙ *Closes at 6 pm Mon. and 9 pm Sun.* ⊹ *1:C4.*

ZONA MINERVA

$ ✕ **Karne Garibaldi.** In the *1996 Guinness Book of World Records,* this
MEXICAN Tapatío institution held the record for world's fastest service: 13.5 seconds for a table of six. Lightning service is made possible by the menu's single item: *carne en su jugo,* a combination of finely diced beef and bacon simmered in rich beef broth and served with grilled onions, tortillas, and refried beans mixed with corn. Don't be put off by the somewhat gritty area surrounding the restaurant at the original location on Calle Garibaldi. There also are three other locations in Zapopan. $ *Average main: $6* ✉ *Calle Garibaldi 1306, Zona Minerva in Sta. Teresita* ☎ *33/3826–1286* ⊕ *www.karnegaribaldi.com.mx* ⊹ *1:A3* ✉ *Plaza Galerias, Vallarta Norte in Zapopan* ☎ *33/3165–2042* ⊹ *1:A3* ✉ *Av. Vallarta 3959, Jardines del los Arcos in Zapopan* ☎ *33/3621–1600* ⊹ *1:A3.*

$ ✕ **La Estancia Gaucha.** Have you been in Mexico for a while and you
ARGENTINE or your stomach is starting to get a bit fed up with the spicy Mexican food? It happens, nothing to feel ashamed of. Been there, done that! Fortunately, Guadalajara's gastronomic scene is one of the best in the country and there are many non-Mexican options. One of the best is definitely La Estancia Gaucha, a delicious Argentinian restaurant with decades of success in the city. The steaks are their specialty, but they offer a wide array of dishes including fishes, pasta and salads. An outstanding cava will also delight wine lovers. $ *Average main: $12* ✉ *Plaza Punto Sao Paulo, Av. de las Américas 1545, Col. Americana* ☎ *33/3817–1808* ⊙ *Mon.–Sat. 1 pm–12 am, Sun. 1 pm–6 pm.* ⊹ *1:A2*

$ ✕ **La Moresca.** While this modern Italian restaurant comes alive at night
ITALIAN when it turns into a hip martini bar, don't pass up a meal before partaking in the revelry. It has the best Italian food in town. The twentysomething Tapatíos like to take their dates here for delicious pasta and pizza dinners and stick around for the scene that follows. Birthday gatherings are common, too, as are simple be-seen excursions. However you do it, this place is Guadalajara at its trendiest, including music played at decibel levels that can sometimes make conversation difficult. Luckily, the Italian kitchen is up to the task. $ *Average main: $11* ✉ *Av. López Cotilla 1835, Zona Minerva* ☎ *33/3616–8277* ⊕ *lamoresca.com* ⊙ *Closed Sun* ⊹ *1:B3* $ *Average main: $11* ✉ *Blvd. Puerto de Hierro 4965, Plaza Andares in Zapopan, Guadalajara, Jalisco* ⊹ *1:B3.*

$ ✕ **Sacromonte.** Elegant atmosphere, decor, and dishes make for a won-
MEXICAN derful dining experience. This isn't the choice if you're looking for an atmosphere that feels Mexican—a significant portion of the other diners will likely be other English-speaking visitors—but the food's delicious anyway. The waiters offer menus in Spanish and in English. If you're into trying local favorites, this is the place to order *la lengua*—the beef tongue—or the chicken mole, which has a sweet twist. The pork loin and barbecue ribs are also worth a taste. For dessert, order the flan with *cajeta* (a local soft caramel sauce); it's homemade—literally made

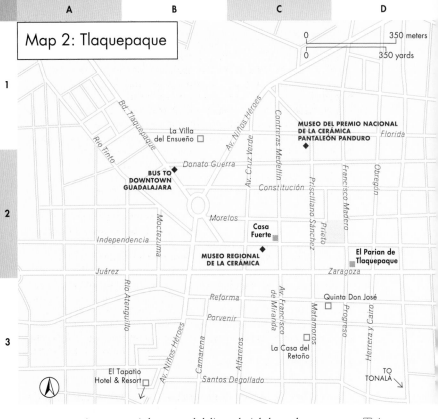

0 ___ 350 meters
0 ___ 350 yards

in someone's house and delivered nightly to the restaurant. $ *Average main:* $10 ⊠ *Pedro Moreno 1398, Col. Americana* ☎ *33/3825–5447* ⊕ *www.sacromonte.com.mx* ☾ *No dinner Sun* ✛ *1:A4.*

$
MEXICAN FUSION

✕ **Santo Coyote.** One of the most sophisticated restaurants in Guadalajara, Santo Coyote offers top-notch Mexican Fusion cuisine, like delicious "tacos el negro" with lobster and traditional Mexican sopa de tortilla. Set in a wide indoor/outdoor space, the atmosphere couldn't be more spectacular with outstanding lighting, a huge palapa, and a beautiful garden. This is the place you would take that date you are trying to impress. Perfect for romantic nights and, all in all, an extraordinary gourmet experience. $ *Average main:* $12 ⊠ *Calle Lerdo de Tejada 2379, Col. Americana* ☎ *33/3343–2266* ⊕ *santocoyote.com. mx* ☾ *Daily 8 am–midnight* ✛ *1:B3.*

$
SEAFOOD

✕ **SantoMar.** A sophisticated seafood restaurant in the heart of the most exclusive commercial area in Guadalajara. Across the street from SantoMar you will find international boutiques such as Burberry, Hugo Boss, Adolfo Domínguez, Lacoste, Tous, and many others. SantoMar shares a stylish food court with several restaurants, but it stands out as the only one offering quality seafood and because of its old dock atmosphere. You'll be hard pressed to find better seafood in Guadalajara. $ *Average main:* $12 ⊠ *Cento Comercial Andares, Blvd. Puerta de Hierro 4965, Col. Americana* ☎ *33/3611–2866* ⊕ *santomar.com.mx* ✛ *1:A1.*

$ ✕ **Tacos Providencia.** When in Mexico, do as the Mexicans do! And there
MEXICAN is nothing more Mexican than eating tacos. However, foreigners usually don't fare well when trying to emulate Mexican gastronomic habits
because they often eat at just any street taco stall, which is definitely not
a good idea. Tacos Providencia offers the authentic Mexican taste, without the Montezuma's revenge pains. A true Tapatío will tell you that
these are the best tacos in town. Don't expect a sophisticated establishment; it's just a clean and functional taqueria where everything is about
those exquisite tacos. $ *Average main: $6 ⊠ Rubén Darío 534, Col.
Americana* ☎ *33/3641–6049 ⊕ www.facebook.com/TacosProvidencia*
⊗ *Closed Mon.* ✛ *1:A1.*

$ ✕ **Tortas Toño.** One of Guadalajara most famous dishes is the "Torta
MEXICAN Ahogada," literally a drowned sandwich. It's a baguette filled with
pork meat served in a kind of bowl with lots (and we are talking lots!)
of hot tomato sauce on top of it. Well, on top, on the sides, on bottom,
the sauce is just everywhere and that's why they are called "ahogadas."
There are two sauces in every establishment serving this kind of "tortas"; one is just tomato sauce and the other one is incredible spicy. It's
very important not to confuse them, because if you are not used to the
kind of chili Mexicans like to eat, you will be crying soon after your
first bite. Add onions, beans and lemon, and you have the best remedy
for a hangover in the world! Tortas Toño serves the best ahogadas in
town and all their branches are very clean and well-managed. $ *Average
main: $4 ⊠ Av. Tepeyac 605, Col. Americana* ☎ *33/3647–6208 ⊕ www.
tortastono.com.mx* ⊗ *After 4 pm* ✛ *1:A1.*

TLAQUEPAQUE

$$ ✕ **Casa Fuerte.** Relax with tasty Mexican dishes at the tables along the
MEXICAN sidewalk or under the palms and by the fountain on the patio. You'll
be tempted by the tables scattered around the sidewalk, but before you
decide, take a peek at those in the oversize garden patio surrounding
a magnificent old tree. Try the house specialty: chicken stuffed with
huitlacoche (a corn fungus that's Mexico's answer to the truffle) and
shrimp in tamarind sauce. Live musicians accompany *comida* (2:30 to
6 pm, approximately) every day except Monday. $ *Average main: $13
⊠ Calle Independencia 224, Tlaquepaque* ☎ *33/3639–6481, 33/3639–
6474 ⊕ www.casafuerte.com* ⊗ *Daily noon–9* ✛ *2:C2.*

$ ✕ **El Parián de Tlaquepaque.** If you are looking for a traditional Mexican
MEXICAN experience, there's no better place to go in Tlaquepaque than El Parián.
This is not actually a restaurant but a large squared building with a cen-
tral patio shared by 18 different restaurants and bars. Here, everyday is
a Mexican fiesta and that's what you come for. Mariachis perform all
day long and tequila flows easily. The cuisine might not be the best in
town, but it's quite good. Founded in 1905, El Parián is as Mexican as
it gets! $ *Average main: $10 ⊠ Calle Independencia 22, Tlaquepaque*
☎ *33/3330–5136* ✛ *2:D2.*

TONALA

$ ✕ **El Rincón del Sol.** A covered patio invites you to sip margaritas while
MEXICAN listening to live *trova* (romantic ballads). Musicians play Tuesday to
Friday evenings between 7 and 9, and on weekends during the leisurely

9

lunch hour (roughly 3 to 5). Try one of the steak or chicken dishes, the burrito, or the classic *chiles en nogada* in the colors of the Mexican flag. The staff is friendly and helpful. ⑤ *Average main: $7* ⊠ *Av. 16 de Septiembre 61, Tonalá* ☎ *33/3683–1989, 33/3683–1940* ⊕ *www. elrincondelsol.com* ⊙ *After 10 pm.*

WHERE TO STAY

CENTRO HISTÓRICO

$ 🏨 **Holiday Inn Centro Histórico.** This branch of the reliable international HOTEL   chain sits in the heart of historic Guadalajara. **Pros:** helpful business center; free Wi-Fi in rooms and public spaces; some free items in the minibar. **Cons:** no heat; small, old gym; no pool. ⑤ *Rooms from: $88* ⊠ *Av. Juárez 211, Centro Histórico* ☎ *33/3560–1200* ⊕ *www. holidaycentrogdl.com* 🛏 *45 rooms, 45 suites* ¶◯╎ *No meals* ✛ *1:D5.*

$ 🏨 **Hotel de Mendoza.** Elegant with its postcolonial architecture, this hotel HOTEL   is on a calm side street a block from Teatro Degollado. **Pros:** great location; comfortable rooms. **Cons:** standard rooms lack tubs; most rooms don't have balconies. ⑤ *Rooms from: $75* ⊠ *Calle Venustiano Carranza 16, Centro Histórico* ☎ *01800/361–2600 toll-free in Mexico, 33/3942–5151* ⊕ *www.demendoza.com.mx* 🛏 *86 rooms, 18 suites* ✛ *1:C5.*

$ 🏨 **Hotel Morales.** After being abandoned for 30 years, this downtown HOTEL   hotel—originally a 19th-century rooming house—has been transformed Fodor's Choice   into one of the city's most luxurious lodgings. **Pros:** relaxed elegance; ★   double-paned windows keep out the noise; Wi-Fi in rooms. **Cons:** lobby restaurant isn't cozy. ⑤ *Rooms from: $75* ⊠ *Ave. Ramón Corona 243, Centro Histórico* ☎ *33/3658–5232* ⊕ *www.hotelmorales.com.mx* 🛏 *59 rooms, 7 suites* ✛ *1:D5.*

ZONA MINERVA

$ 🏨 **El Tapatío Hotel & Resort.** El Tapatío is just how a traditional Mexican HOTEL   hotel should look. ⑤ *Rooms from: $60* ⊠ *Carretera Chapala, Km 6.5, Zona Minerva* ☎ *33/3837–2929, 01800/007–3845 toll-free in Mexico* ⊕ *www.hotel-tapatio.com* 🛏 *123 rooms* ✛ *1:D3.*

$ 🏨 **Fiesta Americana.** The dramatic glass facade of this high-rise faces the HOTEL   Minerva Fountain and Los Arcos monument. **Pros:** airport shuttle (fee); 24-hour room service; Wi-Fi in rooms; ample parking; nice bathroom amenities; AAA discount. **Cons:** some rooms have unpleasant views of roof and generators; no swimming pool. ⑤ *Rooms from: $108* ⊠ *Av. Aurelio Aceves 225, Col. Vallarta Poniente, Zona Minerva* ☎ *33/3818–1400* ⊕ *www.fiestamericana.com.mx* 🛏 *309 rooms* ✛ *1:B1.*

$ 🏨 **Hilton Guadalajara.** This AAA Four-Diamond award-winning hotel HOTEL   is located within Guadalajara's World Trade Center and just across the street from Expo Guadalajara, the city's convention center. **Pros:** set in the World Trade Center; complimentary Wi-Fi; top-notch spa. **Cons:** far from downtown; Mexican feeling is missing; small swimming pool. ⑤ *Rooms from: $89* ⊠ *Av. de las Rosas 2933, Zona Minerva* ☎ *33/3678–0505* ⊕ *www.hilton.com* 🛏 *450 rooms* ¶◯╎ *Multiple meal plans* ✛ *1:D1.*

$ 🏨 **Hotel Plaza Diana.** At this modest hotel two blocks from the Minerva HOTEL   Fountain the rooms are on the small side. **Pros:** free Internet; heated indoor pool; free airport shuttle. **Cons:** gym is on the small side. *Rooms from: $83 ✉ Av. Agustín Yáñez 2760, Zona Minerva ☎ 33/3540–9700, 01800/248–1001 toll-free in Mexico 🌐 www.hoteldiana.mx 127 rooms, 24 suites ⊕ 1:B2.*

$ HOTEL **Hotel Riu Plaza Guadalajara.** One of the newest and trendiest hotels in the city, Hotel Riu enjoys a great location just one mile away from the Gran Plaza shopping mall and two miles from Expo Guadalajara, the city's convention center. **Pros:** centric; brand new; panoramic view of the city. **Cons:** corporate atmosphere; noisy area. *Rooms from: $110 ✉ Av. López Mateos 830, Zona Minerva ☎ 33/3880–7500 🌐 www.riu.com 550 rooms Breakfast ⊕ 1:C1.*

$$ HOTEL **Quinta Real.** Stone-and-brick walls, colonial arches, and objets d'art fill this luxury hotel's public areas. **Pros:** elegant rooms; stately grounds; in-room spa services. **Cons:** pricey rates; no on-site spa. *Rooms from: $160 ✉ Av. México 2727, at Av. López Mateos Norte, Zona Minerva ☎ 33/3669–0600, 866/621–9288 toll-free from U.S., 01800/500–4000 in Mexico 🌐 www.quintareal.com 76 suites ⊕ 1:A2.*

$$$ HOTEL Fodor's Choice ★ **Villa Ganz.** Staying in this neighborhood full of restaurants and nightlife yet away from the gritty historic center might be just the ticket. **Pros:** great location; inviting patios; in-room Wi-Fi; free early-evening wine and canapés. **Cons:** suites must be paid in full when booked; high-season cancellations are charged tax as well as 100% of room fee. *Rooms from: $250 ✉ Av. López Cotilla 1739, Zona Minerva ☎ 33/3120–1416 🌐 www.villaganz.com 9 suites Breakfast ⊕ 1:B3.*

TLAQUEPAQUE

$ B&B/INN **La Casa del Retoño.** This B&B is on a quiet street several blocks from the shopping district. **Pros:** quiet neighborhood; private terraces in some rooms. **Cons:** smallish rooms; lackluster garden. *Rooms from: $79 ✉ Matamoros 182, Tlaquepaque ☎ 33/3639–6510, 33/3635–7636 🌐 www.lacasadelretono.com.mx 8 rooms, 1 suite Breakfast ⊕ 2:C3.*

$ B&B/INN **La Villa del Ensueño.** A 10-minute walk from Tlaquepaque's center, this intimate B&B is near lots of shopping. **Pros:** hot tub; take-out food available from adjacent Mexican restaurant; friendly staff. **Cons:** only junior suites have bathtubs. *Rooms from: $95 ✉ Florida 305, Tlaquepaque ☎ 33/3635–8792 🌐 www.villadelensueno.com 16 rooms, 4 suites Breakfast ⊕ 2:B1.*

$ B&B/INN **Quinta Don José.** One block from Tlaquepaque's main plaza and shopping area, this B&B has a great location. **Pros:** central location; friendly staff who speak excellent English; free calls worldwide; free Wi-Fi; free parking. **Cons:** pool is chilly; some rooms are small. *Rooms from: $85 ✉ Calle Reforma 139, Tlaquepaque ☎ 33/3635–7522, 01800/700–2223 toll-free in Mexico, 866/629–3753 in U.S. and Canada 🌐 www.quintadonjose.com 18 rooms Breakfast ⊕ 2:C3.*

NIGHTLIFE

With the exception of a few well-established nightspots like La Maestranza, downtown Guadalajara quiets down relatively early. The existing nightlife centers on Avenida Vallarta, favored by the well-to-do under-30 set; Avenida Patria, full of bars for young people who party until early in the morning; or the somewhat seedy Plaza del Sol. Bars in these spots open into the wee hours, usually closing by 3 am. Dance clubs may charge a $15–$20 cover, which includes access to an open bar, on Wednesday and Saturday nights. Dress up for nightclubs; highly subjective admission policies hinge on who you know or how you look. The local music scene is less formal and centers on more intimate digs.

BARS

Fodor'sChoice   **i Latina.** One of Guadalajara's hot spots, I Latina is where you will
★   spot a cool, upscale local and international crowd having cocktails. It's been considered for a long time as the best cuisine in all Guadalajara. ⊠ *Av. Inglaterra 3128, at López Mateos, Col. Vallarta Poniente, Centro Histórico* ☎ *33/3647-7774* ⊕ *www.ilatinarest.com* ☉ *Closed Mon.*

La Fuente. Appealing and unpretentious, La Fuente opened in this location in 1950. The cantina draws business types, intellectuals, and blue-collar workers, all seeking cheap drinks, animated conversation, and live music. Above the bar, look for an old bicycle. It's been around since 1957, when, legend has it, one of a long list of famous people (most say it was the father of local newspaper baron Jesús Álvarez del Castillo) left the bike to pay for his drinks. The bar opens at 8—arrive soon after to avoid crowds. ⊠ *Calle Pino Suarez s/n, at Hidalgo, Centro Histórico* ☉ *Closed Mon.*

La Maestranza. For some local color, stop at La Maestranza, a renovated 1940s cantina full of bullfighting memorabilia. ⊠ *Calle Maestranza 179, between López Cotilla and Madero, Centro Histórico* ☎ *33/3613-5878.*

LIVE MUSIC

Rusty Trombone. Rusty Trombone is a great place to relax and enjoy a variety of hip bands. ⊠ *Lerdo de Tejada 2166, Col. Americana* ☎ *33/3630-2294.*

SPORTS AND THE OUTDOORS

GOLF

Clubs are less crowded on Wednesday and Thursday; all rent equipment for around $20 to $30. Golf carts typically cost around $40. Guadalajara's top golf clubs—El Cielo and Santa Anita—are technically for members only, but hotels can get you in.

Atlas Country Club. Atlas Country Club is an 18-hole, par-72 course designed by Joe Finger and is on the way to the airport. Greens fees are about $92 on weekdays, $104 on weekends and holidays. ⊠ *Carretera Guadalajara–Chapala, Km 6.5, El Salto* ☎ *33/3689-2620* ⊕ *country. atlas.com.mx.*

El Cielo Country Club. Private El Cielo Country Club, on a hill outside town, is an 18-hole, 6,765-yard, par-72 course blissfully removed from the city's din and with challenging holes and water features. For non-members it's $115 for 18 holes, including cart. ⊠ *Paseo del Cielo 1, Zapopan* ☎ *33/3612–3535* ⊕ *www.elcielocc.com.*

SHOPPING

The Centro Histórico is packed with shops as well as ambulatory vendors, who compete with pedestrians for sidewalk space. You'll find the most products under one roof at labyrinthine Mercado Libertad, one of Latin America's largest markets. Tlaquepaque and Tonalá are arts-and-crafts meccas. Shoe stores and silver shops are ubiquitous in Guadalajara.

Stores tend to open Monday through Saturday from 10 or 11 until 8, and Sunday 10–2; some close during lunch, usually 2–4 or 2–5, and others close on Sunday. Bargaining is customary in Mercado Libertad, and you can talk deals with some crafts vendors in Tlaquepaque and Tonalá. The ticketed price sticks just about everywhere else, with the exception of antiques shops.

Neighborhood street markets, called *tianguis*, also abound in Guadalajara. They take place at various times throughout the week, with a larger share on Sunday morning. Some focus on specific items like antiques or art, but many have a variety of vendors selling everything from chicken, homemade mole sauce, and fruits and vegetables to flowers, clothing, and housewares.

MARKETS
Tonalá's crafts market, Tlaquepaque's crafts and housewares shops, and Mercado Libertad are the region's top marketplaces. Allot yourself plenty of time and energy to explore all. El Trocadero is a weekly antiques market at the north end of Avenida Chapultepec. Feel free to drive a hard bargain.

Mercado Libertad. Better known as San Juan de Dios, this is one of Latin America's largest covered markets. Its three expansive floors, with shops organized thematically, tower over downtown's east side. Fluctuating degrees of government intervention dictate the quantity of contraband electronics available. Avoid the food on the second floor unless you have a stomach of iron. Be wary of fakes in the jewelry stores. The market opens Monday through Saturday 10–8, but some stores close at 6; the few shops open on Sunday close by 3. ⊠ *Calz. Independencia Sur; use pedestrian bridge from Plaza Tapatía's south side, Centro Histórico.*

ART AND HANDICRAFTS
Ana Lucia Pewter. Ana Lucia Pewter sells beautiful locally made pewter items—from decorative tableware to picture frames—at ridiculously low prices. ⊠ *Calle Ermita 67,* ☎ *33/3683–2794* ⊕ *www.analuciapewter.com.*

Arte Jimenez. Arte Jimenez is a unique shop specializing in decorative art made from fired copper and other metals. ⊠ *Santos Degollado 213, Tonalá* ☎ *33/3562–0291* ⊕ *www.artejimenez.com.*

MASKED CRUSADERS

Lucha Libre. Even if you are not a WWE wrestling fan, attending a Lucha Libre match in Guadalajara is an option few can pass up. But this unique experience is not for the easily offended: while watching the matches between masked heroes and villains, spectators scream obscenities and other uncouth sayings—in Spanish and good fun, of course—at the wrestlers and other spectators. It's about $10 for a ticket to a night of matches, held on Tuesday and Sunday, if you want a seat with the "rich" crowd, or $2 to stand in the balcony with the "poor." Kids' tickets cost $1. ⊠ *Medrano 67, Guadalajara, Jalisco* ☎ *33/3617–3401* ⊕ *www.cmll.com/guadalajara. htm.*

Red Pub. Alternatively, the local bar chain Red Pub offers group trips to the matches for $8, including ticket price, a rather rambunctious bus ride to the event and a beer. Call in advance for reservations. ⊠ *Bernardo de Balbuena 145, Guadalajara, Jalisco* ☎ *33/3616–3474.*

Cadi. Cadi sells awesome stained-glass lamps and other decorative items for the home. ⊠ *Juárez 174, Tlaquepaque* ☎ *33/3343–3682.*

Fodor'sChoice ★ **Galería Sergio Bustamante.** Sergio Bustamante's work is in galleries around the world, but you can purchase his sculptures of human, animal, and fairy-tale creatures in bronze, ceramic, or resin for less at Galería Sergio Bustamante. You'll also find his designs in silver- and gold-plated jewelry. Don't expect a bargain, however; most pieces range from hundreds to thousands of dollars. ⊠ *Calle Independencia 238, Tlaquepaque* ☎ *33/3639–5519, 33/3639–1272, 33/3659–7110* ⊕ *www. coleccionsergiobustamante.com.mx.*

Instituto de la Artesanía Jalisciense. The government-run Instituto de la Artesanía Jalisciense, on the northeast side of Parque Agua Azul, has exquisite blown glass and hand-glazed pottery typical of Jalisco artisans. Prices are fixed here. ⊠ *Calz. González Gallo 20, at Calz. Independencia Sur, Centro Histórico* ☎ *33/3030–9050* ⊕ *www.artesaniasjalisco. gob.mx.*

SIDE TRIPS FROM GUADALAJARA

An hour's drive in just about any direction from Guadalajara will bring you out of the fray and into the countryside. Due south is Lake Chapala, Mexico's largest natural lake. Bordering it are several villages with large expat communities, including Chapala and Ajijic, a village of bougainvillea and cobblestone roads. Tequila, where the famous firewater is brewed, is northwest of Guadalajara. Teuchitlán, south of Tequila, has the Guachimontones Ruins. The placid lakeside area around Chapala makes for a weeklong (expats would say lifelong) getaway, while Tequila and Teuchitlán are great for day trips.

TEQUILA

The drive to tequila country is a straightforward and easy trip. Head west from Guadalajara along Avenida Vallarta for about 25 minutes until you hit the toll road junction (it will say Puerto Vallarta Cuota). The whole trip takes about an hour by car. Take either the toll road (*cuota*) or the free road (*libre*) toward Puerto Vallarta. The toll road is faster, safer, and costs about $10. You can also catch a bus to Tequila from the Antigua Central Camionera (Old Central Bus Station), northeast of the Parque Agua Azul on Avenida Dr. R. Michel, between Calle Los Angeles and Calle 5 de Febrero. Buses marked "Amatitán–Tequila" are easy to spot from the entrance on Calle Los Angeles.

LOCAL HAUNTS

Locals stop at the Mercado Corona, due west of the Palacio Municipal, to pick up fresh produce and meat. The streets north of the market have similar goods, dry merchandise, and school supplies. The Medrano district, starting a block south of the Plaza de los Mariachis and continuing east along Calle Obregón into eastern Guadalajara's nether reaches, is a favorite Tapatío shopping haunt. Though they're short on touristy goods, venturing into these parts is like entering the city's central nervous system.

Another option is to take the Tequila Express train from Guadalajara to Tequila and back for about $80. One of the few passenger trains left in Mexico takes guests on an all-day tour starting and ending with free canned-tequila mixed drinks (like *palomas* and *sangrita*), accompanied by mariachi music. Upon arrival in Tequila, the tour takes visitors to a distillery to learn about the process of making the liquor; the day includes tastings at the distillery, a show of traditional Jalisco dancing and music, and a delicious all-you-can-eat-and-drink Mexican buffet.

Tequila Express ☎ 33/3880–9090 ⊕ *www.tequilaexpress.com.mx*.

TOURS

Servi-Tours Agave Azul offers three different tours every 30 minutes that range from $7 to $11, adding additional stops and time—from one and a half to two hours—depending on what level you choose.

Contact Servi-Tours Agave Azul ☎ 37/4742–0851 ⊕ www.facebook.com/servitour.agaveazul.

Guadalajara Chamber of Commerce ⊠ Av. Vallarta 4095, at Niño Obrero, Guadalajara, Jalisco ☎ 33/3880–9099, 33/3122–7920.

EXPLORING
WORTH NOTING

José Cuervo Distillery. Opened in 1795, the José Cuervo Distillery is the world's oldest tequila distillery. Every day, 150 tons of agave hearts are processed into 80,000 liters of tequila here. Tours are given daily every hour from 10 to 4. The tours at noon and 3 pm are in English, but English-speakers can often be accommodated at other times. The basic tour, which includes one margarita cocktail, costs $8. It's $12 for tours with a few additional tastings as well as an educational catalog,

Tequila isn't just about the local drink; you can easily spend an afternoon taking in the town's colonial architecture.

or $20 if you want to add special reserve tequilas to your tasting. Tours including round-trip transportation can be arranged through the major hotels and travel agencies in Guadalajara. This is a good deal, including several tequila tastings, a complimentary margarita, and time for lunch for about $22. Call at least a day in advance to make arrangements. ■ **TIP➔ Make sure to ask the guide for coupons for an additional margarita, as well as discounts at an area restaurant and in the gift shop.** ⊠ *Calle José Cuervo 73* 🕾 *800/006–8630* ⊕ *www.mundocuervo.com.*

Museo de los Abuelos. The Museo de los Abuelos or Sauza Museum has memorabilia from the Sauza family, a tequila-making dynasty second only to the Cuervos. The museum opens daily 10–3. Admission costs about 50 cents; for this low price they offer tours in English as well as Spanish, depending on the needs of the crowd. ⊠ *Calle Albino Rojas 22* 🕾 *37/4742–0247* ⊕ *www.museolosabuelos.com.*

WHERE TO EAT

$
MEXICAN

✕ **Fonda Cholula.** This typical Mexican restaurant owned by José Cuervo serves up decent quesadillas and other local favorites without leaving your wallet empty. The margaritas are not bad, either. $ *Average main: $10* ⊠ *Calle Jose Cuervo 3* 🕾 *37/4742–1079* ⊕ *www.grupolaposta.mx/ fonda-cholula.html* ⊙ *Daily 12–6, except Christmas and New Year's Day.*

TEUCHITLÁN

50 km (28 miles) west of Guadalajara.

Teuchitlán itself isn't much to see: a small Mexican town like many others, with a few small eateries surrounding a central plaza. But its main draw, the mysterious Guachimontones Ruins, is growing in popularity, and preservation efforts are moving apace. Near the ruins, there are nice lakeside restaurants with decent food and better atmosphere than in town; spending some time here after seeing the ruins makes for a lovely afternoon.

GETTING HERE AND AROUND

To get to Teuchitlán from Guadalajara, drive west out along Avenida Vallarta for 25 minutes to the toll-road junction to Puerto Vallarta, then take the free (*libre*) Route 70 toward Vallarta. Head west along Route 15 for a couple of miles; then turn left onto Route 70 and continue until you reach the town of Tala. Two kilometers (1 mile) past the sugar mill, turn right onto Route 27. Teuchitlán is 15 minutes from the last junction. If you prefer not to drive yourself, it's also possible to hire a car and driver from Guadalajara.

EXPLORING

Guachimontones Ruins. For decades, residents in this sleepy village of sugarcane farmers had a name for the funny-looking mounds in the hills above town, but they never considered the Guachimontones to be more than a convenient source of rocks for local construction projects. Then in the early 1970s an American archaeologist asserted that the mounds were the remnants of a long-vanished, 2,000-year-old community. It took Phil Weigand nearly three decades to convince authorities in far-off Mexico City that he wasn't crazy. Before he was allowed to start excavating and restoring this monumental site in the late 1990s, plenty more houses and roads were produced with Guachimonton rock—and countless tombs were looted of priceless art.

This UNESCO World Heritage Site is most distinctive for its sophisticated concentric architecture—a circular pyramid surrounded by a ring of flat ground, surrounded by a series of smaller platforms arranged in a circle. The "Teuchitlán Tradition," as the concentric circle structures are called, is unique in world architecture. While little is known about the ancient settlement, Weigand believes the formations suggest the existence of a pre-Hispanic state in the region, whereas it was previously held that only socially disorganized nomads inhabited the area at the time. Similar ruins are spread throughout the foothills of the extinct Tequila Volcano, but this is the biggest site yet detected.

Until late 2009, visitors had to find their way to the ruins by asking locals and driving up a hill on an unmarked dirt road. But a large visitor center and museum has been inaugurated, and there are now signs along the highway and through the town of Teuchitlán directing visitors to the site. ⊠ *Carretera Estatal 604, Teuchitlán* ⊕ *www.guachimontones.org.*

WHERE TO EAT

$ ✕ **Restaurant Montecarlo.** This outdoor restaurant is one of a handful of
MEXICAN   eateries along the lakeside in Teuchitlán. While not fancy, it offers a
variety of Mexican dishes, including fish, molcajetes, and fajitas, and
provides a grand view of the lake teeming with fish and birds—including herons and pelicans. There's also a fish pond where kids can bor-
row a homemade rod for some catch and release. As you turn into the
street, don't feel pressured by the parking attendants at the other restaurants who will make attempts to get you into their locales. ⑤ *Average
main: $8 ✉ Calle Las Fuentes 5, Teuchitlán ☎ 38/4733–0257 ⊕ www.
montecarloteuchitlan.com.mx.*

AROUND LAGO DE CHAPALA

48 km (30 miles) southeast of Guadalajara.

Mexico's largest natural lake is a one-hour drive southeast of Guadalajara. Surrounded by jagged hills and serene towns, Lake Chapala is a
favorite Tapatío getaway and a haven for thousands of North American
retirees. The name probably derives from Chapalac, who was chief of
the region's Taltica Indians when the Spaniards arrived in 1538.

The area's main town, Chapala, is flooded with weekend visitors and
the pier is packed shoulder-to-shoulder most Sundays. Its malecón is
often packed with local families and couples on the weekends. Eight
kilometers (5 miles) west is Ajijic, a picturesque village that's home
to the bulk of the area's expatriates. Farther west, San Juan Cosalá is
popular for its thermal-water pools.

GETTING HERE AND AROUND

Driving from Guadalajara, take Avenida Lázaro Cárdenas or Dr. R.
Michel to Carretera a Chapala. The trip takes about an hour. The Carretera a Chapala is the quickest route to Chapala and Ajijic.

Chapala Plus. Chapala Plus serves the lakeside towns for about $4. It's 30
minutes to Chapala and another 15 minutes to Ajijic; there are departures every half hour from 6 am to 9:30 pm. Make sure you ask for the
directo (direct) as opposed to *clase segunda* (second-class) bus, which
makes frequent stops along the highway en route. ☎ *33/3619–5675
⊕ chapalaplus.com.mx.*

CHAPALA

45 km (28 miles) south of Guadalajara.

Chapala was a placid weekend getaway for aristocrats in the late 19th
century, but when then-president Porfirio Díaz got in on the action in
1904, other wealthy Mexicans followed suit. More and more summer
homes were built, and in 1910 the Chapala Yacht Club opened. Avenida
Madero, Chapala's main street, is lined with restaurants, shops, and
cafés. Three blocks north of the promenade, the plaza at the corner of
López Cotilla is a relaxing spot to read a paper or succumb to sweets
from surrounding shops. The Iglesia de San Francisco (built in 1528),
easily recognized by its blue neon crosses on twin steeples, is two blocks
south of the plaza.

On weekends Mexican families flock to the shores of the (for now, at least) rejuvenated lake. Vendors sell refreshments and souvenirs, while lakeside watering holes fill to capacity.

WHERE TO EAT

$ ✕ **Restaurant Cazadores.** This
MEXICAN   grandly turreted brick building was once the summer home of the Braniff family, former owners of the defunct airline. The menu includes slightly overpriced seafood and beef dishes. The house specialty is *chamorro*, pork shank wrapped in banana leaves. A patio overlooks the boardwalk and is inviting in the evening. $ *Average main: $11* ⊠ *Paseo Ramón Corona 18* ☎ *376/765–2162* ⊘ *Closed Mon.*

WHERE TO STAY

$ ☷ **Hotel Villa Montecarlo.** Built
HOTEL   around a Mediterranean-style villa nearly a century old, this hotel has well-maintained grounds with plenty of places for picnics or for the kids to play. **Pros:** huge pools; extensive grounds; outdoor dining under a flowering tree. **Cons:** can be noisy. $ *Rooms from: $90* ⊠ *Paseo del Prado 20* ☎ *376/765–2120* ⊕ *www.hoteles.udg.mx/montecarlo* ⇱ *45 rooms, 2 suites.*

$ ☷ **Lake Chapala Inn.** Three of the four rooms in this restored mansion
B&B/INN   face the shore; all have high ceilings and whitewashed oak furniture. **Pros:** solar-heated lap pool; English-speaking host; sunny reading room. **Cons:** dated furnishings; square tubs not conducive to long soaks. $ *Rooms from: $90* ⊠ *Paseo Ramón Corona 23* ☎ *376/765–4786, 376/765–4809* ⊕ *www.chapalainn.com* ⇱ *4 rooms* ▭ *No credit cards* ⦿ *Breakfast.*

WATER LEVELS

Fifty miles wide but less than 30 feet deep when full, Lake Chapala is the vestige of an ancient inland sea. It's at the tail end (in geological terms) of a natural death from millennia of silt accumulation. This drying process has been accelerated in recent decades by overexploitation of the Lerma River feeding the lake. In 2002, Lake Chapala plummeted to an average depth of four feet, exposing a mile of lake bed stretching from the Chapala pier. Several years of heavy summer rain brought the lake back to near pre-2002 water levels, but what once was a clean place to enjoy lake activities is now much less pristine.

AJIJIC

8 km (5 miles) west of Chapala; 47 km (30 miles) southwest of Guadalajara.

Ajijic has narrow cobblestone streets, vibrantly colored buildings, and a gentle pace—with the exception of the considerably trafficky main highway through the town's southern end. The foreign influence is unmistakable: English is widely (though not exclusively) spoken, and license plates come from far-flung places like British Columbia and Texas.

The Plaza Principal (also known as Plaza de Armas) is a tree- and flower-filled central square at the corner of avenidas Colón and Hidalgo. The Iglesia de San Andrés (Church of St. Andrew) is on the plaza's north side. In late November the plaza and its surrounding streets fill for the saint's nine-day fiesta. From the plaza, walk down Calle Morelos (the continuation of Avenida Colón) toward the lake and peruse the boutiques. Turn left onto Avenida 16 de Septiembre or Avenida Constitución for art galleries and studios. Northeast of the plaza, along the highway, the hub of local activity is the soccer field, which doubles as a venue for concerts.

> **CAUTION**
>
> On both ends of the highway are precarious hilly stretches. Care should be taken while returning to Guadalajara from Chapala on Sunday night, when the largely unlighted highway fills with tipsy drivers.

WHERE TO EAT

$ ✕ **Ajijic Tango.** Considered one of the top, if not the top, restaurants in
ARGENTINE   Ajijic, this Argentine favorite sees locals and tourists waiting in a line down the block to get inside. Many go for the *arrachera* (flank steak), lamb, or carpaccio. Reservations are a must on weekdays—but the eatery doesn't take them on weekends, so get there early. $ *Average main: $10* ⊠ *Calle Morelos 5* ☎ *37/6766–2458* ⊕ *www.ajijictango.com* ⊗ *Closed Tues.*

$ ✕ **Johanna's.** Come to this intimate bit of Bavaria on the lake for German
GERMAN   cuisine like sausages and goose or duck pâté. Main dishes come with soup or salad, applesauce, and cooked red cabbage. For dessert indulge in plum strudel or blackberry-topped torte. Come on the early side, though; this restaurant closes at 8 pm. $ *Average main: $10* ⊠ *Blvd. Ajijic 118-A* ☎ *37/6766–0437* ▬ *No credit cards* ⊗ *Closed Mon.*

$ ✕ **La Bodega de Ajijic.** Eat on a covered patio overlooking a grassy lawn
ECLECTIC   and a small pool at this low-key restaurant. In addition to Mexican standards, the menu has Italian dishes such as pastas; the food here is a bit meager and overpriced. Still, service is friendly, and there's live music—ranging from Mexican pop and rock to blues, jazz, guitar, and harp—most nights. It opens at 8 am, in time for breakfast, every day but Thursday, when it opens later. $ *Average main: $11* ⊠ *Av. 16 de Septiembre 124* ☎ *376/766–1002* ⊗ *Closed Sun.*

$ ✕ **Number 4.** This trendy two-level outdoor restaurant on one of Aji-
ECLECTIC   jic's charming side streets offers beautifully presented dishes, many with an Asian twist. Diners can sit in the modern interior or choose to enjoy the upstairs patio, surrounded by trees and the night sky. Fabulous live piano music accompanies lunch Saturday and Sunday, and there's live music nightly. The bar offers special concoctions, such as a cranberry mandarin martini. $ *Average main: $12* ⊠ *Donato Guerra 4* ☎ *37/6766–1360, 416/907–0609 in U.S. and Canada* ⊕ *www.restaurantnumberfour.com* ⊗ *Hours fluctuate seasonally.*

WHERE TO STAY

$ ☒ **Casa Blanca.** Gracious gardens, tinkling fountains, bright colors, and
HOTEL   arched windows give the traveler a sense of sleeping in a Mexican hacienda while also enjoying the comforts of home. **Pros:** full of character; manicurist and massage therapist by reservation; complimentary shoe shine; on-site Internet service. **Cons:** small rooms. $ *Rooms from: $74* ⊠ *Calle 16 de Septiembre 29* ☎ *376/766–4440, 800/436–0759* ⊕ *www.casablancaajijic.com* ⇄ *8 rooms* ⊙ *Breakfast.*

$ ⛹ **La Nueva Posada.** The well-kept gardens framed in bougainvillea define this inviting inn. **Pros:** uniquely decorated, airy rooms; great restaurant; discounts given for paying with cash. **Cons:** TVs in rooms are small. ⑤ *Rooms from: $72 ⊠ Calle Donato Guerra 9 ☎ 37/6766–1344 ⊕ www.hotelnuevaposada.com* ⇌ *19 rooms, 4 villas* ⏐◎⏐ *Breakfast.*

B&B/INN

NIGHTLIFE

La Bodega de Ajijic. La Bodega de Ajijic has dancing on the weekends and live guitar the rest of the week. It's closed Thursday. ⊠ *Calle 16 de Septiembre 124 ☎ 376/766–1002* ⊠ *$3 cover Fri. and Sun.* ⊗ *Closed Thurs.*

UNDERSTANDING PUERTO VALLARTA

HISTORY

PRE-COLUMBIAN MEXICO

The first nomadic hunters crossed the Bering Straight during the Late Pleistocene Era, some 30,000 or 40,000 years ago, fanning out and finding niches in the varied landscape of North America. In the hot and arid "Great Chichimeca," as the vast area that included the Sonora and Chihuahua deserts and the Great Plains of the United States was known, lived far-flung tribes whose circumstances favored a nomadic lifestyle. Even the unassailable Aztecs were unable to dominate this harsh wilderness and its resilient people.

Mesoamerica, the name given posthumously to the great civilizations of mainland Mexico, spanned as far south of the Great Chichimeca as Honduras and El Salvador. Here, trade routes were established, strategic alliances were formed through warfare or marriage, and enormous temples and palaces were erected on the backs of men, without the aid of beasts of burden or the wheel. Some cultures mysteriously disappeared, others were conquered but not absorbed.

It was in northern Mesoamerica that the continent's first major metropolis, Teotihuacán—which predated the Aztec capital of Tenochtitlán by more than half a century—was built. The gleaming city with beautifully decorated pyramids, palaces, homes, and administrative buildings covered miles and administered to some 175,000 souls; it was abandoned for unknown reasons around AD 700. On the Yucatán Peninsula, great and powerful Maya cities rose up, but like Teotihuacán were abandoned one by one, seemingly at the height of civilization.

During the rise and fall of these great cities, small, loosely organized bands of individuals occupied Mesoamerica's western Pacific coast. By 1200 BC, the culture that archaeologists call Capacha occupied river valleys north and south of what would later be named Bahía de Banderas. From well-positioned settlements, they planted gardens and took advantage of animal and mineral resources from the sea and the surrounding foothills.

These cultures—centered primarily in the present-day states of Nayarit, Jalisco, and Colima—built no large, permanent structures and left few clues about their society. Some of the most compelling evidence comes from artifacts found in tombs. Unlike their more advanced neighbors, the Pacific coast people housed these burial chambers not in magnificent pyramids but in the bottom of vertical shafts deep within the earth. Lifelike dog sculptures were sometimes left to help their deceased owners cross to the other side; servants, too, were buried with their masters for the same purpose. Realistically depicted figures involved in myriad rituals of daily and ceremonial life, most of them excavated only since the 1970s, have given more clues about pre-Hispanic civilizations of western Mexico.

Only so much information can be gleaned, however, especially since the majority of tombs were looted before archaeological research began. North and south of Banderas Bay, the Aztatlán people seem to have established themselves primarily in river valleys between Tomatlán, in southern Jalisco, and northern Nayarit. In addition to creating utilitarian and ceremonial pottery, they appear to have been skilled in at least rudimentary metallurgy. Aside from the Purépecha of Michoacán, to whom the Aztatlán (or Aztlán) are related, no other Mesoamerican societies were skilled in making or using metal of any kind.

The Colonial Period

History favors those who write it, and the soldier-priest-scribe who documented the discovery of Banderas Bay in 1525 gave it a decidedly European spin. According to Padre Tello, four years after the Spanish demolished the Aztec capital at Tenochtitlán, about 100 Spanish troops met 10,000 to 20,000 Aztatlán at Punta Mita (aka Punta de Mita), the bay's northernmost point. Then, by Tello's fantastic account, the sun's sudden illumination of a Spanish battle standard (a large pennant) bearing the image of the Virgin of the Immaculate Conception caused the armed indigenous peoples to give up without a fight. When they lay their colorful battle flags at the feet of Francisco Cortés de Buenaventura, the Spanish commander named the site Bahía de Banderas, or Bay of Flags.

Subsequent adventurers and explorers rediscovered and used the region around the bay, but it wasn't colonized until three centuries later. The name Bahía de Banderas is seen on maps from the 1600s, although whalers in the 1800s called it Humpback Bay, after their principal prey. Boats were built on the beach in today's Mismaloya for a missionary expedition to Baja California, and the long, deep bay was used as a pit stop on other long sailing voyages.

To a lesser extent, Banderas Bay was a place of refuge and refueling for pirates. Around the end of the 16th century, Sir Francis Drake lay in wait here for the Manila galleon—sailing south along the coast laden with wares from the Orient. He sent the booty to his patron, Queen Elizabeth I of England.

The Formative Years

Although adventurers made use of the area's magnificent bay, Puerto Vallarta's story started inland and made its way to the coast. Mining in this part of the Sierra Madre wasn't as profitable as in Zacatecas and Guanajuato, but there was plenty of gold and silver to draw the Spaniards' attention. At the vanguard of Spanish exploration in 1530, the infamous conquistador Nuño Beltrán de Guzmán arrived in the region with a contingent of Spanish soldiers and indigenous allies.

During his tenure in Nueva Galicia (which included today's Jalisco, Zacatecas, and Durango states), de Guzmán seized land that was settled by native peoples and parceled out *encomiendas* (huge grants of land) to lucky *encomendados* (landholders) in return for loyalty and favors to the Crown. The landholders were entitled to the land and everything on it: the birds of the trees; beasts of the forest; and the unlucky indigenous people who lived there, who were consequently enslaved. De Guzmán's behavior was so outrageous that by 1536 he had been stripped of authority and sent to prison.

In exchange for their forced labor, the native population received the "protection" of the encomendado, meaning food and shelter, that they had enjoyed previously without any help from the Spanish. Abuse was inevitable, and many overworked natives died of famine. Epidemics of smallpox, diphtheria, scarlet fever, influenza, measles, and other imported diseases had a disastrous effect. The region's native population was reduced by about 90% within the first 100 years of Spanish occupation.

By the early 17th century, gold and silver were being mined throughout the region; there were bases of operation at San Sebastián del Oeste, Cuale, and Talpa. After the War for Independence (1810–21), Mexican entrepreneurs began to extract gold, silver, and zinc previously claimed by the Spanish. In the mid-1800s, the coast around today's Vallarta was under the jurisdiction of the mountain municipalities.

Independence from Spain brought little contentment to average people, who were as disenfranchised and poor as ever. A prime topic of the day among the moneyed elite was the growing conflict between Liberals and Conservatives. Liberals, like the lawyer Benito Juárez, favored curtailing the Church's vast power. When the Liberals prevailed and

Juárez became Mexico's first indigenous president (he was a Zapotec from Oaxaca), a host of controversial reforms were enacted. Those regarding separation of church and state had immediate and lasting effects.

Settlers on the Bay

The power struggles of the first half of the 19th century had little real impact on relatively unpopulated coastal areas like Banderas Bay. In 1849, a few men from the fishing hamlet of Yelapa camped out at the mouth of the Cuale River, in present-day Puerto Vallarta. A few years later, young Guadalupe Sánchez, his wife, and a few friends were the first official settlers. This entrepreneur made his money by importing salt, vital for extracting mineral from rock. From this business grew the tiny town Las Peñas de Santa María de Guadalupe.

When silver prices dipped between the two World Wars, some of the mountain-based miners returned to their farming roots, relocating to the productive lands of the Ameca River basin (today, Nuevo Vallarta) at the southern border of Nayarit. The fecund land between the mountains and the bay produced ample corn crops, and the growing town of Las Peñas—renamed Puerto Vallarta in honor of a former Jalisco governor—became the seat of its own municipality in 1918.

Development came slowly. By the 1930s there was limited electricity; a small airstrip was built in the 1950s, when Mexicana Airlines initiated the first flights and electricity was finally available around the clock. Retaining the close-knit society and values brought down from the mining towns, each family seemed to know the others' joys and failures. They sat outside their adobe homes to discuss the latest gossip and the international news of the day.

THE MODERN ERA

Honoring a promise made to the Mexican government by John F. Kennedy, President Richard Nixon flew into an improved PV airport in 1970 to sign a treaty settling boundary disputes surrounding the Rio Grande, meeting with his Mexican counterpart, Gustavo Díaz Ordaz. Upon asking for an armored car, he was cheerfully told that the convertible that had been arranged would do just fine. After riding parade-style along the roadway lined with cheering citizens and burros garlanded in flowers, the American leader is said to have asked why, if he was a Republican, the road was lined with donkeys. To which his host sensibly responded, "Well, where in the world would we get all those elephants?"

It took about 500 years for Puerto Vallarta to transition from discovery to major destination, but the city is making up for lost time. "When I was a child here, in the 1950s, Puerto Vallarta was like a big family," the town's official chronicler, the late don Carlos Munguía, said. "When I married, in 1964, there were about 12,000 people." By the early '70s the population had jumped to 35,000 and continued to grow steadily.

Today the greater Puerto Vallarta area has some 220,368, a significant number of them expat Americans and Canadians who vacationed here and never left. The metropolitan area has three universities and a vast marina harboring yachts, tour boats, and the Mexican navy. In 2005 the harbor was expanded to accommodate three cruise ships; the overflow has to anchor offshore. While many folks lament the loss of the good old days before tourism took off, some things haven't changed: Most *vallartenses* (Puerto Vallarta natives) are still intimately acquainted with their neighbors and the man or woman who owns the corner taco stand, which is likely to have been there for years, maybe even generations.

CHRONOLOGY

ca. 350 BC   Oldest evidence of civilization—a ceramic piece from Ixtapa (northwest of Puerto Vallarta)—dates to this time

ca. 1100   Indigenous Aztatlán people dominate region from present-day Sinaloa to Colima states; create first-known settlement in area

1525   First Spanish–Indian confrontation in the region, at Punta Mita. By Spanish accounts, 100 Spanish soldiers prevailed over tens of thousands armed native peoples. Bahía de Banderas (Bay of Flags) was named for the battle flags of the indigenous army that were (according to the Spanish) thrown down in defeat

1587   Pirate Thomas Cavendish attacks Punta Mita, looting pearls gathered from Mismaloya and the Marietas Islands

1664   Mismaloya serves as a shipyard for vessels bound for exploration and conquest of Baja California

1849   Yelapa fishermen are said to have found excellent fishing at the mouth of the Cuale River, making them the first unofficial settlers

1851   Puerto Vallarta founded, under the name Las Peñas de Santa María de Guadalupe, by the salt merchant Guadalupe Sánchez

1918   The small but growing seaside town becomes county seat and is renamed Puerto Vallarta in honor of former Jalisco State governor Ignacio Luis Vallarta (1871–75)

1922   Yellow fever kills some 150 people

1925   Flood and landslides during a great storm form narrow Cuale Island in the middle of the Cuale River in downtown PV

1931   Puerto Vallarta gets electricity (7–10 pm only)

1951   Reporters covering centennial celebrations—marked with a 21-gun naval salute and a wealthy wedding—capture the small-town charm, exposing this isolated coastal gem to their countrymen

1963   Hollywood film *The Night of the Iguana*, directed by John Huston and starring Richard Burton and Ava Gardner, puts PV on the world map, due to the much-publicized affair between Burton and Elizabeth Taylor (who was not in the movie) during the filming here

1970   Vallarta builds a new airport, and improves the electrical and highway systems for Richard Nixon's official visit with President Díaz Ordaz

2000   Census reports the city's population as 159,080

2005   Population rapidly increases to 220,368 in greater metropolitan area

2006   Ground is broken for the 385-slip luxury-yacht marina at La Cruz de Huanacaxtle, north of Bucerías, continuing the trend of converting quiet fishing villages into big-bucks vacation destinations

2007   The "Riviera Nayarit," referring to the real estate between San Blas and Nuevo Vallarta, is officially launched as a newly branded destination

2008   On May 31, Puerto Vallarta celebrates its 40th anniversary as a full-fledged city. Although Puerto Vallarta is largely unaffected, in 2008 gang-related violence escalates on both sides of the U.S.–Mexican border, with the fatality count reaching into the thousands by year's end

2009   In April, U.S. President Barack Obama and Mexican President Felipe Calderon meet to discuss ways to curb gang violence on both sides of the border. Late April also sees outbreaks of H1N1 influenza (swine flu), with Mexico City as the epicenter. Health clubs, nightclubs, stadiums, and many businesses in the Distrito Federal and elsewhere go dark for days, and several international air carriers temporarily suspend service in an effort to prevent the spread of the virus

2010   Mexico played a role in finalizing a successor for the Kyoto Protocol by hosting the UN Framework Convention on Climate Change (UNFCCC) to create the next global agreement on climate change

BOOKS AND MOVIES

Books

Those interested in Mexican culture and society have a wealth of books from which to choose. *The Mexicans: A Personal Portrait of a People*, by Patrick Oster, is a brilliant nonfiction study of Mexican persona and personality. Like Patrick Oster, Alan Riding, author of *Distant Neighbors: A Portrait of the Mexicans*, was a journalist for many years in Mexico City whose insight, investigative journalism skills, and cogent writing skills produced an insightful look into the Mexican mind and culture.

Written by poet, essayist, and statesman Octavio Paz, *The Labyrinth of Solitude* is classic, required reading for those who love Mexico or want to know it better. *The True Story of the Conquest of Mexico*, by Bernal Diaz de Castillo, is a fascinating account of the conquest by one of Cortés's own soldiers.

A collection of essays, *First Stop in the New World*, by David Lida, has contemporary Mexico City as its muse. *The Last Prince of the Mexican Empire*, by C.M. Mayo, explores the motivations and repercussions of Maximilian von Habsburg's disastrous reign as Emperor of Mexico in the mid-19th century. Barbara Kingsolver's *The Lacuna* is an epic set in the Yucatán Peninsula and Mexico City.

There are a few recommended books specifically about Puerto Vallarta. *La Magia de Puerto Vallarta*, by Marilú Suárez-Murias, is a bilingual (English and Spanish) coffee-table book discussing beaches, history, people, and places of Puerto Vallarta. The information is interesting, but the photographs are terribly grainy. For a lighthearted look at life in PV through the eyes of an expat, read *Puerto Vallarta on 49 Brain Cells a Day* and *Refried Brains*, both by Gil Gevins. Along these same lines is *Gringos in Paradise*, by Barry Golson, which evolved out of an assignment for *AARP* magazine and provides a lighthearted look at building the author's dream house in Sayulita,

Nayarit. Those interested in Huichol art and culture might read *People of the Peyote: Huichol Indian History, Religion and Survival*, by Stacy Shaefer and Peter Furst. Also by Stacy Shaefer is *To Think With a Good Heart: Wixarica Women, Weavers and Shamans*.

Movies

The Night of the Iguana (1964), directed by John Huston, is the movie that alerted the world to Puerto Vallarta's existence. Set on the beach and bluffs of Mismaloya, the haunting movie features Richard Burton as a cast-out preacher-turned-tour-guide, Sue Lyons and Deborah Kerr as his clients, and Ava Gardner as the sexy but lonely proprietress of the group's idyllic Mexican getaway. There's no better mood-setter for a trip to Vallarta.

Like Water for Chocolate (Como Agua Para Chocolate) (1992) is a magic-realism glance into rural Mexico during the Mexican Revolution. This visual banquet will make your mouth water for the rose-petal quail and other recipes that the female lead, Tita, prepares. It's based on the novel of the same name by Laura Esquivel, which is equally wonderful. Academy Award winner *The Treasure of the Sierra Madre* (1948), with Humphrey Bogart, is a classic with great mountain scenery. For more fantastic scenery and a great town fiesta, see *The Magnificent Seven* (1960), starring Yul Brynner and Eli Wallach. Nominated for best foreign-language film in 2000, the dark *Amores Perros (Love's a Bitch)* is three intertwined stories portraying corruption and class distinction in urban Mexico. Set in Mexico City with Pierce Brosnan as a failing hit man, *The Matador* (2005) has some good scenes of the Camino Real in Mexico City, a great bullfighting sequence, and is a good drama. More recently, *Rudo y Cursi (Rude and Tacky)* (2008) is a melancholy comedy that follows small-town brothers who become national soccer heroes.

SPANISH VOCABULARY

ENGLISH	SPANISH	PRONUNCIATION

BASICS

Yes/no	Sí/no	see/no
Please	Por favor	pore fah-**vore**
May I?	¿Me permite?	may pair-**mee**-tay
Thank you (very much)	(Muchas) gracias	(**moo**-chas) **grah**-see-as
You're welcome	De nada	day **nah**-dah
Excuse me	Con permiso	con pair-**mee**-so
Pardon me	¿Perdón?	pair-**dohn**
Could you tell me?	¿Podría decirme?	po-dree-ah deh-**seer**-meh
I'm sorry	Lo siento	lo see-**en**-toh
Good morning!	¡Buenos días!	**bway**-nohs **dee**-ahs
Good afternoon!	¡Buenas tardes!	**bway**-nahs **tar**-dess
Good evening!	¡Buenas noches!	**bway**-nahs **no**-chess
Good-bye!	¡Adiós!/¡Hasta luego!	ah-dee-**ohss/ah** -stah **lwe**-go
Mr./Mrs.	Señor/Señora	sen-**yor**/sen-**yohr**-ah
Miss	Señorita	sen-yo-**ree**-tah
Pleased to meet you	Mucho gusto	**moo**-cho **goose**-toh
How are you?	¿Cómo está usted?	**ko**-mo es-**tah** oo-**sted**
Very well, thank you.	Muy bien, gracias.	**moo**-ee bee-**en**, **grah**-see-as
And you?	¿Y usted?	ee oos-**ted**
Hello (on the telephone)	Diga	**dee**-gah

NUMBERS

1	un, uno	oon, **oo**-no
2	dos	dos
3	tres	tress
4	cuatro	**kwah**-tro
5	cinco	**sink**-oh

ENGLISH	SPANISH	PRONUNCIATION
6	seis	saice
7	siete	see-**et**-eh
8	ocho	**o**-cho
9	nueve	new-**eh**-vey
10	diez	dee-**es**
11	once	**ohn**-seh
12	doce	**doh**-seh
13	trece	**treh**-seh
14	catorce	ka-**tohr**-seh
15	quince	**keen**-seh
16	dieciséis	dee-**es**-ee-**saice**
17	diecisiete	dee-**es**-ee-see-**et**-eh
18	dieciocho	dee-**es**-ee-**o**-cho
19	diecinueve	**dee**-**es**-ee-new-**ev**-eh
20	veinte	**vain**-teh
21	veinte y uno/veintiuno	**vain**-te-**oo**-noh
30	treinta	**train**-tah
32	treinta y dos	train-tay-**dohs**
40	cuarenta	kwah-**ren**-tah
43	cuarenta y tres	kwah-**ren**-tay-**tress**
50	cincuenta	seen-**kwen**-tah
54	cincuenta y cuatro	seen-**kwen**-tay **kwah**-tro
60	sesenta	sess-**en**-tah
65	sesenta y cinco	sess-**en**-tay **seen**-ko
70	setenta	set-**en**-tah
76	setenta y seis	set-**en**-tay **saice**
80	ochenta	oh-**chen**-tah
87	ochenta y siete	oh-**chen**-tay see-**yet**-eh
90	noventa	no-**ven**-tah
98	noventa y ocho	no-**ven**-tah-**o**-choh

ENGLISH	SPANISH	PRONUNCIATION
100	cien	see-**en**
101	ciento uno	see-**en**-toh **oo**-noh
200	doscientos	doh-see-**en**-tohss
500	quinientos	keen-**yen**-tohss
700	setecientos	set-eh-see-**en**-tohss
900	novecientos	no-veh-see-**en**-tohss
1,000	mil	meel
2,000	dos mil	dohs meel
1,000,000	un millón	oon meel-**yohn**

COLORS

black	negro	**neh**-groh
blue	azul	ah-**sool**
brown	café	kah-**feh**
green	verde	**ver**-deh
pink	rosa	**ro**-sah
purple	morado	mo-**rah**-doh
orange	naranja	na-**rahn**-hah
red	rojo	**roh**-hoh
white	blanco	**blahn**-koh
yellow	amarillo	ah-mah-**ree**-yoh

DAYS OF THE WEEK

Sunday	domingo	doe-**meen**-goh
Monday	lunes	**loo**-ness
Tuesday	martes	**mahr**-tess
Wednesday	miércoles	me-**air**-koh-less
Thursday	jueves	hoo-**ev**-ess
Friday	viernes	vee-**air**-ness
Saturday	sábado	**sah**-bah-doh

	ENGLISH	SPANISH	PRONUNCIATION

MONTHS

	ENGLISH	SPANISH	PRONUNCIATION
	January	enero	eh-**neh**-roh
	February	febrero	feh-**breh**-roh
	March	marzo	**mahr**-soh
	April	abril	ah-**breel**
	May	mayo	**my**-oh
	June	junio	**hoo**-nee-oh
	July	julio	**hoo**-lee-yoh
	August	agosto	ah-**ghost**-toh
	September	septiembre	sep-tee-**em**-breh
	October	octubre	oak-**too**-breh
	November	noviembre	no-vee-**em**-breh
	December	diciembre	dee-see-**em**-breh

USEFUL PHRASES

	ENGLISH	SPANISH	PRONUNCIATION
	Do you speak English?	¿Habla usted inglés?	**ah**-blah oos-**ted** in-**glehs**
	I don't speak Spanish	No hablo español	no **ah**-bloh es-pahn-**yol**
	I don't understand (you)	No entiendo	no en-tee-**en**-doh
	I understand (you)	Entiendo	en-tee-**en**-doh
	I don't know	No sé	no seh
	I am American/British	Soy americano (americana)/inglés(a)	soy ah-meh-ree-**kah**-no (ah-meh-ree-**kah**-nah)/in-**glehs(ah)**
	What's your name?	¿Cómo se llama usted?	koh-mo seh **yah**-mah oos-**ted**
	My name is . . .	Me llamo . . .	may **yah**-moh
	What time is it?	¿Qué hora es?	keh **o**-rah es
	It is one, two, three . . . o'clock.	Es la una/Son las dos, tres . . .	es la **oo**-nah/sohnahs dohs, tress
	Yes, please/No, thank you	Sí, por favor/No, gracias	**see** pohr fah-**vor**/no **grah**-see-us
	How?	¿Cómo?	**koh**-mo

ENGLISH	SPANISH	PRONUNCIATION
When?	¿Cuándo?	**kwahn**-doh
This/Next week	Esta semana/ la semana que entra	**es**-teh seh-**mah**-nah/ lah seh-**mah**-nah keh **en**-trah
This/Next month	Este mes/el próximo mes	**es**-teh mehs/el **proke**-see-mo mehs
This/Next year	Este año/el año que viene	**es**-teh **ahn**-yo/el **ahn**-yo keh vee-**yen**-ay
Yesterday/today/ tomorrow	Ayer/hoy/mañana	ah-**yehr**/oy/ mahn-**yah**-nah
This morning/ afternoon	Esta mañana/ tarde	**es**-tah mahn-**yah**-nah/ **tar**-deh
Tonight	Esta noche	**es**-tah **no**-cheh
What?	¿Qué?	keh
What is it?	¿Qué es esto?	keh es **es**-toh
Why?	¿Por qué?	pore **keh**
Who?	¿Quién?	kee-**yen**
Where is . . . ?	¿Dónde está . . . ?	**dohn**-deh es-**tah**
the train station?	la estación del tren?	la es-tah-see-on del trehn
the subway station?	la estación del tren subterráneo?	la es-ta-see-**on** del trehn la es-ta-see-**on** soob-teh-**rrahn**-eh-oh
the bus stop?	la parada del autobus?	la pah-**rah**-dah del ow-toh-**boos**
the post office?	la oficina de correos?	la oh-fee-**see**-nah deh koh-**rreh**-os
the bank?	el banco?	el **bahn**-koh
the hotel?	el hotel?	el oh-**tel**
the store?	la tienda?	la tee-**en**-dah
the cashier?	la caja?	la **kah**-hah
the museum?	el museo?	el moo-**seh**-oh
the hospital?	el hospital?	el ohss-pee-**tal**
the elevator?	el ascensor?	el ah-**sen**-sohr
the bathroom?	el baño?	el **bahn**-yoh

ENGLISH	SPANISH	PRONUNCIATION
Here/there	Aquí/allá	ah-**key**/ah-**yah**
Open/closed	Abierto/cerrado	ah-bee-**er**-toh/ ser-**ah**-doh
Left/right	Izquierda/derecha	iss-key-**er**-dah/ dare-**eh**-chah
Straight ahead	Derecho	dare-**eh**-choh
Is it near/far?	¿Está cerca/lejos?	es-**tah** sehr-kah/ **leh**-hoss
I'd like . . .	Quisiera . . .	kee-see-ehr-ah
a room	un cuarto/una habitación	oon **kwahr**-toh/ **oo**-nah ah-bee- tah-see-**on**
the key	la llave	lah **yah**-veh
a newspaper	un periódico	oon pehr-ee-**oh**-dee-koh
a stamp	un sello de correo	oon **seh**-yo deh korr-ee-oh
I'd like to buy . . .	Quisiera comprar . . .	kee-see-**ehr**-ah kohm-**prahr**
cigarettes	cigarrillos	ce-ga-**ree**-yohs
matches	cerillos	ser-**ee**-ohs
a dictionary	un diccionario	oon deek-see-oh-**nah**-ree-oh
soap	jabón	hah-**bohn**
sunglasses	gafas de sol	**ga**-fahs deh sohl
suntan lotion	Loción bronceadora	loh-see-**ohn** brohn-seh-ah-**do**-rah
a map	un mapa	oon **mah**-pah
a magazine	una revista	**oon**-ah reh-**veess**-tah
paper	papel	pah-**pel**
envelopes	sobres	**so**-brehs
a postcard	una tarjeta postal	**oon**-ah tar-**het**-ah post-**ahl**
How much is it?	¿Cuánto cuesta?	**kwahn**-toh **kwes**-tah
It's expensive/ cheap	Está caro/barato	es-**tah kah**-roh/ bah-**rah**-toh

ENGLISH	SPANISH	PRONUNCIATION
A little/a lot	Un poquito/ mucho	oon poh-**kee**-toh/ **moo**-choh
More/less	Más/menos	mahss/**men**-ohss
Enough/too much/too little	Suficiente/ demasiado/ muy poco	soo-fee-see-**en**-teh/ deh-mah-see-**ah**-doh/ **moo**-ee **poh**-koh
Telephone	Teléfono	tel-**ef**-oh-no
Telegram	Telegrama	teh-leh-**grah**-mah
I am ill	Estoy enfermo(a)	es-**toy** en-**fehr**-moh(mah)
Please call a doctor	Por favor llame a un medico	pohr fah-**vor ya**-meh ah oon **med**-ee-koh

ON THE ROAD

Avenue	Avenida	ah-ven-**ee**-dah
Broad, tree-lined boulevard	Bulevar	boo-leh-**var**
Fertile plain	Vega	**veh**-gah
Highway	Carretera	car-reh-**ter**-ah
Mountain pass	Puerto	poo-**ehr**-toh
Street	Calle	**cah**-yeh
Waterfront promenade	Rambla	**rahm**-blah
Wharf	Embarcadero	em-bar-cah-**deh**-ro

IN TOWN

Cathedral	Catedral	cah-teh-**dral**
Church	Templo/Iglesia	**tem**-plo/ee-**glehs**-see-ah
City hall	Casa de gobierno	kah-sah deh go-bee-**ehr**-no
Door, gate	Puerta portón	poo-**ehr**-tah por-**ton**
Entrance/exit	Entrada/salida	en-**trah**-dah/ sah-**lee**-dah
Inn, rustic bar, or restaurant	Taverna	tah-**vehr**-nah
Main square	Plaza principal	plah-thah prin-see-**pahl**

ENGLISH	SPANISH	PRONUNCIATION

DINING OUT

ENGLISH	SPANISH	PRONUNCIATION
Can you recommend a good restaurant?	¿Puede recomendarme un buen restaurante?	**pweh**-deh rreh-koh-mehn-**dahr**-me oon bwehn rrehs-tow-**rahn**-teh?
Where is it located?	¿Dónde está situado?	**dohn**-deh ehs-**tah** see-**twah**-doh?
Do I need reservations?	¿Se necesita una reservación?	seh neh-seh-**see**-tah oo-nah rreh-sehr- bah-**syohn**?
I'd like to reserve a table . . .	Quisiera reservar una mesa . . .	kee-**syeh**-rah rreh-sehr-**bahr** oo-nah **meh**-sah . . .
for two people.	para dos personas.	**pah**-rah dohs pehr-**soh**-nahs
for this evening.	para esta noche.	**pah**-rah **ehs**-tah **noh**-cheh
for 8 PM	para las ocho de la noche.	**pah**-rah lahs **oh**-choh deh lah **noh**-cheh
A bottle of . . .	Una botella de . . .	**oo**-nah bo-**teh**-yah deh
A cup of . . .	Una taza de . . .	**oo**-nah **tah**-thah deh
A glass of . . .	Un vaso de . . .	oon **vah**-so deh
Ashtray	Un cenicero	oon sen-ee-**seh**-roh
Bill/check	La cuenta	lah **kwen**-tah
Bread	El pan	el pahn
Breakfast	El desayuno	el deh-sah-**yoon**-oh
Butter	La mantequilla	lah man-teh-**key**-yah
Cheers!	¡Salud!	sah-**lood**
Cocktail	Un aperitivo	oon ah-pehr-ee-**tee**-voh
Dinner	La cena	lah **seh**-nah
Dish	Un plato	oon **plah**-toh
Menu of the day	Menú del día	meh-**noo** del **dee**-ah
Enjoy!	¡Buen provecho!	bwehn pro-**veh**-cho
Fixed-price menu	Menú fijo o turistico	meh-**noo fee**-hoh oh too-**ree**-stee-coh

ENGLISH	SPANISH	PRONUNCIATION
Fork	El tenedor	el ten-eh-**dor**
Is the tip included?	¿Está incluida la propina?	es-**tah** in-cloo-**ee**-dah lah pro-**pee**-nah
Knife	El cuchillo	el koo-**chee**-yo
Large portion of savory snacks	Raciónes	rah-see-**oh**-nehs
Lunch	La comida	lah koh-**mee**-dah
Menu	La carta, el menú	lah **cart**-ah, el meh-**noo**
Napkin	La servilleta	lah sehr-vee-**yet**-ah
Pepper	La pimienta	lah pee-me-**en**-tah
Please give me	Por favor déme	pore fah-**vor deh**-meh
Salt	La sal	lah sahl
Savory snacks	Tapas	**tah**-pahs
Spoon	Una cuchara	**oo**-nah koo-**chah**-rah
Sugar	El azúcar	el ah-**thu**-kar
Waiter!/Waitress!	¡Por favor Señor/ Señorita!	pohr fah-**vor** sen-**yor**/ sen-yor-**ee**-tah

TRAVEL SMART
PUERTO VALLARTA

GETTING HERE AND AROUND

▌ BY AIR

Flights with stopovers in Mexico City tend to take the entire day. There are nonstop flights from a few U.S. cities, including Atlanta (Delta), Los Angeles (Alaska Air, American Airlines via Mexicana de Aviación), San Francisco (Alaska Air, United, Mexicana), Seattle (Alaska Air), Phoenix (US Airways), Houston (Continental), Dallas (American), Denver (Frontier Air, United), Chicago ORD (American Airlines), and Kansas City, Missouri (Frontier Air).

Air Canada has nonstop flights from Toronto and connecting flights (via Toronto) from all major cities. Web-based Volaris is a Tijuana-based airline with reasonable fares. It flies direct to Puerto Vallarta from Tijuana and between Guadalajara and San Francisco, Los Angeles, and Cancun. You can fly to Manzanillo, just south of the Costalegre, via many airlines with a stop in Mexico City.

If you plan to include Guadalajara in your itinerary, consider an open-jaw flight to Puerto Vallarta with a return from Guadalajara (or vice versa). There's almost no difference in price when you fly a Mexican airline like Aeroméxico, even when factoring in bus fare; sometimes the open jaw is even cheaper.

Flying times are about 2¾ hours from Houston, 3 hours from Los Angeles, 3½ hours from Denver, 4 hours from Chicago, and 8 hours from New York.

Airline and Airport Links.com ⊕ *www.airline andairportlinks.com.*

Airlines Aeroméxico ☎ *800/237–6639 in U.S. and Canada, 01800/021–4000, 01800/021–4010 in Mexico, 322/221–1204 in PV* ⊕ *www. aeromexico.com.* **Air Canada** ☎ *888/247–2262 in U.S. and Canada, 322/221–1823 in PV* ⊕ *www.aircanada.com.* **Alaska Airlines** ☎ *800/252–7522 in Mexico, 322/221–2610 in PV* ⊕ *www.alaskaair.com.* **American Airlines** ☎ *800/433–7300 in U.S., 01800/904–6000 in Mexico, 322/221–1799 in PV* ⊕ *www.aa.com.* **Delta Airlines** ☎ *800/221–1212 in U.S., 01800/266–0046 in Mexico* ⊕ *www.delta.com.* **Frontier** ☎ *800/432–1359 in U.S.* ⊕ *www. flyfrontier.com.* **Interjet** ☎ *01800/011–2345 in Mexico* ⊕ *www.interjet.com.mx.* **United Airlines** ☎ *800/864–8331 for U.S. and Mexico reservations, 01800/900–5000 in Mexico* ⊕ *www.united.com.* **US Airways** ☎ *800/428–4322 in U.S., 322/221–1333 in PV* ⊕ *www. usairways.com.* **Volaris** ☎ *55/1102–8000 in Mexico City, 01800/122–8000 in Mexico* ⊕ *www.volaris.com.mx.*

Airline Security Issues Transportation Security Administration ☎ *866/289–9673* ⊕ *www.tsa.gov.*

AIRPORTS

The main gateway, and where many PV-bound travelers change planes, is Mexico City's large, modern Aeropuerto Internacional de la Ciudad de México (Benito Juárez; airport code: MEX). It's infamous for pickpocketing and taxi scams, so watch your stuff.

Puerto Vallarta's small international Aeropuerto Internacional Gustavo Díaz Ordáz (PVR) is 7.5 km (4½ miles) north of downtown.

Airport Information Aeropuerto Internacional de la Ciudad de México (Benito Juárez) (MEX) ✉ *Mexico DF* ☎ *55/2482–2424, 55/2482–2400* ⊕ *www.aicm.com.mx.* **Aeropuerto Internacional Gustavo Díaz Ordáz** (PVR) ✉ *Tepic Hwy., Km 7.5* ☎ *322/221–1298* ⊕ *www.aeropuertosgap.com.mx/es/ puerto-vallarta-3.*

GROUND TRANSPORTATION

Vans provide transportation from the airport to PV hotels; there's a zone system with different prices for the Zona Hotelera (Hotel Zone), downtown PV, and so on. Outside the luggage collection area, vendors shout for your attention. It's a confusing scene. Purchase the taxi vouchers sold at the stands inside the terminal, and be sure to avoid the time-share vendors who trap you in their vans for a high-pressure sales pitch en route to your hotel. Avoid drivers who approach you, and head for an official taxi kiosk, which will have zone information clearly posted. As in any busy airport, don't leave your luggage unattended for any reason.

Before you purchase your ticket, look for a taxi-zone map (it should be posted on or by the ticket stand), and make sure your taxi ticket is properly zoned; if you need a ticket only to Zone 3, don't pay for a ticket to Zone 4 or 5. Taxis or vans to the Costalegre resorts between PV and Manzanillo are generally arranged through the resort. If not, taxis charge about 200 to 250 pesos ($15–$19) an hour—more if you're traveling beyond Jalisco State lines.

▌ BY BUS

LONG-DISTANCE SERVICE

PV's Central Camionera, or Central Bus Station, is 1 km (½ mile) north of the airport, halfway between Nuevo Vallarta and downtown.

First-class Mexican buses (known as *primera clase*) are generally timely and comfortable, air-conditioned coaches with bathrooms, movies, and reclining seats—sometimes with seat belts. Deluxe (*de lujo* or *ejecutivo*) buses offer the same—sometimes with fewer, roomier seats—and usually have refreshments. Second-class (*segunda clase*) buses are used mainly for travel to smaller, secondary destinations.

A lower-class bus ride can be interesting if you're not in a hurry and want to experience local culture; these buses make frequent stops and keep less strictly to their timetables. Often they will wait until they fill up to leave, regardless of the scheduled time of departure. Fares are up to 15%–30% cheaper than those for first-class buses. The days of pigs and chickens among your bus mates are largely in the past. ▌TIP→ **Unless you're writing a novel or your memoir, there's no reason to ride a second-class bus if a first-class or better is available.** Daytime trips are safer.

Bring snacks, socks, and a sweater—the air-conditioning on first-class buses is often set on high—and toilet paper, as restrooms might not have any. Smoking is prohibited on all buses.

Estrella Blanca goes from Mexico City to Manzanillo, Mazatlán, Monterrey, Nuevo Laredo, and other central, Pacific coast, and northern-border points. ETN has the most luxurious service—with exclusively first-class buses that have roomy, totally reclining seats—to Guadalajara, Mexico City, Barra de Navidad, Chamela, and Manzanillo. Primera Plus connects Mexico City with Manzanillo and Puerto Vallarta along with other central and western cities.

TAP serves Mexico City, Guadalajara, Puerto Vallarta, Tepic, and Mazatlán. Basic service, including some buses with marginal or no air-conditioning, is the norm on Transportes Cihuatlán, which connects the Bahía de Banderas and PV with southern Jalisco towns such as Barra de Navidad.

You can buy tickets for first-class or better in advance; this is advisable during peak periods, although the most popular routes have buses on the hour. You can make reservations for many, though not all, of the first-class bus lines, through the Ticketbus central reservations agency. Rates average 35–76 pesos ($2.70–$5.70) per hour of travel, depending on the level of luxury. Plan to pay in pesos, although most of the deluxe bus services accept Visa and MasterCard.

Bus Contacts Central Camionera ⊠ *Bahia Sin Nombre 363, Las Mojoneras* 🕿 *322/290–1009.* **Estrella Blanca** 🕿 *01800/507–5500 toll-free in Mexico, 322/290–1014 in Puerto Vallarta* ⊕ *www.estrellablanca.com.mx* ⊠ *Carr a Tepic Km 9, Mezcales* 🕿 *329/296–5936.* **ETN** 🕿 *01800/800–0386 toll-free in Mexico, 322/290–0997 in PV* ⊕ *www.etn.com.mx* ⊠ *Plaza Parabien, Av. Tepic sur 1508, Local 5, Nuevo Vallarta* 🕿 *322/297–7552.* **Primera**

Plus ☎ *322/290-0716 in PV, 322/187-0492 in NV* ⊕ *primeraplus.com.mx.* **Transporte del Pacifico (TAP)** ☎ *322/290-0119 in PV* ⊕ *tap. com.mx.* **Vallarta Plus** ✉ *Palma Real 140, Marina Vallarta* ☎ *322/221-3636, 322/306-3071* ⊕ *www.vallartaplus.com.*

CITY BUSES

City buses (6.5 pesos) serve downtown, the Zona Hotelera Norte, and Marina Vallarta. Bus stops—marked by blue-and-white signs—are every two or three long blocks along the highway (Carretera al Aeropuerto) and in downtown Puerto Vallarta. Green buses to Playa Mismaloya and Boca de Tomatlán (7 pesos) run about every 15 minutes from the corner of Avenida Insurgentes and Basilio Badillo downtown.

Gray ATM buses serving Nuevo Vallarta and Bucerías (20 pesos), Punta Mita (30 pesos), and Sayulita (50 pesos) depart from Plaza las Glorias, in front of the HSBC bank and Wal-Mart, both of which are along Carretera Aeropuerto between downtown and the Zona Hotelera.

■TIP→ It's rare for inspectors to check tickets, but just when you've let yours flutter to the floor, a figure of authority is bound to appear. So hang on to your ticket and hat: PV bus drivers race from one stoplight to the next in jerky bursts of speed.

There's no problem with theft on city buses aside from perhaps an occasional pickpocket, which could be said of anywhere in the world.

■ BY CAR

From December through April—peak season—traffic clogs the narrow downtown streets, and negotiating the steep hills in Old Vallarta (sometimes you have to drive in reverse to let another car pass) can be unnerving. Avoid rush hour (7–9 am and 6–8 pm) and when schools let out (2–3 pm). Travel with a companion and a good road map or atlas. Always lock your car, and never leave valuable items visible

in the body of the car. The trunk is generally safe, although any thief can crack one open if he chooses.

■TIP→ It's absolutely essential that you carry Mexican auto insurance for liability, even if you have full coverage for collision, damages, and theft. If you injure anyone in an accident, you could well be jailed until culpability is established—whether it was your fault or not—unless you have insurance.

GASOLINE

Pemex (the government petroleum monopoly) franchises all of Mexico's gas stations, which you can find at most intersections and in cities and towns. Gas is measured in liters. Stations in and around the larger towns may accept U.S. or Canadian credit cards (or dollars).

Premium unleaded gas (called *premium,* the red pump) and regular unleaded gas (*magna,* the green pump) are available nationwide, but it's still best to fill up whenever you can and not let your tank get below half full. Fuel quality is generally lower than that in the United States, but it has improved enough so that your car will run acceptably. At this writing gas was about 12.8 pesos per liter (about $3.78 per gallon) for the cheap stuff and 13.4 pesos per liter ($4.12 per gallon) for super.

Attendants pump the gas for you and may also wash your windshield and check your oil and tire air pressure. A small tip is customary (from just a few pesos for pumping the gas only to 5 or 10 for the whole enchilada of services). Keep an eye on the gas meter to make sure the attendant is starting it at "0" and that you're charged the correct price.

PARKING

A circle with a diagonal line superimposed on the letter *E* (for *estacionamiento*) means "no parking." Illegally parked cars may have the license plate removed, requiring a trip to the traffic-police headquarters for payment of a fine. When in doubt, park in a lot rather than on the street; your car will probably be safer there anyway. There are parking lots in PV at Parque Hidalgo (⊠ *Av. México at Venezuela, Col. 5 de Diciembre*), just north of the Cuale River at the malecón between Calle A. Rodríguez and Calle Encino, and in the Zona Romántica at Parque Lázaro Cárdenas. Fees vary depending on time of day, ranging from 12 pesos (just under $1) per hour to 20 pesos (about $1.50) per hour.

ROAD CONDITIONS

Several well-kept toll roads head into and out of major cities like Guadalajara—most of them four lanes wide. However, these *carreteras* (major highways) don't go too far into the countryside, and even the toll-roads have *topes* (speed bumps) and toll booths to slow you down. *Cuota* means toll road; *libre* means no toll, and such roads are often two lanes and not as well-maintained. A new 33½-km (21-mile) highway between Tepic and San Blas will shorten driving time to about 20 minutes.

Roads leading to, or in, Nayarit and Jalisco include highways connecting Nogales and Mazatlán; Guadalajara and Tepic; and Mexico City, Morelia, and Guadalajara. Tolls between Guadalajara and Puerto Vallarta (334 km [207 miles]) total about $25.

In rural areas roads are sometimes poor; other times the two-lane, blacktop roads are perfectly fine. Be extra cautious during the rainy season, when rock slides and potholes are a problem.

Watch out for animals, especially untethered horses, cattle, and dogs, and for dangerous, unrailed curves. *Topes* (speed bumps) are ubiquitous; slow down when approaching any town or village and look for signs saying "Topes" or "Vibradores." Police officers often issue tickets to those speeding through populated areas.

Generally, driving times are longer than for comparable distances in the United States and Canada. Allow extra time for unforeseen occurrences as well as for traffic, particularly truck traffic.

ROADSIDE EMERGENCIES

To help motorists on major highways, the Mexican Tourism Ministry operates a fleet of more than 250 pickup trucks, known as the Angeles Verdes, or Green Angels, reachable by phone throughout Mexico by dialing 078 or, in some areas near Puerto Vallarta, 066. In either case, ask the person who answers to transfer the call to the Green Angels hotline. The bilingual drivers provide mechanical help, first aid, radio-telephone communication, basic supplies and small parts, towing, tourist information, and protection.

Services are free, and spare parts, fuel, and lubricants are provided at cost. Tips are always appreciated (around 65–130 pesos [$5–$10] for big jobs and 40–65 pesos [$3–$5] for minor stuff; a souvenir from your country can sometimes be a well-received alternative). The Green Angels patrol the major highways twice daily 8–8 (usually later on holiday weekends). If you break down, pull off the road as far as possible, and lift the hood of your car. If you don't have a cell phone, hail a passing vehicle and ask the driver to notify the patrol. Most drivers will be quite helpful.

Emergency Services Angeles Verdes
☏ *078.*

RULES OF THE ROAD

When you sign up for Mexican car insurance, you may receive a booklet on Mexican rules of the road. It really is a good idea to read it to familiarize yourself not only with laws but also customs that differ from those of your home country. For instance: if an oncoming vehicle flicks its lights at you in daytime, slow down: it could mean trouble ahead; when approaching a narrow bridge, the first vehicle to flash its lights has right of way; right on red is not allowed; one-way traffic is indicated by an arrow; two-way, by a double-pointed arrow. (Other road signs follow the widespread system of international symbols.)

⚠ On the highway, using your left turn signal to turn left is dangerous. Mexican drivers—especially truck drivers—use their left turn signal on the highway to signal the vehicle behind that it's safe to pass. Conversely they rarely use their signal to actually make a turn. Foreigners signaling a left turn off the highway into a driveway or onto a side road have been killed by cars or trucks behind that mistook their turn signal for a signal to pass. To turn left from a highway when cars are behind you, it's best to pull over to the right and make the left turn when no cars are approaching, to avoid disaster.

Mileage and speed limits are given in kilometers: 110 kph and 80 kph (66 mph and 50 mph, respectively) are the most common maximums on the highway. However, speed limits can change from curve to curve, so watch the signs carefully. In cities and small towns, observe the posted speed limits, which can be as low as 20 kph (12 mph).

Seat belts are required by law throughout Mexico. Drunk driving laws are fairly harsh in Mexico, and if you're caught you may go to jail immediately. It's difficult to say what the blood-alcohol limit is since everyone you ask gives a different answer, which means each case is probably handled in a discretionary manner. The best way to avoid any problems is simply to not drink and drive.

If you're stopped for speeding, the officer is supposed to take your license and hold it until you pay the fine at the local police station. But the officer will usually prefer a *mordida* (small bribe). Just take out a couple hundred pesos, hold it out discreetly while asking politely if the officer can "pay the fine for you." Conversely, a few cops might resent the offer of a bribe, but it's still common practice.

If you decide to dispute a charge that seems preposterous, do so courteously and with a smile, and tell the officer that you would like to talk to the police captain when you get to the station. The officer usually will let you go rather than go to the station.

SAFETY ON THE ROAD

Never drive at night in remote and rural areas. *Bandidos* are one concern, but so are potholes, free-roaming animals, cars with no working lights, road-hogging trucks, drunk drivers, and difficulty in getting assistance. It's best to use toll roads whenever possible; although costly, they're safer, too.

Off the highway, driving in Mexico can be nerve-wracking for novices, with people sometimes paying little attention to marked lanes. Most drivers pay attention to safety rules, but be vigilant. Drunk driving skyrockets on holiday weekends.

A police officer may pull you over for something you didn't do; unfortunately a common scam. If you're pulled over for any reason, be polite—displays of anger will only make matters worse. Although efforts are being made to fight corruption, it's still a fact of life in Mexico, and for many people, it's worth the $10 to $100 it costs to get their license back to be on their way quickly. (The amount requested varies depending on what the officer assumes you can pay—the year, make, and model of the car you drive being one determining factor.) Others persevere long enough to be let off with a warning only. The key to success, in this case, is a combination of calm and patience.

RENTAL CARS

Mexico manufactures Chrysler, Ford, General Motors, Honda, Nissan, and Volkswagen vehicles. With the exception of Volkswagen, you can get the same kind of midsize and luxury cars in Mexico that you can rent in the United States and Canada. Economy usually refers to a Dodge i10 or similar, which may or may not come with air-conditioning or automatic transmission.

It can really pay to shop around: in Puerto Vallarta, rates for a compact car (Chevrolet Aveo or similar) with air-conditioning, manual transmission, and unlimited mileage range from $19 a day and $120 a week to $50 a day and $300–$400 a week, excluding insurance. Full-coverage insurance varies greatly depending on the deductible, but averages $25–$40 a day. As a rule, stick with the major companies because they tend to be more reliable.

You can also hire a taxi with a driver (who generally doubles as a tour guide) through your hotel. The going rate is about $22 an hour without crossing state lines. Limousine service runs about $65 an hour and up, with a three- to five-hour minimum.

In Mexico the minimum driving age is 18, but most rental-car agencies have a surcharge for drivers under 25. Your own country's driver's license is perfectly acceptable.

Surcharges for additional drivers are around $5 per day plus tax. Children's car seats run about the same, but not all companies have them.

CAR-RENTAL INSURANCE

You must carry Mexican auto insurance, at the very least liability as well as coverage against physical damage to the vehicle and theft at your discretion, depending on what, if anything, your own auto insurance (or credit card, if you use it to rent a car) includes. For rental cars, all insurance will all be dealt with through the rental company.

Major Rental Agencies Alamo ☎ *800/522–9696 in U.S., 322/221–3040 in PV* ⊕ *www.alamo.com.* **Avis** ☎ *800/331–1084 in U.S., 322/221–1112 in PV* ⊕ *www.avis.com.* **Budget** ☎ *800/472–3325 in U.S., 322/221–1210 in PV* ⊕ *www.budget.com.* **Hertz** ☎ *800/654–3001 in U.S., 999/911–8040 in PV* ⊕ *www.hertz.com.* **National Car Rental** ☎ *800/227–7368 in U.S., 322/226–0069 in PV* ⊕ *www.nationalcar.com.*

▌ BY TAXI

PV taxis aren't metered and instead charge by zones. Most of the larger hotels have rate sheets, and taxi drivers should produce them upon request. Tipping isn't necessary unless the driver helps you with your bags, in which case a few pesos are appropriate.

The minimum fare is 40 pesos (about $3), but if you don't ask, you'll probably be overcharged. Negotiate a price in advance for out-of-town and hourly services as well; many drivers will start by asking how much you want to pay or how much others have charged you to get a sense of your street-smarts. The usual hourly rate at this writing was 300 pesos per hour. In all cases, if you are unsure of what a fare should be, ask your hotel's front-desk personnel.

The ride from downtown to the airport or to Marina Vallarta costs about $10; it's $20 to Nuevo Vallarta and $25 to Bucerías. From downtown south to Mismaloya it's about $5 to Conchas Chinas, $10–$12 to the hotels of the Zona Hotelera, $12 to Mismaloya, and $15 to Boca de Tomatlán. You can easily hail a cab on the street. Taxi Tel Flamingos and others provide 24-hour service.

Taxi Company Taxi Tel Flamingos ☎ *322/225–0716.* **Sitio Bucerías** ☎ *329/298–0714.* **Sitio Valle Dorado** ☎ *322/297–5407.*

ESSENTIALS

▌ COMMUNICATIONS

INTERNET

Internet cafés have sprung up all over Puerto Vallarta and even small surrounding towns and villages, making email by far the easiest way to get in touch with people back home. However, the best Internet in town, as in so many other cities of the world, is at Starbucks; nobody will charge you for the Internet service and all you need to do is get yourself a cappuccino. There are several branches within the tourist areas; just look on their website to locate the nearest one.

If you're bringing a laptop with you, check with the manufacturer's technical support line to see what service and/or repair affiliates it has in the areas you plan to visit. Carry a spare battery to save yourself the expense and headache of having to hunt down a replacement on the spot. Memory sticks and other accessories are usually more expensive in Mexico than in the United States or Europe, but are available in megastores such as Sam's Club and Office Depot as well as mom-and-pop computer shops.

The younger generation of Mexicans is computer savvy and there are some excellent repair wizards and technicians to help you with problems; many are bilingual.

Contacts Cybercafes. This website lists more than 4,000 Internet cafés worldwide. ⊕ *www.cybercafes.com.* **Starbucks** ⊕ *www.starbucks.com.mx.*

PHONES

The area code for PV (and the northern Costalegre) and Nuevo Vallarta is 322; San Francisco's is 311; between Bucerías and Sayulita, 329; Lo De Marcos and Rincón de Guayabitos, 327; San Blas, 323. The Costalegre from around Rancho Cuixmala to San Patricio–Melaque and Barra de Navidad has a 315 area code.

The country code for Mexico is 52. When calling a Mexico number from abroad, dial any necessary international access code, then the country code, and then all of the numbers listed for the entry. When calling a cell phone in Mexico from outside the country, dial 01152 (access and country codes) and then 1 and then the number.

Toll-free numbers in Mexico start with an 800 prefix. These numbers, however, are billed as local calls if you call one from a private phone. To reach them, you need to dial 01 before the number. In this guide, Mexico-only toll-free numbers appear as follows: 01800/123–4567. The toll-free numbers listed as 800/123–4567 are U.S. or Canadian numbers and generally work north of the border only (though some calling cards will allow you to dial them from Mexico, charging you minutes as for a toll call). Numbers listed as 001800/123–4567 are toll-free U.S. numbers; if you're calling from Mexico, you'll be charged for an international call.

INTERNATIONAL CALLS

To make an international call, dial 00 before the country code, area code, and number. The country code for the United States and Canada is 1. Avoid phones near tourist areas that advertise in English (e.g., "Call the U.S. or Canada here!"). They charge an outrageous fee per minute. If in doubt, dial the operator and ask for rates.

CALLS WITHIN MEXICO

Directory assistance is 040 nationwide. For assistance in English, dial 090 for an international operator; tell the operator in what city, state, and country you require directory assistance, and he or she will connect you. There's no charge for the former; the latter can be dialed only from a home phone, as the charge appears on the monthly phone bill.

Much less often seen today, a *caseta de larga distancia* is a long-distance/overseas telephone service usually operated out of a store such as a *papelería* (stationery store), pharmacy, restaurant, or other small business; look for the phone symbol on the door. Casetas may cost slightly more to use than pay phones, but you tend to be shielded from street noise, as you get your own little booth. They also have the benefit of not forcing you to buy a prepaid phone card with a specific denomination—you pay in cash according to the calls you make. Tell the person on duty the number you'd like to call, and she or he will give you a rate and dial for you. Rates seem to vary widely, so shop around.

CELL PHONES

If you have a multiband phone (some countries use different frequencies from those used in the United States) and your service provider uses the world-standard GSM network (as do T-Mobile, AT&T, and Verizon), you can probably use your phone abroad. Roaming fees can be steep, however: 99¢ a minute is standard. And you normally pay the toll charges for incoming and outgoing calls. It's almost always cheaper to send a text message (or at least to receive one, which is sometimes substantially cheaper than to send).

If you just want to make local calls, consider buying a new SIM card (note that your provider may have to unlock your phone for you to use a different SIM card) and a prepaid service plan in the destination. You'll then have a local number and can make local calls at local rates. If your trip is extensive, you could also simply buy a new cell phone in your destination, as they go for around $30 and sometimes come with a couple hundred prepaid minutes to start you off. The two cell phone carriers in Mexico are Movistar and TELCEL; minutes can be purchased at their offices or more conveniently at OXXO convenience stores, Guadalajara pharmacies, or other locations.

■ TIP→ If you travel internationally frequently, save one of your old cell phones or buy a cheap one on the Internet; ask your cell phone company to unlock it for you, and take it with you as a travel phone, buying a new SIM card with pay-as-you-go service in each destination.

▌CUSTOMS AND DUTIES

Upon entering Mexico, you'll be given a baggage declaration form and asked to itemize what you're bringing into the country. You are allowed to bring in 3 liters of spirits or wine for personal use; 400 cigarettes, 25 cigars, or 200 grams of tobacco; a reasonable amount of perfume for personal use; one video camera and one regular camera and 12 rolls of film for each; and gift items not to exceed a total of $300. If driving across the U.S. border, gift items shouldn't exceed $75, although foreigners aren't usually hassled about this. ⚠ Although the much-publicized border violence doesn't affect travelers, it is real. To be safe don't linger long at the border.

You aren't allowed to bring firearms, ammunition, meat, vegetables, plants, fruit, or flowers into the country. You can bring in one of each of the following items without paying taxes: a cell phone, a camera, a DVD player, a CD player, a musical instrument, a laptop computer, and a portable copier or printer. Compact discs and/or audio cassettes are limited to 20 total and DVDs to 5.

Mexico also allows you to bring a cat or dog, if you have two things: (1) a pet health certificate signed by a registered veterinarian in the United States and issued not more than 72 hours before the animal enters Mexico; and (2) a pet vaccination certificate showing that the animal has been treated (as applicable) for rabies, hepatitis, distemper, and leptospirosis.

For more information or information on bringing other animals, contact the Mexican consulate, which has branches in many major American cities as well as border towns. To find the consulate nearest you, check the Ministry of Foreign

LOCAL DO'S AND TABOOS

CUSTOMS OF THE COUNTRY

In the United States and elsewhere in the world, being direct, efficient, and succinct is highly valued. But Mexican communication tends to be more subtle, and the direct style of Americans, Canadians, and Europeans is often perceived as curt and aggressive. Mexicans are extremely polite, so losing your temper over delays or complaining loudly will get you branded as rude and make people less inclined to help you. Remember that things move slowly here and that there's little stigma attached to being late. You'll probably notice that local friends, relatives, and significant others show a fair amount of physical affection with each other, but you should be more retiring with people you don't know well.

GREETINGS

Learning basic phrases in Spanish such as *"por favor"* (please) and *"gracias"* (thank you) will make a big difference in how people respond to you. Also, being deferential to those who are older than you will earn you lots of points, as will addressing people as señor, señora, or señorita.

Also, saying *"Disculpe"* before asking a question of someone is a polite way of saying "Excuse me" before launching into a request for information or directions. Similarly, asking *"¿Habla inglés?"* is more polite than assuming every Mexican you meet speaks English.

SIGHTSEEING

In Puerto Vallarta, it is acceptable to wear shorts in houses of worship, but do avoid being blatantly immodest. Bathing suits and revealing clothing are also inappropriate for shopping and sightseeing in general. Mexican men don't generally wear shorts, even in extremely hot weather, although this rule is generally ignored by both Mexican and foreign men on vacation here and at other beach resorts.

OUT ON THE TOWN

Mexicans call waiters *"joven"* (literally, "young man") no matter how old they are (it's the equivalent of the word "maid" being used for the old woman who cleans rooms). Call a female waitress *señorita* ("miss") or *señora* ("ma'am"). Ask for *"la cuenta, por favor"* ("the check, please") when you want the bill; it's considered rude to bring it before the customer asks for it. Mexicans tend to dress nicely for a night out, but in tourist areas, dress codes are mainly upheld only at the more sophisticated nightclubs. Smoking in bars and restaurants is now theoretically illegal, but in some smaller establishments and those with outdoor patios, people still smoke with abandon.

DOING BUSINESS

Personal relationships always come first here, so developing rapport and trust is essential. A handshake and personal greeting are appropriate along with a friendly inquiry about family, especially if you have met the family. In established business relationships, don't be surprised if you're greeted with a kiss on the cheek or a hug. Always be respectful toward colleagues in public and keep confrontations private.

Meetings may or may not start on time, but you should be patient. When you are invited to dinner at the home of a client or associate, it's not necessary to bring a gift; however, sending a thank-you note afterward scores points.

Your offers to pick up the tab at business lunches or dinners will be greatly appreciated but will probably be declined; because you are a guest in their country, most Mexicans will want to treat you to the meal. Be prepared to exchange business cards, and feel free to offer yours first. Professional attire tends to be on the conservative side. Mexicans are extremely well groomed, so you'll do well if you follow suit.

Affairs website (go to the "Servicios Consulares" option).

Information in Mexico Mexican Embassy
☎ 202/728–1600 ⊕ embamex.sre.gob.mx/eua.
Ministry of Foreign Affairs ⊕ www.sre.gob.mx/en.

U.S. Information U.S. Customs and Border Protection ☎ 877/227–5511 ⊕ www.cbp.gov.

▌ ELECTRICITY

For U.S. and Canadian travelers, electrical converters aren't necessary because Mexico operates on the 60-cycle, 120-volt system; however, many Mexican outlets have not been updated to accommodate three-prong and polarized plugs (those with one larger prong), so to be safe bring an adapter.

Blackouts and brownouts—often lasting an hour or so—are not unheard of, particularly during the rainy season, so bring a surge protector.

Consider making a small investment in a universal adapter, which has several types of plugs in one lightweight, compact unit.

▌ EMERGENCIES

If you get into a scrape with the law, you can call your nearest consulate; U.S. citizens can also call the Overseas Citizens Services Center in the United States.

Consulate and Embassy United States Consul ✉ Centro Comercial Paradise Plaza, Paseo de Cocoteros 85 Sur, 2nd fl., Nuevo Vallarta ☎ 322/222–0069, 33/3268–2145 24-hour emergency number ⏱ Mon.–Thurs. 8:30 am–12:30 pm. **U.S. Embassy** ✉ Paseo de la Reforma 305, Col. Cuauhtémoc, Mexico City ☎ 55/5080–2000 ⊕ mexico.usembassy.gov.

General Emergency Contacts General Emergency (Police, Transit, Fire) ☎ 066. **U.S. Overseas Citizens Services Center** ☎ 888/407–4747, 202/501–4444 ⊕ www.travel.state.gov.

▌ HEALTH

FOOD AND DRINK

In Mexico the biggest health risk is *turista* (traveler's diarrhea), caused by consuming contaminated fruit, vegetables, or water. To minimize risks, avoid questionable-looking street stands and bad-smelling food even in the toniest establishments; and if you're not sure of a restaurant's standards, pass up ceviche (raw fish cured in lemon juice) and raw vegetables that haven't been peeled (or that *can't* be peeled, like lettuce and tomatoes).

Drink only bottled water or water that has been boiled for at least 20 minutes, even when you're brushing your teeth. *Agua mineral* or *agua con gas* means mineral or carbonated water, and *agua purificada* means purified water. Hotels with water-purification systems will post signs to that effect in the rooms.

Despite these warnings, keep in mind that Puerto Vallarta, Nuevo Vallarta, and the Costalegre have virtually no industry beyond tourism and are unlikely to kill (or seriously distress) the geese that lay their golden eggs. Some people choose to bend the rules about eating at street stands and consuming fresh fruits and chopped lettuce or cabbage, as there's no guarantee that you won't get sick at a five-star resort and have a delicious, healthful meal at a shack by the sea. If fish or seafood smells or tastes bad, send it back and ask for something different.

Don't fret about ice: Tourist-oriented hotels and restaurants, and even most of those geared toward the locals, use purified water for ice, drinks, and washing vegetables. Many alleged cases of food poisoning are due instead to hangovers or excessive drinking in the strong sun. But whenever you're in doubt, ask questions about the origins of food and water and, if you feel unsure, err on the side of safety.

Mild cases of turista may respond to Imodium (known generically as loperamide), Lomotil, or Pepto-Bismol (not as strong), all of which you can buy over the counter; keep in mind, though, that these drugs can complicate more serious illnesses. You'll need to replace fluids, so drink plenty of purified water or tea; chamomile tea (*te de manzanilla*) is a good folk remedy, and it's readily available in restaurants throughout Mexico.

In severe cases, rehydrate yourself with Gatorade or a salt-sugar solution (½ teaspoon salt and 4 tablespoons sugar per quart of water). If your fever and diarrhea last longer than a day or two, see a doctor—you may have picked up a parasite or disease that requires prescription medication.

PESTS

Mosquitoes are most prevalent during the rainy season, when it's best to use mosquito repellent daily, even in the city; if you're in the jungle or wet places and lack strong repellent, consider covering up well or going indoors at dusk (called the "mosquito hour" by locals).

An excellent brand of *repelente de insectos* (insect repellent) called OFF is readily available; do not use it on children under age 2. Repellents that are not at least 10% DEET or picaridin are not effective here. If you're hiking in the jungle or boggy areas, wear repellent and long pants and sleeves; if you're camping in the jungle, use a mosquito net and invest in a package of *espirales contra mosquitos,* mosquito coils, which are sold in *farmacias* and *tlalpalerías* (hardware stores).

OTHER ISSUES

According to the CDC, there's a limited risk of malaria and other insect-carried or parasite-caused illnesses in certain areas of Mexico (largely but not exclusively rural and tropical coastal areas). In most urban or easily accessible areas you need not worry about malaria, but dengue fever is found with increasing frequency. If you're traveling to remote areas or simply prefer to err on the side of caution, check with the CDC's International Travelers' Hotline. Malaria and dengue are both carried by mosquitoes; in areas where these

illnesses are prevalent, use insect-repellant coiling, clothing, and sprays/lotion. Also consider taking antimalarial pills if you're doing serious adventure activities in tropical and subtropical areas.

Make sure your polio and diphtheria–tetanus shots are up-to-date well before your trip. Hepatitis A and typhoid are transmitted through unclean food or water. Gamma-globulin shots prevent hepatitis; an inoculation is available for typhoid, although it's not 100% effective.

Caution is advised when venturing out in the Mexican sun. Sunbathers lulled by a slightly overcast sky or the sea breezes can be burned badly in just 20 minutes. To avoid overexposure, use strong sunscreens, sit under a shade umbrella, and avoid the peak sun hours of noon to 3. Sunscreen, including many American brands, can be found in pharmacies, supermarkets, and resort gift shops.

Health Information National Centers for Disease Control & Prevention (*CDC*) ☏ *800/232–4636, 877/394–8747 international travelers' health line* ⊕ *www.cdc.gov/travel.* **World Health Organization** (*WHO*) ⊕ *www. who.int.*

MEDICAL CARE

Cornerstone Hospital accepts various types of foreign health insurance and traveler's insurance and is American owned. The other recommended, privately owned hospitals are Hospital San Javier Marina and Hospital Amerimed. Although most small towns have at least a clinic, travelers are usually more comfortable traveling to the major hospitals than using these clinics.

Farmacias (pharmacies) are the most convenient place for such common medicines as *aspirina* (aspirin) or *jarabe para la tos* (cough syrup). You'll be able to find many U.S. brands (e.g., Tylenol, Pepto-Bismol), but don't plan on buying your favorite prescription or nonprescription sleep aid, for example. The same brands and even drugs aren't always available. Prescriptions must be issued by a Mexican doctor to be legal; you can often get prescriptions inexpensively from local doctors located near the pharmacy. You can bring your own medications into the country (as long as you are not into heavy doses of morphine or something like that), but if you need to get more during your stay, you will have to explain to a local doctor your situation and the specific drugs you need, so he can provide you with a new Mexican prescription, which will be valid in any pharmacy in the country.

Pharmacies are usually open daily 9 am to 10 pm; on Sunday and in some small towns they may close several hours earlier. In neighborhoods or smaller towns where there are no 24-hour drug stores, local pharmacies take turns staying open 24 hours so that there's usually at least one open on any given night—it's called the *farmacia de turno*. The Farmacias Guadalajara chain is found throughout the Riviera Nayarit and Puerto Vallarta, and most are open 24 hours; the website provides a full list of all branches.

Hospitals and Clinics Cornerstone Hospital ⊠ *Av. Los Tules 136, next to Plaza Caracol, Zona Hotelera Norte* ☎ *322/226-3700.* **Hospital Amerimed** ⊠ *Bd. Francisco Medina Ascencio 3970, Zona Hotelera Norte* ☎ *322/226-2080* ⊕ *www.amerimed.com.mx.* **Hospital San Javier Marina** ⊠ *Bd. Francisco M. Ascencio 2760, Zona Hotelera Norte* ☎ *322/226-1010.*

Pharmacy Farmacias del Ahorro ⊠ *Blvd. Francisco Medina Ascencio 2740, Zona Hotelera* ☎ *01800/711-2222* ⊕ *www.fahorro. com.* **Farmacias Guadalajara** ⊠ *Insurgentes 261, Zona Romántica* ☎ *322/222-0101* ⊕ *www.farmaciasguadalajara.com.mx.*

MEDICAL INSURANCE AND ASSISTANCE

Consider buying trip insurance with medical-only coverage. Neither Medicare nor some private insurers cover medical expenses anywhere outside of the United States. Medical-only policies typically reimburse you for medical care (excluding that related to preexisting conditions)

and hospitalization abroad, and provide for evacuation. You still have to pay the bills and await reimbursement from the insurer, though.

Another option is to sign up with a medical-evacuation assistance company. Membership gets you doctor referrals, emergency evacuation or repatriation, 24-hour hotlines for medical consultation, and other assistance. International SOS Assistance Emergency and AirMed International provide evacuation services and medical referrals. MedjetAssist offers medical evacuation.

Medical Assistance Companies AirMed International ⊕ *www.airmed.com.* **MedjetAssist** ☎ *800/527-7478, 205/595-6626* ⊕ *www. medjetassist.com.*

Medical-Only Insurers International Medical Group ☎ *866/368-3724* ⊕ *www. imglobal.com.* **International SOS** ☎ *215/942-8226* ⊕ *www.internationalsos.com.* **Wallach & Company** ☎ *800/237-6615, 540/687-3166* ⊕ *www.wallach.com.*

▌ HOURS OF OPERATION

Banks are generally open weekdays 9 to 3. In Puerto Vallarta most are open until 4, and some of the larger banks keep a few branches open Saturday from 9 or 10 to 1 or 2:30; however, the extended hours are often for deposits or check cashing only. HSBC is the one chain that stays open for longer hours; on weekdays it is open 8 to 7 and on Saturday from 8 to 3. Government offices are usually open to the public weekdays 9 to 3; along with banks and most private offices, they're closed on national holidays.

Some gas stations, like those near major thoroughfares, are open 24 hours a day. Those that are not are normally open 6 am–10 pm daily.

Stores are generally open weekdays and Saturday from 9 or 10 to 5 or 7; in resort areas, those stores geared to tourists may stay open until 9 or 10 at night and all day on Saturday; some are open on Sunday as well, but it's good to call ahead before making a special trip. Some more traditional shops close for a two-hour lunch break, roughly 2–4. Airport shops are open seven days a week.

HOLIDAYS

Banks and government offices close on January 1, February 5 (Constitution Day), March 21 (Benito Juárez's birthday), May 1 (Labor Day), September 16 (Independence Day), November 20 (Revolution Day), and December 25 (Christmas). They may also close on unofficial holidays, such as Day of the Dead (November 1–2), Virgin of Guadalupe Day (December 12), and during Holy Week (the days leading to Easter Sunday). Government offices usually have reduced hours and staff from Christmas through New Year's Day.

▌ MAIL

The Mexican postal system is notoriously slow and unreliable; letters usually arrive in one piece (albeit late), but never send packages through the postal service or expect to receive them, as they may be stolen. Instead, use a courier service or MexPost, the more reliable branch of the Mexican Postal Service.

Post offices (*oficinas de correos*) are found in even the smallest villages. International postal service is all airmail, but even so, your letter will take anywhere from 10 days to six weeks to arrive. Service within Mexico can be equally slow. It costs 10.5 pesos (about 80¢) to send a postcard or letter weighing under 20 grams to the United States or Canada; it's 13 pesos (97¢) to Europe and 14.5 pesos ($1.08) to Australia and New Zealand.

Contacts Correos ⊠ *Calle Colombia 1014, El Centro* ☎ *322/222-6308* ⊕ *www.sepomex. gob.mx.*

SHIPPING PACKAGES

FedEx, DHL, Estafeta, and United Parcel Service (UPS) are available in major cities and many resort areas. It's best to

send all packages using one of these services. These companies offer office or hotel pickup with 24-hour advance notice (sometimes less, depending on when you call) and are very reliable. From Puerto Vallarta to large U.S. cities, for example, the minimum charge is around $30 for an envelope weighing 227 grams (½ pound) or less.

Express Services DHL ⊠ *Bd. Francisco M. Ascencio 1046, Zona Hotelera Sur* ☎ *322/222-4720, 01800/765-6345* ⊕ *www.dhl.com.* **Estafeta** ⊠ *Libramiento Luis Donaldo Colosio 122-B, Zona Hotelera* ☎ *322/223-2700, 322/223-2898* ⊕ *www.estafeta.com.* **Mail Boxes Etc.** ⊠ *Calle Ignacio L. Vallarta 130, Local 3, Zona Hotelera Norte [Col. Versalles]* ☎ *322/222-2252* ⊕ *www.facebook.com/ MailBoxes.Etc.PV.*

▌ MONEY

Prices in this book are quoted most often in U.S. dollars. Some services in Mexico quote prices in dollars, others in pesos. Because of the current fluctuation in the dollar/peso market, prices may be different from those listed here, but we've done our best to give accurate rates.

A stay in one of Puerto Vallarta's top hotels can cost more than $350, but if you aren't wedded to standard creature comforts, you can spend as little as $40 a day on room, board, and local transportation. Lodgings are less expensive in the charming but unsophisticated mountain towns like San Sebastián del Oeste.

You can get away with a tab of $50 for two at a wonderful restaurant (although it's also easy to pay more). The good news is that there are hotels and eateries for every budget, and inexpensive doesn't necessarily mean bargain basement. This guide recommends some excellent places to stay, eat, and play for extremely reasonable prices.

Prices throughout this guide are given for adults. Substantially reduced fees are almost always available for children, students, and senior citizens.

ITEM	AVERAGE COST
Cup of Coffee	80¢–$2.50
Glass of Wine	$3.50–$8
Bottle of Beer	$1–$3
Sandwich	$2.50–$5
One-Mile Taxi Ride	$3
Museum Admission	$1

ATMS AND BANKS

ATMs (*cajeros automáticos*) are widely available, with Star, Cirrus, and Plus the most frequently found networks. Your own bank will probably charge a fee for using ATMs abroad; the foreign bank you use may also charge a fee. You'll usually get a better rate of exchange at an ATM, however, than you will at a currency-exchange office or at a teller window. And extracting funds as you need them is a safer option than carrying around a large amount of cash.

Many Mexican ATMs cannot accept PINs with more than four digits. If yours is longer, change your PIN to four digits before you leave home. If your PIN is fine yet your transaction still can't be completed, chances are that the computer lines are busy or that the machine has run out of money or is being serviced. Don't give up.

For cash advances, plan to use Visa or MasterCard, as many Mexican ATMs don't accept American Express. Cash advances are allowed at most local ATMs, however it's the most expensive way to get your money. It may be better to leave cash advances just for emergencies. Large banks with reliable ATMs include Banamex, HSBC, BBVA Bancomer, Santander, Banorte, and Scotiabank Inverlat. Some banks no longer exchange traveler's checks; if you carry these, make sure they are in smaller denominations ($20s or $50s) to make it more likely that hotels

or shops will accept them if need be. Travelers must have their passport or other official identification in order to change traveler's checks.

Banks Banamex ✉ *Calle Juárez, at Calle Zaragoza, El Centro* ☎ *322/226–6110* ⊕ *www.banamex.com* ✉ *Plaza Peninsula, Av. Francisco Medina Ascensio 2485, Zona Hotelera* ☎ *322/226–6103* ✉ *Plaza Caracol L-31, Av. Francisco Medina Ascencio s/n, Zona Hotelera* ☎ *322/224–8710.* **Banorte** ✉ *Paseo Díaz Ordáz 690 at Calle Josefa Ortiz. de Domínguez, El Centro* ☎ *322/222–3210* ⊕ *www.banorte.com* ✉ *Plaza Lago Real, Calle Tepic 430 Ote, Nuevo Vallarta* ☎ *322/223–7796* ✉ *Bd. Francisco M. Ascencio 500, Zona Hotelera Norte* ☎ *01800/226–6783.*

CREDIT CARDS

Credit cards are accepted in Puerto Vallarta and at major hotels and restaurants in outlying areas. Smaller, less expensive restaurants and shops tend to take only cash. In general, credit cards aren't accepted in small towns and villages, except in some hotels. The most widely accepted cards are MasterCard and Visa.

When shopping, you can often get better prices if you pay with cash, particularly in small shops. But you'll receive wholesale exchange rates when you make purchases with credit cards. These exchange rates are usually better than those that banks give you for changing money. U.S. banks charge their customers a foreign transaction fee for using their credit card abroad. The decision to pay cash or to use a credit card might depend on whether the establishment in which you are making a purchase finds bargaining for prices acceptable, and whether you want the safety net of your card's purchase protection. To avoid fraud or errors, it's wise to make sure that "pesos" is clearly marked on all credit-card receipts.

Before you leave for Mexico, contact your credit-card company to alert them to your travel plans and to get lost-card phone numbers that work in Mexico; the standard toll-free numbers often don't work abroad. Carry these numbers separately from your wallet so you'll have them if you need to call to report lost or stolen cards. American Express, MasterCard, and Visa note the international number for card-replacement calls on the back of their cards.

CURRENCY AND EXCHANGE

Mexican currency comes in denominations of 20-, 50-, 100-, 200-, and 500-peso bills. Coins come in denominations of 1, 2, 5, 10, and 20 pesos and 20 and 50 centavos. (Twenty-centavo coins are only rarely seen.) Many of the coins are very similar, so check carefully; bills, however, are different colors and easily distinguished.

U.S. dollar bills (but not coins) are widely accepted in tourist-oriented shops and restaurants in Puerto Vallarta. Pay in pesos where possible, however, for better prices. Although in larger hotels U.S. dollars are welcome as tips, it's generally better to tip in pesos so that service personnel don't have to go to the bank to exchange currency.

At this writing, the exchange rate was 13.43 pesos to the U.S. dollar. ATM transaction fees may be higher abroad than at home, but ATM exchange rates are the best because they're based on wholesale rates offered only by major banks. Most ATMs allow a maximum withdrawal of $300 to $400 per transaction. Banks and *casas de cambio* (money-exchange bureaus) have the second-best exchange rates. The difference from one place to another is usually only a few pesos.

Some banks change money on weekdays only until 1 or 3 pm (though they stay open until 4 or 5, or later). Casas de cambio generally stay open until 6 or later and often operate on weekends; they usually have competitive rates and much shorter lines. By law, no more than $300 can be exchanged per person per day, so plan in advance. Some hotels exchange money, but they give a poor exchange rate.

You can do well at most airport exchange booths, though not as well as at the ATMs. You'll do even worse at bus stations, in hotels, in restaurants, or in stores.

When changing money, count your bills before leaving the window of the bank or casa de cambio, and don't accept any partially torn or taped-together notes: You won't be able to use them anywhere. Also, many shop and restaurant owners are unable to make change for large bills. Enough of these encounters may compel you to request *billetes chicos* (small bills) when you exchange money. It's wise to have a cache of smaller bills and coins to use at these more humble establishments to avoid having to wait around while the merchant runs off to seek change.

▌ PACKING

High-style sportswear, cotton slacks and walking shorts, and plenty of colorful sundresses are the palette of clothing you'll see in PV. Bring lightweight sportswear, bathing suits, and cover-ups for the beach. In addition to shorts, pack at least a pair or two of lightweight long pants.

Men may want to bring a lightweight suit or slacks and blazers for fancier restaurants (although very few have dress codes). For women, dresses of cotton, linen, or other lightweight, breathable fabrics are recommended. Puerto Vallarta restaurants are extremely tolerant of casual dress, but it never hurts to exceed expectations.

The sun can be fierce; bring a sun hat and sunscreen for the beach and for sightseeing. You'll need a sweater or jacket to cope with hotel and restaurant air-conditioning, which can be glacial, and for occasional cool spells. A lightweight jacket is a necessity in winter, and pack an umbrella, even in summer, for unexpected rainstorms.

Bring along tissue packs in case you hit a place where the toilet paper has run out. You'll find familiar toiletries and hygiene products, as well as condoms, in shops in PV and in most rural areas.

PASSPORTS AND VISAS

U.S. citizens reentering the United States by land or sea are required to have documents that comply with WHTI (Western Hemisphere Travel Initiative), most commonly a U.S. passport, a passport card, a trusted traveler card (such as NEXUS, SENTRI, or FAST), or an enhanced driver's license. The U.S. passport card is smaller than a traditional passport (think wallet size), cheaper, and valid for just as long, but you can't use it for travel by air.

Upon entering Mexico, all visitors must get a tourist card. If you're arriving by plane from the United States or Canada, the standard tourist card will be given to you on the plane. They're also available through travel agents and Mexican consulates and at the border if you're entering by land.

TIP→ You're given a portion of the tourist card form upon entering Mexico. Keep track of this documentation throughout your trip; you will need it when you depart. You'll be asked to hand it, your ticket, and your passport to airline representatives at the gate when boarding for departure.

If you lose your tourist card, plan to spend some time (and about $30) sorting it out with Mexican officials at the airport on departure.

A tourist card costs about $20. The fee is generally tacked on to the price of your airline ticket; if you enter by land or boat you'll have to pay the fee separately. You're exempt from the fee if you enter by sea and stay less than 72 hours, or by land and do not stray past the 26- to 30-km (16- to 18-mile) checkpoint into the country's interior.

Tourist cards and visas are valid from 15 to 180 days, at the discretion of the immigration officer at your point of entry (90 days for Australians). Americans,

Canadians, New Zealanders, and the British may request up to 180 days for a tourist card or visa extension. The extension fee is about $20, and the process can be time-consuming. There's no guarantee that you'll get the extension you're requesting. If you're planning an extended stay, plead with the immigration official for the maximum allowed days at the time of entry. It will save you time and money later.

TIP→ Mexico has some of the strictest policies about children entering the country. Minors traveling with one parent need notarized permission from the absent parent. And all children, including infants, must have proof of citizenship (the same as adults; ⇨ *above*) for travel to Mexico.

If you're a single parent traveling with children up to age 18, you must have a notarized letter from the other parent stating that the child has his or her permission to leave the country. The child must be carrying the original letter—not a facsimile or scanned copy—as well as proof of the parent/child relationship (usually a birth certificate or court document), and an original custody decree, if applicable. If the other parent is deceased or the child has only one legal parent, a notarized statement saying so must be obtained as proof. In addition, you must fill out a tourist card for each child over the age of 10 traveling with you.

Info Mexican Embassy ☎ *202/728–1600* ⊕ *embamex.sre.gob.mx/eua.*

U.S. Passport Information U.S. Department of State ☎ *877/487–2778* ⊕ *travel.state.gov.*

RESTROOMS

Expect to find reasonably clean flushing toilets and cold running water at public restrooms in the major tourist destinations and attractions; toilet paper, soap, hot water, and paper towels aren't always available, though. Keep a packet of tissues with you at all times. At some tourist attractions, markets, bus stations, and the like, you usually have to pay 5 pesos to use the facilities. Since the H1N1 flu scare a few years ago, many restaurants, shops, and government offices have had hand sanitizer available for customers to use.

■ TIP→ **Remember that unless otherwise indicated you should put your used toilet paper in the wastebasket next to the toilet; many plumbing systems in Mexico still can't handle toilet paper.**

Gas stations have public bathrooms—some tidy and others not so tidy. Alternatively, try popping into a restaurant, buying a little something (or not), and using the restroom, which will probably be simple but clean and adequately equipped.

▮ SAFETY

Horror stories about drug-cartel killings and border violence are making big news these days, but Puerto Vallarta is many hundreds of miles away. Imagine not going to visit the Florida Keys because of reports of violence in a bad section of New York City. Still, Puerto Vallarta is no longer the innocent of years gone by; pickpocketing and the occasional mugging can be a concern, and precaution is in order here as elsewhere. Store only enough money in your wallet or bag to cover the day's spending. And don't flash big wads of money or leave valuables like cameras unattended. Leave your passport and other valuables you don't need in your hotel's safe.

Bear in mind that reporting a crime to the police is often a frustrating experience unless you speak good Spanish and have a great deal of patience. If you're victimized, contact your local consulate or your embassy in Mexico City.

One of the most serious threats to your safety is local drivers. Although pedestrians have the right-of-way, drivers disregard this law. And more often than not, drivers who hit pedestrians drive away as fast as they can without stopping, to avoid jail. Many Mexican drivers don't carry

auto insurance, so you'll have to shoulder your own medical expenses. Pedestrians should be extremely cautious of all traffic, especially city bus drivers, who often drive with truly reckless abandon.

If you're on your own, consider using only your first initial and last name when registering at your hotel. Solo travelers, or women traveling with other women rather than men, may be subjected to *piropos* (flirtatious compliments). Piropos are one thing, but more aggressive harassment is another. In the rare event that the situation seems to be getting out of hand, don't hesitate to ask someone for help. If you express outrage, you should find no shortage of willing defenders.

General Information and Warnings Transportation Security Administration (*TSA*) ☎ 866/289-9673 ⊕ www.tsa.gov. **U.S. Department of State** ☎ 888/407-4747 from U.S. and Canada, 202/501-4444 from overseas ⊕ www. travel.state.gov.

▮ TAXES

Mexico charges an airport departure tax of $18 or the peso equivalent for international and domestic flights. This tax is usually included in the price of your ticket, but check to be certain. Traveler's checks and credit cards aren't accepted at the airport as payment for this, but U.S. dollars are.

Puerto Vallarta and environs have a value-added tax of 15%, called IVA (*impuesto al valor agregado*). It's often waived for cash purchases, or it's incorporated into the price. When comparing hotel prices, be sure to find out whether yours includes or excludes IVA and any service charges. Additionally, Jalisco and Nayarit charge a 2% tax on accommodations, the funds from which are used for tourism promotion. Other taxes and charges apply for phone calls made from your hotel room.

▌ TIME

Puerto Vallarta, Guadalajara, and the rest of Jalisco State fall into Central Standard Time (the same as Mexico City). Nayarit and other parts of the northwest coast are on Mountain Standard Time.

However, Nuevo Vallarta, Bucerías, La Cruz de Huanacaxtle, Punta de Mita, and most of the Riviera Nayarit have been adjusted to stay in the same time zone as Puerto Vallarta, avoiding the confusions of past years. Bear in mind that Mexico does observe daylight saving time, but not on the same schedule as the United States.

▌ TIPPING

When tipping in Mexico, remember that the minimum wage is just under $5 a day. Waiters and bellmen may not be at the bottom of that heap, but they're not very far up, either. Those who work in international chain hotels think in dollars and know, for example, that in the United States porters are tipped about $2 a bag; they tend to expect the equivalent.

▌ TRIP INSURANCE

Comprehensive trip insurance is valuable if you're booking a very expensive or complicated trip (particularly to an isolated region) or if you're booking far in advance. Comprehensive policies typically cover trip cancellation and interruption, letting you cancel or cut your trip short because of a personal emergency, illness, or, in some cases, acts of terrorism in your destination. Such policies also cover evacuation and medical care. (For trips abroad you should at least have medical-only coverage). Some also cover you for trip delays because of bad weather or mechanical problems as well as for lost or delayed baggage.

Another type of coverage to look for is financial default—that is, when your trip is disrupted because a tour operator, airline, or cruise line goes out of business. Generally you must buy this when you book your trip or shortly thereafter, and it's only available to you if your operator isn't on a list of excluded companies.

Always read the fine print of your policy to make sure that you are covered for the risks that are of most concern to you. Compare several policies to make sure you're getting the best price and range of coverage available.

Insurance Comparison Sites Insure My Trip. com ☎ *800/487-4722* ⊕ *www.insuremytrip.*

TIPPING GUIDELINES FOR PUERTO VALLARTA	
Bartender	10% to 15% of the bill
Bellhop	10 to 30 pesos (roughly 80¢ to $2) per bag, depending on the level of the hotel
Hotel Concierge	30 pesos or more, if he or she performs a service for you
Hotel Doorman	10 to 20 pesos if he helps you get a cab
Hotel Maid	10 to 30 pesos a day (either daily or at the end of your stay); make sure the maid gets it, and not the person who checks the minibar prior to your departure
Hotel Room-Service Waiter	10 to 20 pesos per delivery, even if a service charge has been added
Porter/Skycap at Airport	10 to 20 pesos per bag
Restroom Attendant	5 pesos
Taxi Driver	cab drivers aren't normally tipped; give them 10 to 20 pesos if they help with your bags
Tour Guide	10% of the cost of the tour
Valet Parking Attendant	10 to 20 pesos but only when you get your car
Waiter	10% to 15%; nothing additional if a service charge is added to the bill

com. **SquareMouth.com** ☎ *800/240–0369* ⊕ *www.squaremouth.com.*

Comprehensive Travel Insurers Allianz Travel Insurance ☎ *866/884–3556* ⊕ *www. allianztravelinsurance.com.* **AIG Travel Guard** ☎ *800/826–4919* ⊕ *www.travelguard.com.* **CSA Travel Protection** ☎ *800/711–1197* ⊕ *www.csatravelprotection.com.* **Travelex Insurance** ☎ *800/228–9792* ⊕ *www.travelexinsurance.com.* **Travel Insured International** ☎ *800/243–3174* ⊕ *www.travelinsured.com.*

■**TIP**➔ Okay. You know you can save a bundle on trips to warm-weather destinations by traveling in rainy season. But there's also a chance that a severe storm will disrupt your plans. The solution? Look for hotels and resorts that offer storm/hurricane guarantees. Although they rarely allow refunds, most guarantees do let you rebook later if a storm strikes.

▮ VISITOR INFORMATION

Contacts Abroad Mexican Ministry of Tourism (SECTUR) ☎ *55/3002–6300, 01800/006–8839 toll-free in Mexico* ⊕ *www. sectur.gob.mx.* **Mexican Tourism Board (U.S. and Canada)** ☎ *800/446–3942 in U.S. and Canada* ⊕ *www.visitmexico.com.*

PV and Jalisco Contacts Puerto Vallarta Tourism Board & Convention and Visitors Bureau ✉ *Hotel Canto del Sol, Las Glorias, Local 18, Ground fl., Zona Hotelera* ☎ *322/224–1175, 888/384–6822 in U.S., 01800/719–3276 in Mexico* ⊕ *www. visitpuertovallarta.com.*

Riviera Nayarit Contacts Bay of Banderas/ Nuevo Vallarta Tourism Office ✉ *Paseo de los Cocoteros at Bd. Nuevo Vallarta, between Gran Velas and Marival hotels, Nuevo Vallarta* ☎ *322/297–1006.* **Riviera Nayarit Convention & Visitors Bureau** ✉ *Paradise Plaza, Local Int. 6–A, Paseo de los Cocoteros 85 Sur, Nuevo Vallarta* ☎ *322/297–2516* ⊕ *www. rivieranayarit.com.*

The best of the private-enterprise websites are PV Mirror and Virtual Vallarta, which have tons of good information and short articles about life in PV. Bucerías, Sayulita, and Punta Mita have their own websites, as does the Costalegre region as a whole.

Excellent English-language sites for general history, travel information, facts, and news stories about Mexico are Mexico Online and Mexico Connect. Mexico Guru has news about PV and nearby destinations, interactive maps, and a dictionary of Mexico-specific slang and vocabulary.

The nonprofit site Ancient Mexico has information about western Mexico as well as more comprehensive information about the Maya and Aztecs.

Contacts Ancient Mexico ⊕ *www.ancient mexico.com.* **Costalegre** ⊕ *www.costalegre. ca.* **Mexico Connect** ⊕ *www.mexconnect.com.* **Mexico Guru** ⊕ *www.mexicoguru.com.* **Mexico Online** ⊕ *www.mexonline.com.* **Punta Mita** ⊕ *www.puntamita.com.* **PV Mirror** ⊕ *www. pvmirror.com.* **Sayulita Life** ⊕ *www.sayulitalife. com.* **Virtual Vallarta** ⊕ *www.virtualvallarta. com.*

INDEX

PHOTO CREDITS

Cover credit: karamysh/Shutterstock [Description: Resort in Yelapa]. 1, Mauricio Ramos / age fotostock. 2-3, Mjunsworth | Dreamstime.com. 5, Alija/iStockphoto. Chapter 1: Experience Puerto Vallarta: 8-9, ambient Images Inc./Almy. 10, YinYang/Stockphoto. 11, Bruce Herman/Mexico Tourism Board. 14 (left), Ricardo Villasenor / Shutterstock. 14 (top right), Pierre Rochon / Alamy. 14 (bottom right), Eric James / Alamy. 15 (top left), Barna Tanko / Shutterstock. 15 (right), Douglas Peebles Photography / Alamy. 15 (bottom middle), Danita Delimont / Alamy. 15 (bottom right), Ian Dagnall / Alamy. 16, Fidetur. 17, wadester16/wikipedia.org. 18, Pascal Blachier/wikipedia.org. 19 (left), Alan D. Wilson, naturespicsonline.com/wikipedia.org. 19 (right), Puerto Vallarta Botanical Gardens. 20, Joe Biafore/iStockphoto. 21 (left), YinYang/iStockphoto. 21 (right), Fidetur. 22, Starwood Hotels and Resorts Worldwide. 23, Doug Berry/iStockphoto. 24 and 25, Katherine Wessel/Royal Caribbean International. 26, YangYin/iStockphoto. 27, Andy Hwang/iStockphoto. 29 (left), David Diaz. 29 (right), Kaiser Maximilian. 30, Carlos S. Pereyra / age fotostock. Chapter 2: Exploring Puerto Vallarta: 31, Elena Elisseeva / Shutterstock. 32, Elena Elisseeva / Shutterstock. 38, Chris Howey / Shutterstock 42, Geraldmarella | Dreamstime.com. Chapter 3: Beaches: 51, World Pictures / Alamy 52, YinYang/iStockphoto. 56, Martin Siepmann / age fotostock. 64, Walter Bibikow / age fotostock. 68, dmealiffe/Flickr. Chapter 4: Where to Eat: 73, Andrea Gomez. 74, nicobatista/Shutterstock. 75 (top), E.B.Fladung III/ waywuwei/Flickr. 75 (bottom), SanFranAnnie/Flickr. 76, Robyn Mackenzie/Shutterstock. 102, Jill Negronida Hampton. Chapter 5: Where to Stay: 107, El Careyes. 108, Hotel des Artistes del Mar. 117, Andres Barría. 123, Josef Kandoll W. 127, Hotel des Artistes del Mar. Chapter 6: Nightlife and the Performing Arts: 135, Imagestate/age fotostock. 136, Travel Bug/Shutterstock. 140, Blaine Harrington/age fotostock. 145, csp/Shutterstock. 146 (top left), Alfredo Schaufelberger/Shutterstock. 146 (bottom left), wikipedia.org. 146 (right), Casa Herradura/Brown-Forman. 147 (top left), csp/Shutterstock. 147 (center left), Alfredo Schaufelberger/Shutterstock. 147 (bottom left), Smithsonian Institution Archives/wikipedia.org. 147 (top center), Jesus Cervantes/Shutterstock. 147 (bottom center), Blaine Harrington / age fotostock. 147 (top and bottom right), Jesus Cervantes/Shutterstock. 148 (top left), Eduard Stelmakh/ Shutterstock. 148 (center left), svry/Shutterstock. 148 (bottom left), National Archives and Records Administration. 148 (top right), Andrew Penner/iStockphoto. 148 (bottom right), BlueOrange Studio/ Shutterstock. 149 (top left), Sony Ho / Shutterstock. 149 (bottom left), csp/Shutterstock. 149 (right), Patricia Hofmeester/Shutterstock. 150 (left), The Patrón Spirits Company. 150 (right), rick/Flickr. 151 (top left), Casa Herradura/Brown-Forman. 151 (bottom left), shrk/Flickr. 151 (right), Neil Setchfield / Alamy. Chapter 7: Sports and the Outdoors: 155, steve bly / Alamy. 156, Puerto Vallarta Tours by Johann & Sandra. 159, Vasaleks/Shutterstock. 161, Daniel Mejia/Canopy El Eden. 162, Courtesy of Four Seasons Resort Punta Mita.165, Rancho El Charro. 169, Irene Chan / Alamy. 170, Mark Doherty/ Shutterstock. 175, Keith Levit / age fotostock. Chapter 8: Shopping: 177, Adalberto Rios Szalay / age fotostock. 178, Gena Guarniere & Monroe Davids. 186, tiffa130/Flickr. 192, John Mitchell / Alamy. 193 and 194 (bottom), María Lourdes Alonso. 195 (top), 195 (bottom left and 2 center photos), Ken Ross. 195 (bottom right), Jane Onstott. 196 (top left), patti haskins/Flickr. 196 (bottom left), fontplaydotcom/Flickr. 196 (top right), Wonderlane/Flickr. 196 (center right), José Zelaya Gallery/ArteDelPueblo.com. 196 (bottom right), Jane Onstott. 201, Wonderlane/Flickr. Chapter 9: Side Trips: 203, Jesus/Cervantes/Shutterstock. 204, Holger Mette/Shutterstock. 205 (top), paulhami/Flickr. 205 (bottom, Elena Elisseeva/Shutterstock. 206, www.tour.tk/Shutterstock. 214, Witold Skrypczak / Alamy. 220, Allgöwer Walter/Prisma/age fotostock. 227, W G Allgoewer / age fotostock. 230, csp/Shutterstock. 234, Blaine Harrington / age fotostock. 236, Alija/iStockphoto. 237 (top), Jonathan P. Larsen/Diadem Images/iStockphoto. 237 (center), John Stelzer/iStockphoto. 237 (bottom), Felicia Montoya/iStockphoto. 238 (top left), Ivantsov Ruslan/Shutterstock. 238 (vihuela), wikipedia.org. 238 (guitar), David W Hughes/Shutterstock. 238 (top right), Hannamariah/Shutterstock. 238 (center right), C Squared Studios/Photodisc Green. 238 (bottom right), cowbite/Flick. 239, Jeff Greenberg / Alamy. 240, Ken Welsh/age fotostock. 241 (top), PABLO DE AGUINACO/Mexico Tourism Board. 241 (bottom right), BRUCE HERMAN/Mexico Tourism Board. 250, Jan Halaska / age fotostock. 253, José Fuste Raga/age fotostock. Back cover (from left to right): Ferenz/Shutterstock; Mike Willis/Flickr; Hotel des Artistes del Mar. Spine: Buburuza Productions/iStockphoto.

NOTES

NOTES

ABOUT OUR WRITERS

After years of wandering around Europe and getting a Master's degree in Humanities, **Luis Domínguez** decided to go back home to Mexico, choosing the tropical paradise of Puerto Vallarta to settle in. Ever since, he's been writing about the natural wonders and unique attractions of the Puerto Vallarta and Riviera Nayarit area. Nowadays, he writes both in English and Spanish about football, his travels through Mexico, and foreign affairs, while also teaching philosophy at a local university.

It was surfing waves in foreign countries that initially drove **Federico Arrizabalaga** to hit the road and explore the world, at first around Europe, then overseas. Travel became a passion and his quest to visit new places and learn about different cultures has taken him to South America, Africa, the Middle East, South East Asia and the Pacific, often with his backpack, and other times in a less budget-conscious style. He landed in Puerto Vallarta over half a decade ago where he still surfs almost every week, yet he continues to travel the world, stopping in Spain to visit his family whenever possible and keeping his popular travel blog up-to-date.